Behavioral Neuroscience for the Human Services

Behavioral Neuroscience for the Human Services

FOUNDATIONS IN EMOTION, MENTAL HEALTH, ADDICTION, AND ALTERNATIVE THERAPIES

Harriette C. Johnson, MSW, PhD

OXFORD
UNIVERSITY PRESS

OXFORD

UNIVERSITY PRESS

Oxford University Press is a department of the University of
Oxford. It furthers the University's objective of excellence in research,
scholarship, and education by publishing worldwide.

Oxford   New York

Auckland   Cape Town   Dar es Salaam   Hong Kong   Karachi
Kuala Lumpur   Madrid   Melbourne   Mexico City   Nairobi
New Delhi   Shanghai   Taipei   Toronto

With offices in

Argentina   Austria   Brazil   Chile   Czech Republic   France   Greece
Guatemala   Hungary   Italy   Japan   Poland   Portugal   Singapore
South Korea   Switzerland   Thailand   Turkey   Ukraine   Vietnam

Oxford is a registered trademark of Oxford University Press
in the UK and certain other countries.

Published in the United States of America by
Oxford University Press
198 Madison Avenue, New York, NY 10016

© Oxford University Press 2014

Library of Congress Cataloging-in-Publication Data
Johnson, Harriette C.
Behavioral Neuroscience for the Human Services: Foundations in
Emotion, Mental Health, Addiction, and Alternative Therapies/ Harriette C. Johnson.
pages cm
ISBN 978-0-19-979415-7 (pbk. : alk. paper)   1. Psychiatric social work.   2. Neuroscience.
3. Neuropsychology.   4. Mental illness.   5. Mentally ill—Services for.   I. Title.
HV689.J64 2013
362.2′0425—dc23
2013016587

3 5 7 9 8 6 4 2
Printed in the United States of America
on acid-free paper

To my four lively spirits
Jennifer Elizabeth, Laurie, Diana, and Amy
Biopsychosocial daughters all

{ CONTENTS }

*MEBA items 1-7.

Continued in Part VI, Chapter 45, as Assessing Pat (Completion, MEBA items 8-13): Analysis and Intervention Planning: Thoughts of death, borderline dimensions, and obsessive-compulsive traits in a person with eating challenges.

---

* Continued from Part IV, MEBA items 1-7. MEBA Items 8-13: Thoughts of Death, Borderline
Dimensions, and Obsessive-Compulsive Traits in a Person with Eating Challenges.

{ ACKNOWLEDGMENTS }

First of all, I'm extremely grateful to anonymous reviewers and to reviewers who disclosed their identity (Allen Rubin and Katharine Van Wormer) for important and helpful suggestions.

Acknowledgments are made to the following for reproduction of brain images: Alan Zametkin and colleagues and the *New England Journal of Medicine*; Daniel Weinberger, Clinical Brain Disorders Branch; John Hsiao, Experimental Therapeutics Branch; Mark George, Biological Psychiatry Branch, *National Institute of Mental Health*, National Institutes of Health, US Department of Health and Human Services, Rockville, Maryland; *National Alliance for the Mentally Ill, Campaign to End Discrimination*, Arlington, Virginia; and Lewis Baxter, University of Alabama.

Acknowledgments are made to the following for graphic representations of brain imaging results: Nora Volkow, Joanna Fowler, and Gene-Jack Wang, National Institute on Drug Abuse (NIDA) and *Journal of Clinical Investigation*, for their model of changes from pre-addicted to addicted state; Harry Chugani, Wayne State University School of Medicine, Detroit, Michigan and the *Academic Press* for permission to use a graph of developmental patterns in brain glucose utilization; Gerald Edelman and Yale University Press for permission to include an adaptation of three brain sketches from *Wider than the Sky*; and Tomohiro Ishizu and Semir Zeki for graphs showing concurrence of brain imaging with subject reports of aesthetic judgments.

Steven Hyman, neuroscientist and substance abuse researcher, graciously gave permission to incorporate his lecture material on substance abuse and addiction (1995). I also want to thank him for numerous recent citations from major publications.

Thanks to Gerald Edelman, founder and director of the Neurosciences Institute in La Jolla, California, for his generous consultation, patient explanations, and dazzling metaphors that helped me come closer to understanding his theory of neuronal group selection and its roles in human consciousness.

My thanks to the late Leonard Gibbs (d. 2008) of the University of Wisconsin-Eau Claire for giving us tools to implement evidence-based social work practice, essential skills for new generations of social workers; to Eileen Gambrill of the University of California, Berkeley, for her editorial leadership in introducing complex adaptive systems to social work educators, and for her unique volume on critical thinking with its robust measure of skepticism about professional conventions. Much appreciation goes to Ludwig Geismar, professor emeritus of Rutgers University (d. 2012), for three decades of supportive commentary sprinkled with whimsical humor. These social work researchers/ scholars stand out as inspiring sources of tools for using research to help us offer the best available practice with people.

Elizabeth and Joseph D'Amico, Marcia Brubeck, Jill Haga, and Naomi Pines Gitterman helped me expand the book's connection to practice. Liz D'Amico has a special place as conscientious critic, cheerleader, and contributor of her expertise on trauma, which she generously agreed to share in Part III of this book, despite what sounds to me like a 16-hour workday as an accomplished leader in the Connecticut state child welfare and mental health systems.

Diana Hardina, my computer graphics artist for two earlier books, created the science drawings in Part II and gave assistance on other illustrations and 15 years of invaluable support. I'm grateful to Michie Hesselbrock, first director of the doctoral program at the University of Connecticut School of Social Work, for providing opportunities for me to expand my knowledge of and experience with practice with addiction challenges. David Cournoyer, anthropologist, scholar of child development, associate dean at the University of Connecticut School of Social Work, and then Acting Dean, responded enthusiastically to the first edition of an earlier book on the same subject matter and spurred me on to write another with his three-word injunction: "I want more."

My graphics-for-neuroscience teachers Paul Lindale, Thomas Boisvert, and Jennifer Gutterman-Aviles of Greenfield Community College (computer art) and Neil Carlson of the University of Massachusetts, Amherst (behavioral neuroscience with animations), have inspired and enlightened me. Tom has helped me with his artistic insights about design and lettering. Paul has been a dedicated teacher and mentor of computer modeling and animation to me for 13 years. Jennifer has helped me overcome multiple technical and artistic challenges. President Bob Pura has led and wonderfully enriched this extraordinary place in western Massachusetts. Anyone who is able to spend time at GCC knows it for fine teaching, creative arts, and community mecca for whatever your interests and needs; as host to innumerable specialized events; for a most beautiful third floor library of glass walls with sunlight and views of the surrounding hills, and for friendly and helpful people everywhere. Last but not least, gourmet chef Debbie Herrick and her stellar staff, including Jamie Spencer, have made cafeteria food a daily anticipated delight. Jamie has offered memorable vegetable omelets and summer chats.

Jean Burch Harrison-Siegler, neuroscientist, naturalist, activist, and lifelong friend, added one more gift to the many she's given me, a critical review of my material on the hypothalamic-pituitary-adrenal axis. Before that, she led me across a magical lake in northern New England to see a family of loons, a species known to endorse equality in parental roles. Their chick rode confidently on the back of one of its parents, but I will never know which parent it was.

Two amazing people deserve special mention. Jan Lambert, University of Connecticut social work librarian, has helped me often and tirelessly for the past 20 years, locating resources, instructing me and my students in the use of all manner of electronic tools, resolving computer glitches, ordering books and videos, obtaining elusive materials, and performing countless other tasks, always with unfailing patience and kindness. Virginia Starkie, my secretary for 25 years, has been—well—indispensable. I couldn't even begin to enumerate the range of services she has provided. Like Jan, Virginia is astonishingly patient and kind. I'm not sure how I came to the good fortune of having these two people in my life. Sometimes the dice rolls in our favor.

Many thanks, *of course*, to my students at the University of Connecticut School of Social Work, whose enthusiasm for giving our clients "the best" and for earlier versions of the book has made it all worthwhile.

At Oxford University Press, thanks to Brianna Marron for pre-production help, to Newgen KnowledgeWorks, and to members of the production staff for their patient efforts. I've been very fortunate to have the assuredly most indispensable contributors of literary class and good-natured admonitions in my three editors. Maura Roessner lured me into this project and guided the framing of its structure. Nicholas Liu, her science-and-technology whiz, filled in admirably for her after she departed for another job. Dana Bliss has shepherded the final year of writing and creating graphics with aplomb, wisdom, and impeccable taste (and patience with my quirks). What incredible help—how did I get so lucky?

Harriette C. Johnson, October 8th, 2013

{ PREFACE }

Purpose and Perspective

Should a preface comprise most or all relevant information about what readers can expect and learn from a book? I believed so (without ever thinking about it) for previous books. But now I'm not so sure. The chapters themselves are engaging, whereas the inventory of topics in the preface seems—well, let's just say "utilitarian." So this time I've restrained my urge to tell you about all the aspects of this book I think are important and am offering an abbreviated version.

One of the anonymous reviewers described this book as a "page turner." I was delighted that she (revealing her identity after the fact) was not just respectful, but downright turned on. That is exactly what I want for readers, because neuroscience has been turning me on for years! But you probably do want a quick and painless summary to help you decide whether and what to read or use for students.

This book's purposes are (1) to advance practitioner assessment and intervention planning skills by incorporating neuroscience knowledge, (2) to provide information that agency administrators and policy-makers can access to inform their choices about services deserving investment of precious agency, private, or public resources, and (3) to enhance our own knowledge about ourselves—as everyday people—and our loved ones.

Thus the target audiences extend to readers who may not need neuroscience for their work, but who have had their appetites whetted by this new knowledge about human life that's increasingly enlivening national media.

Major neuroscience roles in mental health, substance use, drug and non-drug forms of addiction, child development, parenting, violence, criminal behavior and other human issues are well established by research in "hard" sciences and social sciences. Because most researchers now appear to accept the proposition that neuroscience knowledge is a sine qua non of evidence about human behavior in the social environment, we lay out steps for searching neuroscience aspects of emotions, behavior, and cognition and for incorporating the information into practice when relevant.

Words that characterize the book's perspective—biopsychosocial, ecological, multisystemic, and, of course, focus on person-in-environment—are very familiar to practitioners in social work and other human services. Neuroscience fits seamlessly into these perspectives. Recent initiatives to help people lead happier lives by bringing together scientific research with practices in the human services, called *translational research*, have advanced the quality of educational programs in the "helping professions" (see, for example, McGartland-Rubio, Schoenbaum et al., 2010).

Practice examples in this book with respect to individuals and families are indicated by a human group icon (⛉). These narratives are material for assessment, intervention planning, or other problem-solving behaviors by practitioners, educators, and persons with an interest in any of the fields of practice listed earlier. The examples here touch on a few of the vast number of systems of different sizes—family dynamics; agendas and procedures of important organizations such as schools and workplaces; cultures expressed in language, religion, behavioral norms, aesthetic preferences, and humor; social psychological processes such as prejudice, persuasion, and social cognition; economic power and powerlessness; global dimensions of some of these; and others. Any of these multiple influences on emotions, behavior, and cognition may occupy space in a systems analysis of a specific individual, group, or institution.

Audiences for this book include students in nonmedically oriented helping professions (using the book as a course text) and practitioners in a range of human services (using the book as a self-teaching tool). As a social work educator, I present applications in social work. When the editorial "we" is used in the book, it denotes a consensus of the invited social work authors Elizabeth D'Amico, Joseph D'Amico, Marcia Brubeck, and Jill Haga, who have contributed client vignettes and part or all of a chapter.

However, the book's subject matter is equally relevant for guidance counselors, family therapists, school and clinical psychologists, forensic specialists, rehabilitation counselors, and even medically trained practitioners already familiar with elementary neuroscience. In the absence of basic knowledge about the influences of neurobiology in peoples' struggles, it is all too easy for any of us to attribute willful incompetence or to assign blame to people with emotional or behavioral challenges or their families.

The comprehensive and multisystemic approach to human service practice spelled out in this book may thus offer strategies to workers from diverse educational and social backgrounds. Some of us enthusiastically, others reluctantly, are embracing neuroscience knowledge as we discover it is essential to assess and intervene competently (see, for example, Johnson, Atkins, Battle et al., 1990; Rubin, Cardenas, Warren et al., 1997; Beless, 1999; Spence, DiNitto, and Straussner, 2001; Taylor, 2003; Nower and Blaszcinzcski, 2004; Johnson, 2004; Farmer, 2009; Matto, Strolin-Goltzman, and Ballan, 2013).

Evidence-Based Practice as a Cross-Disciplinary Approach

It's unusual today to find a helping discipline that does not at least give lip service to the importance of evidence-based practice (EBP) (Satterfield, Spring,

Brownson et al., 2009). This book is founded on evidence bases for psychological phenomena (emotions, behavior, cognition) as they occur in the presence of neurobiological events on the micro end of the spectrum. Neuroscience processes themselves are in continual flux in response to mid- and large-sized forces impinging on individuals and families (e.g., organizations, cultures, economic power, and even weather conditions!). Environmental inputs are central to psychological events happening in the brain and entire nervous system.

How Will the Book Achieve Its Goals?

PART I depicts the historical and philosophical context prior to incorporation of neuroscience into ecosystem frameworks. We introduce early and contemporary conceptual models in social work as they've advanced toward current intellectual trends. An amalgamation of old and new is now defining practices of the helping professions, including social work, for the 21st century. Many of our familiar themes of practice, such as multicultural, multisystemic, and collaborative work for promoting justice and alleviating miseries, continue on center stage. Neuroscience made its debut decades ago, but only in the past few years has it become a media favorite. New trends within neuroscience itself have swept onto the stage and are sharing the spotlight with numerous time-honored helping traditions.

Among the newer thrusts, in addition to translational research mentioned above, are *epigenesis, study of neural networks* (now superceding previous emphasis on individual brain structures and functions), *evidence-based human behavior in the social environment* (HBSE), and *evidence-based assessment and intervention planning*. We use the terms *evidence-based* and *evidence-informed* interchangeably in this book, since evidence-based practice simply means using research evidence to inform (*not dictate*), our practice.

The general systems theoretical framework for this book encompasses knowledge both about human psychology (emotions, behavior and cognition) and about social work practice (what methods are likely to be effective, for whom, under what conditions). We show readers how to combine *multisystem* and *evidence-based* components to improve assessment of individual and family clients, and we spell out practical skills for choosing interventions that are most likely to address client needs uncovered in the assessment process. This process must be collaborative and respectful of clients' own goals, preferences, situations, and cultures (Woolf, 2008, p 213).

The book is not a text on social work methods overall. Starting in Part I and continuing throughout the book, we:

- identify specific worker behaviors needed to access state-of-the-art information pertaining to client concerns;

- integrate neuroscience knowledge into assessment and intervention planning, demonstrate ways for readers to educate themselves and their clients, and help them access this information, understand it, and relate it to their own issues;
- encourage readers to facilitate clients' independent decision-making skills;
- provide information that can be easily disseminated to colleagues;
- advocate for agency policies consistent with neuroscience-informed best practices; and
- emphasize the need to work to bring public policies more in line with the best interests of service users through collective social action.

PART II sets forth basic information about brain structures and processes that mediate psychological functions of emotion, behavior, and cognition. These structures seldom have solo roles; usually they are actors within larger neural systems. It also includes introductory information about actions of classes of drugs in the brain, explaining a few mechanisms by which these drugs—antipsychotics (neuroleptics), opiates, stimulants, antidepressants, mood stabilizers, hallucinogens—are believed to work. Attention is given both to drugs designated "therapeutic" (medically sanctioned) and to drugs for pleasure, referred to as "recreational" (sold on the street or, in the case of alcohol, tobacco, and coffee, in liquor stores, supermarkets, and convenience stores). The book is not intended as a compendium of therapeutic and side effects of specific drugs; manuals that compile this information are available elsewhere (see, for example, Labbate, Fava, Rosenbaum, and Arana, 2010; National Institute of Drug Abuse [NIDA], 2011).

PART III on *neural networks* reports on the recently expanded domain of neuroscience that looks beyond specific structures and pathways to brain systems that process and often direct human experience. We examine the roles of two examples of neural networks that mediate pleasure and stress/trauma, respectively. This section refers to circuits or networks of real neurons that are connected or functionally related in the central nervous system and/or peripheral nervous system to one or more specific physiological functions. The other type of neural network modeling uses artificial neurons to solve artificial intelligence problems and is beyond the scope of this book.

Parts IV to VII explore dimensions of four areas of practice: substance use and addiction, child and adult development, psychiatric conditions and illnesses, and multiple routes to quality of life. Each area involves a spectrum from typical/usual to atypical/problematic, such as "mental health and mental illness," "typical and atypical development," "benign and injurious substance use," and "nonviolent versus violent behavior."

These four sections of the book acquaint readers with a wealth of examples of research knowledge that can advance assessment validity and deepen understanding of client behavior, emotions, and intervention needs.

Multimedia Animations

The book is enhanced by multimedia-animated mini-lectures available online, illustrating some of the brain structures and functions mediating psychological life. When we illustrate two neural networks, three-dimensional neuroscience animations are projected with brief videotaped segments of people living common moments in daily life. That is, three-dimensional animations of neurobiological events simulate invisible brain actions that underlie observable human experiences.

Instructors, if they wish, can show these lecture/animations/video clips to classes or can assign this web-based material as homework. The animations combined with the reading can reduce instructor class prep time—in fact, instructors not well versed in this material can learn it from the book and animation sets shown to students.

Behavioral Neuroscience for the Human Services

PART I

Our Professions Come of Age

NEUROSCIENCE KNOWLEDGE AND TOOLS FOR BIOPSYCHOSOCIAL PRACTICE

{ 1 }

Why Should I Care about Brain Science?
I'm a "People" Person

That's a good question. For most of our nation's history, few people thought we should or even could try to learn about how our brains work. Although roots of the discipline we now call *neuroscience* pushed a few sprouts up into visibility every once in awhile before and during the 19th century, almost all research in this area of knowledge dates from the early 20th century, gathering astonishing momentum in the final two decades of the 1900s—only to accelerate even more during the early 21st century. Invention of various technological tools, especially electronic scanners that allow us to watch our living brains in action through time, have spearheaded this frenzy of research activity. So now that new scientific knowledge continues to burst forth, why should human service practitioners tune in?

Suppose a teacher refers a five-year-old boy to you because he's hyperactive in class. How can you determine if he's just one of those many kids who are often restless, impulsive, and overactive? Or is his hyperactivity a reaction to a stressful family or school situation? Or does he have a neurobiological condition called attention-deficit hyperactivity disorder? How will the answer to that question affect your ideas about intervention? Will a behavior management plan do the job? Should the family situation be explored to see whether there are some acutely stressful events taking place? Is medication likely to be needed?

Here's another example. What will happen when your client, or a family member of your client, asks you to explain what's wrong with her? Or asks you how a particular medication works? Your client says that unless you can explain to her what this drug is supposed to do and how it works, she's going to stop taking it. Why should she risk putting this powerful (and mysterious) chemical into her body? Will you shrug and say she'd better talk to her doctor? You work with this doctor, and you know he doesn't take the time to give more than a cursory explanation. He's too busy.

What will happen when you have a strong opinion that your client's medication isn't doing what it's supposed to? When the psychiatrist asks you why you think so, and you don't understand how the medication is expected to work in the first place, what are you going to say? How credible will you be in the eyes of the prescribing physician who has so much power over your client's well-being? What basis will you have for making judgments about the course of action the doctor has set forth?

Or you have a client who is in recovery. He really wants to stay clean and sober, because his wife is threatening to leave, and his boss has given him an ultimatum. He keeps relapsing. He wants to know why the cravings are so strong—why can't he stay clean and sober? What's going on in his head that he can't control? If you don't understand the neurobiological basis of addiction, how can you explain it to him? Is urging him to Just Say No the answer?

What about your client with posttraumatic stress disorder (PTSD), who was in combat in Afghanistan and is now having flashbacks, night sweats, and waves of paralyzing terror? Are you still thinking in the old way about PTSD ("it's functional") because it's caused primarily by overwhelming environmental stressors? Are you aware that the person's brain has actually changed? How might it help you to work effectively with this client if you know that the intensity or persistence of PTSD symptoms arises from neurobiological changes induced by the stressful situation? What do the neurobiological underpinnings of PTSD have to do with the types of interventions you recommend?

Here's one more example. You are assigned a client with a diagnosis of borderline personality disorder. She has a reputation among your colleagues for being impulsive and prone to suicidal gestures such as cutting and overdosing. She's been involved with your agency for a long time. They've assigned her to you because she's burned out the other workers. What is going on with this person? Do you understand her? What role does neurobiology play in her borderline characteristics? How are you going to help her? What reason do you have for thinking your interventions may be successful?

Neuroscience is still a long way from having all the answers. In fact, it's only recently made its entrance. But it offers explanations that can help you answer some of these questions better than you could without it. This book suggests a few of these explanations, lays the groundwork for you to seek out many more on your own, and gives you some of the scientific background you'll need to help you understand the science-based material that you find.

Brain biology directly affects the well-being of those real people you're trying to help, and knowledge about it can directly affect how you practice. Part I presents the practice milieux, the changing ideologies, and in general the historical environments into which neuroscience entered and began to take root. It explains a few important tools for learning and teaching this new human science as a multisystem method of assessment. This method incorporates neuroscience into larger social science frames as core information for human services. Why are we the way we are? Part II presents basic brain structures and functions. Part III places these individual structures and small-unit functions into their systemic contexts within the brain. The two human experiences of pleasure on the one hand, and trauma and stress on the other are probed in Part III as examples of the work of the brain's systems in these experiences. Each neural system is made up of numerous structures and connecting pathways that carry out one or more specific functions. And among the responsibilities of the brain as a whole is to mediate *all our psychological functions, without exception.*

Are you wondering how the previous statement can possibly be true?

You're not alone. Millions of observers of human nature have shared your skepticism over the years, and even today millions still do. This book is one of an expanding body of research findings that support the contention that all psychological events are implemented by brain systems. A major contributor to this belief is the discovery of actual devices the brain uses to take in forces from the outside environment, convert these messages into brain functions, and then dispatch responses back to environments. One of the major achievements of neuroscience in the last few years is the acceleration of identification of specific intermediary events that are transforming environmental forces into internal human (and other animal) events.

Parts IV, V, VI, and VII summarize, respectively, some current neuroscience research on substance use/addiction, child development, psychiatric conditions, and multiple routes to quality of life. Those chapters will familiarize you with evidence that has led neuroscientists and medical researchers to their conviction that neurobiology is the foundation of all emotions, behavior, and cognition (psychological functions)—the external observable expressions of internal physiological events.

Neuroscience Knowledge: How Is It Faring in the Second Decade of the Millennium?

Steven E. Hyman, Director of the National Institute of Mental Health (1996–2001) and Provost of Harvard University (2001–2012), was kind enough to contribute a foreword to my earlier book *Psyche and Synapse* (1999, 2004).

I had occasion to talk to him late in 2010 when he was a panelist on the topic "The Future of Higher Education" (Boston, MA, November 7), at my own high school, from which I had graduated many decades earlier. Our school's good fortune in having him participate in this event arose from his being the father of two daughters attending the school.

I chatted with Dr. Hyman before the panel discussion. I told him I had first heard him speak in the mid-1990s at a workshop on the neuroscience of addiction at Harvard, where he chaired the Interfaculty Initiative on Mind, Brain, and Behavior. Not only was that presentation a milestone in my own development; it also electrified the more than 400 human service practitioners in the audience, who lined up after the program in the lobby and down long hallways to introduce themselves, pick up some reprints lying on the table, and, I would guess, express their delight and conviction about the importance of his material for their work in community agencies.

However, on this evening 15 years later at my high school, Dr. Hyman's reply to my reference to that workshop was terse: "Now we *really* know something."

In a similar vein, Daniel R. Weinberger, Chief of the Clinical Brain Disorders Intramural Research Program at the National Institute of Mental Health since 1998, stated without equivocation that "we have learned more about the brain and behavior in the past five years than in *all of history* before then" (Weinberger, 2011, emphasis in presentation).

Research published in neuroscience in recent years is daunting in its enormous volume, diversity of specializations, and relevance to contemporary human services. It readily became obvious to me that an "update" of my most recent book on neuroscience for human services (2004) would not suffice. There is simply too much new knowledge about human behavior that is changing some of the premises of psychological theory.

What I'll try to do is to familiarize you with basic neuroscience knowledge, describe the intellectual and professional contexts in which neuroscience has emerged as front and center knowledge for hands-on work with people, and provide strategies for integrating this core information into your own assessment, intervention planning, and managerial activities. As we explore this together, it will almost certainly be fun. Actually I'm hoping you'll have a few "Wow!" moments as you make discoveries about this most exciting, amazing science of living creatures. If you've already had an exhilarating experience with brain science, don't stop now—there's always so much more to learn.

You'll soon discover (if you haven't already) that emotions, behavior, and cognition are just as physical in essence as heartbeat, respiration, or infection. They're misleading, though—they're so associated with specific "affects" (psychiatry's label for observable emotions), with specific behaviors whose psychological meanings often appear obvious, and with cognitions (thoughts) coursing through our minds (by the way, where *is* your mind located?)—that we continue to put all these human functions under the rubric of "psychological," implying a distinction from bodily events.

You've just seen me refer to a divide between "mental" and "physical" function for the last time in this book. If you catch me or a contributing author doing so, please be charitable enough to make allowances for our "mature" brains, which were conditioned during our youth when the so-called *dichotomous model* was an almost unchallenged dogma in psychiatry, social work, and other disciplines.

This book is intended to help you acquire some tools, whether you have a limited scientific background or are well versed in the biological sciences. The book's style is conversational, but its message is always serious. The research from which the information has been drawn is referenced as a composite at the end of the book. Sometimes, in cases where the information is widely accepted and validated "common knowledge" among scholars, and in order to enhance readability, it is not cited in the text itself. Much of the knowledge conveyed is essential as state-of-the-art content related to human behavior in the social environment, mental health/mental illness, substance abuse/addiction, child development, actions of therapeutic and street drugs in the brain, and so-called "natural" or "alternative" therapies and interventions relevant to these areas.

Often segments contain examples or vignettes from research that traditionalists might argue are not *indispensable*, but that are exciting, funny, or thought-provoking. Such additions, I believe, are really important to communicate the sense of wonder and fascination that neuroscience can inspire. To get the most out of this book, you should practice applying what you're learning (1) to assess and understand more about your clients, and (2) to develop interventions that respond directly to this understanding. By the time you finish this journey, don't expect that you'll have an inventory of answers—you'll just be better equipped to ask the *right questions*. Unless we can first identify the essential questions our clients need us to raise, issues that matter greatly in their daily lives may go unattended.

As noted in the Preface, beginning neuroscience information is necessary to enhance human service practice not only with individuals/families/groups, but also for administrative and policy making practice—necessary, I would argue, for providers to direct organizations and leverage resources wisely.

I emphasize "beginning" neuroscience. Leaders such as Nobel Laureates Eric Kandel (2011) and Gerald Edelman (2004) and neuroscience scholar Steven Hyman (cited above), have described the human brain as the most complex entity in the known universe. It would be the height of folly to suggest that assessments involving such complexity, much of which is not yet well understood, could be conclusive or certain.

Isn't there a contradiction here? On the one hand we're declaring neuroscience knowledge essential for practice, but on the other, we're pointing out its large areas of uncertainty. This contradiction exists in the context of a new and growing emphasis on evidence-based knowledge for practice.

My response is that in the midst of a vast universe of questions, we do already have some answers relating well-documented scientific findings to psychological and practice knowledge. We'll present what we do know while advocating caution about what we don't know. Evidence-based practice does not consist of a set of facts; it is a process of learning through time (Gambrill and Gibbs, 2009; Gibbs, 2003; Haynes, Sackett, Gray, Cook, and Guyatt 1996).

One question that must be clarified right from the start is that we present information that can help human service practitioners *better understand underlying psychological and social dynamics, and use that understanding* to identify and choose interventions in collaboration with our service users. The skills we outline here do not depend on prevailing conventions for insurance reimbursement, whether DSM-5, DSM-IV-TR, or earlier versions of official manuals. Practitioners must certainly learn how to obtain payment for services, but that is not what this book is about.

At this point, I should warn you about an aspect of this volume that might make you uncomfortable. Although the book is intended as a textbook for graduate and undergraduate students, it deviates fairly substantially beyond what I think people consider the boundaries of a sound respectable college textbook: step-by-step clear information with a relatively impersonal/objective presentation. It appears that the traditional textbook's purpose is to impart knowledge, not to create enjoyment (except in the sense that learning itself is fun).

I too believe that giving clear step-by-step information is very important educationally, and I think this book does that. However, amid segments of information, it intersperses conversational, playful dialogues between me and the reader, whose replies to my queries I am not privileged to hear. These stylistic features may violate common expectations for a textbook, incorrectly leading some readers to think it lacks gravitas. To the contrary, I believe it not only conveys serious scientific information (the gravitas part) but also adds humor and whimsy, so that readers with varying levels of interest in the subject matter can discover that neuroscience can be fun and fanciful.

As an example, color image E. depicts a simple concept: to wit, "a core focus of this book will be to explore collaborative efforts between certain *inner brain structures* and specific outer regions in the *prefrontal cortex* in conducting and mediating our emotions, behavior, and cognition." The simplicity of this concept requires only a tiny measure of working memory to hold the concept in mind while flipping from the text page to the color image insert section.

Turn now to color image A., Three Mauras in the Lagoon: Reflections on the Self. We see the two important regions, inner *brain structures* and outer *cerebral cortex*, each occupying its space in Maura's brain separately. That's because it's easier to see them in isolation when trying to show their locations with the least amount of distortion or clutter.

So why are the three Mauras *in the water*? What does a tropical lagoon have to do with neuroscience? Well…my honest reason is that to me it adds whimsy and fantasy to simple images of cortex and inner structures—biological entities that inspire me with wonder as I explore their amazing capabilities.

But if I have to come up with a serious academic rationale, I could say it symbolizes that our bodies are composed of more water than anything else, 57% up to 65% or higher for typical adults (Wikipedia, 2012)—so what more fitting milieu for creatures like us than a tropical lagoon?

3

Normality, Professional Culture, and Psychiatric Disorders

DIAGNOSING JARED

What's "normal" and what's "abnormal"? Issues such as concepts of normality, diagnosis, and influence of professional cultures appear to heavily influence modes of practice. Client material illustrates professional dilemmas and potential conflicts between organizational imperatives and client needs.

In Part VI, we consider psychological indicators and other "signs and symptoms" (APA, 2000) of the person's emotional, cognitive, and behavioral status. When, as providers in mental health settings, we're called upon to evaluate that status, we are asked to judge whether a "disorder" is or is not present, and if we believe it is, what disorder it is.

One or more tentative diagnoses are usually made at the time of the first meeting with a mental health professional, sometimes including a mental status exam (short list of verbal questions to the client testing his or her orientation to reality). Tests deemed necessary by medical staff such as blood draws, chemistries, and other procedures may be done to answer questions about the person's condition(s).

A person is believed to have a certain "disorder" when he or she shows characteristics that are specific signs and symptoms typical of that particular disorder. Since many signs and symptoms are listed as criteria for more than one diagnostic category, the practitioner considers which diagnosis or diagnoses best fit the person, then records one or more diagnoses for which the person fully qualifies by meeting at least the minimum required number of criteria listed in the diagnostic manual. For example, to meet criteria for a diagnosis of borderline personality disorder in the DSM-IV-TR (in use at the time of writing), the individual had to show at least five of nine specified criteria (APA, 2000).

As practitioners, we mentally assign individuals to one of two groups characterized in psychiatric diagnosis as showing either "normal human variation" (no disorder) or "abnormal human variation" (may have a disorder). When we go beyond our mental activity to making entries on actual electronic or paper records denoting a psychological challenge needing therapeutic attention, we've made an implied judgment that something is wrong enough to consider for professional intervention.

As I explained above, I replace characterizations such as "normal/abnormal" or "functional/dysfunctional" with the terms "typical" and "atypical," which evoke an image of a location on a bell-shaped curve where the measured item falls, rather than an attribution of inferior status, badness, or "them and us." This preference reflects my own cultural perspective that concepts of "normality" reflect subjective, culturally determined judgments, whereas the same level of function (however measured) can be represented as typical or atypical without a connotation of good versus bad or healthy versus disordered.

Whether or not a diagnosis is assigned depends on which side of some cutoff point on a mental-health-to-mental-illness continuum the person's combination of emotions, behavior, and cognition is judged to fall. This cutoff point can vary from having very specific numeric criteria (score on a psychological test performance was 29), less numerically precise criteria (falling within a 20–50 range), or nonnumerical levels indicated by fuzzy quantities such as "a lot," "very few," "rarely," or "often."

Our overall or summary judgments of the person being evaluated are likely to have been arrived at from looking at several different characteristics, such as severity, duration, or frequency of signs and symptoms; presence across diverse settings; situations in which the behavior or emotional reaction occurs or fails to occur; contexts at the time of onset; economic stressors; indicators of neurobiological functions; cultural forces; and of course the nature of the challenges themselves, such as rageful outbursts or constant motion or social distance or persistent despair or false perceptions of sounds or visions. We give an example below of a client diagnosed or assessed very differently by people from two different cultural perspectives.

> Jared, age 29 and African American, is kneeling on his back porch talking audibly to someone whom no one else can see or hear. He does this several times a week. His next-door neighbor Beatrice is sitting on her back porch, which is almost identical to Jared's on this street of row houses. She scowls and mutters under her breath. "When is he going to see a shrink? He's a nut case." Jared's neighbor Edna on the other side, however, nods approvingly and crosses herself. "Praise the Lord, praise the Lord, he's found the Lord," she says to her sister as they both relax on their lawn chairs and enjoy the late afternoon sun. Edna and Jared's mother attend the same church.

Who's right? Is Jared mentally ill? Is he hallucinating? Does he have a diagnosis of schizophrenia? Or is he having a life-expanding spiritual experience? In Jared's neighborhood, no one has ever taken any action against him, although his behaviors are well known to everyone on the street. He is not violent, has never hurt or even frightened anyone, and he's lived there for years.

Jared does not work. He stopped attending school when he was 14 because his mother didn't like the way the school was treating him. Efforts by attendance officers to enforce his attendance were circumvented by his mother and Jared until his 16th birthday. His mother was not convinced that school attendance could benefit him in light of humiliating encounters with certain staff and peers.

His mother supports them both by working in a local store and by part-time housekeeping at a motel. When she is not at work, they spend a lot of time visiting family members who live nearby. Jared has never received mental health treatment. Family members haven't urged Jared's mother to "do something about Jared"—he is viewed as one of them and acceptable as he is, with his idiosyncracies.

One American subculture, that of psychiatry, would probably look at his behavior in light of DSM criteria and find him to have schizophrenia, chronic undifferentiated type.[1] Members of another subculture of American society, the religious group that Jared's mother and next-door neighbor Edna are part of, might interpret his behavior as a spiritual experience, not an illness. Probably some of the residents of the neighborhood would characterize Jared in a third way, as an odd or peculiar but harmless young man.

But let's consider what may happen when a new element is introduced into this history.

Jared attacks two little girls on a street in his town when they laugh at him and taunt him with words such as "you're crazy" and "you've got a loose screw." He flies into a rage, punches both girls, and grabs one of them and pounds her repeatedly on her back and legs. Both girls are bruised but there is no evidence of serious injury. Jared is apprehended, spends eight months in jail, and is released to his mother's home with a mandate to receive court supervision and psychiatric treatment. He receives a diagnosis of schizophrenia, chronic paranoid type. He is required to attend a day treatment program and to report to his parole officer regularly. Jared and his mother are warned that if Jared violates the conditions of his parole, he will be sent to prison for a long time. Jared says he is very sorry and won't do anything like that again.

No further incidents occur, but Jared's mother is now on tenterhooks. She's afraid to leave him alone and has had to reduce her work hours to be with him when day treatment is not open. Under these altered conditions, subcultures redefine the individual. Psychiatry defines him with a more severe diagnosis than he probably would have received over the years prior to the incident. Many in the local neighborhood, who formerly perceived him as odd or different, now see him as insane, violent, and dangerous to children. Neighborhood parents warn their children to stay away from Jared.

---

[1] As of December 1st 2012, the long-in-preparation DSM-5 was finalized by the APA Board but was not disclosed to the public until the publication date in May 2013 (APA, 2012, http://www.dsm5.org/Pages/Default.aspx).

How did Jared's status change from being odd, but acceptable, to mentally ill, dangerous, and an ex-offender? The concepts "abnormal" and "pathological" are usually not invoked for all unusual psychological functions, but specifically for those behaviors, emotions, or cognitions that cause trouble for the individual and/or the people who must interact with him or her. Had Jared remained the same person, without the incident having occurred, it's quite likely in our view that he might never have been defined as having a specific mental illness, because he would not have encountered the professional subculture that defines people through that lens.

Dominant cultures and subcultures strongly influence a wide range of beliefs, values, and meanings in most areas of human society, including mental health and mental illness. The National Institute of Mental Health's Culture and Diagnosis Group defines culture as "meanings, values, and cultural norms that are learned and transmitted in the dominant society and within its social groups. Culture powerfully influences cognition, feelings, and self-concepts *as well as the diagnostic process and treatment decisions*" (Sadock and Sadock, 2003, pp. 168–169, emphasis added). That is, concepts of pathology implicit in the notion of diagnosing mental illnesses are strongly influenced by a particular American subculture, that of mental health professions such as psychiatry, clinical psychology, and clinical social work. (The meaning of the word *clinical* is beyond the scope of our discussion. The term is used here to refer to subsets within the disciplines that designate themselves as *clinical*, usually connoting engaging in treatment of individuals using the nomenclature of the medical tradition.)

Where do we draw the line between normal and abnormal, mentally intact and mentally ill? Are suicide bombers mentally ill? Would an American who voluntarily dies in order to inflict death on others be considered mentally ill? Might committing suicide be a rational act, given its cultural and political context? What if this suicide bomber's cause is so compelling that he believes the price of death is worth it? What if his culture applauds death for that cause, and assures the individual of rewards in the hereafter? We'll return to some philosophical and political issues of mental health and illness later (Part VI).

4

Breaking Through: Is It Nature or Nurture?

DOMAINS OF BIOLOGICAL INFLUENCE
ON PSYCHOLOGICAL FUNCTIONS

Are biology and psychology inseparable? For many decades, purveyors of psychological wisdom did not seriously entertain this notion. Social workers educated in the 1950s, 1960s, and 1970s will remember that the closest scholars came to attributing any connection between human psychology and biology was in Sigmund Freud's developmental stage theory of oral, anal, and genital phases, a belief that remained popular until discredited by scientific research (see, for example, Johnson, 1991; Torrey, 1992). To his credit, Freud did recognize that psychology had some connection to biology, but technical tools at that time did not facilitate discovery of the real connections. Followers of Freud came more and more to believe in psychological constructs devoid of biology.

During the middle decades of the 20th century, it was assumed (without proof) that psychological disorders were either *organic* (as in senile dementia or drug-induced psychosis) or else *functional*, a term that denoted environmentally induced states of mind. Nearly all mental disorders and emotional difficulties were assigned to the functional category (Smith College School of Social Work, 2008). The word *environment* itself was shorthand for psychosocial environment, roughly translated as "the people in my life that affect my 'psyche,'" the poetic term from Greek mythology meaning *self, soul,* or *mind* (Mish, 1988). More specifically, with respect to emotional and cognitive development, *the environment* was thought to consist chiefly of parental behaviors, feelings, and thoughts continually bombarding developing offspring.

Few mental health professionals in the 1950s and 1960s seemed to have difficulty with such puzzling questions as how a disembodied mind might actually work (Torrey, 1992). It didn't seem important. What social workers, psychologists, and psychiatrists did deem important were, first, parental sins of commission and omission (mostly by mothers) that led inexorably to emotional damage in their young (Caplan and Hall-McCorquodale, 1985). Second, the clue to any number of adult woes could be an unresolved intrapsychic conflict (Arlow and Brenner, 1964; Bale et al., 2010) stemming from a failed opportunity in childhood to resolve the conflict at the appropriate stage of development. The result was that it was carried relentlessly forward into adulthood. Clinician/detectives were charged with finding these pathogenic forces presumed to be responsible for their clients' unhappiness.

Today, few researchers in the fields of child development and mental health still accept the mind/body dichotomy, that is, the separation of mind from body. The so-called *biopsychosocial paradigm* is now a cornerstone of behavioral theory.

However, Miresco and Kirmayer (2006) studied case vignette analyses by mental health professionals indicating that despite attempts to adopt an integrative biopsychosocial model, mind/body dualism is still pervasive, operating in accordance with a mind/brain dichotomy in ways that are often "covert and unacknowledged." Social workers were not included in the study; subjects were psychiatrists and psychologists. However, earlier comparative studies of all three professions indicated similar beliefs among social workers (Cournoyer and Johnson, 1991; Johnson, Cournoyer, Fisher et al., 2001; Johnson and Renaud, 1997). We'll return to this subject later.

Biopsychosocial and person-in-environment. What *is* a "biopsychosocial person-in-environment"? This increasingly popular tripartite creature had long exhibited psychological and social characteristics (although definitions differed according to diverging theoretical beliefs). Yet the nature of our tripartite creature's "bio" components remained vague and fragmented—scarcely even disputed, because these components were so few and far between. The profession acknowledged that biological aspects of personhood were important, but it seldom developed specific accounts of what these might be, let alone how our biological selves could be integrated with familiar "psycho," "social," cultural, and environmentally molded, selves (Johnson, 1991; Taylor, 2003; Torrey, 1992).

The "person"—the human organism whose emotions, behaviors, and cognitions characterize "who I am"—is perceived as a biopsychosocial entity *shaped by environments* and *acting upon them*. The person is embedded in and at the same time continuously interacting with the world outside. In social work shorthand, this concept is expressed as our familiar "person-in-environment." In the 1960s and 1970s, the person-in-environment in social work lingo typically referred to a psychosocial person, evolving into a "*biopsychosocial*" person in the last decades of the 20th and first decade of the 21st centuries (Johnson, 1980; Taylor, 2003).

For example, during the 1990s (and for some of us, even earlier), we mostly endorsed the axiom that schizophrenia develops in part from a genetic predisposition—but what about the more than 200 other psychiatric diagnoses catalogued in successive versions of the DSM (*Diagnostic and Statistical Manual of Mental Disorders*)? We considered that children with attention-deficit hyperactivity disorder (ADHD) characteristics might have a temperamental (inborn) bent for inattention, impulsivity, and disinhibition—but how was that different from active energetic boys at the upper end of a continuum whose high activity levels were nevertheless within "normal" limits? Wasn't it unethical to prescribe Ritalin for such children rather than create the kinds of environments within which they could develop into upstanding adults?

Scholars have roamed and stumbled along the multiple routes leading from their familiar psychological homes to more and more complex networks of muddy roads, foggy pathways, and dead ends. These extra layers of complexity are in part an inevitable consequence of trying to integrate the "bio" into an authentic, balanced biopsychosocial frame.

In the late 19th century, a famous explorer declared that the human mind was biological, only to be turned back by lack of tools for unearthing the recesses of the mind. His colleagues were derisive. They greeted his excited proclamations with stony silence. And so he gave up the quest for scientific truth and found an eager horde of followers who loved his metaphors and vignettes about postulated universals of human development. His theories of human behavior became a cornerstone of psychology for much of the 20th century.

In the last years of the 20th century and first years of the 21st, those formerly missing tools were discovered and made operational by human ingenuity. New generations of scientists applied these tools to long-postponed exploration of the roots of human emotions, intelligence, initiative, action, and humor. (Thousands could have been cited here—see for example Bailey, Bartsch, and Kandel, 1996; Hope, Kosofsky, Hyman, and Nestler, 1992; Hyman, Comb et al., 1988; Insel and Shapiro, 1992).

Had Freud lived to discover and use these tools, would he once again have become a leader in the search for the mind and the brain? Undoubtedly. Only this time he most likely would have made sure that his theories were supported by contemporary scientific evidence.

In a similar fashion, albeit at a much slower rate of progression starting much earlier in history, theories in the social sciences (e.g., psychology, political science, and economics) emerged from inferences that scholars made about ways that social, political, and economic forces operate. Inferences almost entirely based on historical information and individual observations were replaced more and more by inferences based on data gathered according to rules of empirical science.

In social work, the impetus to bring the "bio" into the "biopsychosocial" as a meaningful tripartite concept has shown some modest progress. At least three books on neuroscience for social work appeared during the first decade of the 21st century (Applegate and Shapiro, 2005; Farmer, 2009; Johnson, 2004), compared to one book each decade during the 1980s and 1990s (Johnson, 1980, 1999).

Another obstacle to embracing the new integrated person-in-environment model is that biology has been a vehicle for oppression, linked to characteristics such as skin color, facial characteristics, gender, and ethnicity. A few dismal examples are the enslavement of African Americans, horror of Holocaust genocide, racially motivated hate crimes, imprisonment of Japanese Americans in concentration camps, victimization of Native Americans, blaming women victims of physical and sexual abuse for their abuse, and most recently, visual representations of Barack Obama, first African American President of the United States, as Adolf Hitler (Tea Party protests televised on all major networks, 2009, 2010). Yet clearly these atrocities are not caused by biology itself; they are social psychological responses to real or attributed biological differences (Aronson, 2008).

In earlier writings I've addressed universal neurobiological phenomena—events similar for all human beings regardless of race or ethnicity. Here we consider information that helps us begin to understand *how societal goods or evils actually affect our neurobiology* to give us strength, pleasure, fun, or serenity, or to cause us stress, anxiety, grief, conflict, or trauma.

How are influences in childhood or adulthood received by our brains and translated into psychological events? How do individual differences interact with environmental forces to mold our lives? How can we make connections between the conditions we encounter every day in our work, such as substance abuse, psychiatric challenges, or family violence, and the invisible changes in our brains that lie behind these visible psychological events? The more we can learn about these connections, the better equipped we'll be to help people we serve.

Emotions, behavior, and cognition are processes that take place at the nexus where the individual human organism ("person") interfaces with the world outside that individual ("environment"). It's important to remember that the biology/environment dichotomy itself is not accurate, because environments can be biological as well as psychosocial.

For example, viruses and bacteria (which sometimes cause mental illnesses), or meats and vegetables laced with environmental toxins, are biological aspects of our environments. (Most of the food we eat is material of organic origin, such as grains, meats, fruits, vegetables, eggs, fish, and dairy, with or without added inorganic compounds such as preservatives or colors.) Physical nonbiological aspects of the environment such as heat, cold, dryness, light, and darkness also influence our moods and behaviors.

And any interpersonal relationship, whether loving, antagonistic, or oppressive, involves one individual with his or her multitude of biopsychosocial attributes, and *environmental biopsychosocial* forces emanating from the second individual, whether his or her behaviors are loving, playful, or nurturing; hostile; domineering, submissive, or abusive; or showing indifference or detachment. So much for biological humans versus nonbiological environments!

Hypothetically, if we wanted to bring about a change in behavior by the "other" person, we should assess the nature of this environmental source of influence by conducting an in-depth assessment of this "other" in addition to the individual whose needs we want to see met. And so on ad infinitum. Now back to the real world.

Risk factors and protective factors. During the 30 years since the publication of the first book on neuroscience for social work (Johnson, 1980), advances in research on psychiatric illnesses, substance abuse and addiction, and child and adolescent development have accelerated at an extraordinary pace. It is now known that there is no single cause for most psychiatric conditions and most instances of addiction. With rare exceptions (such as Huntington's Disease), these conditions and states arise from complex multifactorial interactions through time between *risk factors* and *protective factors.* Risk factors and protective factors can be biological or nonbiological and can arise within or outside the human body.

Here, risk factor is defined as a biological or nonbiological variable that

a. contributes to a problem occurring,
b. makes the problem worse, and/or
c. makes the problem last longer.

The converse, protective factor, is defined as a biological or nonbiological variable that

a. contributes to preventing a problem from occurring,
b. lessens its severity, and/or
c. helps it get better faster.

It's important to note that *biological* risk and protective factors themselves can emanate either *from within the individual* (e.g., as a configuration of specific genes, a level of a particular neurotransmitter, or a temperamental characteristic, any of which may be potentially harmful or beneficial), or *from the external environment,* such as illness-producing bacteria contaminating human drinking water (risk factor), or bacteria that enhance healthful aspects of foods such as yogurt (protective factor).

And we shouldn't leave out the most common biological risk and protective factors in our environments—human beings.

Both biological and nonbiological risk and protective factors emanating from the external environment are processed by the individual himself or herself, becoming—sometimes almost instantaneously—a part of that individual's own biopsychosocial internal self. This transformation of environmental inputs can be temporary, lasting only for a brief moment, or long-term, ongoing influences on the individual's emotions, behavior, and cognition.

Internal influences toward risk or protection may be chemical (such as a low level of serotonin, which influences mood and other states) or nonliving biological substances (such a recently consumed meal of cheeseburger, fries, and a chocolate shake). This tasty but unhealthful meal is not a part of the eater's biopsychosocial self when eaten, but is quickly converted and incorporated into the person's own biological system.

Major risk factors and protective factors, both for illnesses and for social problems, have been identified through epidemiological, clinical, and laboratory research. The list of candidates is legion. Risk and protective factors arise from genetics; viruses; birth events; nutrition; economic resources; social and emotional supports; organizational forces, both risk- and support-generating (e.g., families, schools, workplaces, health care– and social service–providing organizations), spiritual resources, and cultural forces.

How might culture cause risk factors for social problems? When culture is defined to include beliefs, values, and norms, culturally derived risk factors are illustrated by ethnocentrism (for example, perceiving one's own ethnicity as superior, or imposing beliefs derived from one's own cultural background on persons of other cultures); heterosexism (perceiving people with same sex preferences as inferior, pathological, or not entitled to equal protection under the law); or ableism (perceiving persons with disabilities as alien, incapable, or equivalent to the disability itself rather than ordinary people who have a disability).

The concept of risk and protective factors counters our human tendency to dichotomize (for example, "psychiatric conditions are caused by either biology or environment"). A fundamental difference between older theories of psychology or child development and contemporary ecosystems theories is the replacement of an "either/or" mindset with "both/and." And the "both/and" itself is inadequate—we are almost always looking at multivariable phenomena in any given ecosystem, phenomena created by variables acting and influencing up and down through hierarchies of systems sizes and complexity.

Take the dichotomy of gender. We've long known that psychological and cultural factors converge to create persons with many combinations of so-called *masculine* and *feminine* characteristics, straight and gay orientations. But even leaving this socially defined variability aside, when we define gender solely by presence of male or female genitalia, there's still no absolute truth in a dichotomous view—some persons are born with combinations of both (see for example Koken, Bimbi, and Parsons, 2010; Reis, 2009; Sanchez, Sanchez, and Danoff, 2009; Wiesemann, Ude-Koeller, Gernot, Sinnecker, and Thyen, 2010).

Yet old theories die hard. Human nature seems to crave simplicity and certainty in an overwhelmingly complex and uncertain world. Incorporating neuroscience knowledge into already complex ecosystems just makes matters more difficult for many of us.

BOX 4.1 My Risk Factor and Protective Factor Midsummer Night

I am sleeping in a charming Victorian mansion in the New Hampshire White Mountains. The lacy crocheted curtains blow gently in the moonlit chamber. I and my professorial colleagues have spent the day in civilized discourse about permutations of risk factors and protective factors.

I find myself on the spacious lawn looking out over sunny fields leading up to a mountain. I'm not in the least surprised to see two demure ladies in floor-length Victorian dress, facing each other with boxing gloves—pictures of composure and gentility (see Figure 4.1). Each lady was the embodiment of one side of a two-sided contest, RF on my left and PF on my right, equally demure and genteel. Oh my, they're starting to spar!

Now I'm watching a continual series of split-second actions—footwork, body motions, and jabs back and forth—as each adversary responds to the other's action. This rapid nonstop action will continue until one warrior lady knocks down the other. If the Risk Factors prevail over the Protective Factors, an observable condition or crisis will occur. If the Protective Factors prevail by fending off the onslaught of the Risk Factors, no identified "disorder" or condition will emerge and/or an impending crisis will be averted.

I've just realized that this drama is taking place inside my own brain and body. These are my own risk and protective factors. My mental and physical state is the prize for the winner of the match. My heart is pounding faster and faster and I start to breathe heavily. My brain is processing every step the combatants take, every facial expression, every punch. I watch my brain doing high-speed calculations about the effects of one protagonist's latest move, the likely next move of the other, the effect every move has on my own physical and mental state, the sensations I'm experiencing with every move of the combatants. How can I respond to improve the odds that my protective factors will win?

All of a sudden I hear a thud. The ladies have disappeared. I realize that the boxing match fell short of representing reality. It combined all the risk factors into one entity and all the protective factors into the other. That's not the way the real world works.

Risk Factors   **Protective Factors**

FIGURE 4.1

FIGURE 4.2

> But my brain has come through, once again. Its versatility never ceases to amaze me. The boxing ring morphs instantaneously into a giant arena with many players, each interacting with several of the others, each containing both risk and protective components (see Figure 4.2). There's no way I can keep up with all of this. I might as well sit back and watch this astonishing performance.

Many combatants each embody both risk and protective factors. Some players act simultaneously as agents of both risk and protection. For example, when an individual is addicted to cocaine or alcohol, user friends supply social support and friendship, but at the same time may (inadvertently or openly) undermine the individual's attempt to get clean or sober.

In epidemiology, the risk factor/protective factor model pertains specifically to assessment of physical illness versus health, and social illness (such as crime, violence, danger) versus social well-being (such as order, civility, safety). That is, it explicitly uses the concepts of physical and social pathology to frame data about populations.

In social work, as in epidemiology, the scope of systems analysis includes medical pathology and social pathology, spanning a wide range of practice issues such as life-threatening contagious disease (AIDS), family violence, teen substance abuse, or adult criminality. The domains of both disciplines entail states of being, broad scope, and often, extreme complexity.

Human states of being can be designated in terms of a spectrum from typical/usual to atypical/not usual, as, for example, "mental health and mental illness," "typical and atypical development" (replacing the judgment-based constructs of "normal" and "abnormal"), "benign and injurious substance use," and "nonviolent versus violent behavior." These states of being vary in space and time; intensity; level of coherence; mobility; capacity for change; cultural and ethnic difference; degree of power; access to resources; propensity for wellness and for specific illnesses; temperament; and neurobiological and muscular endowments in areas of human endeavor such as music, athletics, visual arts, mathematics, language, information processing, mechanics, and many other abilities.

We really have no idea about the molecular processes that led us to this complex inventory of possible contributing factors. Should we even care? How do we avoid becoming overwhelmed by this complexity?

Just *recognizing* the complexity of human psychological functions in their environmental contexts is the first step. Perhaps the second step is to acknowledge that in any situation there will always be factors operating that we're not aware of, and that our understanding will always be imperfect. The myth that we can "master" a content area such as human behavior in the social environment or mental health must be dispelled.

In a well-known text on human biology for social workers, Ginsberg, Lackerud, and Larrison (2004) integrated diverse human biological information on health and illness into a truly biopsychosocial context, encompassing relevance for macro- as well as micro-level practice, social policy issues, and the growing body of evidence-based knowledge that must become familiar to providers of human services. With respect to the mental health/human behavior area, they write:

> There has been a slow but perceptible shift in the theories concerning the origins of mental health problems that have been based on a complex and evolving understanding of the causes underlying human behavior... The growth in understanding the biological factors associated with mental health disorders has called into question some of the techniques used by social workers in helping people with mental health problems. (p. 155)

Ginsberg et al. (2004) have identified above two key characteristics of emerging neuroscience knowledge: *complexity*, which will immediately become apparent to readers of this book on neuroscience for practice, and *evolving*. Although their text was published only nine years prior to the completion of this book, the evolution they noted has occurred at a rate much faster than many of us could have imagined. What was "new" in 2004 has been revised, expanded, and in some areas proven incorrect.

Here's where this book comes in. As we increasingly recognize the complexity of these areas of knowledge and then acknowledge how little any of us knows, we can begin to identify specific kinds of knowledge that can help us in our work of helping others. We can recognize that we need to know more, especially in certain areas, than we had previously believed.

The neurobiological foundation of human psychological functioning is one kind of knowledge we once ignored. Now we're stepping up to the plate and informing ourselves. But we have to keep learning about as many of the recent advances as we can. Lifetime learning is not just icing on your favorite to-die-for chocolate cake—it's a mixture of exciting new, ingredients mixed *in the cake itself.*

How can this book help? The purpose of the book is to make available some knowledge about the role of neurobiology in psychological functioning that can be integrated with psychosocial and life contextual knowledge. How often in our everyday lives do we unconsciously integrate knowledge from different areas into our assessments? Wouldn't it be preferable to be more aware of knowledge that we're integrating? What do we do when an accurate assessment requires some expertise or piece of information that we don't have? Do we pause in the assessment to try to obtain that information? What happens if we *don't even know* that we're missing an important piece of information? Is our assessment off target?

Yes, probably. Owing to the complexity of human situations, most of the assessments we make continually every day, knowingly or unknowingly, in our work and our personal lives, are probably less than fully accurate. But in situations with clients, we want to reduce inaccuracies as much as possible while recognizing the limits of our access to important information.

Does a neurobiological understanding of psychic phenomena explain away the roles of emotions, behavior, and thought? *Not at all!* Does it take away the need for psychosocial interventions? *Not at all!* On the contrary, it helps us understand psychic phenomena (mental functioning) more fully so that we can integrate this knowledge with our psychosocial expertise.

We attempt to incorporate highlights of the information derived from a knowledge base that has grown exponentially during the past decade, in both scope and depth. Thousands of publications in scientific journals can be accessed through databases such as PubMed. The sheer volume of available information, not to mention the technical complexity of much of the research, might tempt us to throw up our hands. Do we really need to be conversant with all this? Surely there's no way most of us can understand much of the research on genetics or the neurobiology of medication actions, and do we really have to?

Here, my response is both yes and no. No, we don't need to understand advanced scientific treatises on genes and alleles, and no, we don't need to master much of this highly technical information to help our clients. So where's the "yes"?

The "yes" is that our service users do need to understand what their own or their family member's condition is, how it can affect behavior and emotions, how the condition may manifest itself in the future, and what the new knowledge about these issues may mean for themselves and their loved ones. They need to learn how a specific treatment or intervention is thought to work, and what interventions have been shown to be effective for some people with similar conditions. That is, clients need to have at least a basic understanding of the "hows" and "whys." How is treatment X or Y likely to address the problems of concern, and why? How can clients make informed choices? And on a more existential level, clients want answers to questions like "Is my situation hopeless?" "What did I do to cause this problem?" "Am I just a loser?" "Am I a bad parent?" "Did I fail as a partner?" "What can I do to make things better?" "Who can help me?"

Is it the social worker's responsibility to facilitate clients in making informed choices and resolving existential issues? If so, then we as professionals need to understand *enough* about the way the condition operates (biologically as well as psychosocially) and *enough* of how possible interventions work (biologically as well as psychosocially) to convey *enough* of that information to clients so they can better understand, learn, and take action.

DOMAINS OF BIOLOGICAL INFLUENCE ON
PSYCHOLOGICAL FUNCTIONS

This introduction to biopsychosocial knowledge would not be complete without information on the domains of biological influence on psychological phenomena. Table 4.1 presents biological functions that may act in concert with nonbiological factors to influence emotions, behavior, and cognition, and mechanisms through which they wield this influence. Examples are included of specific conditions or symptoms that can arise from each domain.

In the early decades of the 1900s, most psychiatrists in Europe and America believed that mental disorders were illnesses of the brain. By the 1950s and 1960s, this view had been largely supplanted by new ideas proposed by Freud and his followers. As I noted earlier, mid-20th-century psychiatric dogma, along with social work's conventional wisdom, now categorized all mental disorders either as *organic* (biological in origin, such as senile dementia, drug intoxication, and mental retardation) or as *functional* (arising from psychosocial stressors). I'll refer to this formulation as the *dichotomous theory of etiology*.

In the decades before the 1970s, every psychiatric disorder not in the organic category was automatically assigned to the functional category, from autism to schizophrenia to manic-depressive psychosis (as bipolar disorder was then called) to character pathology (now known as personality disorder). Cognitive differences, too, were often viewed as functional. For example, what we now might call a "learning disability" was then thought to be a learning problem caused by emotional factors. Every condition not designated organic was assumed to be functional, that is, caused by toxic environments, most typically rejecting, overcontrolling, overindulgent, distant, or otherwise inadequate mothers. Fathers were seldom mentioned in those days.

In the 1970s, tiny cracks appeared in this fortress of beliefs, as a few people questioned the popular concepts of the "schizophrenogenic mother" (assumed

TABLE 4.1 Domains of Biological Influence

Domain	Mechanisms of Influence	Examples of Conditions Sometimes Related To Domain
Genetic	genetic programming	bipolar disorder, schizophrenia, obsessive-compulsive disorder, Down's syndrome, major depression, attention-deficit hyperactivity disorder, tic disorders, Huntington's chorea, panic attack, dementia, autism, dyslexia, alcoholism, borderline personality, anxiety disorders
Endocrinological	hormone imbalance	some mood disorders, post partum psychosis, extreme aggressivity (when due to excess testosterone), premenstrual syndrome
Allergic/ Immunologic	autoimmune reactions antigen/ antibody reactions	attention-deficit hyperactivity, depression
Metabolic	biochemical processing burning for energy (diabetes, hypoglycemia)	depression, anxiety, dementia, retardation, autism, schizophrenia
Infectious	viral or bacterial disease (e.g. encephalitis, rubella)	attention-deficit hyperactivity, cognitive impairment
Head injury	oxygen deprivation damaging or destroying neurons	attention-deficit hyperactivity, impulsivity, aggressivity,
Nutritional	lack of needed nutrients (proteins, vitamins, minerals)	impaired cognitive functions, apathy, dementia, aggressivity, depression
Neoplastic	new tissue (as in cancer/ tumor),	pressure from tumors in brain
Toxic	lead, mercury, street drugs, prescribed meds, workplace or home chemicals,	retardation, attention-deficit hyperactivity, dementia, aggressivity, learning disability, autism

Separation into domains is for purpose of clarity only. Domains are highly interactive with each other.
Behavioral and cognitive problems are increasingly being related to proliferating environmental toxins.

to have caused her child's schizophrenia), the "refrigerator mother" (Bruno Bettelheim's characterization of mothers of autistic children), and the idea that mental illness was a myth of attribution thought up by culpable families to cover up their dysfunctional family systems. Bettelheim (1903–1990) also likened mothers of autistic children to SS guards in Nazi concentration camps. He continued proclaiming his views to sellout audiences of social workers and other service providers until his death.

In the late 1950s and early 1960s, schizophrenia began to be treated with Thorazine and other antipsychotic drugs. A large number of long-term sufferers improved so much with these medications that psychiatric hospitals discharged them after years of hospitalization (although, unfortunately, communities at that time had not been adequately prepared and funded to meet their needs).

In the 1970s, early neuroscientists proposed that schizophrenia, autism, and bipolar disorder were neurobiological illnesses in the organ of the brain. Studies by Kety (1979) and others supported the importance of genetics in schizophrenia, noting that most identical twins of persons with schizophrenia either also developed schizophrenia (about 50%) or had other mental disorders along a "schizophrenia spectrum." Fieve (1975) found rates of genetic influence in manic-depressive disorder to be even higher than those for schizophrenia. Cantwell (1972), Wender (1971), and others documented strong genetic and other biological influences in minimal brain dysfunction, a global term that encompassed what we now call attention-deficit hyperactivity disorder (ADHD) and learning disability. Ritvo and colleagues (1976) demonstrated multiple brain abnormalities in children with autism. Lewis and Balla (1976) went so far as to obtain neurologic data suggesting that brain dysfunction often played an important role in delinquent behavior. By 1981, major biological substrates of borderline personality disorder had been identified by Andrulonis, Glueck, Stroebel, and colleagues.

Mental health practitioners and educators largely ignored these prophets of science. At most, they conceded that there might be a "biological predisposition" to these disorders. Still, many held tenaciously to the notion that toxic family environments (read "bad mothers") made the decisive contribution both to major mental illnesses such as schizophrenia and bipolar disorder, and to nonpsychotic conditions such as obsessive-compulsive disorder, panic attack, and mood dysregulation—conditions that often inflicted misery on sufferers and their families (see Part VI, Mental Health and Mental Illness: Medical Conventions, Recent Research, from Assessment to Intervention Planning).

The convergence of new methods for studying mental illness and the formation of the National Alliance for the Mentally Ill (NAMI) led in the 1980s to widespread questioning of whether mothers were really schizophrenogenic, prone to "refrigerate" their children, or perpetrating the myth that mental illness was a biological disease to conceal their culpability. Research evidence increasingly supported the view that the origins of learning disabilities and ADHD were neurobiological, not responses to parental ambition, marital conflict, or other family dynamics.

At least two eminent psychiatrists made public apologies in major professional journals to parents of mentally ill youth for having erroneously blamed them for their children's illnesses. Kenneth Terkelsen (1983) apologized to parents of persons with schizophrenia for his unfair and denigrating views about parents' supposed roles in causing their children's illnesses. Fourteen years later, John Gunderson published a similar apology with respect to parents of people with borderline personality disorder.

> I...was a contributor to the literature that led to the unfair vilification of the families and the largely unfortunate efforts at either excluding or inappropriately involving them in treatment. So it is with embarrassment that I now find myself presenting a treatment [psychoeducation] that begins

with the expectation that the families of borderline individuals are important allies of the treaters (Gunderson, Berkowitz, and Ruiz-Sancho, 1997, p. 451).

Brain-scanning techniques, developed in the 1980s and 1990s and perfected during the 2000s, brought the history of theories about mental disorders around full circle to the beliefs of the pre-Freudians. Leaders in the neuroscience revolution now asserted unequivocally that psychiatric disorders were biological diseases of the brain, just as nephritis is a disease of the kidney. They claimed that these neurobiological diseases were not caused by toxic families any more than toxic families cause nephritis. Unlike the pre-Freudians, however, these neuroscientists had masses of scientific data to support their claims.

But there was a problem. Thousands of practitioners had been born, raised, and immersed in the old dichotomous mind versus body paradigm. They had spent years of their lives developing treatment strategies and techniques founded upon that model. Now they were being asked to give up a lot of what they had been taught and had used as axioms to guide their practice, to learn to think about things differently.

To make matters worse, the domain of neurobiological research extended further and further beyond its original focus on major mental illnesses to encompass what had once been perceived as the turf of nonmedical psychotherapists—nonpsychotic conditions mentioned previously, addiction, and personality disorders. One by one, each diagnosis was removed from the *functional* column and placed in another category—not the old *organic* column, but an entirely new category dubbed *neurobiological disorder*. This new designation assumed that persons suffering from any of these conditions had an underlying, biologically based condition that continually interacted with environments through time, with the biological organism influencing the environment and the environment influencing the biological organism, back and forth, in endless flux. In fact, the time had come to deep-six the old organic/functional classification system.

The new knowledge generated by the neuroscientists called for major shifts in practice approaches for people with mental illnesses, including those with less severe conditions that could be subsumed under the rubric *psychological problems*, or those with deficits or differences in cognitive processing, such as learning disabilities.

Rather than simply helping people gain insight into their emotions and ventilate their feelings, therapists were now called upon to use a range of interventions for clients with diverse diagnoses, usually including a combination of some of the following: education about the condition; medication; training in social, communication, self-control, or daily living skills; support groups; special educational strategies; individual counseling; and active ongoing advocacy to help clients obtain employment, find housing, or access other financial, material, and service benefits. The one-time mainstay of psychiatric treatment, psychotherapy, was now supplemented with many other interventions. Educational supports and techniques targeting specific neuropsychological functions replaced psychological counseling as first-line interventions for learning deficits.

In addition, psychotherapy itself now had to take a variety of forms, depending on the condition. A client with schizophrenia might require education, supportive counseling, and coaching about how to be successful in tasks of daily living. Cognitive restructuring might be indicated for depression, in vivo exposure therapy for acute anxiety, self-control skills training for impulsivity problems, or relapse-prevention techniques for addiction.

The simpler days of sitting in an office helping clients express their feelings were over. A much wider repertoire of techniques was now required. This expanded menu of interventions was consistent with the findings of the new neuroscience, and these therapeutic techniques could be used in conjunction with medication or without it.

By the late 1990s, scholars had achieved a deepening understanding of all psychological conditions as outcomes of the interactions between biological and nonbiological risk and protective factors. Psychological distress or dysfunction was not, as previously assumed, an inevitable consequence of a single variable, BP or "Bad Parenting". In fact, persons with psychological or cognitive problems, whether severe or relatively mild, often had families who were concerned, loving, and persistent in their efforts to help their loved one. These parents, who usually had other perfectly typical children, were remarkable not for their pathogenic qualities but for their dedication to the needs of their ill or challenged family member.

Parents who were angry, critical, depressed, or in denial about their child's condition were now seen not as pathogenic agents, but as deeply worried and sad people who felt helpless to make their family member better. They were experiencing vicarious pain for the child's seemingly endless suffering, chronic grief about the loss of a child they once had or hoped to have, or they felt overwhelmed by crushing life circumstances.

Professional helpers now increasingly subscribed to the view that all parents, including the most supportive, can certainly do things that make their loved one's condition worse—not as pathogenic agents but as people in need of emotional support, validation, and specialized skills for relating effectively to the challenged family member. Accordingly, as the persons with the mental illness or psychological distress were now known to need a range of interventions, family members also were found to need professional services quite different from what social workers and other service providers were accustomed to offering.

5

Why Do We Know So Much More Now Than in the 1980s and 1990s?

At least four factors have contributed to rapid advances in neuroscience knowledge: (1) a technological revolution; (2) accumulating evidence about neurobiological structures and functions underlying psychological problems; (3) experiences with new medications; and (4) public education by mental health family and consumer advocacy groups.

1. The technological revolution

- Brain imaging techniques allow us to see not only structures but also actual functions or processes in the living brain.
- Electron microscopes allow us to see and record minute structures in the brain such as neurons, synapses, and even molecules.
- Microelectrodes allow us to wire and measure the activity of a single neuron (nerve cell).
- Biochemical assays (tests and analysis of brain and body chemistries and prospective medications) can provide essential data for learning about biological and chemical properties related to symptoms of emotional, behavioral, and cognitive dysfunctions.

Brain imaging has brought about unprecedented breakthroughs in our knowledge. These techniques measure brain characteristics using computers to see "slices" of living brains. This information is transformed into visual images on monitors or into printouts of numerical values. Examples of techniques that show structures are computed tomography (CT) and magnetic resonance imaging (MRI). CT scans are cheaper and can detect calcified lesions better than MRIs. MRIs give a clearer picture (have superior resolution), can distinguish subtle differences in brain tissue, and can represent thinner slices of brain tissue.

Examples of techniques that show functions or processes are positron emission tomography (PET), single photon emission computed tomography (SPECT), and functional magnetic resonance imaging (fMRI). Glucose compounds, incorporating radioactive substances acting as markers that PET and SPECT can read, are injected into the blood, allowing PET and SPECT to track glucose concentrations in different brain regions. In PET scans, reds, oranges, and whites represent areas of high activity (increased glucose metabolism). Greens and blues represent areas of low activity (decreased glucose metabolism) (see color image B., PET Scans of Adults without and with Attention-Deficit Hyperactivity Disorder, second page of the color image insert section).

SPECT scans are similar to PET and cheaper, but they provide less clear pictures (poorer image resolution).

Functional MRIs (fMRIs) give a series of rapid MRI images that can measure regional oxygen levels in blood vessels without injecting anything, so that no radioactive substance is administered. In addition, fMRIs can show more detail than PET about the activity of a particular region. For these reasons, fMRIs are typically the imaging of choice. Please turn to color image B. again.

A person with ADHD has more areas of greens and blues, indicating underactivity in certain areas of the brain where less glucose is being burned up. A person without ADHD has more areas of reds, oranges, and whites, where there's more glucose being burned up. In typical persons, the brain systems that inhibit behaviors balance the effects of systems that excite behaviors. The scan shows underactivity in more brain regions of the person with ADHD than in the brain without ADHD. But people with ADHD are often *overactive*.

So why should that be? In specific brain regions, some inhibitory forces that are supposed to balance excitatory forces appear to be underactive, allowing some excitatory forces to get revved up. This in turn is believed to be associated with behavioral disinhibition or overexcitation. I'll explain more about excitatory and inhibitory actions in the brain in Parts II and IV.

Radiologists and neuroscientists have debated the merits of the techniques mentioned above for a range of specific diagnostic questions. Readers who want to learn more about a particular technique can search PubMed and also cautiously search for the answers with keywords such as "compare" "fMRI" "SPECT," and "PET."

If we are to have any confidence that the difference between the two brain images has anything to do with ADHD, we need corroborating data from multiple sources such as individual and family history, response to previous treatment, reports of scans of the brains of several people from each of the two groups (those with and without ADHD), and comparisons of medical and demographic variables. In relation to this particular study, safeguards for validity were in place (Zametkin et al., 1990).

2. *There is new evidence about neurobiological structures and functions that underlie psychiatric illness.* Scanning technology advances have allowed us to see that psychiatric disorders involve certain specific brain structures or functions that differ from those of typical brains. Anatomical (structural) and physiological (functional, process) characteristics of

the brains of people with psychiatric disorders are phenomena that we can't see without technology. These phenomena, now visible in scans, relate directly to the psychiatric symptoms that we do see in daily life.

3. *Experiences with new medications* have shown that specific symptoms— such as hallucinations, delusions, hyperactivity, despair, compulsive rituals, or paralyzing fear in the absence of a real threat—respond to specific medications associated with each type of symptom.

4. *Mental health family and consumer advocacy groups are educating the public.* The work of these groups has increased public awareness of brain/behavior relationships and the role of neuroscience in mental illness and mental health. The following examples of national groups with local affiliates around the country have all been in existence 20 years or more: National Alliance for the Mentally Ill (NAMI), Federation of Families for Children's Mental Health (FFCHM), CHADD (Children with Attention Deficit Disorder), and Learning Disabilities Association (LDA). These groups have collaborated with professionals in agencies, with the National Institute of Mental Health (NIMH), and with national educational organizations, to dissemi- nate information about neurobiological disorders. These groups have also lobbied for legislation, such as parity in third-party reimburse- ment. There are many other support/advocacy groups sponsored locally around the country that can usually be accessed through local government lists or national advocacy organizations on the web.

{ 6 }

What Can We Make of Jenny's Rages?
Biology-Environment Disputes Among Mental Health Social Work Specialists
By Marcia Brubeck, MSW, JD

Nine-year-old Jenny has severe, intense tantrums at home with her single-parent mother. During these episodes, which are characterized by prolonged rages, she throws things, swings the cat by the tail so that its head bangs against the floor, becomes very physically agitated, and screams at the top of her lungs. The episodes occur at least once every couple of days and last an hour or two. Immediately prior, the child becomes hot and reports feeling lightheaded. When the episode passes, she falls asleep and wakes without any recollection of what happened.

She has been seen in a hospital day treatment facility and an agency day treatment facility, where therapists have diagnosed her with oppositional defiant disorder (ODD) and have advised the mother that she has poor parenting skills. The mother and I have obtained copies of all medical records and have synthesized them with developmental, medical, and family history to demonstrate that the child qualifies for a diagnosis of bipolar disorder (nowadays sometimes called "mood disorder NOS" (not otherwise specified) because of the diagnostic inadequacies of the current DSM-IV-TR, particularly where children are concerned. (The NOS categories are expected to be eliminated from the DSM-5)).

Providers, however, are often unwilling to make this diagnosis, regardless of the evidence. Particularly in complex, difficult cases, each institutional provider wants to affirm the diagnosis assigned by the previous provider, because making a new diagnosis, regardless of the justification, exposes the provider to potentially greater liability in the event of mishaps (there's safety in consensus).

This is particularly the case when the pharmacological problems are complex, as with juvenile onset bipolar disorder and seizure disorder, which are sometimes difficult to distinguish. This is not to mention the insistence by professionals that Jenny's problem is not a biological disorder at all, as implied by the ODD diagnosis. The child in question was unstable on medications administered by an outpatient psychiatrist specializing in juvenile onset bipolar.

If pharmacology is diagnosis-driven, there's added reason to stick with diagnoses for which there are relatively "safe" medication options. And the medication question itself, as I always explain to parents, is handled differently depending on the prescriber's philosophy and value system. For example, if mental illness has robbed the child of executive functions, making it impossible for her to perform academically or to play a game of checkers with peers, do you (1) medicate conservatively, because the child is nine and you worry about the potential long-term effects of the neuroleptic? Or do you (2) medicate more aggressively, because the child is suffering not only from the illness's symptoms and the stigma of having the illness, but also from the foregone opportunity to succeed at important developmental tasks of childhood? The second option entails the hope that medical advances will both improve knowledge of long-term effects of current medications and bring onto the market new, more effective, and more benign pharmaceutical options.

To sum up, the institutional question is this: Which gets priority, consideration of the client's needs, or consideration of the institution's exposure to risk? The medication question is this: Which consideration should govern present assessment, possible future costs or known, here-and-now quality-of-life issues?

Afterthoughts. I don't know whether electroencephalograms (EEGs) are routinely done when children are receiving only day treatment. Certainly they would not be done at an agency; whether hospital day treatment programs order them or not, I don't know. And I also don't know whether EEGs are routinely ordered when a diagnosis of juvenile onset bipolar is suspected. It's important to bear in mind that diagnoses not only *may* but *must* be made even without medical tests. As a social worker, I cannot order tests, but I must supply a diagnosis if my services are to qualify for reimbursement by managed care. Outpatient clinics and agencies under contract to our state's child protective services, which also assign diagnoses, may have medical personnel who ask the primary care provider (outside the hospital or agency) to order one or more tests. However, whether or not the medical personnel are involved with the case, and whether or not tests are ordered, some diagnosis will certainly be assigned. In other words, anyone who wants mental health care from *any* source and is not prepared to pay for it out of pocket must anticipate that the provider *will* assign a diagnosis—and that this diagnosis will enter the patient's medical record somewhere with no indication of supporting evidence.

Comment (HC Johnson): Readers will appreciate this forthright analysis of both bureaucratic and medical dilemmas. I have one difference of opinion with the writer concerning the diagnosis, which appears to me to be a seizure disorder rather than childhood bipolar.

It is well known that these different conditions overlap in some ways, as some of the anticonvulsants are used for both.

Wait! I'm not even entitled to an opinion! I haven't read the medical records collected by the child's mother and the author of this summary (family's counselor and advocate), nor have I done a question-focused search in a premier medical database to compare juvenile onset bipolar and seizure disorder. Yet I'm considered a social work mental health expert after many years of practice and teaching and multiple mental health-related publications. I could go on television right now and give my "expert" opinion, and the chances are that many of the viewers would believe it, without any clinical or research documentation to substantiate the opinion.

However, an in-depth diagnostic evaluation for this indigent child and mother by experts in child neurology and child psychiatry conversant with current research in their respective fields, and who have years of experience in specialist practice guided by scientific knowledge, might have contributed knowledge that makes informed treatment choices by families and practitioners possible. This system of care didn't even consider a neurobiological evaluation, preferring a diagnosis of "oppositional defiant disorder" while blaming the mother for "poor parenting skills." Do you think this was malpractice? If you were a worker for this family, what would you do?

The Biopsychosocial Perspective

THEORETICAL FRAMEWORKS, UNIFYING THEMES

The simplest animated environment-brain-behavior model involves a circular pathway from an environmental stimulus via a peripheral nerve to the spinal nerve column and directly back out via another peripheral nerve to direct a responding muscle to deliver the person's response back out to the environment. (If the target is an internal organ, that organ's action may impact internal body processes rather than the external environment.)

This circuit is called a *reflex arc*. It doesn't actually involve the brain at all! This reflex arc doesn't even let your brain ponder what kind of response would work the best. Nerves outside the brain are running the show and giving split-second commands to muscles: "Act, don't think."

Up one level from the simplest reflex arc is an environmental stimulus to a peripheral nerve to the spinal cord to the *sensory cortex* in the brain (input), a processing action in the *sensory association cortex* (intermediary), which then sends edited messages to the *motor cortex*, which in turn sends commands out to muscles to act (output). Figure 7.1 below illustrates this process with a generic environmental input, a route in and out, and a generic environmental response. Any number of different brain structures can be consulted along the way, with corresponding additional branches of pathways en route to the destination. We'll see a few as we progress through the book.

New information about brain/psychology/environment interactions comprises several conceptual models or frameworks. Let's review a few of them briefly.

General systems theory (GST) represents the world as a giant living system composed of interacting and mutually influencing components (systems, suprasystems, and subsystems) that range in size from very small particles (electrons, atoms, molecules) to very large national and international forces (economic, political, cultural). The arrangement of these components is hierarchical. A *system* is defined as an entity with more than a single part, separated from other systems by physical or metaphorical boundaries, that receives inputs and dispatches outputs. A system exchanges inputs and outputs with

1 environment impacts individual
2 receptors in skin and surface membranes pick up environmental signals
3 transmission to brain via sensory neurons, spinal cord and/or cranial nerves
4 relayed to relevant type of sensory cortex (one of five senses)

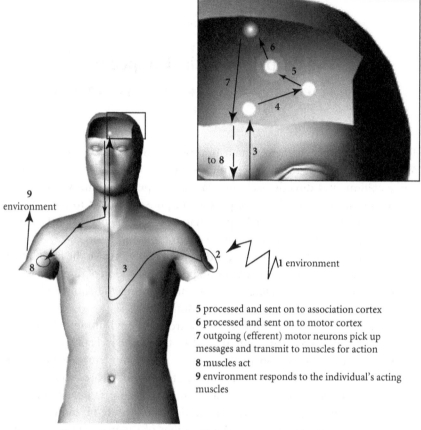

5 processed and sent on to association cortex
6 processed and sent on to motor cortex
7 outgoing (efferent) motor neurons pick up messages and transmit to muscles for action
8 muscles act
9 environment responds to the individual's acting muscles

FIGURE 7.1 *From environments to peripheral nerves to spinal cord and brain, then back out to the world outside.*

other systems outside its own boundaries to carry out functions necessary for the system's survival (Bertalanffy, 1956; Miller, 1978).

Almost all systems contain smaller component systems within themselves, called *subsystems*. The system itself is also a part of larger systems, called *supra-systems*. Other systems on the same level within a hierarchy of systems are called *parallel systems*.

According to general systems theory, systems can be living or nonliving. For example, a thermostat, a single computer, and a network of computers are examples of *nonliving systems* at different levels of complexity. An amoeba, a human being, a support group for would-be dieters, a family business, an elementary school, the United States Senate, a multinational corporation, and the International Monetary Fund are examples of *living systems* at different levels of complexity.

The thermostat (nonliving system) and the amoeba (living system) represent very simple systems that may have few or no subsystems embedded in them. Our other examples of systems act both as subsystems to larger systems (a single computer is a subsystem to a network of computers, a person is a subsystem to the weight-control support group she belongs to) and as suprasystems to their smaller component systems (the single computer is a suprasystem to its built-in modem, the person is a suprasystem to her circulatory and reproductive systems). Any system that includes living systems within it is itself defined as a *living system*; hence, organizations and government bodies are living systems. For example, the U.S. Senate is a suprasystem to the Senate Finance Committee, and the Senate Finance Committee is a suprasystem to each of its members.

Psychologist James Grier Miller (1978), in a monumental 1,000-plus page exposition, showed how general systems theory applies to human systems of all sizes. Warren, Franklin, and Streeter (1998) explain how concepts from two contemporary theories (chaos theory, complexity theory) can enhance systems theory as a foundation for social work practice by strengthening nonlinear analysis of human behavior in its environmental contexts. Their perspective was prescient of a young scientific discipline in the making—neuroscience is a domain in which chaotic and complex neurobiological events morph into orderly processes, probably through natural selection (see Chapter 38, Consciousness: An Evolutionary Perspective).

The Multisystem Evidence-Based Assessment (MEBA), together with the EPICBIOL matrix supplying multilevel systems information for MEBA (item #9), is used for both breadth and in-depth analysis of client situations. I apply it with a young woman with multiple conditions (Pat, Chapters 32 and 40–45). These chapters combine time-honored assessment questions well known to social workers (Chapter 32) with questions for which answers can be found by searching research databases (Chapter 40–45). This joining of the old and the new acknowledges the value of both and takes a beginning step in training student practitioners to carry out evidence-based assessment in the context of multisystem milieux.

By applying the evidence-based multisystem assessment tools to real people, students can gain proficiency in genuine biopsychosocial assessment and intervention planning. In all applications, the approach will be collaborative and respectful of the client's knowledge of his or own needs and wants, constraints, and culturally based preferences.

Contemporary developmental psychology, as conceived by some of its leading proponents, incorporates reciprocally influencing biological, interpersonal, cultural, organizational, economic, and political variables into an understanding of human development (Kagan, 1994). These developmental psychologists expand the general systems theory constructs of interlocking, interacting systems by emphasizing the time dimension, that is, systems interacting through time. Jerome Kagan's work exemplifies a biopsychosocial perspective that meaningfully incorporates research on child and adult development through time. Rather than progression through universal stages from birth to death, development is viewed as ever-changing and highly variable between individuals, depending on their temperaments and social contexts. Development is highly responsive to "winds of change" and is seldom predictable by the kinds of demographic and interpersonal variables we typically observe and measure (Kagan and Zentner, 1996).

Epidemiology (approaches to knowledge building in the field of public health) views the human organism in interaction with the environment. Epidemiology originated the concept of risk factors and protective factors for human conditions, problems, and disorders. We return here to further discussion of this core feature of epidemiological theory.

The concept of risk and protective factors pertains to biological and non-biological variables in individuals and in environments, interacting through time, to prevent or minimize (protective factors) or cause or exacerbate (risk factors) problems of health/mental health and social problems (World Health Organization, 1992). Little stretching is required to meld Kagan's (1994) developmental model with epidemiological research, as these two approaches are fundamentally similar to each other and to Strohman's epigenetic model (2003), discussed later (Chapter 8). Protective and risk factors are variables that induce changes through time (for better or worse). Epidemiology emphasizes quantitative tools for data collection and analysis to generate knowledge and predict the likelihood of future events in light of differing initial conditions.

Ecological theory considers mutually influencing interactions between people (human organisms) and their environments (Germain, 1991; Mattaini, 1999). In its social work applications, ecological theory has stressed the concept of environments as contexts for psychological functions. It has helped generations of social work students appreciate the interdependence between individuals, families, and their social and physical contexts. Empirical studies of ecological theory by other disciplines, such as epidemiology and cellular biology, have supplied research data that support the validity of the underlying concepts of ecological theory and theories of living systems (Strohman, 2003; World Health Organization, 1992).

The *Strengths perspective* is qualitatively different from the other approaches we've considered, in that it is primarily a philosophy or way of interpreting information about bio-, psycho-, and social factors rather than a theory that attempts to describe and explain the world. According to Saleebey (2001, pp. 13–18), the principles of strengths-based approaches are the following: (1) Every individual, group, family, and community has strengths. (2) Trauma, abuse, illness, and struggle may be injurious, but also may be sources of growth. (3) We must stop assuming that we know the upper limits of people's capacities to grow and change. (4) Collaboration is a more helpful posture than a posture of professional expertise. (5) Environments are full of resources if only we take the time to find and exploit them. (6) Caretaking is a natural and essential condition for human well-being. There is nothing wrong with wanting to be taken care of and accepting caretaking, the social norms of independence and self-sufficiency notwithstanding. All people who need care must get it. "Dependence," once equated with psychological deficit, is viewed from the strengths perspective as a natural human need.

Strengths-based social work practice and ecological practice can be congruent with a biopsychosocial perspective, assuming they are based on multifactor assessment that includes the "bio" component together with respect for scientific knowledge about mental health gleaned from decades of cross-disciplinary research (Taylor, 2006, p. 3). Taylor commends strength-based advocates for reminding workers that "in spite of difficulties, clients are individuals with skills, personal insights, feelings, hopes, and civil rights." However, he cautions us that when strength-based approaches fail to include evidence-based analysis, as is happening increasingly often in constructivist or postmodern strengths-based social work, scientific research is likely to be denigrated or dismissed in favor of narrative practice.

Some of the harmful consequences of this dismissal of science include doubting that mental illnesses are neurobiological conditions and withholding medications, which are often the only known effective treatments. Historically, the failure to provide essential medication has resulted far too often in flagrant and often physically destructive psychotic behaviors, refusal of treatment by clients who end up living marginal lives on the street, and otherwise preventable deaths. Numerous studies of the views of families with mentally ill members report years of anguish because their loved one with an untreated mental illness is living a life of excruciating psychic pain and degradation. Taylor writes that "A visible minority of social construction, postmodernist, and strengths theorists . . . summarily dismiss decades of mental health knowledge. . . . [substituting] a simple answer to extraordinarily complex questions. With little debate or introspection, some professional educators, agencies, and clinicians are endorsing treatment methods and professional ethics largely built on the foundation of a single, unproven, practice notion" (Taylor, ibid., p. 3).

Other theories mentioned above (general systems theory, research-based developmental psychology, and epidemiology) are inherently consistent with beneficial mental health treatment since they include knowledge from neuroscience and have been validated by multiple sources of evidence (see Figure 7.2).

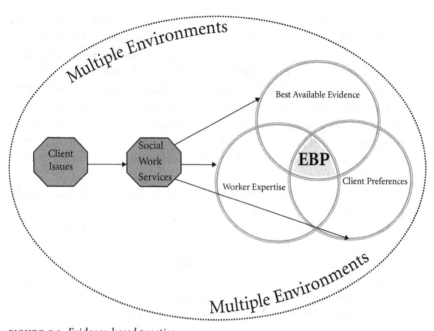

FIGURE 7.2 *Evidence-based practice.*

Adapted from Haynes et al., Gibbs, Gambrill (see References for these sources) Harriette C. Johnson, February 2006

Unifying Themes

Some unifying themes of the biopsychosocial perspective appear frequently in the theoretical frameworks we've just summarized.

1. *Human emotions, behaviors, and thoughts are biopsychosociocultural events.* That is, they respond to complex multilevel biological, psychological, social, and cultural environments through time. *Environment* comprises not only interpersonal milieux, such as family and peers, but also economic, political, cultural, legal, and organizational forces.

Biological environments supply both risk factors (such as chemical toxins or viruses in the air, water or food supply), protective factors (such as fruits and vegetables and therapeutic organically based medicines), and interpersonal environments—themselves strongly *neurobiological*, whether comprised of families, co-workers, bosses, church fellows, neighbors, acquaintances, or even strangers.

2. *Human development is constantly in flux, in a continuous, recursive process.* Personality is not a stone statue. It is not fixed at birth or age 3, or age 10 or 21, or even 50. It is more like a lump of cold dough, solid but not frozen, changing shape as the world presses on it at one point or another. It can change shape at any time, depending on what part

of it is pressed, how heavy the pressure, and how malleable it may have become from the warm hands of its modelers. The brain is plastic, that is, amenable to change, and can produce changing emotions, thoughts, and behaviors.

3. *The once popular separation of the physical (body) from the psychological (mind) is a false dichotomy.* Psychological events always, without exception, represent body/environment interactions. Emotions, behaviors, and cognitions are not manifestations of either nature or nurture. They are responses to complex ongoing interactions between nature and nurture.

4. *Feelings, behaviors, and thoughts are situation-specific.* That is, a person responds to what he or she perceives as the requirements of the situation at that moment in time, influenced not just by his or her "personality" but also by the real attributes of the present situation. One result of this process is that when we believe we can predict people's responses based on some salient personality characteristic (for example, Eve is an "anxious" person, Jeff is a "hostile" person, or MacKenzie is a "calm" person), we are incorrect. Eve isn't anxious in every situation, only when she's in danger of being late for an appointment or when she has to speak in public. Jeff isn't always a hostile person, only when someone cuts in front of him in line or calls him a wimp. MacKenzie's calm all right when she's chatting with her friends, but not when she loses her glasses or misses the bus to work.

5. *The ways we think, learn, interpret, and feel are influenced by our temperaments* (inborn, biological characteristics) interacting with learned information and specific characteristics of the present situation.

6. *In any instance of psychological function, the relative contributions of biological and nonbiological variables to the interactive process may vary.* Influence on some psychic functions may be predominantly biological, with contributions from nonbiological environmental factors (as in brain conditions such as schizophrenia, bipolar disorder, attention-deficit hyperactivity disorder, obsessive-compulsive disorder, learning disability, pervasive developmental disorder, Tourette syndrome, panic attack, and some instances of major depression).

Influence on some psychic functions may come predominantly from non-biological environmental forces, with contributions from biology; posttraumatic stress disorder is the most salient example.

Finally, there may be major contributions both from biological and from nonbiological environmental factors in the creation of a problem, as in addiction, some kinds of violence, and conduct disorder. No matter which influence predominates, biology and environment are involved in virtually all psychic phenomena. *Nature versus nurture, biology versus environment, physical versus psychological—all these are false dichotomies!*

7. *Human services practice needs science-based knowledge.* A final unifying theme of this book is its search for strategies to integrate findings of science into our thinking about practice. We dismiss or remain ignorant of the findings of scientific inquiry—findings derived from neuroscience, social psychology, child development, public health, and other fields—at the peril of our clients.

Translational research is a fairly new characterization of initiatives to help people lead happier lives by bringing together scientific research with practices in the human services (see for example McGartland-Rubio, Schoenbaum et al., 2010). Social work has embraced ecosystems perspectives on Human Behavior in the Social Environment (HBSE) since the late 1960s, but for the most recent two decades, the profession has struggled to find a meaningful place for biological knowledge within multisystemic frameworks. In this area, human service practice can benefit from translational research.

By contrast, during these last two decades, most of the scientific community seems to have taken it as a given that basic neuroscience is essential to understand human psychological functioning. But scientists can learn from us as well. What are the realities of people's life struggles, and how can scientific advances be most effectively brought to bear in their behalf? What are the multiple obstacles we all face, especially under conditions of poverty or discrimination, in which the most helpful responses are often different from what we've been able to do in both macro and micro areas?

Purveyors of translational research share a mission to overcome the science/practice divide. They note that scientists and practitioners alike must take steps to find each other and collaborate in bringing together their respective domains. Translational research advocates have taken funding sources for basic sciences research to task for spending precious resources on esoteric albeit fascinating studies that do nothing to advance human health and welfare (see, for example, Woolf, 2008).

Examples of efforts illustrate the model by advancing from both ends toward the center of a metaphorical spectrum, where they can meet in the middle. From a medical perspective, Steven H. Woolf (2008) has taken a leading role in advocating priority funding for biological research that demonstrates applicability for improving human health and well-being. Ty Tashiro and Laura Mortensen (2008), coming from a nonmedical discipline, explain how *social* sciences (with social psychology the case in point) can contribute to innovative treatments for mental conditions now known to be illnesses of the organ called the brain.

This book intends to advance the goals of translational research by educating nonscientists in human services practice about fundamentals of neuroscience and showing ways to integrate this knowledge into multisystem frontline practice. Although our focus is on the one-way direction from science to practice, instances of the converse (practice to science) are mentioned when appropriate.

Detailed practice applications with clients introduced throughout the book demonstrate how integrating neuroscience and social science may help make sense of puzzling behavior, social learning/behavioral principles, social psychological phenomena, economic forces, and other factors (yes, there's now a specialty within economics dubbed *economics neuroscience*!).

Some of these applications also exemplify what we call *multiple routes* to well-being (sometimes referred to by professionals as *alternative therapies*). These routes to well-being are helpful to large numbers of people completely outside medical-therapeutic contexts and professionally directed services. It seems fairly obvious that professional helpers should routinely consider these approaches in order to enrich our resources when a spiritual pursuit, physical exercise, or companionship of a pet seems to have potential for helping a specific service user (see Part VII, Multiple Routes to Quality of Life).

At least four core principles of translational research are relevant to the learning and practice agendas of social work and other nonmedically oriented helping professions.

First, as Fontanarosa and DeAngelis (2002) have noted, effective translation of the new knowledge generated by basic science research into new methods of prevention, diagnosis, and treatment of disease is critically important for improving health. Social work, epidemiology, and other disciplines use broader definitions of disease and health to include social diseases such as poverty, crime, and related social ills.

Second, practice-based research, with consumers participating in design and implementation whenever possible, is important for successful transfer of knowledge to practice (Westfall, Mold, and Fagnan, 2007).

Third, researchers and practitioners together must ensure that new interventions and research knowledge *actually reach* the clients or populations for whom they are intended and that these new interventions are *correctly implemented* (emphasis added). This component of translational research requires improving access, coordinating or even reorganizing systems of care, helping clinicians and clients change behaviors and make better-informed choices, providing point-of-care decision support tools, and strengthening client-provider relationships (Cochrane Collaboration, 2007; Davidoff and Batalden, 2005; Woolf, 2008). These authors note that multiple challenges beset this phase, such as human and organizational inertia and constraints on resources and infrastructure.

A fourth principle, sometimes overlooked by medical systems mounting translational initiatives, is that not only new biotechnological knowledge and therapies, but also other basic sciences, such as epidemiology, behavioral science, communication, cognition, social marketing, economics, and political science, must be made available, with funding priorities that make this possible (Woolf, 2008). As Woolf has written (p. 213), "Poverty matters as much as proteomics[1] in understanding disease. Discovering better ways to ensure that patients receive the care they need—safely, compassionately, and when they need it—is not easy. . . . Scientific discoveries and spectacular new devices are more fascinating to the public and more lucrative for industry."

This book emphasizes, respectively, the first and fourth components of translational research: *incorporating new scientific knowledge* into professional practice and *integrating research findings from all disciplines* relevant to particular clients or consumer populations into multisystem understanding, assessment, intervention planning, and agency policy. These aspects obtain not only for individual practitioners but also for service provider agencies and funding sources.

The book also includes *helping clinicians and patients change behaviors and make better-informed choices* and according *priority to consumers' preferences* with providers in supportive, not directive, roles.

---

[1] Proteomics: "the large-scale study of proteins, particularly their structures and functions. Proteins are the main components of the physiological metabolic pathways of cells. The proteome is the entire set of proteins produced or modified by an organism or system." *Wikipedia*, October 26th, 2013. http://en.wikipedia.org/wiki/Proteomics

{ 8 }

The Biopsychosocial Perspective: Genetics, Epigenetics, and Complex Adaptive Systems

The dichotomous perspective has framed the "causes" issue as nature versus nurture rather than nature/nurture interaction. That is, it has posed the question "What percentage of condition X is due to biology, what percentage to environment?" By contrast, the biopsychosocial frame asks, "How does biology interact with environment over time to arrive at condition X?"

At least two errors have sometimes accompanied the dichotomous perspective. First, the word *genetics* has been substituted for *biology*. The question now reads: "What percentage of condition X is due to genetics, what percentage to environment?" Second, the dichotomous perspective has incorrectly assumed that genes are always deterministic. That is, once you have a gene for trait X, Y, or Z, the trait will appear. These two misconceptions diminish the importance of the "bio" *as an ongoing, interactive force that is continually modified by environmental inputs*, and also ignore the multiple roles played in emotions, behavior, and thought by *nongenetic* biological variables.

The apparent persistence of these beliefs among social work educators was addressed in a lead article in the *Journal of Social Work Education* by cell biologist Richard C. Strohman (2003; Gambrill, 2003). Strohman points out that a simple linear progression from single gene to specific disease accounts for only about 2% of diseases, including sickle cell anemia and Duchenne muscular dystrophy. The remaining 98% of human diseases involve multiple genes and/or continuous interactive processes through time (Strohman, 2003).

Some social work scholars have always valued information from other disciplines (see for example Gambrill, 2003; Kendall, 1950). However, those of us who have long endorsed the concept of a nature/nurture interactional process have lacked the biological knowledge that could explain the *mechanisms* by which environmental forces impact human psychological functions. Cell biology has offered social work a scientific model that validates social work's long-held conviction about the primacy of environment in psychological functioning. Cell biology demonstrates that all aspects of human health, body organs, and body systems, including the brain and the central nervous system, are candidates for environmental impacts.

Current knowledge has dispelled the myth that psychology is separate from biology. Research during the decades of the 1980s and 1990s has shown that neurobiological events take place in conjunction with all psychological events, without exception. Every emotion, behavior, and cognition that we can observe is the manifestation of invisible neurobiological events.

This parallel process (visible affects and behaviors, invisible actions in the brain) takes place in the context of continuous transactions between the human organism and environmental variables (both biological and nonbiological). Environmental inputs strongly influence the ways the brain functions, evoking changes in chemistry and levels of activity in different brain structures and regions. The brain's responses to the environment's inputs (*emotions, thoughts*) lead to *behaviors* that in turn impact the environment, a process encompassed by the concept of *epigenetic*.

The epigenetic model includes three pathways in the body: the genetic, which is familiar to most of us; the polygenetic; and the epigenetic (not to be confused with Erikson's epigenetic model, which strongly favors environmental causation, not biology/environment interaction, in psychological development, and in many instances attributes child psychiatric disorders *now known to be neurobiological illnesses* to toxic parenting) (Schriver, 1995).

The recent influence of epigenetic analysis is suggested by its prominence in scientific journals. Our PubMed searches using the terms "epigenetic" or "epigenesis" yielded 4,151 hits in 2004 and 21,254 hits in 2011. Most abstracts pertained to interactions of genes with environments that influence and alter the process of *gene expression* (how genes are made manifest in visible phenomena). By contrast, *Social Work Abstracts* listed only seven citations for "epigenetic" in 2004 and only eight in 2011, with only three of these pertaining to the contemporary gene x environment interactional meaning of the concept (Bracha, Torrey, Gottesman, Bigelow, and Cunniff, 1992; Ishijima and Kurita, 2007; Neigh, Gillespie, and Nemeroff, 2009).

The *genetic* pathway is the route by which a specific single gene influences a *phenotype*, defined as "what the organism looks and behaves like" (Strohman, 2003, p 190). The process is initiated within cells as transcription, the copying of genetic information from the DNA molecule (deoxyribonucleic acid) to particular forms of RNA molecules (ribonucleic acid). RNA then transfers the information to sequences of protein molecules that form the structures of cells.

The *polygenetic* pathway involves several genes acting along pathways from the level of genotype to the level of phenotype. The most serious premature killers in the United States (cancer and cardiovascular disease), as well as most psychiatric disorders and addicted states, are polygenetic, that is, subject to influence from multiple genes.

However, the polygenetic model cannot explain phenotypal outcomes unless it is understood to operate through the third pathway, the *epigenetic*. Figure 8.1 shows how the epigenetic model incorporates inputs from the

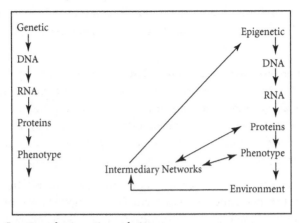

FIGURE 8.1 *Genetic and epigenetic regulation.*

Adapted from RC Strohman (2003). Genetic determinism as a failing paradigm in biology and medicine: implications for health and wellness, *JSWE* 39(2): 175, 191. Original in MS Jamner and D Stokols (eds), *Promoting Human Wellness: Frontiers for Research, Practice and Policy.* University of California Press.

environment by inserting intermediary steps between genetically coded proteins and phenotypic structures and functions (Strohman, 2003).

Epigenetics currently refers more broadly to any change in gene function not associated with DNA sequence variation (Bale et al., 2010). The neuroscience community has embraced it as a means of integrating the roles of environments in influencing gene expression that may or may not be heritable (ibid.).

The epigenetic model emphasizes the role of networks that influence the ways genes are *expressed*, that is, manifested in functions. These networks, which receive, incorporate, and process inputs from the environment, form parts of what are referred to as *complex adaptive systems*. Cellular structures, entire cells, and organs operate within these larger complex systems.

How many of us believe that all inherited characteristics come from genes that we acquire from our parents? Or that the only exception to that rule is gene mutation? Those of us who haven't taken courses in biology in recent years are often surprised to learn that changes can be inherited that *don't come from gene mutation*. In complex adaptive systems, epigenetic changes in cells are often heritable. This is because initial cell responses not involving genetic mutation may persist over time and become stable. Change is then transmitted to daughter cells during mitosis (cell division) (Strohman, 2003, p. 175).

Several layers of networks, such as gene circuits, metabolic networks, cell structures, membranes, and networks of cells, are distributed at many levels in the human organism. These levels receive inputs from external environments either directly or indirectly, and dispatch outputs to external environments. Thus cells, body organs, and the entire organism interact with the outside world (see genetic and epigenetic pathways in Figure 8.1).

Gottesman, a leading expert on the genetics of schizophrenia, notes the applicability of a complex adaptive systems model to the etiology of schizophrenia.

> The variation observed in individual differences for normal and pathological behaviors has genetic factors as a major contributor at the most distal end of a complex gene-to-behavior pathway. Research into the etiologies of such major mental diseases as schizophrenia is facilitated by adopting the approach used for complex adaptive systems as pursued by those who study coronary artery disease and diabetes. (Gottesman, 2001, p. 867)

Two facts about genes are central to our knowledge. First, the activity of genes does not stop at conception or birth. Genetic activity can be turned on (or off) throughout the life cycle. Second, changes in gene expression (how a gene manifests itself in a phenotype) occur through changes in *cytoplasm* (the part of the cell that surrounds the nucleus). These changes can be passed on to offspring. In addition, enzymes, catalysts of many transactions at different levels, can change chromosome structures by marking sections of DNA chemically without actually changing the genetic code. What this appears to mean is that although gene codes themselves change only through mutation, the pathways through which they wield their influence are subject to other inputs beside genetic, and sometimes these other influences prevail.

An estimated 20,000 to 30,000 different genes are present in each person. Estimates made up to three years prior to the release of results of the Human Genome Project in 2003 had been far higher, as high as 100,000 (Pennisi, 2003).

Let's consider that each of these genes may work together with other genes to produce polygenetic effects. Numerous interactive intermediary networks control polygenetic actions. As if that weren't complicated enough, *each of these intermediary networks has its own rules and procedures, and all levels are interactive with each other* (Edelman, 2004; Strohman, 2003). How can our bodies make sense out of anything so complex? How can our brains put together coherent, purposeful behaviors and thoughts?

It should be immediately apparent that the level of complexity for anything beyond the progression from single gene to single protein tests the boundaries of the human imagination. Not only is it expecting too much of social workers to carry out assessments of these complex processes but the state of the art of neuroscience itself is far from being able to trace all or even most of the complex pathways from genes to phenotypes.

What neuroscience has been able to show are correlations between alterations in *specific brain regions, structures, and functions* and common human experiences, both typical (such as learning, affiliation, attachment, and aggression) and atypical (such as disturbed emotions, bizarre or antisocial behavior, addiction, childhood developmental disorders, adult personality change, and elderly dementias) (Fuster, 2008; Miller and Cummings, 2007; Purves et al., 2008).

That is, neuroscience has succeeded in identifying connections between activities in the brain and these various observable phenomena. Tracing exact pathways and sequences of pathways by which these connections are made is very difficult, but neuroscientists collectively have made progress in this area as well. As we write, probably some investigator is jumping up and down for joy in his or her lab because a new neuroscience discovery has just occurred!

The *ways* we respond to the environment are strongly influenced by genetically based psychological characteristics, often called temperament. Children with different *temperaments* not only respond differently to their environments, but also evoke different patterns of response *from* their environments, responses that are repeated over and over. Tense, shy, or irritable children elicit a different set of responses from those evoked by outgoing, relaxed children, thus partially shaping their own environments (Kagan, 1994).

These findings in no way suggest that family environments are not important in children's emotional well-being. Most of us know from our own experience that our families were critical to our sense of security, emotional well-being, and interpretation of the world. What the findings do indicate is that biological factors are much more important than we previously thought and operative in ways never imagined by once-popular developmental theorists such as Sigmund Freud and Erik Erikson.

Ironically, Freud, a neurologist, believed strongly in the primacy of biology as a determinant of psychological function, but was unable to grasp the real nature of biological influences. The lack of research tools available during his lifetime to identify neurology/psychology connections led him to metaphors (such as ego, id, superego) associated inaccurately with early biological developmental events (such as oral and anal "fixations"). Were he alive today, he would have seen many of his ideas discredited, but neuroscience has validated his early conviction about the importance of biology in mental functions.

A small number of the best-validated complex adaptive systems (CAS) applications, such as the processing of trauma and stress and the functions of the hypothalamic pituitary adrenal (HPA) axis, are presented in this book. Since so many of the complex adaptive systems that process human behavior are still not well understood, CAS will sometimes be applied as *likely descriptions or explanations* rather than empirically validated networks of structures and functions.

Developed in medicine in the mid-1990s and first introduced to social work in summer 2003 as lead article in the *Journal of Social Work Education* by then-editor Eileen Gambrill, the CAS model emphasizes serial transactions between environmental forces and the human organism through the action of *intermediary systems.*

These intermediary systems within the human body receive, process, and transform messages from the world outside into actual physical functions within the individual. Not only do these transformations produce a ripple effect among human physiological and even anatomical components, but they are also transformed into behaviors, cognitions, and emotions that are exported back to the world outside. Cell biologist Richard Strohman deplores the uninformed dichotomous gene-environment view of human behavior in the social environment so long prevalent in the social sciences and offers us a more scientific view, showing ways that genes and environment interact and mutually influence through time.

CAS is a faithful representation of ecosystems theory that tries (and has had some beginning success at) explaining *how*—by what mechanisms—the environment affects psychological processes. It rejects a dichotomous biology versus environment perspective and assumes, based on vast evidence, that all psychological events arise in the context of interactional biopsychosocial processes.

For how long have we in social work been saying that the environment is a crucial influence on human behavior? That's a cardinal tenet of ecosystems theory. But how does that *work* inside the human brain and entire body? To the best of my knowledge, the Strohman article is the first instance in social work journals to propose a credible theory to address that question.

Neither Strohman nor this book makes any claim that we now have "answers." To the contrary, remaining questions vastly outweigh known information at present. Rather, we now have a method of inquiry in which science has advanced our understanding by peeling off a few layers of the onion's skin. Much of the interior remains mysterious.

{ 9 }

Assessment and Intervention Planning
with Individuals and Families

THREE TOOLS FOR COMBINING MULTISYSTEMS
AND EVIDENCE-BASED ANALYSIS

This chapter is unique among the chapters in this book because it is strictly a how-to-do-it (methods) exposition that addresses the questions of *What* are these tools? *Why* do we need them? and *How* do we use them? The Whats, Whys, and Hows are described for each tool.

The tools are being introduced here so they can be applied *in part* or *in full* in client examples, throughout the book and in real situations encountered by readers. The purpose is to teach a method for doing assessments and intervention planning that (1) takes into consideration *multiple levels of systems* interacting with an individual or family, (2) draws on *research-based knowledge* to understand clients and to develop interventions collaboratively with clients, and (3) builds client *cultures, preferences, real-life situations, and hoped-for outcomes* into the assessment method.

The *worker's practice expertise* is critical to tailoring interventions to be responsive to clients' agendas, using research findings not as directives but as ideas for intervention that worker and client can collaboratively consider, use, or decide not to use.

The three tools are EPICBIOL, Multisystem Evidence-Based Assessment (MEBA), and Search Skills for Digging Up Evidence with Help from MOLES (methodology-orienting locators for evidence search) by Leonard Gibbs (2003).

The second and third of these three tools emphasize finding and using evidence-based information to (1) understand emotions, behavior, and cognition (psychological variables) and (2) use this understanding to construct, collaboratively with clients, a plan for a combination of interventions.

This "package" of interventions incorporates knowledge gained from face-to-face conversations with clients and others involved with them, life histories, information about larger systems affecting the clients, and searches of contemporary scientific databases about the neuroscience of human emotions, behavior, and cognition that appear to be salient for this client and family. Neuroscience itself is a prototype of evidence-based knowledge.

Why should we focus on using evidence-based knowledge to assess? Because competent practitioners need up-to-date research findings both to provide the most effective service possible and to share this knowledge with their service users in everyday language. Why do clients need this information? To answer a question with another question, how else can they make informed choices?

Evidence-based search skills are necessary not only for neuroscience questions but also for everyday issues pertaining to psychology, epidemiology, medical questions, sociology, anthropology, political science, economics, and other disciplines as well.

A) EPICBIOL (see EPICBIOL Matrix Outline below).

What? EPICBIOL is a simple screening tool comprised of a grid of categories of *risk factors* (needs/challenges/problems) and *protective factors* (strengths/supports/ assets). These influences emanate from individuals/significant others ("micro" or small size factors), organizations/institutions ("mezzo" or mid-level size), and societal/national/global ("macro" or large scale) forces. The EPICBIOL matrix generates a quick bird's-eye view of areas of challenge and strength for individuals and families.

These multilevel systems influence people's lives in positive and negative ways and shape their psychological reactions (emotions, behavior, and cognition). Examples include temperament or inborn genetic predisposition for or resilience to a major mental illness (micro individual factors); policies and procedures of schools, workplaces, or social agencies (mezzo organizational factors); and cultural traditions, economic policies of corporations or government, and political imperatives (macro large-scale forces).

EPICBIOL creates a broad spectrum of possibly important aspects of the client system to guide problem definition. Details are not necessary for this grid because they will be supplied in the MEBA tool.

Why? When assessing clients in direct services, our natural tendency as practitioners is to focus on items that "jump out" at us, and to build our assessment around those items (Johnson, 1978), while forgetting to look at issues less salient to us, such as influences of neurobiological processes at the micro end of the spectrum or corporate and government economic policies on the macro end. Thinking about these aspects of influence on individuals as a routine part of assessment could, we believe, reduce the kind of individual- and family-blaming still continued by some professionals. Miresco and Kirmayer (2006, p. 917) have put it succinctly.

The more a behavioral problem is seen as originating in "psychological" processes, the more a patient tends to be viewed as responsible and

EPICBIOL

Category	Risk Factors	Protective Factors
ECONOMIC		
POLITICAL		
INTERPERSONAL		
CULTURAL		
BIOLOGICAL		
INTERNAL/MENTAL		
ORGANIZATIONAL		
LUCK (CHANCE EVENTS)		

blameworthy for his or her symptoms; conversely, the more behaviors are attributed to neurobiological causes, the less likely patients are to be viewed as responsible and blameworthy (Miresco and Kirmayer, ibid).

Evidence indicates that the same inverse relationship applies to *families* of persons with mental illness, addiction, and other conditions (Johnson et al., 2001).

This tool is a structured outline of broad *categories* to consider in the process of assessment, acting as a memory jog analogous to problem-oriented client records (PORs) (see for example De Vriendt, Clays et al., 2011; Winters et al., 2009). The latter are extensive lists of *specific* detailed daily life items, inventories that are now highly sophisticated technologically (Jacobs, 2009; Uzuner et al., 2010; Xiao et al., 2011). Unlike PORs, the EPICBIOL categories, by contrast, are broad and general.

On the EPICBIOL, workers and clients must either write entries into each empty box on the grid or leave it blank—as they go over it together, it helps the client and the worker/assessor remember otherwise overlooked areas of potential risk and protection. Because EPICBIOL is a simple screening device, no high-tech installations are needed.

How? Quick and easy. Client and worker fill out the grid collaboratively with paper and pen or pencil. For the greatest benefit, they should do this together, but an alternative is for the client to do it at home, bring it to a meeting or session, and then go over it together.

B) Multisystem Evidence-Based Assessment (MEBA)

What? MEBA is a set of questions that combines several components: a traditional psychosocial evaluation format, used for decades in social work practice; expanded attention to multisystem information (cultural, organizational, and political/economic); up-to-date research about the neurobiological aspects of clients' challenges and the effectiveness of different interventions; and giving priority to the clients' agendas. That is, the instrument gives directives intended to ensure that the process between worker and client is collaborative. The items include the following:

1. traditional psychosocial evaluation items (questions 1–6);
2. sociocultural and organizational information (questions 7–8);
3. individual and family risk and protective factors, including environmental, compiled on EPICBIOL above (MEBA question 9);
4. individual risk factors relating to neurobiological aspects of any substantial difficulty with emotion, cognition, or behavior (question 10);

5. evidence-based information comparing possible intervention choices with respect to effectiveness, which are then evaluated by worker and client for suitability for this particular individual and/or family clients (questions 11–12); and

6. guideposts for collaborative practice and giving priority to client preferences (question 13).

This synthesis of the old and the new is intended to maximize benefits of (1) long-used systems-oriented assessment tools, (2) contemporary evidence-based information, and (3) a philosophy of assessment and intervention planning conducted in a collaborative fashion with the complementary expertise that worker and client bring to joint brainstorming.

Why? A world of new knowledge has recently emerged about *causes of and contributors to* mental, emotional, and behavioral challenges and *effectiveness of interventions* for these challenges. Etiological and effectiveness items elicit answers to the questions "for which problems, in which populations, under what conditions, are these interventions likely to be effective?"

We need to integrate the acquisition of this knowledge seamlessly into our routine assessment and intervention planning behaviors. Questions on the MEBA attempt to capture this information.

How? Some of the process of filling out the MEBA can usually be done by clients, changing the wording on most parts of items 1–6 from third person to direct questions to clients. A Spanish version is being developed. Items 7–13 require action by the worker to elicit or clarify information and to do database searches, with the client participating as much as possible.

C) Search Skills for Digging Up Evidence with Help from MOLES

Why should we consult research findings as part of client assessment and intervention planning? The underlying premise was summarized in this quote.

> I've worked for 8 years in [my field of practice]. I feel I know quite a lot about it. However, I'm only one person. The knowledge from all my sources over the years still adds up to only a small fraction of the world's knowledge about my area of practice.
>
> Can I really assume, with my personal experience, knowledge from clients and colleagues, and a few workshops that I've attended, that I know most of what's really important?
>
> I'd like to think so—and maybe I do! But how can I be confident about that if I haven't also kept up with knowledge that's continually growing, changing, and being disseminated through research publications? (MSW student, 2013, on condition of anonymity)

Multisystem Evidence-Based Assessment (MEBA)
Assessment and Intervention Planning with Individuals and Families
Harriette C. Johnson (revised 2012). All rights reserved.

This instrument teaches components of evidence-based assessment
and intervention planning with individuals and families in
the context of multiple systems.

1. What are the client's presenting problems and strengths?
   Client's view
   Views of significant others
   Worker's/assessing person's view

2. What do the individual client and/or significant others want?
3. What is the history of the presenting problem(s)?
4. What is the client's current life situation and family history (family, work and school, health issues in family, economic security, religious involvement, social interaction outside family)?
5. How have previous helpers, if any, tried to alleviate the problem(s)? With what results?
6. How do members of the client's family appear to interact with each other? (give specific behavioral details to document your judgments).
7. How do stressors from environments outside the family appear to impact family members and influence the dynamics between them?
8. How does cultural diversity seem to influence the situation? (Be sure to include the *worker's subcultures* and the *organizational subcultures of agencies providing services*). (Hint: "organizational subculture" refers to values, beliefs, and behavioral norms for service delivery).
9. What environmental and individual risk and protective factors seem to be associated with challenges that concern individual, family, worker? To answer, fill out EPICBIOL to visualize multiple factors.
10. *Individual risk factors*: If the individual or family member(s) show *serious dysfunction* in behaviors, emotions, and/or cognitions (such as violence, depression, delusions), what are some major associated neurobiological factors? Do EBP searches, using MOLES keywords for *assessment* and *risk/prognosis*.
11. *Individual and family interventions*: What psychosocial and/or biological interventions have been shown by research to decrease the problem(s) or risk factors? Do EBP searches, using MOLES keywords for *effectiveness* and *prevention*.
12. *Environmental interventions*: What environmental/situational interventions might enhance or create new protective factors? Enter a particular environmental factor that you think might be important for this specific client situation. Do EBP searches, using MOLES keywords for *effectiveness* and *prevention*.
13. How can we (client system and worker) use the information we've compiled in the service of the clients' goals and preferences? (see Question 2). Plan intervention(s) collaboratively with client(s).

If you're not quite convinced, let's see if you still feel that way after you've done an exhaustive review of research literature on a major topic in one of your own areas of practice expertise.

1. If you discover that you already know everything that came up in the searches, you're amazing.
2. If you discover information that you didn't know before, but that seems inconsequential for practice, you can continue doing what you were doing until new studies offer something better. You now have peace of mind—"I'm doing everything I can."
3. If you discover information that you didn't know before, but that requires you to consider doing something additional or different for an individual client or an agency population, bingo! The winners are your clients!

There are basically two kinds of searches, *general searches* on your topic (throw out a wide net, get broad-based information often relevant to a large number of people) and *searches to obtain answers to specific questions*. If you're in direct practice, these specific questions are ordinarily about an individual or family you're currently working with. If you're an administrator overseeing decisions about individual clients or making agency policy, you'll want answers to questions that can enlighten your decisions about agency client populations, programs, and agency policy.

Two major components of this knowledge are about challenges faced by individual clients and the agency's overall client constituency, and about interventions that have and have not been demonstrated to be most likely to help. Research study abstracts usually summarize results of the study being reported, and if those results look promising, your next question is whether the study subjects are sufficiently like your client(s) to consider applying the same strategies.

Do you possess the skills to use the practice method(s) employed in the study that you want to use? If yes, so far, so good. Otherwise, you should connect the client with one or more resources that offer that service after brainstorming with their intake worker as to whether it's appropriate in this situation.

Questions may pertain to particular populations, situations, conditions, etiology, challenges, strengths, diagnoses, if any, and the relative effectiveness of different interventions. Both general and client-specific searches are important and necessary. Instructions for both kinds of searches that we set forth draw heavily from Gibbs's (2003) exposition of EBP, *Evidence-Based Practice for the Helping Professions*, Chapters 3–4. The acronym MOLES stands for Methodology-Orienting Locators for an Evidence Search.

This methodological filtering strategy spelled out by Gibbs is not a time-consuming task (you just use the one-page matrix to add methodological

TABLE 9.1 Methodology-Orienting Locators for an Evidence Search (MOLES)

Effectiveness Questions	Prevention Questions	Risk/Prognosis Questions	Assessment Questions	Description Questions (with Qualitative Studies a Subset)	Syntheses of Studies (These work primarily with effectiveness and prevention questions but may work with others.)
random*	(random*	(risk	(inter-rater	(random*	meta-anal*
OR	OR	assessment*	OR	select	OR
controlled	controlled	OR	inter-observer	OR	meta anal*
clinical trail*	clinical trial*	predictive	OR	survey	OR
OR	OR	validity	true positive*	OR	metaanal*
control	control	OR	OR	representative	OR
group*	group*	predictive	specificity	sample)	systematic
OR	OR	value	OR	AND	review*
evaluation	evaluation	OR	false positive*	(client	OR
stud*	stud*	receiver	OR	satisfaction	synthesis of
OR	OR	operat*	false negative*	OR	studies
study design*	study design	ROC	OR	patient satisfaction	OR
statistical*	OR	OR	sensitivity*	OR	study synthesis
significan*	statistical*	sensitivity	OR	needs assessment)	
OR	significan*	OR	predict*	to retrieve	
double-blind	OR	specificity	OR	qualitative studies:	
OR	double blind	OR	receiver	(qualitative stud*	
placebo	OR	false positive*	operate*	OR	
	placebo)	OR	OR	qualitative	
	AND	false negative*	ROC)	analys*OR	
	prevent*	OR	AND	content analys*	
		prognos*)	(asses*	OR in depth	
		AND	OR	interview*	
		predict*	diagnos*)	OR in-depth	
				participant*	
				OR participant	
				observation	
				OR focus group*)	

Note: The MOLES appear in rough descending order of their utility; so you might start with those at the top and, if you find few references, add more MOLES downward with the OR command to enlarge the MODELS set. Also, some of the columns at their bottom include another set connected by the AND command. These additional terms generally mark the topic for their respective question type. MOLES reflect my search experience, ideas from Gibbs (1991), and ideas in *PDQ Evidence-Based Principles and Practice*, by A. McKibbon, A. Eady, and S. Marks, 1999, Hamilton, U.K.: B.C. Decker.

keywords right off Table 9.1 to the content keywords you've chosen). MOLES is easy to learn. It's important for human service work as it increases *exponentially* the ease and speed with which searches can yield the highest probability of snaring methodologically sound studies—that is, short of *reading every candidate study* and drawing on your undoubtedly profound knowledge of research methods to grade each study's competence!

Limits menus in databases often use a catchall filter such as "Research Articles," but the criteria for inclusion do not typically ask for user inputs about type of study and a range of several types, each paired with statistical methods most commonly used for that type of study.

This procedure, known by its acronym MOLES, makes it possible for workers, therapists, administrators, clients, family members, advocates, and writers to go straight to the best experts around the world and retrieve knowledge pertaining to almost any condition or challenge. Want biological and environmental risk and protective factors (for assessment)? Or research-based estimates of the relative effectiveness of possible interventions (for intervention planning)? What interventions, for what types of clients, with what specific challenges, under what conditions?

MOLES won't collate all of that information for you—you'll still have to compile the elements–but it will supply you with most of the methodologically sound abstracts of studies that contain the keywords you enter. The Gibbs matrix to which I'm referring is reproduced in this chapter (Table 9.1). The one-page instrument for using MOLES to refine database searches, with the history of its creation by a group of statisticians in the mid-1990s, are included here so that users can understand how to use it and why it works. I haven't found anything that can come close to the little rodents in overcoming one of the gigantic impediments to systematic use of research findings in everyday practice: the need to evaluate every study for its methodological acceptability.

We'll give an example from practice that informs assessment and intervention planning at the end of the chapter: neurobiology of delinquency in youth gamblers identified as falling into one of three groups.

To go through the steps outlined here, we'll use the database PubMed. It's the premier medical/psychiatric database and contains more than 22 million abstracts as of 2013. You can get a running start on your general search by looking at articles designated "Review" or "Meta-analysis," which have already analyzed numerous studies and summarized them for you. You'll need to pull abstracts of the reviewed studies so you can do your own review, but you seldom need to read the actual articles when you're giving a simple overview of many different studies. Methodology and findings are typically summarized in the abstracts.

The situations in which you will want to pull up the actual articles (full text) are when a study seems important enough for your work for you to delve into details and gain solid understanding of what was done and how, in each particular instance. For studies of great relevance to your own work, you should also carefully read the authors' views of implications of the findings, noting differences of opinion.

Search conventions vary among databases. All databases return fewer abstracts as you add limiting keywords. Additional keywords help you zero in on the specifics of a question while excluding more and more abstracts that may be interesting and important but do not help you answer your question(s).

Two important keyword techniques in PubMed are (1) the Boolean terms OR, AND, and NOT (always in upper case), and (2) the use of the asterisk (*) at the end of a root that has several possible endings. When you use the word OR, you are asking for *all studies* that include *any* of the terms separated by OR, with the list starting and ending with parentheses; for example, (teenage OR adolescent OR youth); (intervention OR treatment). You want any and all of the terms.

When you want the computer only to include studies that contain *both terms or all terms separated by a Boolean term*, replace the word OR with AND. OR helps you be more exhaustive (increases number of abstracts), whereas AND helps you be more restrictive (decrease number of abstracts). Don't misunderstand—AND should *only* be used because you want both terms (or more than two if you've listed them) *together* in your sources to convey the correct meaning, not because you want to get rid of a pile of abstracts! The AND command is intended to exclude articles that have one or the other, but not both.

The term NOT allows you to exclude a particular entity from a category of items you are searching. To take an example from this book: Part VI, Chapter 42, p. 313: "(dialectical behavior therapy) NOT (borderline personality OR bpd)," which I used to find all other conditions or diagnoses that had been treated with dialectical behavior therapy (DBT) *except* BPD. That is, I eliminated all references pertaining to BPD to find the applications of DBT for people with any challenge other than BPD.

Root words with an asterisk are used to call up all abstracts having at least two forms of the keyword, in order to get as much information as possible in as few as possible search runs. For example, *delinquen** calls up any references that use either *delinquency* or *delinquent*. As of November 27, 2011 (numbers change continuously), *delinquency* received 5,248 hits, *delinquent* 3,369, and *delinquen** 8,080. The difference between the number with the asterisk term (8080) and the sum of the two separate forms of the word (8,617) is 537 abstracts, indicating the number of abstracts that were counted twice for containing both terms, *delinquency* and *delinquent*. Instances of each term are added to its own count, so that the total counts for each alone, summed and added together, shows 537 more abstracts than the 8,080 in which no hit (abstract) is counted more than once.

Don't be alarmed! You're not going to read 8,080 abstracts! There are specific acceptable techniques for filtering out studies with questionable methodologies, and, as a by-product, reducing the number of abstracts to manageable size *without doing the very time-consuming evaluations of studies yourself*. We'll give our delinquency example later.

Your search must be *evidence-based*. Articles that are purely theoretical, philosophical, or narrative do not qualify (although qualitative research may qualify if it meets certain criteria). That means you must "cover the territory" by compiling candidate studies in as many searches as necessary to make sure you haven't left out any important studies (searches must be *systematic* and *exhaustive*).

If you only look at a few of many abstracts on your topic, how will you know what you've missed? Since there's no way to know what you have left out, *you haven't reviewed the existing evidence.* You have only selected a few citations haphazardly. That's not evidence-based or evidence-informed. Evidence means *the* existing evidence, not just a fragment of it here or there.

In Gibbs 2003, page 59 (matrix of COPES question types) and page 100 (matrix of MOLES keyword terms related to each type of question) will give you the essential information for doing the searches and filtering out information lacking safeguards for reliability and/or generalizability. COPES or its variants are used to answer specific questions, whereas MOLES should be used in *both* general *and* specific searches.

Study these two pages from the Gibbs book and make sure you understand them. These two acronyms refer to the following words: Client-Oriented Practical Evidence Search (COPES) and Methodology-Oriented Locators for an Evidence Search (MOLES). MOLES are methodological filters used to screen out unreliable or otherwise weak information. MOLES terms have the double advantage of *giving a much higher probability of reliability, validity, and generalizability* than the universe of articles on your topic, *and greatly reducing the number of studies that must be reviewed.*

MOLES addresses an important impediment to evidence-based practice, namely that users of research findings need to have both the *expertise* and the *time* to evaluate the quality of research studies they use to inform their practice. Medical statisticians designed MOLES to overcome this major obstacle, adapted by Gibbs (2003) for human services.

Gibbs (2003, pp. 98–99) reports that MOLES are terms marking the best evidence for retrieval in any electronic database. Haynes, Wilczynski, and colleagues (1994) demonstrated MOLES's strength by going through 10 journals for 1986 and 1991 to identify studies related to the five question types (Table 9.2), including effectiveness, prevention, risk/prognosis, assessment, and description (the description category can utilize qualitative research).

Once these studies were identified by hand (laboriously), Haynes's team applied their MOLES to electronic databases for the same years and journals to see how many of their "gold standard" studies were picked up by the MOLES. The MOLES identified 93% of studies found in the hand search (93% sensitivity). Readers can decide whether this very time-consuming hand search process would be worth finding the additional 7%. Gibbs (2003, p. 100) footnoted his MOLES matrix as follows:

> The MOLES appear in rough descending order of their utility; so you might start with those at the top and, if you find few references, add more MOLES

TABLE 9.2 Five COPES Question Types and Four Corresponding Features of a Well-Built Question

Five Question Types	Four Elements in a Well-Formulated Question			
	Client Type and Problem	What You Might Do	Alternate Course of Action	What You Want to Accomplish
	How would I describe a group of clients of a similar type? Be specific.	Apply a treatment; act to prevent a problem; measure to assess a problem; survey clients; screen clients to assess risk.	What is the main alternative other than in the box to the left?	Outcome of treatment or prevention? Valid measure? Accurate risk estimation, prevented behavior, accurate estimation of need?
Example Effectiveness Question	If disoriented aged persons who reside in a nursing home	are given reality orientation therapy	or validation therapy,	which will result in better orientation to time, place, and person?
Example Prevention Question	If sexually active high-school students at high risk for pregnancy	are exposed to baby think-it-over	as opposed to being exposed to didactic material on the proper use of birth control methods,	will they have fewer pregnancies during an academic year? Knowledge of birth control methods?
Example Assessment Question	If aged residents of a nursing home who may be depressed or may have Alzheimer's disease or dementia	are administered depression screening tests	or short mental status examination tests,	which measure will be the briefest, most inexpensive, valid, and reliable screening test to discriminate
Example Description Question	If members of a hospital team who are concerned about team functioning	take the preliminary checklist (clinical) team effectiveness test	or take the interdisciplinary team weekly inventory,	which measure will most reliably and validly reflect the team's ability to accomplish tasks?
Example Risk Question	If crisis line callers to a shelter for women who have been battered	are administered a risk-assessment scale by telephone	as opposed to practical judgment, unaided by a risk assessment scale, being relied upon,	will the risk-assessment scale have higher reliability and predictive validity for violent behavior?

Note. This table follows *Evidence-Based Medicine: How to Practice and Teach EBM*, by D. L. Sackett, W. S. Richardson, W. Rosenberg, and R. B. Haynes, 1997, p. 29, New York: Churchill Livingstone. Adapted with permission.

downward with the OR command to enlarge the MOLES set....MOLES reflect my [Gibbs'] search experience, ideas from Gibbs (1991, and ideas in *PDQ Evidence-Based Principles and Practice*, by A McKibbon, A Eady, and S Marks, 1999, Hamilton UK, BC Decker.

Suppose we want to learn about assessment-related information. Table 9.3 shows possible reductions in numbers of abstract hits when we add the two most frequently used MOLES terms for *risk/prognosis* (risk assessment OR

TABLE 9.3 Results of MOLES Keyword Screenouts of Studies with Questionable Methodologies

Keyword	Total hits without MOLES terms	Total hits with MOLES terms	Hits with MOLES terms as a percentage of hits without MOLES terms
Delinquen* (includes delinquent & delinquency)	864	92	10.7%
delinquent only	510	71	13.9%
delinquency only	699	93	13.3%

Note: when you use either "neuro*" or "neur*" as a root, PubMed truncates your search at 600 abstracts, often omitting large numbers of abstracts. Therefore, to avoid random abstracts omissions, it is necessary to use the more restrictive root "neurobio.*"

predictive validity) and *assessment* (inter-rater OR inter-observer) questions respectively. A few keywords and multiple word terms follow on the general subject of neurobiological aspects of youth delinquency. These are illustrations, not an exhaustive list (see Table 9.4).

Now, if we add keywords (neurobio* OR brain), youth, and delinquen* with the MOLES terms, we get 126 hits for delinquen*. We're in the range of manageability now, depending on your purposes for the searches. Of course, you can reduce the numbers further by adding keywords such as female (98), violen* (73), or arrest* (32). These added keywords return no hits with all three keywords separated by ANDs (arrest* AND female AND violen*), and 118 hits when separated by ORs (arrest* OR female OR violen*). (Why?)

Try replicating what I did here. The best route to acquiring skill is to practice. Your numbers won't be the same because of the time lapse between original runs and your new trials, but it should be interesting to see whether the percentages remain similar.

Finally, I arbitrarily selected a few references that appeared interesting to me (listed below), and from among these, I've reprinted three abstracts (interesting and relevant findings were numerous, but space dictated limiting these to three).

TABLE 9.4 Keywords for Searching for "Delinquency Neurobiology"

Keywords (used in combination and separately—many possible, combinations)

delinquen*	(teenage OR adolescent OR youth)
brain	impulsive*
neurobio*	(anger OR angry)
antisocial	Trauma
CU [refers to callous unemotional]	moral*
brain callous unemotional	
addict*	

Combination of keywords to locate abstracts that contain multiple variables.

trauma brain neurobio* antisocial (substance abuse)
One variable not on the list above has been added.
What is the investigator trying to find out?

Examples of studies retrieved:

Caspers S, Heim S, Lucas MG, Stephan E, Fischer L, Amunts K, and Zilles K (2011). Moral concepts set decision strategies to abstract. *Neuropsychologia 48*(7):2018–2026.

Ferguson CJ (2010). Genetic contributions to antisocial personality and behavior: a meta-analytic review from an evolutionary perspective. *J Soc Psychol 150*(2):160–180.

Harenski CL, Harensk KA, Shane MS, Kiehl KA (2010). Aberrant neural processing of moral violations in criminal psychopaths. *J Abnormal Psychol 119*(4):863–174.

Moll J, De Oliveira-Souza R, Zahn R (2008). The neural basis of moral cognition: sentiments, concepts, and values. *Annals of NY Acad of Science 1124*:161–180.

Shirtcliff EA, Vitacco MJ, Graf AR, Gostisha AJ, Merz JL, Zahn-Waxler C (2009). Neurobiology of empathy and callousness: implications for the development of antisocial behavior. *BehavSciLaw 27*(2):137–171.

Sommer M, Rothmayr et al. (2010). How should I decide? The neural correlates of everyday moral reasoning. Neuropsychologia. 2010 Jun;48(7):2018–2026.

Abstracts of three of the references listed above

Ferguson CJ (2010). Genetic contributions to antisocial personality and behavior: a meta-analytic review from an evolutionary perspective. *J Soc Psychol 150*(2):160–180.

Abstract

Evidence from behavioral genetics supports the conclusion that a significant amount of the variance in antisocial personality and behavior (APB) is due to genetic contributions. Many scientific fields such as psychology, medicine, and criminal justice struggle to incorporate this information with preexisting paradigms that focused exclusively on external or learned etiology of antisocial behavior. The current paper presents a meta-analytic review of behavioral genetic etiological studies of APB. Results indicated that 56% of the variance in APB can be explained through genetic influences, with 11% due to shared non-genetic influences, and 31% due to unique non-genetic influences. This data is discussed in relation to evolutionary psychological theory.

Shirtcliff EA, Vitacco MJ, Graf AR, Gostisha AJ, Merz JL, Zahn-Waxler C (2009). Neurobiology of empathy and callousness: implications for the development of antisocial behavior. *BehavSciLaw 27*(2):137–171.

Abstract

Information on the neurobiology of empathy and callousness provides clinicians with an opportunity to develop sophisticated understanding of mechanisms underpinning antisocial behavior and its counterpart, moral decision-making. This article provides an integrated in-depth review of hormones (e.g. peripheral steroid hormones such as cortisol) and brain structures (e.g. insula, anterior cingulate cortex, and amygdala) implicated in empathy, callousness, and psychopathic-like behavior. The overarching goal of this article is to relate these hormones and brain structures to moral decision-making. This review will begin in the brain, but will then integrate information about biological functioning in the body, specifically stress-reactivity. Our aim is to integrate understanding of neural processes with hormones such as cortisol, both of which have demonstrated relationships to empathy, psychopathy, and antisocial behavior.

The review proposes that neurobiological impairments in individuals who display little empathy are not necessarily due to a reduced ability to understand the emotions of others. Instead, evidence suggests that individuals who show little arousal to the distress of others likewise show decreased physiological arousal to their own distress; one manifestation of reduced stress reactivity may be a dysfunction in empathy, which supports psychopathic-like constructs (e.g. callousness). This integration will assist in the development of objective methodologies that can inform and monitor treatment interventions focused on decreasing antisocial behavior.

Sommer M, Rothmayr C, Döhnel K, Meinhardt J, Schwerdtner J, Sodian B, Hajak G (2010). How should I decide? The neural correlates of everyday moral reasoning. *Neuropsychologia* 48(7):2018–2026.

Abstract

The present fMRI study is the first that investigates everyday moral conflict situations in which a moral standard clashes with a personal desire. In such situations people have to decide between a morally guided and a hedonistic behaviour. Twelve healthy subjects were presented with verbal stories describing conflicts with either moral or neutral content. The moral stories described conflicts requiring a decision between a personal desire and a conflicting moral standard, whereas the neutral conflicts required a decision between two conflicting personal desires. When compared to neutral conflicts, moral conflicts elicited higher activity in a wide spread neural network including the medial frontal cortex, the temporal cortex and the temporo-parietal junction and the posterior cingulate cortex.

Further analyses of the moral conflicts revealed that hedonistic decisions in contrast to morally guided decisions were associated with significantly higher rankings of uncertainty and unpleasant emotions and induced significantly more activation in the amygdala/parahippocampal region. The present results generalise findings on the neuroscience of moral understanding by extending it to everyday moral decisions. Furthermore, the results show that the amydala region plays a central role in the processing of negative emotional consequences associated with immoral decisions.

10

Complementary Roles of Quantitative and Narrative Approaches

HOW WE USED THEM TOGETHER TO LEARN ABOUT PARENT/PROFESSIONAL RELATIONSHIPS

One of the premises of this book is that research-based knowledge is essential for social work practice—hardly a novel point of view. This belief is a central tenet of both the National Association of Social Workers (NASW) Code of Ethics and the Council on Social Work Education's Educational and Policy Accreditation Standards (EPAS, 2008). Yet studies suggest that research and practice are still in separate worlds, in which research findings that could advance and strengthen practice and policy go unused, even dismissed (Biegel, Johnsen, and Shafran, 2001; McGuire, 2006; Scott, 2002).

In a study of attitudes and barriers to evidence-based practice in social work, McGuire (2006) found that common reasons given among 433 LCSW survey respondents for low rates of evidence-based practice utilization included lack of time to read research, lack of time to implement new ideas, results not being generalizable to practice, and difficulty understanding the research. Thirty-six percent reported reading social work literature less than three times per year.

Those not in private practice and those in high bureaucracy structures reported experiencing more barriers to using research in practice than others, but together with those who graduated after 1992, were more willing to try new interventions if required by an authority.

Generalizability of this study was limited by a 25% response rate among 1,728 randomly selected recipients of mailed surveys. However, the results from those who did respond constituted an interesting exploratory study of workers' perceived reasons for low utilization of research findings. In the absence of nonresponder follow-up data, we speculate that the 75% nonresponder group who did not find the time or energy to do the survey would have comprised practitioners on average *less* interested in and attributing *less* importance to research as a practice tool, than the responders, who made time to respond.

Research findings are the foundation of this book. They are used to provide practice-relevant information about neurobiological aspects of individual behavior, emotions, and cognitions that take place in everyday ordinary life, in typical child and adult development, and in atypical (psychiatric) conditions, substance abuse, addiction, criminal behavior, violence, and many other life circumstances. They are drawn from the disciplines of neuroanatomy and neurophysiology, psychiatry, developmental psychology, genetics, molecular biology, epidemiology, pharmacology, and radiology.

Yet integrated biopsychosocial knowledge requires major reliance on social sciences such as social psychology, anthropology, sociology, economics, political science, and family studies. The scope of this book does not allow for "equal treatment" of material from the social sciences. However, that in no way implies that the authors undervalue this vast knowledge—rather, the subject matter of this book, neuroscience for human services, is so enormous itself that it is accorded a central role. Social science content in research studies is included to provide balance and context to neuroscience findings.

Much of the research reported in this book has been generated by numerical (quantitative) methods. That is because the kinds of data related to roles of neurobiology in psychological functioning mostly rely on numerical methods—they are obtained through brain scans, laboratory experiments, epidemiological studies of populations, tests of safety and efficacy of different interventions, blood studies, genetic studies, and correlations between some of these areas. Our choice of types of research is directed by the subject matter.

In our series of studies about parent/professional relationships, on the other hand, both quantitative and qualitative methods were essential. We conducted a set of studies of views about professionals by parents of children with psychiatric disabilities and views about parents of children with psychiatric disabilities held by professionals (Cournoyer and Johnson, 1991; Johnson, 1991; Johnson et al., 2001; Johnson, Cournoyer, and Fisher, 1994; Johnson and Renaud, 1997). Our qualitative work, derived from videotaped interviews with individual parents, enabled us to learn in depth about their beliefs and experiences and to at least partially understand the complex situations that engendered their views.

For example, in their interviews for the video *Our Fight: Parents Tell It Like It Is* (Deerfield Valley Publishing, 1999), parents told us about their expectations for their newborn child; how the developing child fell short due to the disability; how the child's suffering was prolonged and intense; how parents coped with their own grief, overpowering at times, arising from the child's pain; how they feared for the child's future and experienced chronic worry about the limits of their abilities to protect the child from failure and rejection; how exhausted and discouraged they often felt from demands of daily caretaking; and the cascade of emotions that professional behaviors elicited, too often negative.

These interviews produced many illustrations of actual behaviors toward parents that practitioners engaged in, sometimes with negative impact, sometimes with positive. Parents reported the contexts of these professional behaviors so that we could understand the situations in which these behaviors were likely to emerge. We obtained a wealth of examples of different specific behaviors—what worker A, B, or C said and did—together with descriptions of practice situations that brought forth the behaviors. It's unlikely that those contextual insights could have been gained by quantitative methods alone.

We used the themes uncovered in these interviews to choose variables for study of the views of large numbers of parents. The quantitative approach allowed us to draw conclusions about the relative importance and ubiquity of specific views among populations of parents and among cohorts of professionals.

For example, the results showed that large numbers of parents felt that professionals had blamed them for their child's disability. A smaller number of parents reported more obvious ethical violations such as workers' questionable fee charging or failure to observe appropriate client/worker boundaries.

Most parents reported that workers were courteous, *even some of those workers perceived by parents to hold attitudes of blame or devaluation of the parents.* The negative communications were often subtle in that they did not take place in a context of overt discourtesy. That information helped us recommend changes in certain practice behaviors that could diminish subtly negative and increase positive communications by providers.

The procedures we followed in choosing databases varied by subject matter. We consulted Social Work Abstracts in some of the areas. For child and adult development, we used major psychology, sociology, and anthropology databases. For psychiatric and substance abuse disorders, we used medicine and psychology databases as well as websites for federal agencies such as the National Institute of Mental Health (NIMH), the National Institute on Drug Abuse (NIDA), and the National Institute on Alcohol Abuse and Alcoholism (NIAAA). For multiple routes to quality of life, we used those already mentioned and (with caution) added a few general Internet sources.

We emphasized the following questions as guides to including or excluding abstracts. (1) Does the abstract address a topic relevant to human services such as social work? (2) Does the research appear in a (blind) peer-reviewed journal? (3) Does the reported research appear to conform to well-established principles of quantitative or qualitative methodology? We were very interested in research on the views of service consumers or that had been carried out in part by consumers.

We referred to works on evidence-based practice now being published in social work journals more frequently than a few years ago. From among five question types (effectiveness, prevention, risk/prognosis, assessment, and description) (Gibbs, 2003), our reviews of research most often involved *risk/prognosis, assessment* of etiologies, and *effectiveness* of interventions. I highly recommend the Gibbs reference for readers who want support in finding reliable and valid evidence. Historically, statistical inference, based not on certainty but on probability, increasingly has become the basis for testing beliefs.

To be sure, in an intellectual world fraught with uncertainty, scholars from the hard sciences and the social sciences alike have sometimes been guided by their human strivings to be *certain* by going beyond their data. However, our human tendencies notwithstanding, the goal of grasping "the whole truth" has generally been replaced with finding information with the *highest probability* of being valid. No guarantees, no claims of infallibility.

Although *evidence-based* refers to information derived from both quantitative and qualitative research, *it is not a collection of research findings*. Rather, it is a *process of inquiry* that allows helping professionals to access up-to-date, scientifically valid information *relevant to any specific client, in any practice setting*, whom they may be trying to help. That's because this process of inquiry helps workers and those they serve accurately assess the "whole" (biopsychosocial) person-in-environment and choose among *state-of-the-art as well as familiar "tried and true" interventions* for specific individual, family, or group clients. Let's look at an example.

A recent study of approaches for helping youth gamblers compiled research on these teenagers with a range of characteristics and situations (Nower and Blaszcinzcski, 2004). The authors found that the youth clustered into three categories, differentiated by their individual personal traits interacting with their differing environments. Two tried-and-true interventions were appropriate for all three groups (youth and parental education about gambling, behavioral methods to provide incentives for "pro-social" behavior).

Different additional approaches were useful depending on which of the three groups of personal traits and individual situations the youths fit into: (1) gambling had developed only through environmentally and culturally based reinforcements in the absence of any psychiatric vulnerability, (2) gambling had developed in response to a combination of [biologically based] anxious and depressive temperaments and certain environmental conditions, and (3) gambling had developed in response to a combination of [biologically based] impulsivity, excitement, or stimulus-seeking interacting with certain environmental conditions. Different interventions were required for youth in each of the three groups in addition to the two interventions common for all. Knowledge about the roles of neurobiological factors was *necessary* to understand the importance of the recommended interventions that addressed multiple idiosyncratic factors.

But, you may say, even if practitioners look up research about their clients' issues, most of them have minimal competency in evaluating reliability and validity of that research. How can they judge whether the research findings they locate are trustworthy guides to assessment and intervention planning? How can they "trust" the published information they find? How can they systematically sift through possibly hundreds of abstracts and concisely summarize the collected findings? (see the section Search Skills for Digging Up Evidence with Help from MOLES in Chapter 9, p. 56, where we offer some possible answers to these questions).

None of our research tools is perfect, but in my view the combination we present here increases the probability that our searches in behalf of our clients can yield better assessment and intervention information than the haphazard searches many social workers are likely to use, given their taxed resources of time and energy.

The late Leonard Gibbs deserves great credit for providing tools that busy, caring, practitioners even with limited research know-how can use to expand their helping skills. They will be able to give their clients the benefits of state-of-the-art research-based information in ways that have seldom been possible in the past.

Attributing value to a screening process for research methodology does not imply contempt for individual anecdotes as possible sources of knowledge about my client Emma's real experiences. For many decades, social work has recognized the importance of individual narratives not only in generating research questions that can yield generalizable findings, but also in expanding our insights into the issues and meanings for individual respondents.

However, social work researchers widely accept the belief that in the absence of further inquiry, such accounts are not generalizable *yet*—that is, the probability is extremely low that the highly complex specific biological and environmental conditions that converged to mold my client Emma *are similar enough* to conditions that have shaped my clients Frieda, Gertrude, and Hannah that we can directly transfer to these other women a package of interventions that helped Emma.

PART II

Fundamentals of Neuroscience

BRAIN WORKS[1]

Introduction

As stated in Part I, neuroscientists such as Nobel Laureates Eric Kandel (2011) and Gerald Edelman (2004), as well as former director of the National Institute of Mental Health and Harvard University Neuroscience Professor Steven Hyman (1997) have described the human brain as the most complex entity in the known universe. Technological developments from the 1970s to the present have dramatically advanced our understanding about how the brain mediates our feelings, behaviors, and thinking, and how some medications and street drugs can influence and alter this mediation. However, there's still a lot that we don't know. We'll look at a little of the amazing reservoir of knowledge about how the brain works that is already widely accepted by scientists, and occasionally we'll consider current controversies about these beliefs as well.

The brain's functions include receiving messages, making decisions, and sending out commands. The brain works around the clock. It never stops for rest. The fuel that keeps its motors running is a simple sugar called glucose, which circulates around the brain through blood vessels to locations where it is needed, in proportion to the level of activity at each site. When any part of the brain becomes very active, it burns lots of glucose, using the oxygen it gets from the lungs. Different glucose levels show up on PET, fMRI, and SPECT scans (see Chapter 5), color-coded for varying levels of glucose, indicating the areas of high and low activity, continually in flux, in response to changing

---

[1] Material in Part II relies heavily on several current neuroscience texts, but seldom cites them directly. Since they all cover similar fundamentals, the number of citations would be unmanageably large. These texts are listed in the References: Carlson, 2011; Fuster, 2008; Miller and Cummings, 2007; Pinel, 2011; and Purves et al, 2008. They are useful for readers who want to dig deeper to understand complicated neural actions, at a level of detail beyond the scope of this book.

inputs or environmental conditions. Thanks to these scanners, researchers can now watch events in the brain in real time.

The brain accounts for only 3% of the body's weight but consumes 20% of the body's oxygen. That means it burns a lot of calories to do its work. (Want a crash diet? Maybe try thinking harder?)

Part II summarizes a few of the most important individual brain structures and functions, including two kinds of structures: (1) those that are large enough to be visible to the human eye, and (2) those that are microscopic in size. Part III, a sequel to this section on brain fundamentals, introduces complicated combinations of these structures and functions referred to as *neural networks* or *neural systems*. There we present two examples of neural systems that enact, respectively, Pleasure and Stress/Trauma.

Now, in Part II, we'll look at some of the smaller units that collaborate to form systems that engage psychological functions of emotion, behavior, and cognition. The information in Part II will help you understand Part III and the substantive areas that follow it (Parts IV–VII). For more advanced and comprehensive understanding of the brain, there are many thousands of articles in scientific journals and numerous neuroscience texts that reveal inner dynamics of human behavior. This recent set of advances has often led to the replacement of terms like "physiological psychology" with "behavioral neuroscience" (Carlson, 2011).

Organic wiring connects our brains with every corner of our bodies as well as environments outside, sending and receiving electrical and chemical messages far and wide—a theater of intertwining moving and darting players that animate the human person.

11

Brain Structures: Larger
(Visible to the Human Eye)

As you read about larger and microscopic brain structures and systems, you'll want to look at color illustrations for Part II in addition to the many black and white line drawings of neurons, synapses, neurotransmitters, and enzymes embedded within the text. Printing needs required placing all color images in a single section, so one black and white surrogate of a full-page color illustration (color image D.) has been placed within the text to reduce page-flipping while you match the text you're reading to a nearby visual.

The color image C., Cerebral Cortex, represents the outer surface of the brain, while color image D., Larger Inner Brain Structures and Cerebellum, includes major inner structures and one outer regional structure, the cerebellum. Color image E., Team Players: Prefrontal Cortex and Inner Brain Structures, shows areas where the cerebral cortex, especially the prefrontal cortex, and the inner structures communicate as they process psychological events (emotions, behavior, cognition). In image E., cortical regions have been displaced to outside the head to show the areas of interaction more clearly than is possible with superimposed transparencies of one in front of the other.

Take a look at these now before embarking on the study of organs of the brain. Some of the most important neural networks for psychological functions include combinations of structures and pathways connecting the cortex, outer layers of the brain, with inner regions: limbic system, midbrain, and brainstem. All such structures perform specific functions in consort with other structures to which they connect through pathways.

An in-text surrogate of color image D., Larger Inner Brain Structures and Cerebellum, black and white version, follows (Figure 11.1). Most specific structures are now known to carry out their tasks interactively. Before you try to learn about complex connections across brain regions, you should familiarize yourself with the most important structure names, the building blocks of neural networks. Doing that should help you begin to visualize how and where some important events in your own and everyone else's emotional, cognitive, and behavioral life are happening.

Many but not all structures are bilateral, meaning that one is found in each of the two hemispheres (left and right). In the descriptions that follow,

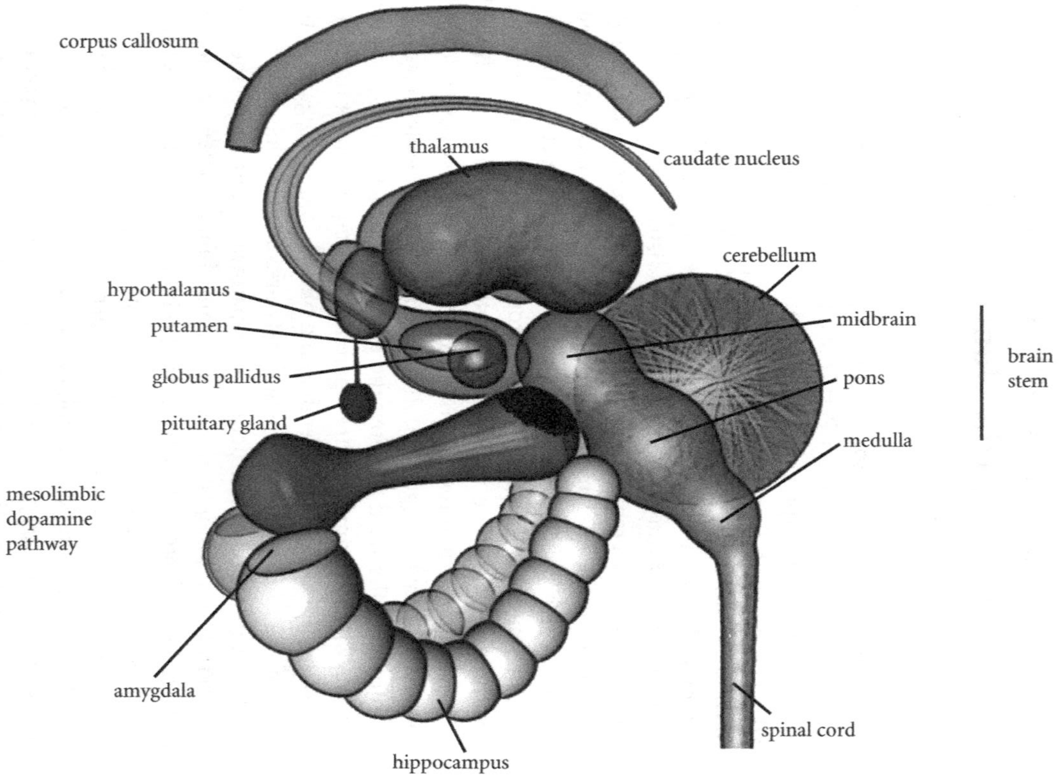

FIGURE 11.1 *Larger inner brain structures and cerebellum, see color image D.*

substructures within regions of the brain such as cortex, diencephalon, limbic, basal ganglia, and brainstem, are named according either to *location* (e.g., *medial orbitofrontal cortex*) or *function* (e.g., *primary motor cortex*).

Various structures collaborate with different combinations of structures and pathways within their particular regions and outside it, across the brain, to perform many psychological functions. For example, to generate pleasure, the mesolimbic dopamine pathway connects points in the midbrain (*meso* means "middle") with points in the limbic system, whereas the mesocorticolimbic circuit adds a third region, the cortex (much of it concerned with cognition and also emotion) to the meso and limbic regions.

Two words seen continually in neuroscience texts are *afferent*, meaning bringing messages *to* a structure or region, and *efferent*, carrying messages *away from* a structure or region.

The Cerebral Cortex, the Frontal Cortex, and the Prefrontal Cortex. The outer surface of the brain, called the cerebral cortex, has multiple functions. It is 2–4 millimeters (0.08–0.16 inches) thick and is convoluted with many folds and grooves, so its actual surface area is about 2½ square feet and its depth some fraction of an inch hovering around one-tenth of an inch (Kandel, Schwartz, and Jessell, 2000).

In humans, the frontal cortex comprises nearly a third of the entire cortex. The frontal cortex continually receives messages from and sends messages to other brain regions, including the limbic system. By our old-fashioned methods of comparisons of human intelligence to that of other animals, the percentage of frontal area in the entire cortex was used to measure "intelligence" (ability to do complex cognitive tasks like planning and reasoning), With humans averaging 29% frontal cortex as part of the entire cortex, chimps 17%, dogs 7%, and cats 3.5%, we were about 1.7 times as intelligent as our nearest competitors the chimps, and for cat lovers, the numbers were disheartening. On average, dogs scored twice as intelligent as cats. But . . . .

New research suggests that we've given our co-inhabitants of the Animal Kingdom a bad rap. Human hubris again? Frans de Waal, primatologist, professor at Emory University and Director of the Living Links Center at the Yerkes National Primate Research Center in Atlanta, has just published a book reporting, among other things, a multitude of recent experiments with chimps, elephants, rats, octopuses, and other creatures performing ingenious problem-solving tasks. It turns out that the apparent explanation for why we haven't previously discovered these impressive intellectual feats by so many and such diverse nonhumans, is because we weren't perspicacious and empathetic enough to recognize the need for and devise zoologico-centric strategies for testing nonhuman intelligences (de Waal, 2013).

Joaquin Fuster (2008), leading scholar on the prefrontal cortex, devotes much of his introduction to what he views as confusing and muddled definitions of "prefrontal," which he disentangles for readers at great length.

Because of its central roles in psychological events (emotions, cognitions, behaviors), this book will focus on the actions of structures of the prefrontal cortex as (1) similar but separate functions in the region of the frontal lobe, and (2) located anterior to (in front of) motor-related areas (motor association/premotor and primary motor cortices). That is, both *specific functions* and a fairly broad *frontal location* loosely define the *prefrontal* structures.

Various sections of *sensory* cortex, posterior to (behind) the prefrontal cortex, and other parts of the brain receive information from sensory organs (for vision, hearing, touch, taste, smell) via axons projecting through spinal and cranial nerves. The strip of cortex called the *primary motor cortex* sends out behavioral commands to muscles that can do their bidding, again via axons in spinal and cranial nerves but in the opposite direction from the incoming sensory messages.

Intermediary neurons in sections called the *association cortices* (plural of *cortex*) process incoming messages from parts of the *sensory cortices*. Association cortex regions translate messages into communications that different regions of the brain can interpret. For example, in response to sensory inputs that inform the individual of approaching danger, the *motor cortex* that was warned by an association cortex then sends out commands around the body: "Leg muscles! Run, run!" There's an even faster way to get safe: the danger message can go to a reflex arc in the spinal cord which gets your muscles running instantly without going up to the brain for authorization.

The cortex is comprised of many different regions specializing in different functions. In order to follow the discussion of the different cortical regions and of larger brain structures in general, it is necessary to know the terms describing location.

---

anterior versus **posterior** (at the front versus at the back)
rostral versus **caudal** (near the frontal/facial end versus rear or tail end)
dorsal versus **ventral** (on or near the back versus on or near the belly)
medial versus **lateral** (in the middle versus on the side)

These distinctions are important because most larger brain structures perform multiple functions implemented in different sections of these structures. Within a single structure such as the hypothalamus, it is even possible to find different sections of the same structural organ performing opposite functions, such as one hypothalamic nucleus telling the organism to eat more while another nucleus is telling it to stop eating! (Who wins?) Locations of one section relative to another within a structure, or locations of two different structures vis-à-vis each other, are designated by the terms in the box above.

The **prefrontal cortex** as defined above has subdivisions such as the orbitofrontal cortex, the medial prefrontal cortex, and the subgenual anterior cingulate cortex (see color images C. and E. in color section). These structures are involved in complex cognitive functions and the expression of personality and social behavior (Purves et al., 2008). These subsystems of the prefrontal cortex mediate such activities as perceiving, learning, remembering, evaluating the importance of pleasurable or aversive stimuli, planning, and executing plans. The nomenclature can be confusing, because these subsections have their own names ending in the word *cortex*, falsely implying that they're *parallel* systems to the prefrontal cortex when in fact they're different regions performing many different functions *within the larger region* of the prefrontal cortex.

We provide more information about prefrontal cortex activities in various sections of the book on pleasure, addiction, executive functions, and other topics.

The **diencephalon**, an interior region of the brain near the limbic system and the basal ganglia, is made up of the *thalamus* and the *hypothalamus*, located below the thalamus. The hypothalamus has a close relationship with the pituitary gland, to be discussed below.

The **thalamus** has a complex role in information processing. It is a relay station that frequently receives information from the environment and transmits it to different regions of the cerebral cortex and other parts of the brain. A simple map illustrates a typical sequence of transmission of a message from and back out to the environment, often through the thalamus (see Figure 7.1).

Transmission of information back to the environment takes place via behaviors of the individual that environments interpret. However, environments do not always interpret accurately. When this happens, the message has been misunderstood.

The thalamus, like the hypothalamus, contains multiple nuclei (groups of specialized neurons) that perform functions in numerous neural networks spanning the cortices, limbic system, basal ganglia, and brainstem, especially relaying information.

The **hypothalamus** ("low" thalamus or "under" thalamus) in humans is about the size of an almond, yet its importance, versatility, and power in the brain's hierarchy are legendary. A miniature Napoleon of the brain? Probably not—it seems more interested in promoting equilibrium and well-being than in conquest of neural domains. It is made up of a large number of *nuclei* (neuron bundles), each of which occupies a domain of its own, with its own pattern of connections and function. The various nuclei are grouped into regions.

The hypothalamus is a watchdog of homeostasis around the body. The principle of homeostasis has long been one of the brain's gold standards as it enacts its job description of maintaining balance between competing forces—for example, the body's energy intake versus expenditure of energy is intended to be virtually equal. We'll see in Part III how this feisty little structure seems to have lost that particular battle over homeostasis to some mighty adversaries. The hypothalamus monitors and/or adjusts blood flow, energy metabolism, reproductive behaviors, hunger and appetite, and coordinates responses to threatening conditions (Purves et al., 2008, p. 528). In Part III we'll also take up a concept that some neuroscientists increasingly prefer to homeostasis, called *allostasis*.

Various hypothalamic nuclei manage sleep; manufacture neuropeptides that control secretion of a variety of hormones by the pituitary gland; secrete the "urge to cuddle" transmitter/hormone oxytocin and its cousin vasopressin into the bloodstream; are involved in feeding, reproductive, and parenting behaviors; and direct thermoregulation and water balance. These nuclei receive inputs from the limbic system as well as visceral sensory inputs from the *nucleus of the solitary tract*. This latter structure has an important role in eating, as we'll see in Part III.

Hypothalamic structures organize behaviors to regulate body temperature, blood pressure, aggression, and sexual behavior. Stimulation of the hypothalamus can produce upsurges in sexual behavior. Hypothalamic hormones stimulate the pituitary gland to release *its* hormones that also include the brain's natural opioids, the endorphins and the enkephalins (see Table 11.1, Families of Neurotransmitters and Neuromodulators). And much of the time, the pituitary takes its orders from the hypothalamus. Are you asking yourself how all those nuclei of the little nut-sized hypothalamus can keep track of and manage so many different activities? I am—but I can't claim to have the answer. Sort of like a microchip in a computer (probably *much* more complex)?

Recent studies have shown that the hypothalamus has a sensing mechanism that identifies the hormone and nutrient fuel components of energy in order to regulate both food intake and glucose homeostasis (Chari, Lam, and Lam, 2010). Some neuroscientists believe the chief eating-related function of the hypothalamus is not to regulate eating, but rather to regulate energy metabolism (Pinel, 2011).

The **pituitary gland** manages other endocrine glands, such as those in reproductive organs (testes and ovaries). It is only the size of a blueberry, but

TABLE 11.1 Families of Neurotransmitters and Neuromodulators

Amino acids: gamma-aminobutyric acid (GABA), glutamate, glycine

Monoamines: dopamine, norepinephrine, epinephrine, serotonin, histamine

Acetylcholine

Neuropeptides:
  endogenous opioids:
    α-endorphin, β-endorphin, γ-endorphin (γ is the Greek letter gamma), dynorphin, leu-enkephalin, metenkephalin
  hypothalamic hormones:
    corticotropin-releasing factor (CRF), vasopressin, oxytocin, somatostatin, thyrotropin-releasing hormone (TRH), luteinizing-hormone-releasing hormone (LHRH)
  other peptides:
    substance P, delta sleep-inducing peptide (DSIP), glucagon, bradykinin

Other substances that generally act as neuromodulators:
  growth hormone, prolactin, adenosine, prostaglandins, corticosteroids, estrogens, androgens

it is pivotal in creating and regulating hormones. However, this "master" gland is largely controlled by the hypothalamus. Hormones produced in the hypothalamus are packaged in vesicles and propelled down to the end of axons, where they are stored in nerve endings and picked up by blood vessels that directly connect the hypothalamus with the pituitary gland.

The hypothalamus and the pituitary gland connect via the circulatory system with the *adrenal glands* located on the kidneys, in a complex feedback loop known as the hypothalamic-pituitary-adrenal (HPA) axis (see color images K. and L., and a detailed account of the action of the HPA axis in stress and trauma, pp. 155–156).

The HPA axis is one of the body's two major neural circuits for processing stress. It processes stress from short-term events and also serves as a staging site for biochemical and cellular changes that give rise to the long-term outcome known as posttraumatic stress disorder (PTSD).

The HPA axis functions are spelled out as noted above. The HPA axis also has significant influence over the immune system; intense or prolonged stress or trauma can damage immune function.

The **limbic system** is the deep inner section of the brain, known as the "primitive" brain. It's essentially a region that includes structures from the frontal cortex, medial forebrain, midbrain, basal ganglia, and temporal lobe, grouped loosely by physical proximity to each other as well as specific functions performed by neural circuits within and reaching beyond the limbic region. Animal species that predated *homo sapiens* had limbic systems, and most animal species, including those much less neurologically developed than humans, such as reptiles, have them today. Limbic systems occur in species across levels of complexity and differentiation. They do not depend on consciousness.

Limbic structures regulate drives (hunger, thirst, sex), emotions and passion (love, rage, joy, fear, sadness), arousal, and levels of attentiveness. The limbic system mediates fear and transmits messages of pleasure or pain into memory. It plays a key role in determining what is salient enough to be remembered. Intensely positive memories, such as a drug high, can cause people with addictions to have cravings and risk relapse even after years of abstinence. Intensely negative memories are activated even years later as symptoms of PTSD. These memories are put into storage by biochemical processes that result in actual changes in microscopic brain structures—changes that are invisible to the naked eye but occur in tandem with behaviors and affects (emotions) that *are* observable. Here are some actions of important limbic system structures.

The **amygdala** is a small but complicated structure whose most prominent function seems to be promoting survival. It's located just in front of the hippocampus bilaterally. Many environmental inputs converge in the amygdala via transmission by the thalamus and/or from the cortices for the five senses. It links cortical regions that process sensory information with motor nerves that signal muscles to act and integrates behavioral and hormonal components of emotions with involuntary body events such as heart rate, respiration, and intestinal activity. It's essential for decoding emotions and setting off alarms when danger lurks. Ability to decode emotions means perception and understanding of one's own or another creature's intentions and emotions.

The amygdala alerts us to both beneficial and harmful stimuli. The beneficial signals include the presence of food, water, and salt, potential sexual partners, and needs of infants for care. It's also thought to be involved in the paths that recognize pheromones (sexually stimulating odors).

The amygdala is particularly stimulated by events that signal imminent danger—we need it to protect us. It notifies individuals of approaching pain, rivals, or the presence of a predator likely to have chosen the individual for its next meal (or in the case of humans, for its next scam?). Fight-or-flight reactions are mediated by the amygdala, as are rage reactions. When a person flies into a rage, his or her amygdala is revved up.

The amygdala allows us to feel certain emotions, especially fear, and to recognize them in others. However, like most brain organs, it does not constitute a "center" for fear because it collaborates with numerous other structures in all its functions. The amygdala is a "hub" where many of the body's alarm circuits are grouped together (University of Washington Digital Anatomist Program, 2011),

The **hippocampus** derives its name from the similarity of its shape to a seahorse. It is located in the medial temporal lobe of the brain, is a major component of the brains of humans and other mammals, and is part of the limbic system. There is now almost universal agreement that the hippocampus plays an important role in memory, spatial coding and navigation, detecting novel events, places and stimuli, and specifically in forming new memories from experiences and memory for facts (VanElzakker, Fevurly, Breindel, and Spencer, 2008). However, the process of building memories is still not fully understood, nor is it known which neural circuits are responsible for acquisition, consolidation, and recall of memories.

The form of neural change known as long-term potentiation (LTP) was first discovered in the hippocampus. LTP is a persistent increase in synaptic strength following high-frequency stimulation of a chemical synapse, often involving the neurotransmitter glutamate (Paradiso, Bear, and Connors, 2007). A change in synaptic responsiveness, induced by brief strong activation and lasting for hours, days, or longer, was first produced by researchers Bliss and Lømo (1973). This increase in synaptic strength lasts a very long time compared to other processes that act on synaptic strength.

A graph comparing the response to stimuli in synapses that have undergone LTP versus synapses that have not undergone LTP shows that those that have undergone LTP have stronger electrical responses to stimuli than do other synapses (Paradiso et al., 2007). LTP in the hippocampus is "the vanguard and the best documented neuronal substrate for memory formation" (Kumar, 2011). LTP can help you hold and savor happy memories, but the converse is also true. It can prolong and amplify memories of pain, fear, rage, or humiliation.

It would be hard to overstate the importance of memory in our lives, because most learning throughout life requires memory. Diseases causing severe memory loss lead to people no longer recognizing their families and to becoming unable to live safely on their own.

Severe damage to the hippocampus in both hemispheres results in inability to form or retain new memories (*anterograde amnesia*) and often also affects memories formed before the damage occurred (*retrograde amnesia*). The mechanism of transferring memories from the hippocampus to the cortex as part of memory consolidation is still unknown (Vadakkan, 2011). In some cases, older memories remain intact despite hippocampal destruction, a fact that led to the idea that consolidation of memories over time might involve the transfer of memories *out* of the hippocampus to other better protected parts of the brain, such as the cortex (ibid.).

Amnesic persons frequently show "implicit" memory for experiences (i.e., without conscious recollection). For example, a person with hippocampal damage is asked to guess which of two faces he or she has seen most recently. The person believes that he or she has never seen either face previously, yet gives the correct answer most of the time. Neuroscience researchers sometimes distinguish between *conscious recollection*, which depends on the hippocampus,

---

BOX 11.1 Attack of the Adrenals—A Metabolic Story

The ambulance siren screams its warning to get out of the way. You can't move your car because you're stuck in a bumper-to-bumper traffic jam that reaches as far as the eye can see. There must be an accident up ahead. Meanwhile the road construction crew a few feet from your car is jack-hammering the pavement. You are about to enter the stress zone.

Inside your body the alert goes out.

"Attention all parasympathetic forces. Urgent. Adrenal gland missile silos mounted atop kidneys have just released chemical cortisol weapons of brain destruction. Mobilize all internal defenses. Launch immediate counter-calm hormones before hippocampus is hammered by cortisol."

Hormones rush to your adrenal glands to suppress the streaming cortisol on its way to your brain. Other hormones rush to your brain to round up all the remnants of cortisol missiles that made it to your hippocampus. These hormones escort the cortisol remnants back to Kidneyland for a one-way ride on the Bladderhorn. You have now reached metabolic equilibrium, also known as homeostasis.

Resources for Science Learning: The Franklin Institute,
August 24, 2011. http://www.fi.edu/learn/brain/stress.html.

and *familiarity*, which depends on other regions of the medial temporal cortex (Diana, Yonelinas, and Ranganath, 2007).

Recent discoveries in rodent brains have given rise to the "cognitive map hypothesis" (Moser, Kropf, and Moser, 2008; Solstad, Boccara, Kropff, Moser MB, and Moser EI, 2008). In people, more active hippocampi were shown when they navigated correctly in a computer-simulated "virtual" navigation task (Maguire, Burgess et al., 1998; Maguire, Gadian et al., 2000). There is also evidence that the hippocampus plays a role in finding shortcuts and new routes between familiar places.

For example, London's taxi drivers have to pass a strict test, "Knowledge of London Examination System," informally known as "The Knowledge," before being licensed to drive the traditional black cabs. They must show they've learned a large number of places and the most direct routes between them (Wechsler, Morss, Wustoff, and Caughey, 2004).

A study at University College London by Maguire, Gadian et al. (2000) showed that part of the hippocampus is larger in taxi drivers than in the general public and that more experienced drivers have bigger hippocampi! Whether having a bigger hippocampus helps an individual to become a cab driver in the first place, or if learning lots of shortcuts for a living makes an individual's average-sized hippocampus grow, is not yet known. There was a positive correlation between the length of time an individual had spent as a taxi driver and the volume of the right hippocampus. Could it be that cabbies have found a secret to fight back memory decline as they get older?

The hippocampus contains high levels of glucocorticoid receptors, which make it more vulnerable to long-term stress than most other brain areas (Joels, 2008). Aging, diseases, stress, and other pathological conditions are now known to negatively influence learning and memory capabilities (Kumar, 2011).

Although many species have hippocampi, we typically believe that less differentiated creatures cannot really perform cognitive tasks.

The lateral pallium of a typical fish is considered a fish equivalent of our hippocampus. Several types of fish, particularly goldfish, have been shown experimentally to have strong spatial memory abilities, even forming *cognitive maps* of the areas they inhabit (Jacobs, 2003). But damage to the lateral pallium in fish impairs spatial memory.

Have we been unfairly assessing the capabilities of the goldfish all these years? Steven Hyman, former director of NIMH (the National Institute of Mental Health), once jokingly dubbed this kind of attribution "species-ist" (Brain-Behavior Workshop on Addictions, Harvard Medical School, 1995).

The **basal ganglia,** a system of structures deep within the brain in the area of the limbic system, include the *striatum* (*caudate nucleus* and *putamen*), the *globus pallidus*, and the *substantia nigra*. Regions of the basal ganglia have long been known to regulate typical as well as atypical movement. Atypical examples are hyperactivity or paucity of movement.

Also, convergent data from neuroimaging, neuropsychology, genetics, and neurochemical studies indicate that the frontostriatal network is a likely contributor to the pathophysiology of attention-deficit hyperactivity disorder (ADHD), involving the caudate nucleus and putamen, lateral prefrontal cortex, and anterior cingulate cortex (Emond, Joyal, and Poissant, 2009). They and other researchers have emphasized poor behavioral inhibition as the central impairment of ADHD. Disinhibition, characteristic of disorders of impulsivity and control such as ADHD, is sometimes a result of inadequate activity by basal ganglia structures, resulting in failure to inhibit inappropriate outbursts as well as motor activity.

More recently, the basal ganglia have emerged as important players in the processing of pleasure. When we consider the neuroscience of pleasure in Part III, we'll discuss this third role of the basal ganglia, which often confers the gift of having fun.

The Brainstem. The brainstem arises in the *midbrain* and descends through the *pons* and the *medulla* to connect with the spinal cord. The pons, a bulge in the brainstem, is important in sleep and arousal and in relaying information from the cerebral cortex to the cerebellum. The medulla regulates the cardiovascular system, respiration, and muscle tone. The *nucleus of the solitary tract* in the medulla has a central role in managing food intake (see Pleasure, Chapter 21, p. 135).

Corpus Callosum. This structure is composed of bundles of neurons carrying messages from the cerebral hemisphere on one side of the brain to the other, permitting communication between the two hemispheres.

We've just introduced readers to a few very important brain structures—but there are many more for which we don't have space here. Among these others, a few will appear for the first time when we look at neural networks in Part III, and a few more in the later sections of the book on addictions, child development, mental health and illness, and multiple routes to the quality of life.

{ 12 }

Brain Structures: Microscopic (Neurons, Synapses, and Other Amazing Brain Actors)

Neurons (see Figure 12.1 and color image G., Neuron on Stage). These tiny cells in the brain, spinal cord, and throughout the body carry out the brain's functions of receiving messages, making decisions, and sending out commands. Estimates of the total number of neurons in the human organism vary; one commonly heard estimate is 100 billion. Neurons connect with other neurons through tiny spaces, called *synapses*, that are filled with gelatinous fluid. Each neuron is thought to make from several up to hundreds or even thousands of such connections with other neurons. The estimate of the total number of connections made by neurons altogether is often 100 trillion, but neither the

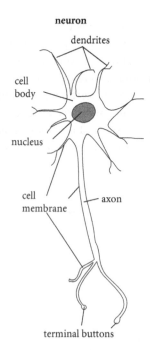

FIGURE 12.1 *Neuron.*

number of neurons nor the number of connections is known precisely, and, presumably, both can vary from person to person.

In the brain and spinal cord, neurons are tightly packed together in bundles. The basic structures and functions of human neurons are similar to those of less differentiated species, such as the squid, the snail, and the leech (our first cousins?).

The neuron, like other cells in the body, is covered around its entire surface with a thin *cell membrane*. It has a cell body containing a nucleus, which is distinct from the nuclei we met earlier, the *bundles of neurons* performing a specialized function. The nucleus of a cell body is its core, which has critical functions in the maintenance of that single cell, whereas the nuclei that form bundles of neurons are groups of whole cells, not parts of a cell.

In the neuron, many tiny filaments (threads) called *dendrites* receive chemical messages from adjacent neurons. Each neuron has many dendrites but only one *axon*. The axon is also a threadlike structure. It sends chemical and electrical messages to receiving neurons (although messages can also go from the axon of one neuron to the axon of another neuron, or from an axon to the cell body of an adjacent neuron). We will discuss mostly the more common transmission route from the axon of one neuron to dendrites of adjoining neurons.

We often hear about our *gray matter* as a stand-in for "brain." Gray (or grey) matter (spelled both ways) refers technically to neuronal cell bodies, neuropil (dendrites and unmyelinated axons), glial cells (astroglia and oligodendrocytes), and capillaries (tiny blood vessels). White matter does not include cell bodies. It's mostly myelinated axon tracts in which myelin shields on axons are white. Gray matter has a gray-brown color from capillary blood vessels and neuronal cell bodies (Purves et al., 2008 pp. 15–16). When reductions in gray matter are found, there usually is a deficiency in some brain tissue somewhere in the brain. Neurons come in different sizes and shapes. There are as many as 200 different varieties. Some neurons have long axons (as much as a meter in length when stretching down the spine), and some have short axons. Although there is only one axon per neuron, at its end the axon divides into numerous projections with tiny bulbs at their ends. These are called *terminal buttons*. At these terminal buttons, chemical messengers called *neurotransmitters* are manufactured and then dispatched to other neurons.

Vesicles are round containers that store neurotransmitter molecules in the terminal buttons. Vesicles are made of the same material as cell membranes. They are manufactured in the cell body by tiny factories called *Golgi apparatus*, then transported down the axon to the terminal buttons.

Synapses (see Figure 12.2) are tiny spaces between the cell membranes of adjacent neurons. The dendrites of neurons are very near (but don't actually touch) the axons of adjacent neurons. They are separated by these tiny spaces filled with gelatinous liquid. As noted above, there are an estimated 100 trillion or more synapses in the human body. Synapses are where the action is!

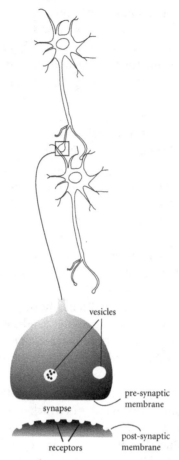

vesicles

pre-synaptic
membrane

synapse

post-synaptic
membrane

receptors

FIGURE 12.2 *Terminal button and synapse.*

Although synapses make up less than 1% of the total volume of the brain, they are the sites where the most important actions influencing emotions, thoughts, and behavior take place. Even though very important functions take place in the nucleus and the cell body, the task of transmitting messages from neuron to neuron—which happens for every activity of our psychological lives—takes place at junctures between neurons, not in the cell body.

Presynaptic membrane. The section of the sending neuron's cell membrane (the thin membrane that covers the entire surface of the neuron) that is adjacent to the synapse.

Postsynaptic membrane. The section of the receiving neuron's cell membrane that is adjacent to the synapse.

Receptors. Protein molecules embedded in the surface of postsynaptic and presynaptic membranes. Receptors have many different chemical structures. Receptors are the sites where many psychoactive drugs do their work.

Each receptor molecule combines only with those neurotransmitter molecules that fit with its chemical structure, like a lock (the receptor molecule) and a key (the neurotransmitter molecule). The chief function of postsynaptic receptors is to alter the electrical forces (called *action potential*) that either increase or decrease the electrical current set off in the receiving neuron. How action potentials work is fairly complex, so rather than possibly overwhelm you with the *hows* and *whens*, we refer you to any of the current introductory neuroscience texts as well as multiple entries on the web, found using the keywords "action potential" (see for example Carlson, 2011; Pinel, 2011; Purves et al., 2008).

{ 13 }

The Brain's Natural Chemicals: Precursors, Messengers, and Enzymes

Glucose is the simple sugar that the brain uses as energy to do its work. Remember, some of the brain scans that measure how much activity is taking place in different regions of the brain do so by forming color-coded images of glucose metabolism in those regions.

Enzymes are compounds that trigger chemical reactions without themselves being chemically changed. We have many enzymes throughout the body that perform essential functions. Names of enzymes can be recognized because they end in the letters *-ase*. For example, *monoamine oxidase* is the enzyme that causes monoamine compounds to be broken down chemically. Enzymes in neuronal structures are synthesized in the cell bodies of neurons and transported down axons to the terminal buttons.

A precursor is something that comes before something else. *Precursor substances* in the brain are building blocks for neurotransmitters. They are protein molecules that come from digestion of protein-containing foods. Many of these proteins have been broken down during digestion into amino acids. They are transported to the brain by blood vessels, cross over into the neuron, and are transformed into neurotransmitters inside the neuron through chemical reactions.

Neurotransmitters, also referred to as transmitters, are molecules that act as chemical messengers (see Chapter 11, Table 11.1, Families of Neurotransmitters and Neuromodulators, and color images M. and N. referenced in Part IV).

The messages of transmitters enact all our psychological functions. Neurotransmitters are manufactured from precursor substances either in the axon terminal buttons (most transmitters) or in the cell body (neuropeptides). They are stored in synaptic vesicles, then released from the vesicles into the synapse where they cross the synapse and combine with postsynaptic receptor molecules to start off a chain of events in the receiving neuron. Until recently, it was believed that neurons produced only one kind of transmitter, but we now know that many neurons contain and dispatch more than one type. Different types of vesicles within the same terminal button contain the different transmitters.

The total number of different neurotransmitters is unknown, but more than 100 have been identified. Others are believed to exist. In addition, we keep discovering "new" (hitherto unknown) effects of already identified transmitters.

Some transmitters are considered putative because it has not been possible to determine whether they meet all criteria for neurotransmitter status. According to widely accepted criteria, in order to be dubbed *neurotransmitter*, a molecule must be present within a presynaptic neuron, must be released in response to an electrical current involving influx of calcium ions into the terminal button, and must have specific receptors at its target site on the postsynaptic neuron with which it can combine chemically. To carry out this function, a transmitter must be chemically constructed to fit with the chemical construction of its receptor, as described earlier. This process will be explained in Chapter 14 on neurotransmission.

Neuromodulators are cousins of neurotransmitters. They act like transmitters, but their action is not limited to the synaptic cleft. They diffuse much more widely through extracellular fluid (fluid outside the cell membrane).

The picture is confusing because a substance can act as a neurotransmitter in one situation, a neuromodulator in another, a hormone acting in the brain, or a hormone acting at distant sites in the body.

Transmitters often have multiple functions and behave differently in different contexts. A transmitter may combine with several different receptors, all dedicated to that particular transmitter. For example, serotonin has at least 14 different receptors and changes its effects depending on which receptor is receiving it. The neurotransmitter epinephrine in the brain is the same substance as the adrenaline your adrenal gland secretes when you get "butterflies" in the stomach. The histamine that makes you sneeze, itch, or have watery eyes is also a neurotransmitter that regulates sleep/wake cycles, hormonal secretion, and other functions. Estrogens and androgens are neuromodulators as well as sex-related hormones that make you feel—well, you know what we mean.

For our purposes, becoming familiar with what these substances do to influence our emotions and behavior is more important than arguments about which substances fall into one or another category. Therefore, we list some of the more common neurotransmitters and neuromodulators together in Chapter 11, Table 11.1, grouped in "families." Readers are referred to neuroscience texts for more detailed discussions.

Neurotransmitters are "first" messengers, bringing signals from neuron to neuron. In order for the transmitter to act, the first-messenger signal must often be translated by the action of ***second messengers*** into a signal the receiving neuron can interpret.

Second-messenger molecules are activated when a neurotransmitter combines with a postsynaptic receptor, initiating a cascade of steps that allow transmission of the impulse to the receiving neuron to occur. Second messengers have other functions such as traveling to the cell nucleus and initiating biochemical changes. Examples of second-messenger molecules are calcium ions ($Ca++$) and cyclic adenosine monophosphate (cAMP). The actions of these and many other second messengers are detailed in neuroscience texts referenced throughout this book (see for example Carlson, 2011; Pinel, 2011; Purves et al., 2008).

The three most common neurotransmitters in the central nervous system (CNS) are glutamate, GABA, and glycine. These transmitters have a general role in determining how fast receiving neurons fire.

Glutamate, also called *glutamic acid*, is the principal excitatory transmitter in the brain and spinal chord.

Gamma-aminobutyric acid (GABA) is the most abundant inhibitory transmitter in the brain and is actually manufactured from (excitatory) glutamate by the action of an enzyme that removes *one chemical component* from the glutamate compound! That is, the most common excitatory transmitter is a close relative of the most common inhibitory transmitter—similar but not identical chemical structures, opposite actions. GABA is the transmitter in as many as one-third of the synapses in the brain. It is most often found in local circuits, where it acts through networks of short connecting neurons called *interneurons* that link many neurons in the brain.

Glycine is a more localized inhibitory transmitter used in the spinal cord and lower brain.

All other neurotransmitters transmit directives through circuits of neurons that carry out diverse specific brain functions.

GABA receptors are essential to the effects of some anxiety-reducing drugs (called *anxiolytics*) such as alprazolam (Xanax), lorazepam (Ativan), and diazepam (Valium) of the benzodiazepine family (popularly known as "benzos"). The type A GABA receptor (GABA A) has not one but five binding sites, one for GABA itself, one for benzos, one for barbiturates, and two others. Figure 13.1 is a sketch of a GABA A receptor in the membrane of a postsynaptic neuron, with these three binding sites labeled. These drugs enhance inhibitory actions in reducing anxiety, promoting sleep, reducing seizures, and promoting muscle relaxation.

How could the brain possibly know to grow receptors for specific drugs that don't occur naturally in the brain? The brain is amazing, but is it that amazing?

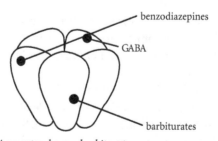

FIGURE 13.1 *GABA A receptor, benzo, barbiturate.*

Has the pharmaceutical industry pulled off an extraordinary coup? Not likely. It is believed that some substances, called *ligands*, exist within the brain that have an affinity for certain receptors. Whatever these ligands may be, presumably the brain, not the drugs, "grew" these receptors for the ligands. The drugs thus resemble the natural ligands sufficiently to trick the receptors into accepting them.

All muscular movement results from release of **acetylcholine** (**ACh**), which also facilitates dreams in REM sleep, perceptual learning in the cerebral cortex, memory function in the hippocampus, and arousal and alertness in the frontal cortex and striatum. There is no need to remember examples such as the ones given for acetylcholine. You can always look up actions of specific transmitters if you need the information, and it would be impossible (and serve no useful purpose) to try to memorize the myriad functions of different brain chemicals. In any case, researchers keep discovering new substances with new actions. We merely give a few examples to illustrate for readers how incredibly complex and how amazing an instrument the human brain is!

In the monoamine neurotransmitter family, **dopamine** (**DA**) produces both excitatory and inhibitory responses in postsynaptic neurons, depending on which of several different dopamine receptors is involved. Dopamine mediates the reinforcing effects of pleasures from food, sex, drugs, music, art, and other sources, as well as movement, attention, and learning. Cell bodies of dopaminergic neurons in the substantia nigra project axons to the striatum (caudate nucleus and putamen), affecting movement and inhibition. (The suffix *-ergic* designates a specific neuron by the kinds of transmitters it secretes.)

Dopamine (DA) cell bodies in the ventral tegmental area (VTA) project to the nucleus accumbens, amygdala, and other structures, where they promote reward and reinforcement, and to the prefrontal cortex, where they stimulate formation of memories and carry out executive functions such as planning and problem solving (see Figures 13.2a and 13.2b, Dopamine and Serotonin Pathways, and color images F., J., M., and N. as referenced in Parts III and IV).

Almost all regions of the brain receive **norepinephrine** (**NE**) as input from noradrenergic neurons. *Noradrenergic* is the label used to refer to neurons that produce norepinephrine, because adrenaline and noradrenaline are synonymous with epinephrine and norepinephrine respectively, and because the alternative phrase, *norepinephrinergic*, with seven syllables, is hard to pronounce! Norepinephrine is a much more important neurotransmitter than epinephrine. Epinephrine is a minor transmitter in the brain, but it is a major hormone in the body where it is called adrenaline, sent out when needed for "fight or flight" by the adrenal glands located on the kidneys.

Many of the cell bodies of noradrenergic neurons originate in the **locus coeruleus** in the brainstem and project axons to most regions (cortex, limbic system, basal ganglia, diencephalon, cerebellum). Although receptors for norepinephrine produce both excitatory and inhibitory effects, the primary

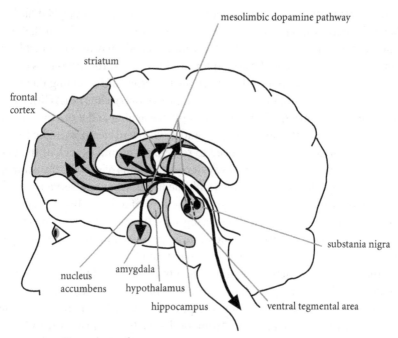

FIGURE 13.2A *Dopamine pathways.*

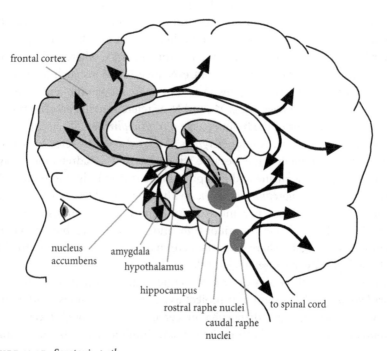

FIGURE 13.2B *Serotonin pathways.*

behavioral effect of norepinephrine is to increase vigilance and attentiveness to the environment, an excitatory function. Norepinephrine also increases the individual's responsiveness to other excitatory transmitters.

Serotonin (also called *5-HT*, for its chemical name 5-hydroxytryptamine) has complex behavioral effects. It has become well known for its role in regulating mood, through the popularity of antidepressant drugs like fluoxetine (Prozac), sertraline (Zoloft), and paroxetine (Paxil), designated by their function as *selective serotonin reuptake inhibitors*. These functions will be explained in Chapter 17 on actions of classes of drugs.

In addition to regulating mood, serotonin also plays important roles in control of sleep, eating, arousal, and anxiety. Drugs to change serotonin levels have been used to treat obsessive-compulsive disorder, panic attack, and nicotine addiction; prevent or ameliorate nausea in cancer chemotherapy; curb alcohol cravings; regulate pain; and suppress appetite in obesity. Hallucinogenic drugs such as lysergic acid diethylamide (LSD) appear to produce their effects by affecting serotonin transmission. Serotonin is able to carry out these diverse functions because of its 14 or more different receptors mentioned above. The effects of the messages it transmits to receiving neurons change, depending on which receptor is active.

The cell bodies of serotonergic neurons are located in clusters in the middle and lower brain regions including the pons and upper brainstem, mostly the **raphé nuclei** (*nuclei* is plural for *nucleus*, particularly in the context of nucleus as a bundle of neurons, not a single core structure within the central part of the cell body). Neurons from the raphé region project to the frontal cortex, thalamus, cerebellum, medulla and spinal cord, hypothalamus, amygdala, and hippocampus (see Figure 13.2b). Again, it is not necessary to memorize this information; it can be readily accessed as needed.

The three monoamine transmitters—dopamine, norepinephrine, and serotonin— have a great deal to do with psychological activity. They are extremely versatile and play multiple roles in our lives. For example, dopamine is active in the pleasures of eating, drinking, and sex. It combines with several different dopamine receptors (known as D1, D2, D3, D4, and so on). It is often *too* abundant in schizophrenia. It is also overabundant when a person is high on street drugs such as amphetamine. Too much dopamine can make you feel terrific, or it can make you mentally ill. Sometimes people who come into an emergency room from overdosing on amphetamines are misdiagnosed as having an acute episode of schizophrenia because the symptoms can look a lot alike.

Serotonin and norepinephrine are believed to be released from varicosities (swellings) in branches of axons rather than from terminal buttons. However, some do so near postsynaptic membranes, so they appear to behave as they would in conventional synapses.

Histamine neurons are concentrated in the hypothalamus and are involved in transmitting signals from the hypothalamus to the cerebellum. These neurons send a small number of projections to the brain and spinal cord, mediating arousal and attention and explaining the drowsiness side effect of antihistamine drugs. Histamine is released from cells around the body in response to allergic reactions.

Neuropeptides consist of chains of 3 to 36 amino acids linked together in a mix-and-match fashion. Amino acids are molecules with different arrangements of carbon, nitrogen, hydrogen, and oxygen. Neurons manufacture their own precursors for these neuropeptides by building giant molecules called polypeptides. Enzymes break down polypeptides into smaller segments of amino acids and then reconstitute them into diverse molecules, each one some form of amino acid chain. These new amino acid molecules are peptide neuromodulators and neurotransmitters.

Many peptides known to be hormones also act as neurotransmitters. Peptides often cohabit terminal buttons with other types of transmitters, such as monoamines, and are released in conjunction with these other transmitters.

Among the neuropeptides listed in Table 11.1, a range of different functions are carried out. The ***endogenous opioids*** are thought to be agents of alternative treatments such as hypnosis, acupuncture, and yoga. The word *opioid* refers to natural (endogenous) brain chemicals, whereas the word *opiate* refers to drugs such as heroin and morphine. They got their names from the opium poppy, cultivated for 5,000 years and used as an analgesic since at least the 16th century. The neural systems activated by opioids may suppress the perception of pain, inhibit defensive reactions in some species such as fleeing and hiding, and stimulate reward circuits ("pleasure pathways" or "pleasure circuits"). Typically opiate drugs multiply manyfold the effects of the similar natural opioids.

Hypothalamic hormones (hormones synthesized by neurons in the hypothalamus and dispatched to the pituitary gland) regulate secretion of hormones by the pituitary gland at target sites all around the body. Two neurotransmitters in the group, ***oxytocin*** and ***vasopressin***, are manufactured in the hypothalamus, then transported to and then released from the pituitary. Oxytocin not only initiates the birth process in human mothers and stimulates milk production in the breast, but also stimulates "affiliation"—sexual attraction, pair bonding, and paternal caretaking in animals, as well as the urge to cuddle! We discuss this remarkable potion in more detail in Part V, Chapter 34, see pp. 222–223.

{ 14 }

Neurotransmission: How the Brain
Sends and Receives Messages

The brain sends messages through the firing action of neurons, a process that goes on continuously, day and night, waking and sleeping, 24 hours a day, 365 days a year. The firing action of a neuron consists of sending electrical impulses through the entire neuron, and then setting off chain reactions of similar firing action in adjoining neurons. In neurons, action potentials often produce nerve impulses at speeds of one-thousandth of a second, with speed variations depending on the properties of the nerve fiber and its environment.

Neural (nerve) impulses are motions of electrically charged particles called *ions* that pass back and forth across the neuron's membrane. Ions are created by atoms or molecules of chemical substances losing or gaining electrons, thereby becoming electrically charged.

Typically, the impulse travels the entire length of the neuron (starting with the dendrites and ending at the axon's terminal buttons). It is propelled down the neuron like a row of dominoes, as exchange of each ion across the cell membrane sets off another ion exchange in the next section of the neuron.

These electrical impulses are then set off in adjoining neurons by chemical messengers, or neurotransmitters, that cross synapses from one neuron to another. This network of interconnecting neurons is so complex that by comparison, the world's most complicated computer looks like a child's toy.

The process of neurotransmission. Several events take place in this process.

1. Neurotransmitters enter a receiving cell by crossing the synapse from sending neurons and binding with receptors on the postsynaptic membrane of dendrites of receiving neurons (see Figure 14.1a).
2. When the neurotransmitters bind with postsynaptic receptors, an electrical impulse is set off in the receiving neuron and travels as electrical current down the neuron, from the dendrites, through the cell body and the axon, to the receiving neuron's terminal buttons (see Figure 14.1a).

(a)

FIGURE 14.1A *Neurotransmitters bind with receptors.*

3. Electrical current arrives at the terminal buttons (Figure 14.1b).
4. When this electrical message arrives at the terminal buttons, it sets off biochemical events in the terminal buttons that cause neurotransmitters to be released into the synapse (see Figure 14.1c). These messages are carried by the neurotransmitters from the

(b)

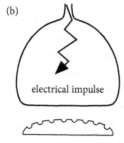

FIGURE 14.1B *Electrical impulse down dendrite to axon.*

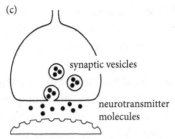

FIGURE 14.1C *Vesicles spill contents into synapse.*

presynaptic membrane of the sending neuron, across the synapse, to the postsynaptic membrane on the dendrites of the receiving neuron.

To understand neurotransmission, it is sometimes helpful to think of the process in two phases: transmission of electrical current down the neuron and biochemical events at the terminal buttons. (The process is actually much more complicated, but this simplified model is intended to give an overall sense of the process to readers not versed in physiological psychology.) It is important to remember that the electrical activity itself is also biochemical.

These messages can be either excitatory (telling the receiving neuron to fire at a faster rate) or inhibitory (telling the receiving neuron to fire at a slower rate). The rate of responding of the receiving neuron depends on whether there is a preponderance of excitatory or a preponderance of inhibitory messages coming into the receiving neuron. Remember, the neuron may be receiving several hundred messages at the same time from other neurons adjacent to it.

When the chemical messengers called neurotransmitters arrive at the postsynaptic membrane, they combine with postsynaptic receptor molecules. Each kind of postsynaptic receptor molecule receives the specific neurotransmitter molecule whose chemical structure fits with it.

However, sometimes receptor molecules can be fooled. Sometimes they accept imposters, such as therapeutic or street drugs that are similar but not identical in chemical structure to the natural neurotransmitter that fits with the particular receptor. This is explained more fully in sections on substance abuse and mental illness.

The concentration of various neurotransmitters in the synapse is regulated by *reuptake* and *enzymatic deactivation*. In reuptake of transmitters into presynaptic terminals, other molecules at the surfaces of the presynaptic membrane called *transporters* carry transmitters back up from the synapse into presynaptic neurons. By removing transmitters from the synapse, the reuptake process ends one round of electrical impulse and release. Reuptake causes the overall amount of the transmitter substance in the synapse to diminish.

Enzymatic deactivation consists of an enzyme setting off a chemical reaction that destroys the neurotransmitter by breaking it down into end products, called *metabolites*. The end result here is the same: decrease in the amount of transmitter substance available to do its work of crossing the synapse and combining with postsynaptic receptors on the surface of the receiving neuron.

Pathways for sending messages. Pathways are bundles of interconnecting neurons that perform specific tasks. Transmission pathways for different neurotransmitters extend throughout the brain. Examples are dopamine pathways and serotonin pathways (see Figures 13.2a and 13.2b).

Notice that in many areas the different transmitter systems run parallel to each other. That means they pass through and act in many of the same regions of the brain. An example of a bundle of neurons is the mesolimbic dopamine pathway, which carries pleasure messages from the ventral tegmental area (VTA) in the midbrain to the nucleus accumbens (NAc) in the forebrain and also the limbic system (see color image D.).

Neurotransmitters: Synthesis
Through Release in Four Steps

Synthesis of neurotransmitters (or how your hamburger or tofu is transformed into neurotransmitters). First, you eat protein-containing foods. Second, your digestive system breaks the foods down into its protein components, amino acids, which are the building blocks for neurotransmitters.

Third, your circulatory system carries these amino acids to your brain. These molecules are called precursor substances because they are precursors—they come before—neurotransmitters. The blood vessel wall acts as a filter called the *blood brain barrier*, because it allows some but not all molecules to pass through (see Figure 15.1a).

The precursor substances cross through the walls of blood vessels and through the cell membrane of terminal buttons of neurons. Neurotransmitter factories are inside the terminal buttons. Once these precursors get into the neuron, the neurotransmitter factory swings into action with the help of enzymes.

Fourth, enzymes in the terminal buttons promote chemical reactions that convert the precursor molecules into a new substance (precursor + enzyme = new substance) (see Figure 15.1b). Let's call the first enzyme that acts on the precursor substance *enzyme 1*.

Fifth, the transformation from precursor substance to neurotransmitter molecule can involve one change (using one enzyme), or there can be a series of changes, a series of different new substances, using several different enzymes. Let's call the second enzyme in this chain of events *enzyme 2*.

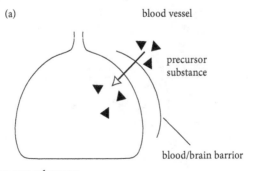

FIGURE 15.1A *Precursor substances.*

(b)

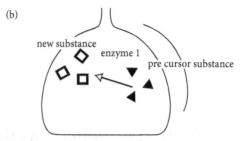

FIGURE 15.1B *Precursor substances and enzyme transformation.*

(c)

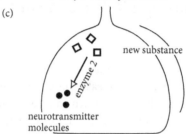

FIGURE 15.1C *New substance transformed by enzyme.*

Enzyme 2 promotes chemical reactions that convert the new substance either into neurotransmitter molecules or into another new substance. We are using the term "new substance" as a generic term for any chemical compound that is produced during this process of transformation from precursor substance to neurotransmitter (see Figure 15.1c). Once the final products have been manufactured (neurotransmitter or neuromodulator molecules), the life cycle of the neurotransmitter is at phase (2), storage.

Storage of neurotransmitter molecules. To prevent various enzymes from continuing to change neurotransmitters into other compounds, the newly created little transmitter molecules need protection, so they get into the round containers called vesicles. They are stored in the vesicles until the next phase of release (see Figure 15.2a).

Electrical impulse. The electrical impulse coming down the axon stimulates release of the neurotransmitters from their vesicles into the synapse. Here's how. Electrically charged calcium particles (calcium ions) sit outside the neuron's

(a)

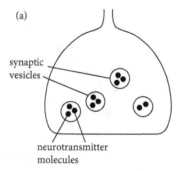

FIGURE 15.2A *Terminal buttons with vesicles and neurotransmitters.*

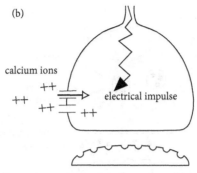

(b)

calcium ions

electrical impulse

FIGURE 15.2B *Calcium ions enter neuron as impulse arrives at terminal button.*

cell membrane in the region of the presynaptic membrane (see Figure 15.2b). The electrical impulse comes down the neuron (starting from the dendrites, through the cell body, and on down to the terminal button via the axon).

Release. When the electrical message hits a terminal button, the electrical current stimulates channels in the cell membrane to open and let the calcium ions into the neuron (Figure 15.2b). There, the calcium ions cross the neuron's cell membrane, stimulating the vesicles to move down the terminal button to the presynaptic membrane. The vesicles fuse with the presynaptic membrane, open up, and spill their contents (the neurotransmitter molecules) into the synapse (see Figures 15.2c and 15.2d).

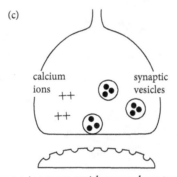

(c)

calcium ions

synaptic vesicles

FIGURE 15.2C *Calcium ions ++ in neuron, vesicles move down toward presynaptic membrane.*

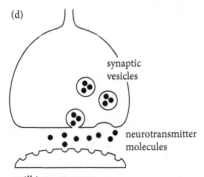

(d)

synaptic vesicles

neurotransmitter molecules

FIGURE 15.2D *Transmitters spill into synapse.*

(e)

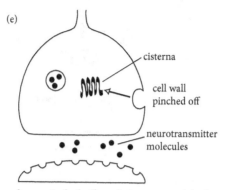

cisterna

cell wall
pinched off

neurotransmitter
molecules

FIGURE 15.2E *Cell membrane pinched off, made into new vesicles by cisternae.*

After dumping their contents into the synapse, the vesicles cease to exist. The membranes of vesicles are made of the same material as the cell membrane itself, so as they fuse, they become part of the cell membrane. In order to replace lost vesicles, chunks of the terminal button's cell membrane are pinched off and then recycled to form new vesicles by *cisternae* (a part of the Golgi apparatus) (see Figure 15.2e). The exact mechanisms of manufacture and transport are still uncertain; Golgi apparatus is typically located in cell bodies.

{ 16 }

Outcomes: The Fifth Step in Neurotransmission

Once neurotransmitters have been released into the synapse, several outcomes are possible.

1. Neurotransmitter molecules can *bind* (combine) with postsynaptic receptor molecules to excite or inhibit the receiving neuron's firing action (see Figure 16.1a).
2. Neurotransmitter molecules can be taken back up into the sending neuron, a process called *reuptake* (see Figure 16.1b).

(a)

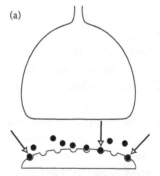

FIGURE 16.1A *Transmitters crossing over and combining with postsynaptic receptors.*

(b)

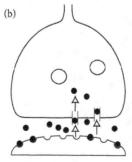

FIGURE 16.1B *Reuptake of transmitters in synapse.*

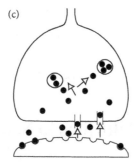

FIGURE 16.1C *Reuptake of transmitters in synapse; transmitters then move into vesicles.*

3. Some of the reuptaken neurotransmitters *move back into vesicles* and
   are recycled through the process again (see Figure 16.1c).
4. Other reuptaken molecules don't make it into the vesicles because
   they *get broken down by the action of an enzyme* (let's call this
   enzyme 3) into end products of chemical degradation, called *metabolites*. Now they're out of circulation. They're not neurotransmitters
   anymore (see Figure 16.1d). The metabolites are removed through
   the blood stream or reabsorbed in some other way.

Still other neurotransmitters don't make it out of the synapse at all. They *get
broken down by the action of an enzyme right in the synapse* (let's call this
enzyme 4) into end products called *metabolites*. Now they're out of circulation too. Putting neurotransmitters out of circulation by breaking them
down into metabolites is called *inactivation or deactivation* (see Figures 16.1d
and 16.1e).

Although the sequence of events just outlined is the typical route for
many neurotransmitters, there are several other possible routes. For example, serotonin and norepinephrine are released through varicosities (swellings) in branches of the axon. Some of them are released near postsynaptic

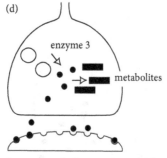

FIGURE 16.1D *Transmitters in neurons don't move into vesicles, so they are broken down by
enzymes.*

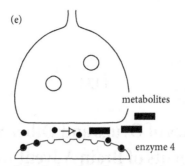

FIGURE 16.1E *Transmitters being broken down by enzymes in synapse.*

membranes, so they appear to behave as in the process just described. Others are released diffusely throughout the extracellular region, thus acting as neuromodulators.

Peptides (see Chapter 11, Table 11.1) make a different voyage. They are manufactured in the cell body rather than in terminal buttons. The biological activity of each peptide depends on its particular sequence of amino acids as well as on which of three kinds of receptors it attaches to. After release into the synapse, neuropeptides are not reuptaken and recycled. Those that don't reach their postsynaptic receptors are destroyed by more enzymes.

17

Some Classes of Drugs and Other Substances: Agents of Brain Adventures

Psychoactive drugs (legal and illegal, therapeutic and recreational) and other chemical compounds can interfere with normal processes of neurotransmission at any stage in the life span of neurotransmitters. Here we introduce some actions of different classes of drugs, expanded in Parts III and IV. Table 17.1 lists classes of prescribed drugs.

Drugs can

1. *interfere with the synthesis of neurotransmitters.* Example: Low levels of lead, ingested over time, impede the action of enzymes that promote the synthesis of neurotransmitters from precursor substances (see Figure 17.1a).

2. *facilitate or inhibit the release of transmitters.* Example of a release facilitator: amphetamine promotes release of dopamine into the synapse. Example of a release inhibitor: Calcium channel blockers, such as verapamil, sometimes used to treat bipolar disorder, affect the action of the calcium by blocking the channels on the cell membrane that allow calcium ions (Ca^{++}) to pass through (see Figure 17.1b). If the calcium ions can't get into the presynaptic neuron, vesicles won't

TABLE 17.1 Categories of Therapeutic Drugs

Categories of Therapeutic Drugs	Conditions for Which Drug is Used
Neuroleptics (antipsychotics)	schizophrenia, and as adjuncts in other conditions
Antidepressants	depression, obsessive-compulsive and eating disorders, aggressivity, attention-deficit hyperactivity disorder (if stimulants can't be used), some addiction cravings
Mood stabilizers (lithium)	bipolar and schizoaffective
Anticonvulsants	disorders, episodic
Calcium channel blockers	aggression
Anxiolytics (anti-anxiety)	anxiety
Psychostimulants	attention-deficit hyperactivity disorder

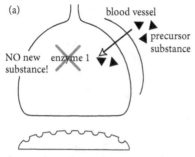

FIGURE 17.1A *Lead interferes with synthesis of precursor substance into neurotransmitter.*

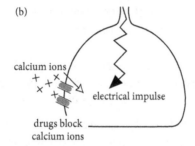

FIGURE 17.1B *Verapamil blocks entrance of Ca⁺⁺ into neuron so vesicles can't go down to presynaptic membrane.*

fuse with the presynaptic membrane and won't be able to dispatch their loads of neurotransmitters into the synapse.

3. *potentiate (increase, strengthen) the action of transmitters.*
   Example: Opiates such as heroin and morphine have molecular structures similar enough to structures of natural neurotransmitters (endorphins, enkephalins) that they can fool natural opioid receptor molecules into thinking they are the natural transmitters. *Opioid* refers to natural transmitters in the brain, whereas *opiate* refers to drugs. Opiate drugs work by combining with the same receptors used by the natural opioids. These drugs behave like natural opioid transmitters but in stronger concentrations than the natural chemicals, to give a heroin rush or to numb pain from an injury or illness. Opiate drugs act in similar fashion to the natural opioid transmitters, thereby adding to the action of the transmitter. In this situation, you have natural transmitters doing their work plus opiate drugs doing the same work. Drugs and other chemicals that increase the effects of a substance are called agonists (see Figure 17.1c).

4. *block action of transmitters at postsynaptic receptor sites.*
   Example: *Neuroleptics*, also called *antipsychotics*, include newer drugs that block both serotonin and dopamine (called *serotonin-dopamine antagonists*, or *SDAs*), and older drugs that block dopamine only (called *dopamine antagonists*). The latter group,

(c)

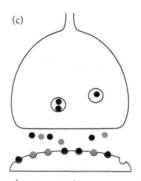

drug + transmitter
= bigger bang for transmitter buck!

FIGURE 17.1C *Opiates potentiate effects of natural opioids.*

including chlorpromazine (Thorazine), haloperidal (Haldol), flu-
phenazine (Prolixin), and many others, were the primary tools for
reducing symptoms of schizophrenia until the 1990s.

The newer serotonin-dopamine antagonists, also called *atypical antipsychotics*, include risperidone (Risperdal), clozapine (Clozaril), olanzapine
(Zyprexa), and others. They are now used more often than dopamine antagonists because they not only can ameliorate a larger range of symptoms, but also
have a much more favorable side-effect profile.

These drugs also fool receptors. However, unlike the previous group of
drugs, they do not act like the natural transmitters they resemble. They grab
receptor slots *away from* the natural transmitters by binding more quickly and
more tenaciously to the receptors, thereby preventing the natural transmitters
from doing their work. This postsynaptic process is called *competitive binding at the receptor site*. Drugs that diminish the effects of other substances are
called *antagonists* (see Figure 17.1d).

(d)

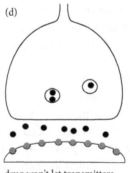

drug won't let transmitters
into their post-synaptic
homes (receptor sites)

FIGURE 17.1D *Drugs block dopamine at post-synaptic receptor sites.*

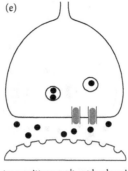

transmitters can't get back up!

FIGURE 17.1E *Drugs block reuptake of serotonin and/or norepinephrine into presynaptic Neuron.*

5. ***block reuptake of transmitters into the presynaptic neuron.***
   Example: Selective serotonin reuptake inhibitors (SSRIs) block the
   reuptake of the neurotransmitter serotonin into the sending neuron,
   thereby increasing the amount of serotonin available in the synapse
   to combine with receptors on postsynaptic membranes. The SSRIs
   relieve symptoms of depression, obsessive-compulsive disorder, and
   other psychiatric conditions by remedying the inadequate supply of
   serotonin that is causing the symptoms (see Figure 17.1e).

These drugs have come into widespread use since the beginning of the 1990s,
replacing older drugs (such as *tricyclic antidepressants*) that had multiple
unpleasant side effects. Well-known SSRIs are fluoxetine (Prozac), sertraline (Zoloft), paroxetine (Paxil), citalopram (Celexa), and numerous others.
Sometimes these drugs have the specific troublesome side effects of preventing orgasm or decreasing libido, so it may be necessary to substitute
other drugs.

Some drugs also alleviate depression by blocking reuptake of norepinephrine as well as serotonin into the presynaptic terminal, such as venlafaxine
(Effexor), mirtazapine (Remeron), bupropion (Wellbutrin), and nefazodone
(Serzone). Cocaine and its relatives achieve their effects by blocking reuptake
of dopamine. Reuptake blocking of these different transmitters increases the
amount of neurotransmitter left in the synapse to combine with postsynaptic receptors to give symptom reduction or, in the case of recreational drugs,
a high.

6. ***prevent inactivation of transmitters by enzymes.*** Some enzymes
   promote the degradation (breaking down) of neurotransmitters into
   the end products called metabolites. When levels of a transmitter are
   too low, inhibiting the enzyme that is breaking the transmitter down
   increases the supply of that transmitter in the synapse. As a result,
   more is available to combine with postsynaptic receptor molecules.

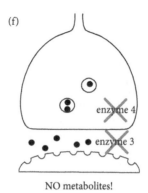

NO metabolites!

FIGURE 17.1F *Drugs block enzymes that destroy transmitters.*

Example: *Monoamine oxidase* (note ending -*ase*, designating an enzyme) breaks down (inactivates) monoamine neurotransmitters. *Monoamine oxidase inhibitors (MAOIs)* block the action of the enzyme monoamine oxidase. They stop it from breaking down monoamine transmitters. Thus they increase the amount of monoamines available to do work (see Figure 17.1f). Serotonin, dopamine, and norepinephrine are major monoamine neurotransmitters (see Chapter 11, Table 11.1). The MAOIs relieve symptoms of depression related to inadequate supply of serotonin and norepinephrine by blocking the breakdown of these transmitters.

These monoamine neurotransmitters have a great deal to do with psychological activity. They are extremely versatile and play multiple roles in our lives. As mentioned earlier, for example, dopamine is active in the pleasures of eating, drinking, sex, and many other common pleasures. It combines with several different dopamine receptors.

Do you enjoy these? Thank your pleasure circuits!

18

🏛 Using Neuroscience Information to Empower (excerpt from process recording): José, 38, Angry, Abused, and Court-Mandated

By Joseph D'Amico, MSW

Brief Profile. José is a 38-year-old Latino male who was mandated to attend individual psychotherapy by the court. José had gotten into an altercation with his girlfriend's ex-husband and was subsequently arrested for breach of peace.

He is very loyal to those he considers his friends, and his self-image is built upon his word. If he makes someone a promise, he will keep it—no matter what the cost.

Brief History. José is one of two children born into a family with a history of alcoholism and depression. His earliest memories, of which he can barely speak, involve being sent to foster homes, juvenile facilities, and physical and emotional abuse by his father. Between foster homes and juvenile detention centers he "ran the streets," where he learned how to fight and survive.

He left school before graduating, drank, did drugs, worked at various jobs, and became a semi-pro boxer. José is from New York and came to his current residence in New England approximately seven years ago.

Treatment Background. The first several sessions with José consisted mainly of getting to know him and, thus, building a therapeutic relationship. Engagement was easy as José is a bright and very likeable person. Although his attitude appeared to be totally negative, in that he was quick to anger and his speech was interspersed with swearing, it was not difficult to ascertain that this was his way of socializing. José had a volatile temper and would go from making a joke to immediately switching to anger. Once he was "set off," he would begin to rant and rave in a loud voice, loudly swearing and gesticulating with his arms and hands.

Session : José enters my office and sits down and we exchange greetings.

T: How are you doing, José?
J: Lousy. My boss is screwing me around and has me driving all over the place and owes me back money.

T: Oh. [A pause ensues with room for José to continue.]

J: You haven't heard the worst of it! I went to make a delivery in Bridgeport and pulled in where it said trucks enter. I blew my horn and waited. Nothing happened so I kept blowing my horn and finally this big fat B. . . . comes out and starts yelling that deliveries are around the corner. So I drive around the corner and find the entrance. I walk in and there's a guy standing behind a cage and I ask if this is where I'm supposed to drop off my supply. He gave me some smart answer and I lost it. I told him I'd jump over that cage and rip his arms off as well as that rotten tie he had on. [I'm omitting all the swearing that went with this.]

T: [José went on with this for a few more minutes before I intervened.] So, José, who is it that's so angry?

J: What do you mean?

T: I mean that I'm listening to a guy called "Mr. Anger," and that's not you. It seems to me that when Mr. Anger comes, José leaves. Make any sense to you? [José takes a few moments before answering.]

J: Yeah, it sort of does. When I get angry I seem to disconnect from myself, then nothing else matters. I'm so worked up that not only does nothing else matter, but all that exists is pure, blind rage.

T: We don't have to name Mr. Anger as he isn't any one person or event. Rather, he's a totality of years of trauma or abuse in various forms as well as parts of family, friends, and environment. Now I realize that you truly want to get a handle on your temper as you're tired of losing it and then going through the emotional torment of feeling guilty and ashamed of your behavior. What I'd like to do now is explain what it is I think is going on in your brain. Sometimes just knowing that what is happening is grounded in your body and your brain and can be explained logically and scientifically makes a difference.

J: That would be great!

T: Well, to begin with, José, you have to sort of stretch your imagination. Our brains have been evolving for thousands of years and are pretty complex. The part of the brain that we're concerned with here is a part called the limbic system. This is an inner section of the brain, and animals that predated humans had limbic systems. What I'm alluding to is that this is a much less developed part of the brain but it is very important because it's a major part of the brain systems that regulate things like hunger, thirst, sex, as well as emotions and passions such as love, joy, fear, sadness, and rage. This limbic system also has other functions including transmitting messages of pleasure and pain into memory. These memories are put into storage by a biochemical process that results in actual changes in microscopic brain structure.

Whew...break time.

J: Joe, I'm not sure I got all of that...

T: I'll bet—I'm giving you a lot of information pretty quickly.

Let's look at it from another angle. Being that our main concern is your anger, let's just focus on one part of the limbic system called the amygdala. The amygdala mediates rage reactions.

When you get angry the amygdala is really revved up. If we take this one step further, we know that you have memories in storage in your brain that get activated by cues that at times you may not be consciously aware of. Since you have a trauma history, José, you have loads of memories you've pushed out of your mind—that is, memories of things you aren't even aware of—and your buttons can get pushed a hundred times a day. The amygdala is going into overdrive. Make any sense?

J: Yeah! I get the gist of it, I do know what you mean. But now, how do I deal with it?

T: Well, perhaps just having some information is the first step.

You've got plenty to reflect on till our next session.

PART III

Hidden Circuits

NEURAL NETWORKS TODAY, CONNECTOMES ON THE HORIZON

Human Neural Systems: Working for You Day and Night

Human neural systems activate every nook and cranny of your body. They engage structures from the many neural systems you, I, and everyone rely on to electrify our bodies—yes, our nerves carry electrical charges that we're seldom even aware of. (When was the last time you checked your volts and amps?)

Complex cognitive and emotional networks linked to behavioral structures extend *across* as well as *within* brain regions. These labyrinths of structures, pathways, and interactive systems have been labeled *neural networks* (Fuster, 2008, p. 191). Extensive reciprocal connections and collaborative efforts among many cortical, subcortical, and brainstem structures manage every kind of human experience. The theater for the action includes the human brain and spinal cord (central nervous system or CNS), the body outside the CNS (body organs and the peripheral nervous system), and the person/environment interface where inputs and outputs are dispatched in both directions.

Here, we use the term *neural network* to refer to *natural networks of real biological neurons connected or functionally related in the central nervous system and/or peripheral nervous system, for the purpose of performing one or more specific physiological functions.* The other kinds of neural networks, called *artificial neural networks* for solving artificial intelligence problems, are beyond the scope of this volume.

Among the multitude of chores neural networks perform on our behalf is the integration of emotion, cognition, and behavior. That is, they generate, monitor, balance, tweak, create pleasure or introduce caution in our psychological selves. Sometimes they even unleash a cascade of glittering fireworks in our psychological lives so exciting, beautiful, or dangerous that we remember them for a lifetime.

To illustrate how our neural networks are known or believed to work, Part III introduces you to two examples of natural neural networks, servicing Pleasure and Stress/Traumatic Stress respectively. As of the time of writing, no one knows how many neural networks are in the human brain. How could we discover what they all are and how each works to implement common human experiences? *Star Wars* fantasy or realistic scientific goal? Moreover, it is difficult to be sure of where the line crosses between ordinary everyday stress (which can be mild or intense) and "traumatic" stress.

Sebastian Seung, professor of Computational Neuroscience at the Massachusetts Institute of Technology, has made the Human Connectome known to the public through lectures, videotapes, and writings (see for example the video *I Am My Connectome* (Seung, 2010) and a new book, *Connectome: How the Brain's Wiring Makes Us Who We Are* (HS Seung, 2012). As a physicist and neuroscientist, he proposes that not only will the technology for mapping the connections in the human brain become available as ultra high-capacity and high-speed computer technology is developed, but also that this ultimate achievement in mapping will unlock the clues to our identities, or selves. The Human Connectome map of neural connections takes its name from its predecessor, the Human Genome, released in 2003, the map of human genes constructed over many years by many scientists.

The National Institutes of Health (NIH) launched their Human Connectome Project as a five-year project sponsored by sixteen components of the NIH in July of 2009. It was the first of three Grand Challenges of the NIH's Blueprint for Neuroscience Research. It awarded two grants, $30 million over five years, to a consortium led by Washington University in Saint Louis and the University of Minnesota, and $8.5 million over three years to a consortium led by Harvard University, Massachusetts General Hospital, and the University of California at Los Angeles, with contributions from dozens of investigators and researchers from nine other institutions. The data that result from the NIH-sponsored research will be made available to the public in an open-source internet neuroinformatics platform (National Institutes of Health (NIH), 2010).

The goal of the Human Connectome Project is to build a "network map" that will shed light on the anatomical and functional connectivity within the healthy human brain, as well as to produce a body of data that will facilitate research into brain disorders such as autism, Alzheimer's disease, and schizophrenia (NIH, 2010). As we go to press, breaking news of the results of an NIMH-funded genetics study of the five most-common mental conditions has just been published that may be a giant preparatory step for future Connectome research. Autism, attention-deficit hyperactivity disorder (ADHD), bipolar disease, schizophrenia, and major depression all share similar genetic components, despite their very different symptoms (National Institute of Mental Health, 2013). The meaning and importance of this discovery for understanding causes of mental illness and finding new and stronger treatments is discussed in Part VI on Mental Health and Mental Illness.

Meanwhile, we've already identified a few of the neural networks that will form small parts of the gigantic human Connectome when it is created. Two such networks are the subject of Part III. Although some scientists may distinguish between *neural networks* and *neural systems*, we use the terms interchangeably in this book. I haven't yet found clearcut distinctions between the two concepts, both of which are defined by the functions they perform for the brain and entire body. The inventory of functional roles for hitherto unidentified networks/systems is still expanding as they continue to be discovered.

Neural networks are the sites where your own and your clients' joys, challenges, tribulations, and hour-to-hour events take place. Because many of these topics are very large, we've chosen one specific, familiar example from each of the two areas of experience to explore in more detail.

In previous sections, we summarized a few characteristics of some brain structures, both microscopic and "large" (meaning visible by the human eye) that perform functions central to human behavior in the social environment. Just as the profession of social work increasingly championed a view of human behavior profoundly rooted in multiple external systems (an advance spearheaded by the social movements of the 1960s), so neuroscience advanced from focusing on specific functions performed by each brain structure, to a systems view of brain functions performed by collaborations among several *structures* or parts of structures, *pathways* connecting these structures both close and far apart in the brain, and *influences from external environments*.

As technology has advanced, neuroscience researchers have increasingly become able to identify neural networks or systems as the context in which individual structures can accomplish their work. Brain imaging is the single technological tool most responsible for scientists now being able to watch these processes as they happen in the brain (see Part I, Chapter 5).

During the last three or four decades of the 20th century, a new theoretical model surged in popularity in social work from its origins in cybernetics in the first half of the 20th century (Bertalanffy, 1950). This paradigm, *general systems theory* or *GST*, was much more comprehensive than its predecessors. It spawned related conceptual frameworks in social work and other disciplines for decades to come, from ecosystems to living systems to life model to complex adaptive systems (see Chapters 7 and 8).

Before the term *neural networks* had even come into use, GST as a multidimensional conceptual framework had been widely endorsed across disciplines. Neural networks, the neuroscience *subsystems* to living creatures and *suprasystems* to smaller inner parts, plugged into GST with a seamless fit.

Neural networks, with their component cell bodies, dendrites, axons, synaptic connections, and molecules of very diverse chemicals, all taking off and landing every minute of every day and night 24/7, would challenge the world's most skillful air traffic controllers. Who could direct and manage such a complex entity to ensure arrivals at intended destinations and avoid collisions, engine failures, and random errors? Somehow our brains manage to do this successfully most (not all) the time. The process is sometimes error-prone—but the brain is amazingly successful in many instances. In Part V, the chapter on consciousness gives us a few insights into the process, dubbed *neural Darwinism* by Nobel Laureate Gerald Edelman (2011), that many believe explains the air traffic controller puzzle of who's in command.

To appraise the continuous ongoing interactions back and forth between individual factors and factors external to the individual, it's often important to be able to assess the relative influence of different variables, either risk or protective factors, on a particular outcome. Researchers in fields such as epidemiology and biological sciences have been doing this for some time. These interactive factors are both biological and nonbiological, from the moment of conception until the moment of death.

It has long been known that many psychological events (emotions, behaviors, and cognitions) are motivated by survival goals for individuals and species, and (extending to human institutional domains), the survival of organizations, cultures, economic and political entities, and enclaves of power. Neural systems within individuals appear to be pursuing an overall—but not sole—objective of survival.

Certainly food, sex, fear, problem-solving, planning, and executing, all processed by neural networks, often serve the purpose of survival—but where do sadness or greed or killing in the absence of threat fit in? There are many complex functions falling within the purview of "psychological" that do *not* appear to make contributions to survival (although some of these other functions are referred to as "adaptive," that is, helping the individual "adapt" to some circumstance).

In fact, we label some psychological functions as outright "self-destructive," implying physical or metaphorical sabotage of one's own survival. But many emotions, behaviors, and cognitions, while not as extreme, appear to be self-defeating, risky, random, irrelevant to our high-priority interests, or at best trivial. Did your parents, in their effort to guide you to the happiest life possible, ever try to dissuade you from a course of action they perceived as deserving of one of those adjectives? As a parent yourself, or as a friend or mentor, have you ever done that?

What more do we want from life over and above surviving? If the responses of a substantial global cohort of people representing every form of diversity were to be surveyed and their replies to this question quantified, it is perhaps safe to assume that a relatively small number of answers would be given by many respondents *across* cultures, together with a long list of not-so-frequent but strongly held wishes *endemic to particular cultures* or *idiosyncratic to individuals*.

As we ponder these questions, we need first to be aware of principles and concepts that characterize today's knowledge about the brain's "policy-making" in pursuit of life goals.

A Few Principles of Brain Systems Policy-Making

1. *The principle of homeostasis has long been viewed as a brain's gold standard*, as it enacts its job description of maintaining equilibrium—balance—in the entire body. Numerous neural networks have been characterized as including the promotion of homeostasis as one of their functions. The axiom is that survival of individuals and species requires balance between competing forces— for example, the body's intake versus expenditure of energy must be virtually equal. And for most people in the history of the world (as far as we know), scarcity, not overabundance of food, has been a compelling threat to that balance, as it still is today in many parts of the world. True, some of the wealthy and powerful during the medieval and Renaissance eras—who had abundance of venison and rabbit from their hunts and servants to grow, harvest, and prepare grains, vegetables, meade, and elegant desserts—ate gargantuan amounts of rich foods and became obese and in pain with gout. But their numbers were a small fraction of the populace.

In the decade since 2000, a subset of neuroscientists and other biological scientists have questioned the validity of homeostasis as a descriptor of typical human neural processes, for a number of reasons proposed by Ganzel, Morris, and Wethington (2010), McEwen (2007), and many others, which we'll look at in more detail later. In this book we continue to use the homeostasis concept when citing neuroscientists who use it, but plan to follow the dialogues as they unfold before choosing one to the exclusion of the other just yet.

2. *Redundancy, not parsimony, is one of the brain's guiding principles of growth and development* from a tiny cluster of cells shortly after conception, through the birth process of an already highly complex infant, and becoming increasingly versatile, more complex, and—yes—redundant.

What does that mean? It means that a given objective can often be met in one of several possible ways, using different structures and pathways. If one strategy doesn't work, due, perhaps, to an incompatible environment or a poorly functioning brain component, the resourceful brain will find another route. The brain has redundant structures and functions that sometimes come in handy.

But how does the brain get that way? When two parallel neurons fire in sync by pure chance, this synchronized firing leads to ongoing synchronized firing, which promotes bonding and working together by these "cooperative" neurons. Some neuroscientists find the most plausible explanation of how the brain arrives at adult states of consciousness is through a process of natural selection that takes place over many generations (Edelman, 2004). By contrast, those structures and processes that rely on failing blueprints do not survive or procreate, leaving the species with the "fittest" choice of capabilities.

3. *Heritable changes can be passed down from parent to offspring without any gene mutation.* How? By a process called *epigenesis*, where the form by which the gene expresses itself can change and be passed to offspring because some aspect of the gene's environment changes, *not the gene itself*. Often the cytoplasm of cells transmits such changes (for an introduction to epigenesis, see Strohman, 2003, summarized in this volume, Chapter 8).

The relevance of these principles will become apparent as the analysis develops. What can science teach us about our clients and ourselves? Our first topic is pleasure, also called *reward* (words we'll use interchangeably). What knowledge can science give us that might help us increase (our clients', our own) pleasure and diminish (their, our own) pain? Is that the meaning of "quality of life"?

Before you embark on an excursion into pleasure, rate each of the following pleasures in your own life as (1) really, really important; (2) somewhat important; or (3) not very important.

- sensory and aesthetic enjoyment
- laughing
- sharing life with one or more loved ones
- making money
- mastering skills to find "self-fulfillment"
- learning new things not for any life purpose but strictly to have fun

[Author's "confidential" disclosure: I rated all items above except one as "really, really important." The remaining item I rated as "somewhat important"—which item do you suppose that was? How do your own ratings compare?]

20

Pleasures: Your Favorites, My Favorites, and How Brain Ingenuity Puts Them on the Map

Hedonic experience is arguably at the heart of what makes us human

MORTEN KRINGELBACH, 2005

Some folks enjoy sex the most, others food, and, most recently, Internet games have joined the growing list of behaviors that for some are so captivating that they preempt most of their devotees' waking hours.

Is there one neural network for all different kinds of pleasure? No—different combinations of brain structures mediate different types of pleasure, each combination having chemical/electrical pathways that make connections among specific structures and to points outside the circuit, including outer body surfaces interfacing with external environments.

This chapter provides a brief overview of pleasure in general, with some information relevant to many kinds of pleasure. The next chapter, Chapter 21, focuses on one example of a source of pleasure. (What's your guess about what that will be?) For surveying the territories where rewarding experiences prosper, neuroscientist David Linden's menu of widely enjoyed pleasures mediated by neural networks looks like a pretty good start to me: "How our brains make fatty foods, orgasm, exercise, marijuana, generosity, vodka, learning, and gambling *feel so good*" (subtitle to *The Compass of Pleasure*, 2011, emphasis in original). I've completed my own list by scratching off a couple of those items, then adding a few of my own not on the list. Chances are you'd do the same to develop your own list. Before you continue reading, take a couple of minutes to do that.

Certain structures and substances in the brain reappear so often in these combinations, mediating different kinds of pleasures, that a few brain structures and chemicals have become renowned for their contributions to our happiness. Do nucleus accumbens, ventral tegmental area, striatum, or dopamine, endorphins, oxytocin ring a bell?

Current neuroscience research on the anatomy and physiology of pleasure (see references in text Chapters 20–22) identify a few circuits specializing in pleasure that reappear very often across the range of pleasurable

activities—food, sex, and gambling, for example. These have some major pleasure structures and pathways in common, not just with each other but also
with recreational drugs, leading many neuroscientists to believe that we can
become addicted to food, sex, or gambling just as we do to both legal and
illegal drugs.

Another characteristic of experiencing pleasure is that *anticipation* of neural feel-good rewards stimulates the release of some pleasure-carrying neurochemicals before you've even tasted the food, made love, won a jackpot at
the casino, or seen that your favorite player's hit is actually a grand slam home
run. The anticipation that the pleasure is *about* to happen is sufficient in many
instances to initiate some of the neurochemical reactions that make the actual
experience itself so pleasurable.

But what about the disappointment that ensues when the expected event
doesn't happen? Does that feel like waking up joyfully from a dream of ecstasy,
only to discover it was just a dream?

Do You Know Where Your Hedonic Hotspots Are?

Are pleasure, fun, enjoyment, feeling good, laughing, euphoria, satisfaction,
accomplishing, winning, and just plain good luck all part of the human condition? Some of us brought up in certain religious traditions were taught that
the word *hedonism* referred to crass, self-centered, sensual, often exploitative
physical gratifications—a kind of pleasure that often harmed others and sig-
naled bad character on the part of the hedonist.

In fact, that connotation is also prevalent today, according to the
Merriam-Webster Online Dictionary (retrieved 2011), whose synonym list
for hedonism consists of "carnality, debauchery, sybaritism, voluptuous-
ness," and its brief definition of the word itself "excessive pursuit of fleshly
pleasures <their spring break trip to Mexico became an exercise in heedless
hedonism>." Related words included "venery, wantonness; greed, rapacious-
ness, rapacity, ravenousness; dissipation, gluttony, immoderation, intemper-
ance, self-indulgence," and antonyms were "abstinence, asceticism, sobriety,
and temperance".

However, the discipline of neuroscience seems to have adopted the adjective *hedonic* without unsavory or immoral connotation—in fact, we're apparently now allowed to *celebrate* moments in life when our brain circuits activate
"hedonic hotspots" and the larger areas we're dubbing "feel-good fields" (see
color images F., H., I., and J(1).).

The official hedonic hotspots, thought to be about a cubic centimeter in
humans (Kringelbach and Berridge, 2010), are in the nucleus accumbens
shell (a single hotspot), one in the posterior ventral pallidum lying under the

nucleus accumbens, and one in the parabrachial nucleus of the brainstem (see color image E., Team Players: Prefrontal Cortex and Inner Brain Structures, and J., Hedonic Hotspots). Others are suspected and in the process of being confirmed. It's fortunate for us that the larger areas of feel-good fields are there too, because with nothing but the few *official* hedonic hotspots, we'd be missing a lot of fun.

Hedonic responses (pleasure, reward in feel-good fields and hotspots) can be elicited by many possible stimuli, not just food or sex. Not only do hedonic drives motivate getting nourishment for survival of the individual or procreating for the survival of the species—but also, more generally, they make life worth living despite experiences of pain, frustration, disappointment, sometimes despair, that most people feel at least for some periods in their lives.

By themselves, with no intervention, the hotspots arouse facial expressions in response to sweet and bitter flavors in human infants, monkeys, and rodents, all of whom show similar facial reactions for liking (sweet) and disliking (bitter). When the hotspots were activated by injected chemicals that increase pleasure, the human infants', monkeys', and rodents' natural liking for sweet-tasting substances (sucrose) doubled—twice the reward effect of the natural sucrose by itself. These cross-species tasters are displayed in color image J(2)., Sweet Tastes, Bitter Tastes. These injected chemicals resembled natural substances in animal brains. They were natural versions of drugs of abuse: opioids (mu-opioid); the endocannibinoid anandamide, a natural relative of marijuana; and a hypothalamic neuropeptide neurotransmitter/ hormone called *orexin*, formerly known for its regulation of sleep and now also celebrated in the food pleasure market. To create their rewards, these substances combine with receptors dedicated to a particular neurotransmitter and its look-alikes.

The *orbitofrontal cortex (OFC)* is an important center for *judging the value* of a stimulus to the individual ("value assignment") and the integration of these hedonic responses (see color image E., Team Players: Prefrontal Cortex and Inner Brain Structures). The OFC takes note of how good a stimulus is, how much I want to do the behavior that produced it again, and other "implicit" (not conscious) thoughts.

Berridge (2007), Berridge and colleagues (2009), together with associates, developed a classification for components of pleasure/reward into three groups: (1) "liking" (known as hedonic response, conscious pleasure, affect, or emotion); 2) "wanting" (technical label "incentive salience," meaning a motivation or urge to get a liked thing or enact a certain behavior or achieve some goal); and 3) "learning" (associations, representations, and predictions about future rewards based on past experiences that have colored our memories and influenced ongoing reward-seeking behavior).

Referring to a very important pleasure circuit of the brain, David Linden (2011, p. 18) has explained the learning function well: "So what does this brain

circuit....mean for the feeling of pleasure? Here's the central insight: experiences that cause the dopamine-containing neurons of the VTA to be active and
thereby release dopamine in their targets (the nucleus accumbens, the prefrontal
cortex, the dorsal striatum)...will be felt as pleasurable, and the sensory cues
and actions that preceded and overlapped with those pleasurable experiences
will be remembered and associated with positive feelings." Steven E. Hyman (see
Introduction, Part I), articulated this process from the perspective of substance
users: "That felt *good*, let's remember how we did it, and *let's do it again!*"

With respect to the liking and wanting functions, Havermans (2011) agrees
that differentiating appetitive motivation from liking is important, but cites
laboratory evidence supporting the contention that it is impossible to reli-
ably distinguish liking from wanting—and concludes that this distinction *isn't
important anyway* for developing useful applications such as reducing obesity
and overweight.

Although brain imaging studies have shown that liking and wanting don't
follow identical neural circuits, usually both are necessary for the experience
of reward and pleasure—they tend to happen together. Yet there are even times
when we want things we don't like—for example, in addiction, once tolerance
has developed to a substance and it no longer gives pleasure, some addicted
brains urgently want it to avoid or escape withdrawal sickness (a classic example of negative reinforcement). The opposite of tolerance can also occur, called
sensitization, meaning that the brain gets increasingly revved up over time by
a previously enjoyed stimulus. The stimulus now confers more and more pleasure over time, as contrasted with less and less in the case of tolerance (Fuster,
2008; Kringelbach and Berridge, 2010).

Freud believed a pleasure center or pathway existed in human brains, but
couldn't prove it; it turns out he was right about that (except that there are
several different kinds of structures in different circuits spread out around
the brain that collaborate in the creation of pleasure, not a single entity called
the "id").

Decades after Freud's death, technologies have enabled us to learn a great
deal about the brain's virtuosity in transmitting pleasure messages. Poor
Freud—wouldn't he have been thrilled and excited to learn so much of what
we now know by our sheer good luck to be alive during the decades of the
brain (1990–2000 was actually officially declared "Decade of the Brain" by
then President George H. W. Bush). Throughout the history of the human
species, unbeknownst to our grandparents, we would never have been able
to enjoy *anything* without the actions of certain neurotransmitters and other
chemical substances in our brain pleasure locations!

According to Kringelbach and Berridge (2010), pleasure is never merely
a sensation or a thought until an additional hedonic "gloss" is generated
("painted") by the brain. The metaphorical gloss evokes a shiny surface of a
polished apple, a newly washed and sprayed human coiffe, or the finest piece

of recently polished antique furniture in your grandmother's living room. That is, receiving a pleasure-creating stimulus doesn't translate into a subjective feeling of pleasure until the brain has painted the gloss.

Neuroscience research has repeatedly confirmed that brain mechanisms involved in fundamental sensual pleasures (notably food and sex) overlap with mechanisms for *higher-order pleasures* such as artistic, musical, intellectual, humorous, spiritual, altruistic, and monetary. (Do you think getting money deserves the label of a "higher-order" pleasure?)

With respect to aesthetic pleasures from *music* and *visual arts*, can we assume that people who describe a work in one of these media as "beautiful" have experienced some pleasure while hearing or seeing it? And where do our brains process this experience? When we pool results from recent experiments, we seem to be finding some answers.

Neuroscientists Tomohiro Ishizu and Semir Zeki (2011) set up experiments to learn whether activity in one particular area of the brain correlates with the experience of beauty derived from *different* sources. They wanted to see if there were common brain patterns in people from different cultures while seeing paintings or hearing musical works that the people described as beautiful.

Ten western Europeans, four Japanese, three Chinese, two Indians, and two Americans rated 30 paintings and 30 segments from musical compositions on a 9-point scale: beautiful 7–9, neutral 4–6, and ugly 1–3. Researchers recorded the subjects' brain patterns via fMRI (functional magnetic resonance imaging) (Ishizu and Zeki, 2011), in response to a 16-second flash for each painting and a 16-second musical clip for each segment of music. Images and music clips rated by subjects as somewhat to very beautiful corresponded to a comparably strong spark of activity in a tiny 15-to 17-millimeter-wide section of the medial orbitofrontal cortex (mOFC) (*PLoS ONE*, July 6, 2011).

The overlaps between brain activations for music and visual art scans were unmistakable. The *strength of activation* in the medial region of the OFC was *proportional to the intensity of the experience of beauty* reported by the subjects for both visual and musical trials, with linear relationships between brain activation and participants' beauty ratings scores: the more beautiful the piece was rated, the greater the spark in the mOFC. (See Figure 20.1.)

Nadal (2011) and Di Dio and Gallese (2009) agree that aesthetic experience is a multilevel process. Di Dio and Gallese imaged people viewing visual art and found (using other neurophysiological evidence as well) that aesthetic preference involves activations of sensorimotor, core emotional, and reward-related centers of the brain. In short, aesthetic experience goes beyond cognitive appraisal of a work of art to integrate *emotion* as a core ingredient through connections with the insula (Damasio and colleagues, 2000) and the amygdala (Phelps and LeDoux, 2005). Pleasure is usually an essential component. *Preferred* stimuli selectively activated the right amygdala relative to

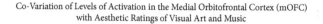

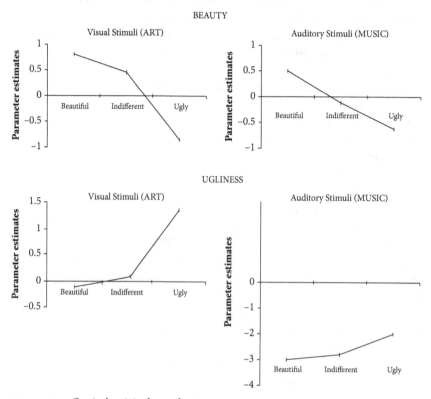

FIGURE 20.1 *Cortical activity by aesthetic rating.*

disliked stimuli, indicating an emotional component (Phelps and LeDoux, 2005). This information reminds us that the amygdala, whose activities in aversive experience are widely publicized, also processes positive experience. Acceptance for services by the amygdala seems to require salience of an emotion, whether negative or positive.

The OFC is the brain organ most known for attaching a value either to a reward or to an aversive object or event. As noted above, the medial region of the OFC has been linked to perception of beauty as well as judging a stimulus as pleasurable, with "beauty" being processed independently of pleasure. Fans who find reggae or rap more rewarding and beautiful than an 18th-century string quartet or a romantic symphony would most likely get a much greater zing in brain pleasure centers from their individually preferred artistic creations.

Music rated beautiful seemed to spur the brain's pleasure locations more quickly than did art (each medium also activated its respective sensory region, auditory or visual). However, beautiful paintings also triggered the caudate nucleus, which has been linked to feelings of romantic love. Why would visual art, but not music, be linked to romantic love, if in fact there is such a link in the caudate? We don't know, and Ishizu and Zeki (2011) state that as of the time of writing, they didn't know either why the caudate nucleus excluded music. (Haven't many of us associated certain pieces of music with experiences of romantic love? Perhaps the neuroscientists just haven't discovered that connection yet.)

But what about the paintings and music that participants found *ugly*? Those experiences not only received the lowest rating scores, but also showed the lowest activation in the mOFC (Ishizu and Zeki, 2011).

Salimpoor, Benovoy, Larcher, Dagher, and Zatorre (2011) found that music can arouse feelings of euphoria and craving, similar to tangible rewards involving the striatal dopaminergic systems (*dopaminergic* means processor of dopamine). Dopaminergic structures in these circuits include the ventral tegmental area (VTA), nucleus accumbens (NAc), septum (which the NAc leans against, hence the adjective *accumbens*), and dopaminergic projections from the VTA and substantia nigra (SN, adjacent to the VTA), to the striatum (caudate nucleus and putamen) in the basal ganglia.

Neuroscientists today widely recognize these mesolimbic and mesocorticolimbic dopamine circuits as preeminent neural systems in the pursuit of pleasure (see for example Grant, Potenza, Weinstein, and Gorelick, 2010; Kringelbach and Berridge, 2010; Linden, 2011; Wang, Volkow et al., 2009).

Humor. Laughter, "the best medicine," long recognized as such around the world, was permanently imprinted in the American public consciousness by the *Reader's Digest*'s popular page of human vignettes, read eagerly every month by my mother and her friends. Isn't laughing a lot of fun?

Despite the seemingly obvious fact that humor and laughing are *fun*, neuroscientists struggled for many years to show that laughter (mirth) actually activates pleasure centers in the brain. Gregory S. Berns (2004) wrote:

> The human reward system has been shown to be activated by a wide range of reinforcers, including food, money, sex, drugs, and beauty. Now, a recent fMRI study has found mesolimbic reward activation associated with humorous cartoons, providing a neurobiological link between theories of humor and hedonic processes in the brain.
>
> Two cows were standing in a field, and one said to the other, "Those humans are sure getting worked up about this mad cow disease. It is an unfortunate state of affairs. What do you think?" To which the other replied, "Don't ask me. I'm a chicken."

Was this joke funny? Before you answer, let's ask your nucleus accumbens; it may surprise you. Berns, a celebrated American neuroeconomist, neuroscientist, professor of psychiatry, psychologist, and writer, went on to laud Mobbs, Greicius, Abdel-Azim et al. (2003) from the Stanford University Neuroimaging Laboratory for being the first to find evidence that humor modulates the mesolimbic reward centers, using functional MRI. Berns noted that humor-induced activation of the mesolimbic reward system was significant because it provided the first tentative link to the hedonic aspects of humor.

Mobbs, Hagan, Azim, Menon, and Reiss (2005) also found that the degree of humor intensity was positively correlated with intensity of electronic signals in these regions and with extroversion in discrete regions of the frontal and temporal cortices, and was connected with emotional stability in the mesocortical-mesolimbic reward circuitry (right orbital frontal cortex, caudate, and nucleus accumbens). Conversely, introversion correlated with increased activation in the bilateral amygdala, indicating that personality styles can either facilitate or work against humor appreciation.

Moran et al. (2004) showed full-length episodes of the television sitcoms *Seinfeld* or *The Simpsons* using functional magnetic resonance imaging (fMRI) to dissociate humor detection ("getting the joke") from humor appreciation (the affective experience of mirth). Humor detection moments revealed increases in left inferior frontal and posterior temporal cortices, whereas brain activity in humor appreciation revealed increases in bilateral regions of insular cortex and the amygdala.

Osaka and Osaka (2005), also using fMRI with human subjects, demonstrated that visualization of mimic words and emotional facial expression words, suggesting laughter, significantly activated striatal reward centers, including the putamen/caudate/nucleus accumbens, prefrontal cortices, dorsal anterior cingulate cortex, and the supplementary motor area, while nonmimic words that did *not* imply laughter did not activate these areas. (A propos of our personal lists of pleasures, did you include laughter on your list?)

Graham (2011) investigated *social play*, a source of enjoyment for young mammals (including our human offspring, of course). She found that the relative *volume* of the dorsal striatum, a structure tied to experience and anticipation of pleasure and reward, correlated with the rate of *social but not nonsocial* play behavior across species. The caudate and putamen connect to regions associated with social play behavior (e.g., neocortex, cerebellum, limbic system).

Gambling is a nondrug behavior that activates pleasure locations in the brain. On the neurobiological level, Reuter et al. (2005) found groups of pathological gamblers to have dysregulation of brain areas linked to reward and emotion, including the ventromedial prefrontal cortex (vmPFC) and ventral striatum (nucleus accumbens) as well as alterations in dopamine neurotransmission, when compared with healthy controls. Specifically, very low levels of dopamine in these areas are thought to motivate individuals to try to induce homeostasis in dopamine levels by pleasure-seeking combined with diminished impulse control.

Dopaminergic involvement in gambling has been reported in several studies as a side effect of dopamine *agonists* (substances that increase dopamine's effects) used as medication in patients with Parkinson's disease to treat symptoms of tremor and loss of muscular control (Steeves et al., 2009). Van

Eimeren et al. (2009) propose that these dopamine agonists prevent pauses in dopamine transmission, and *thereby impair the negatively reinforcing effect of losing*. Subjects don't emotionally experience their losses because the artificially induced constant influx of dopamine maintains a sense of pleasure. Thus, pathological gambling in persons with Parkinson's disease may stem in part from an impaired capacity of the OFC to correctly evaluate the negative consequences of gambling.

Sexual pleasure happens in some of the most widely activated pleasure locations, the parts of the medial forebrain circuit from the VTA to the nucleus accumbens and from the VTA to the dorsal striatum (Georgiadis et al., 2006). Some types of sexual pursuits have also been defined as addiction in recent years. Garcia and Thibaut (2010) report several proposed classifications of sexual pursuits considered excessive, related to obsessive-compulsive disorder, impulse control disorder, out-of-control sexual disorder, and addictive disorder. Although scientific data are limited, a number of characteristics— frequent preoccupation with sex, much time spent in sexual activities, continuation despite negative consequences, and repeated and unsuccessful attempts to reduce these behaviors—support a designation of addiction (by itself or in conjunction with any of the other designations). As many studies have shown, circuits transmitting pleasure experiences often include the same pathways involved in substance abuse and addiction (Grant et al., 2010) (see Part IV).

Debating Dopamine. Debate continues about the precise causal contribution made by dopamine to our experiences of pleasure and reward. Among three possibly competing explanatory categories are liking, learning, and wanting. Does dopamine mostly mediate the hedonic impact of reward ("liking"), the learned predictions of future reward, prediction error signals, and associative links with the pleasurable stimulus ("learning"), or attributing incentive salience to reward-related stimuli ("wanting")? Each hypothesis was evaluated by Berridge and colleagues (Berridge, 2007; Berridge, Robinson, and Aldridge, 2009), who concluded that the incentive salience or "wanting" hypothesis of dopamine function appears to be consistent with more evidence than either "liking" or "learning." That is, dopamine's contribution to pleasure in humans and other animals appears to be chiefly to cause *wanting*, more than causing *liking for* or *associative learning about* those rewards. Contrary to popular belief, this view holds that dopamine's chief function is *not* to generate pleasure through hedonic "liking," even though the nucleus accumbens dopamine-using shell holds one of the three known pearls of pleasure (hedonic hotspots), but rather to facilitate "wanting" (incentive salience).

Small, Jones-Gotman, and Dagher (2003) found by PET scan that seven healthy volunteers in an eating experiment gave meal pleasantness ratings that correlated with levels of dopamine release in the dorsal striatum (putamen and caudate nucleus). There were no changes elsewhere in the striatum, including the ventral striatum (nucleus accumbens and proximate structures). Assuming these pleasantness ratings measure "liking," if dopamine affects wanting only, what is creating the *liking* and why do these meal pleasantness ratings ("I liked that") correlate with levels of dopamine?

We have not been able to ascertain from the literature how widely the various beliefs about dopamine functions are shared by contemporary neuroscientists. One fact is clear. Dopamine is present much of the time that pleasure is reported. It's there! Yet its actual roles appear to remain in doubt. Like numerous other transmitters, dopamine has a few variants and multiple different receptors with different functions. We know that dopamine can both excite and inhibit. Might dopamine perform more than a single pleasure function, directly giving rise to promoting wanting, taste rewards (liking), and/or learning about eating-related pleasure through memory-building?

In studies of intracranial self-stimulation (ICSS) summarized by Carlson (2001), laboratory animals whose brains were wired to the medial forebrain bundle connecting the VTA and the NAc, energetically pressed levers to release dopamine—again and again—and if this weren't enough evidence that dopamine has something to do with the animals' fervor, then we'd expect that injections of drugs that block the dopamine receptors would cause them to decrease their lever pressing. Stellar, Kelley, and Corbett (1983) decided to test this belief—and the animals did slow down their lever pressing!

Many structures in addition to those just mentioned have been demonstrated through ICSS studies to process pleasure, notably the prefrontal cortex, olfactory bulb, several nuclei of the thalamus, reticular formation, amygdala, and locus coeruleus, involving not only dopamine but also serotonin, acetylcholine, and norepinephrine (Carlson, 2001).

So whenever something or someone makes us feel good by activating our hedonic hotspots or feel-good fields in our pleasure pathways, we want to experience these feelings again. Therefore we become more likely to repeat *behaviors* that we believe generated these feelings (the definition of positive reinforcement). The behaviors that allow or actively promote a pleasurable taste, sexual experience, hearing beautiful music, shopping, being in the company of a certain person or—perhaps—helping someone in need—these behaviors are "positively reinforced" by the moments of pleasure, satisfaction, or "rush" that follow the behaviors, making the behaviors more likely to recur in the future.

What jumps into your mind as one such behavior that almost everyone enjoys? Is it on your own list of favorites?

21

Eating: The Pleasures That Keep on Pleasing

As a preamble to neuroscience's spotlights on the pleasures of eating, we want to remind ourselves that many millions, probably billions of the world's people, are too poor to enjoy even minimally adequate calories and nutrition, let alone the panoply of seductive flavors that we in the middle class have in such abundance. They struggle just to stay alive, day after day. Corporate and national greed that promote these inequities in pursuit of ever-greater profits have been explored by some neuroscientist authors in the context of the neuroscience of eating (Linden, 2011). We applaud this work, which is totally in sync with the social work codes of ethics that mandate us to fight injustices of egregious inequality.

In the "tempted brain," Berridge, Ho, Richard, and DiFeliceantonio (2010) list numerous brain sites activated by pleasant foods in the *frontal cortex* (orbitofrontal, anterior cingulate, and insular cortices with the insula straddling the frontal and temporal lobes); in *subcortical forebrain structures* (nucleus accumbens, ventral pallidum, and amygdala); and in *lower brainstem systems* (corticolimbic dopamine projections from the ventral tegmental area and the parabrachial nucleus of the pons). To this list we'll add the *dorsal striatum* (caudate and putamen) in the basal ganglia, two adjacent structures that have recently attracted attention as purveyors of pleasure. The orbitofrontal region of the prefrontal lobe is also the reported leader in coding taste and smell pleasures. However, not all brain activations that code food pleasure necessarily *give rise* to that pleasure, and there are more codes for pleasure in the brain than there are causes for it (Kringelbach and Berridge, 2010).

We want to mention as a general principle that olfaction (smell) often combines with gustatory (taste) stimuli to contribute to the reward (or aversiveness) of an edible. For knowledge about our world of aromas and how they affect eating pleasure, we refer you to texts referenced in this book and to the database PubMed, which together supply detailed information about olfaction.

Many brain sites participate in eating extravaganzas. I've given examples above but don't want to overload readers with technical details that seem of lesser importance, in the interest of clarity and simplicity. We've included the following major regions of neural networks that manage eating: nucleus of the solitary tract, hypothalamus, amygdala, dorsal striatum, thalamic nuclei, orbitofrontal cortex, insular cortex, and the nucleus accumbens/septum/ventral pallidum area.

Built-in brain food processors *evaluate* the edibility of available objects and *motivate* us to eat if the candidate food passes its evaluation (or if it fails, *instruct us to disdain it*). Our brains *decide* what to eat, *draw on* our experience, and maybe even *follow recipes* from world-renowned chefs to reward ourselves with a smorgasbord of good-tasting foods and drinks, *watch* the level of energy intake to *determine* whether it's commensurate with our energy output, *send messages to structures* that modify behaviors so that inputs and outputs of energy will be balanced, *send and receive messages* that our stomach is stretching (distended with food) or wanting to be fed, *disperse biochemicals* (often hormones) that *tell motor neurons* either to eat more or stop eating, and *warn us* when a food we're about to eat may make us sick. And our brain's food processors enhance all this with a *lifetime of memories of food pleasures*, often associated with specific environmental influences that prevailed at the time a certain food was relished. (All that? I thought I just see food, it looks good, and I eat it, no big deal.)

Visual Representation of a Network of Gustatory Delight

Look at color images H., Neural Circuits for Eating, and I. Neural Circuits for Eating: Zooming in on some Hypothalamus and Brainstem Contributors. Then watch the 3-D animation of neuroscience events that take place as we eat

Box 21.1

Emotions, Cognitions, and Behaviors
Hedonic Hotspots Lit Up by a McDonald's Banquet
CHEESEBURGER
FRIES WITH KETCHUP
EGGNOG SHAKE
(IT'S HOLIDAY SEASON.)

Emotion while eating, feeling happy, yum-m-m
Cognition while eating ("It's delicious")
Behavior while eating: biting into cheeseburger and fries, chewing, sipping shake, savoring the taste, swallowing.

Emotion while eating comes to the end, sense of loss, all gone, want more
Cognition while eating comes to the end ("darn, it's all gone, would love to start all over again")
Behavior while eating comes to the end: last bite of cheeseburger, last fry, last sip.

Emotion after eating: regret and anxiety about pile-up of calories or sat fat
Cognition after eating: "really bad for me, I'm disgusted with myself"
Behavior after eating: going for a walk to try to mitigate the damage.

[see pp. 134–137] so you can follow the progression of nerve impulses occurring along the different paths and recurring loops of neural networks for eating. It won't be important for you to remember all the details of this brain rollercoaster ride, but you should try to follow it to become familiar with the ways neural networks work to produce a range of our human experiences.

The *first projection* of hundreds or thousands of neurons in the peripheral nervous system (outside the brain and spinal cord) begins when ingested food or drink touches any of the estimated 10,000 taste buds on our tongues and nearby surfaces in the mouth. Receptors on *sensory cranial neurons* pick up messages from taste buds and convey them to rostral (read "toward the head") and medial (read "in the middle") regions of the *nucleus tractus solitarius* (NTS) in the brainstem medulla. This region of the NTS processes taste-related information and is dubbed the *gustatory nucleus* of the solitary tract complex (Purves et al., 2008).

The other main part of the NTS is the *visceral motor system* (also called *autonomic*), at the caudal ("toward the tail") or bottom region of the NTS. This system receives signals from the gastrointestinal system via the vagus nerve, such as when the stomach becomes full, then communicates with other brain structures concerned with *energy homeostasis*, the body's balance between relative amounts of energy intake (food and drink) and energy expenditure (metabolism).

In the NTS region, these gustatory and visceral sections of the NTS meet and send out action signals via the gustatory/visceral reflex arc, which Purves and colleagues (2008) say is a really good idea. This is so because reflex arcs are the nervous system's fast track to action—they bypass the brain's time-consuming deliberations and order muscles to act, *right now*, which creatures need to do quickly when, for example, they're eating something bad for them and better stop right away!

A *second projection* goes out from the visceral motor signals region (caudal) of the NTS to the *hypothalamus*. The hypothalamus has a major role in eating. It monitors and adjusts energy metabolism, hunger, and appetite as its various nuclei receive sensory and contextual information; it compares that input with biological set points; and it activates various systems where adjustments may be needed to restore homeostasis or carry out needed behaviors.

As an example, studies have recently shown that the hypothalamus has a sensor to identify hormones and energy nutrients that regulate both food intake and glucose homeostasis (Chari, Lam, and Lam, 2010). When the *ventromedial nucleus* of the hypothalamus, a satiety center in laboratory animals, received bilateral lesions and stopped sending satiety messages, hyperphagia (overeating) and obesity resulted. Had the ventromedial nucleus of the hypothalamus not been tampered with, the animals probably would have contentedly ambled away from the feeder and still have their girlish or boyish figures today.

As another example, the *arcuate nucleus*, a tiny region within the hypo-thalamus, receives multiple signals from different paths. It contains mixed types of neurons that keep busy sending out opposing messages—"eat, eat" or "stop, stop"! How does the brain know what to do? (For a detailed account, see Linden, 2011, p. 75.) A large number of variables can tip the balance here, such as mood, exercise, aromas, even the time of day. We don't know exactly how the brain makes a decision. Which forces prevail? Why?

A *third projection*, this one from the gustatory nucleus in the NTS, sends messages to the ventral posterior medial nucleus of the thalamus (VPM), whose job is to relay information to certain specific cortical areas.

A *fourth projection* carries out this relay by proceeding from the VPM of the thalamus to taste-directed regions of the *insular cortex* and *orbitofrontal cortex* that are part of the larger area of the prefrontal cortex. The *insular cortex* (*insula*) is hidden beneath the frontal and temporal lobes and can only be seen if these are pulled apart (Purves et al., 2008). It is buried in the fissure separat-ing these two lobes, and thus it is sometimes assigned by neuroscience authors to one or the other lobe.

The insular cortex is the *primary gustatory area in the brain*. It participates in many aspects of eating of which tasting palatable foods is one. In smokers, damage to the insula disrupts the urge to smoke (Wang, Volkow et al., 2009), suggesting malfunction in the pleasure pathway for smoking.

The orbitofrontal cortex (OFC) also has important roles in taste. Its neurons respond to combinations of visual, olfactory, and gustatory stimuli (sight/smell/taste) to perform the functions of *evaluating* and *integrating diverse sensory inputs* (Kringelbach, 2005; Purves et al., 2008). It also modulates autonomic reactions and contributes to learning, prediction, and decision-making in the areas of emotional and reward-related behaviors.

The orbitofrontal cortex functions as part of multiple neural networks. Circuits for the *actual* reward value, *expected* reward value, and *subjective pleasantness* of foods and other reinforcers all are represented in the orbito-frontal cortex, providing a basis for further exploration of our conscious expe-rience of pleasure and reward (Kringelbach, 2005).

Food cues increase metabolism in the OFC, presumably by stimulating motivation for food consumption ("wanting") (Wang, Volkow et al., 2009). The OFC is what's referred to as an "association" area, managing messages con-necting sensory and motor events.

Kringelbach (2005), noting that the OFC as of 2005 was among the least understood regions of the human brain, probed its role in linking a pleasur-able stimulus to hedonic experience, generating the actual feeling of pleasure. The OFC, amygdala, and cingulate cortex contribute to emotional process-ing in the human brain. The links of the OFC to the sensory and reward-ing properties of reinforcers, could, Kringelbach believes, offer important insights into the widespread obesity epidemic and emotional disorders such as depression. By the time of writing this book (2013), the OFC had attracted much more research attention than was the case when Kringelbach's article was published—the OFC is now viewed as a pivotal area of the prefrontal cortex.

Measuring emotions relies on a scientific strategy of dividing the concept of emotion into two parts: the emotional state (measured through physiological changes such as autonomic and endocrine responses) and feelings (the subjective experience of emotion). What's important here, we think, is to remind readers that pleasures of eating have complex connections with human emotion—shades of Marcel Proust's madeleines (little tea cakes) remembered from childhood (Proust, 1913). When we eat or think about eating, myriad emotions are triggered, such as joy or longing or nostalgia, and after eating, possible examples of emotion are satisfaction for normal weight people or, for dieters, either pleasure with themselves because of their restraint, or satiated but rueful.

Last but far from least, a *fifth group of projections* involve the regions of the *mesolimbic* and *mesocorticolimbic* neural networks, which include the medial forebrain pleasure circuit and those hedonic feel-good havens such as the nucleus accumbens, the caudate nucleus and putamen, the ventral pallidum, the insula, the parabrachial nucleus, the OFC, and others, receiving dopamine from the brain's fountains of delight (with poetic names like ventral tegmental area or substantia nigra). It is in these linked structures in the networks that pleasure and reward experiences happen. "That was *good*," or "that was *really tasty!*" or "*Wow! That was awesome, incredible, the best food experience I've ever had!*" One of our video participants actually exclaimed that last sentence while getting a high on a Mexican entrée!

Pleasure and reward vary according to the kind of food eaten, individuals' hunger states, stress levels, and other conditions at the time of eating. We show unrehearsed, unscripted, unprompted video clips of persons eating—this participant was indeed very hungry! The videos incorporate animations of the major activated neural networks simulating the real neural systems at work.

22

Eating and Obesity: Has Pleasure
Vanquished Homeostasis?

The average weight of an adult in the United States has increased by about 26 pounds from 1960 to the present (Linden, 2011, pp. 82–83), and according to Wang, Volkow et al. (2009) approximately 90 million Americans are obese. Other countries, especially wealthy ones, have also experienced increases in overweight, although my colleagues and I (anecdotally) have heard recent visitors to major European and Asian cities report how many fewer overweight people they saw on the streets than was the case in the United States.

Body mass index (BMI), expressed as a person's weight in kilograms divided by the square of his or her height in meters (kg/m^2), is the measure commonly used by government and other health care centers to report prevalence estimates of overweight and obesity. Common classification for overweight is a BMI of 25.0–29.9, for obesity a BMI greater than or equal to 30.0, and for extreme obesity, a BMI greater than or equal to 40.0. Results from the 2007–2008 National Health and Nutrition Examination Survey, using measured heights and weights, indicate that an estimated 34.2% of U.S. adults aged 20 years and over are *overweight and not obese*, 33.8% are *obese*, and 5.7% are *extremely obese*. Prevalence of obesity for women is 35.5%, for men, 32.2%, and for children 2 to 19 years of age, 16.9%.

Clearly the numbers of people meeting criteria for obesity can be reduced by using higher cutoff points to qualify for the designation, but even with less stringent cutoffs, there would still be seriously high prevalence of obesity and overweight. More than two decades of research by dozens of respected researchers have shown that even mild to moderate overweight significantly increases the risk of heart and vascular disease, cancer, and diabetes.

Or does it? JAMA (*Journal of the American Medical Association*) published results of a meta-analysis of 97 studies from all over the world, based on data from more than 2.88 million people. The team studied 270,000 deaths in the United States, Canada, Europe, Australia, China, Japan, Brazil, Israel, and Mexico. The study was conducted by the U.S. Centers for Disease Control (CDC) (Flegal, Kit, Orpana, and Graubard, 2013).

The study concluded that slightly to moderately overweight people as measured by BMI have a *lower* mortality rate than normal-weight and thin people. These results contradicted the preponderance of research showing correlations between the risk of death and being overweight, even mildly or moderately, once factors such as lower weight from cigarette smoking, chronic disease, and wasting from frailty in the elderly are taken into account.

The problem with the gigantic study was that researchers at the CDC *didn't* take these conditions into account. They couldn't, because so many of the studies on which the meta-analysis was based did not contain that kind of breakdown of the data. Flegal defended the study's viability by its [perfectly true] statistical significance. But any study based on faulty design can produce false results that are statistically significant. Once normal-weight and thin people who are already ill are removed from the sample of "healthy" people, these statistical results no longer hold (Gavomali, 2013; Nursing Times.net, 2013).

Nevertheless, the announcement was dynamite. Not only was it the occasion for joyful celebration by many of the two-thirds of American adults who are overweight or obese—who understandably would love to be relieved from the deprivation of dieting—but also the many giant corporations who make fortunes off the food and weight-loss industries. Packs of hungry media sleuths triumphantly announced the health scoop of the year, Overweight People Live Longer, based on results from the JAMA study and published in dozens of media outlets, as a cursory scan of Google with keywords such as "overweight people live longer" clearly demonstrated.

Members of a panel convened by the Harvard School of Public Health (HSPH) evaluated the findings. They identified methodological errors in the study that they said resulted in the "artificial appearance" of a protective benefit in being overweight or even "mildly" obese. Walter Willett, Chair of the HSPH Nutrition Department, called the study "rubbish," and Frank Hu, Chair of its Obesity Department, invoked the well-known observation that if something is too good to be true, it's usually false (see for example Miller, 2013; Hughes, 2013).

It is hard for me, and I'm sure many others, to understand how such an enormous study conducted by the research arm of the U.S. Centers for Disease Control (CDC)—a prestigious federal government agency—and involving many researchers, could make and stick to their assertions of validity (their earlier similar results were released in 2007) (Flegal, Kit, Orpana, and Graubard, 2013; Gavomali, 2013; Nursing Times.net, 2013). Isn't there a serious ethical violation in falsely reassuring overweight people that being somewhat fat is not only okay, but it's also better for your health?

Other studies involving obesity are less newsworthy and have less ubiquitous public health implications, but they are of interest here. In one of a series of experiments by Eric Stice and colleagues, pleasure responses were recorded through fMRI (functional magnetic resonance imaging) as young women subjects, one group obese, the other lean, lay in the scanner and received chocolate milkshake sips through a straw. Chocolate is known to be a strong activator of pleasure locations in the brain. The women also participated in genetic testing for the presence of the TaqIA A1 allele (Stice, Spoor, Bohon, and Small, 2008).

Several interesting findings emerged. Obese women had much lower pleasure activation in the dorsal striatum from milkshake sips than did lean women. The striatum, a part of the basal ganglia we've encountered earlier, is also known to process large amounts of dopamine.

And to add insult to injury, tests of anticipatory pleasure just *before* acquiring tasty food showed greater anticipatory activation of reward circuitry in obese than in lean individuals—"a cruel double-edged sword of increased craving coupled with decreased pleasure" when actually eating (Linden, 2011, p. 82). The same phenomenon of anticipatory pleasure occurs for persons addicted to drugs when they have an immediate prospect of using (Volkow et al., 2010). At follow-up a year later, the allele TaqIA A1 carriers showed the greatest weight gain.

Volkow et al. (2010), leaders in the addiction field, compared obese subjects to drug addicts and found strong neurobiological similarities. They propose that a major motivator for food addiction, as is true for persons addicted to drugs, is "blunted" pleasure responses related to abnormally low dopamine levels, causing an ongoing sense of pleasure deprivation for which they try to compensate with compulsive pleasure-seeking behaviors.

Attribution of causality for overweight and obesity is a subject of controversy in the fields of neuroscience, epidemiology, endocrinology, psychology, and others. A few findings from the work of Eric Stice and colleagues may give us some clues (Stice, Spoor, Bohon, and Small et al., 2008; Stice, Yokum, Burger, Epstein, and Small 2011; Stice, Yokum, Zald, and Dagher 2011):

- Obese humans, compared with normal-weight humans, have *fewer striatal D2 receptors* and *lower striatal pleasure response* to food intake, which predicts weight gain, consistent with the *reward-deficit theory of obesity* (people overeat to try to compensate for low levels of experienced food pleasure).
- Presence of the TaqIA A1 allele, a fairly common gene variant, decreases the density of D2 dopamine receptors in pleasure networks (*thinner dopamine D2 receptors caused by a gene*).
- Overeating reduces D2 receptor density, D2 sensitivity, reward sensitivity, and striatal response to food (*thinner dopamine D2 receptors are also caused by overeating in addition to being caused by a gene; other consequences of overeating are lowered responsiveness to food reward*).

The prominence of the striatum (caudate nucleus and putamen) in food pleasure has only recently been discovered, whereas its involvement in controlling motor movement has long been recognized. Recent experiments by Schloegl, Percik and colleagues (2011), Balleine, Delgado, and Hirosaka (2007), and Stice and colleagues (2008, 2011A, 2011B), have brought to light new evidence that the dorsal striatum is also involved in higher cognitive functions, especially those relevant to reward, pleasure and addiction, as it integrates sensorimotor, cognitive, and motivational/emotional information.

In addition, citing multiple sources, Balleine and colleagues (2007) state that although there is an extensive literature linking the cognitive control of executive functions specifically to the prefrontal cortex (Fuster, 2000; Goldman-Rakic, 1995), these more recent studies suggest that these functions also depend on reward-related circuitry linking prefrontal, premotor, and sensorimotor cortices with the striatum.

Other parts to the puzzle. Medical sciences have thus implicated neurobiological variables as contributors to obesity and overweight. What is the culpability of external systems? Who are the perpetrators?

The food industry has been remarkably successful at developing and marketing tasty, high fat, high sugar foods, a "superaddictive" combination with a pleasure effect greater than the summed effects of each component alone (fat, sugar). Thus, these products activate pleasure circuits intensively (Linden, 2011). One dismal consequence of the technologically driven enhancement of pleasure by the food industry, bonanza for its bottom line but deleterious to health and welfare, is the estimated prevalence of mild to severe overweight in about two-thirds of the U.S. population.

The Center for Science in the Public Interest health newsletter on food and nutrition, *Nutrition Action,* has continued to provide extensive documentation and detailed food product information on this subject for many years, in my view a very good investment at $20 a year for anyone trying to foster the health of families.

The diet industry is another multibillion dollar sector of the economy that profits from overeating. Sales promotions for any number of methods hold out "carrots" of success to would-be fat-losers, but realistic information about long-term success rates, if disseminated, may have a depressing effect on the diet business. This is not to discount what successful dieters have sometimes accomplished by dint of heroic efforts over long time periods, but promises of a multitude of routes to slimness have been notoriously unfulfilled on a societal level.

Biological reasons discovered by neuroscience and other sciences have thus interacted with commercial and societal realities to explain why the gold standard of homeostasis, in the instance of food and eating, has been violated for a likely majority of people in our culture.

In contrast to many countries of the world where poverty, lack of employment, malnutrition, and vulnerability to illness are the rule, industrialized countries, led by the United States, have created and implemented production technologies sufficient to feed the entire planet were the resources distributed in an equitable manner (which of course has never been the case). The result has been epidemic levels of overweight in the United States and other industrialized countries due, most studies show, to overeating, with lack of exercise an important but smaller contributor.

With regard to individual factors, which of the following is the Obesity Devil—Weak Willpower, or Complex Neurobiological Systems? Do these evildoers conspire to do in our best-laid plans? These issues matter to clinicians because they have enormous implications for treating conditions of obesity and overweight. Although the BMI (body mass index) is about 80% heritable, gene/environment interactions appear to be critical for trying to explain why the average weight of an adult in the United States has increased so dramatically (Linden, 2011).

Perhaps a better way to formulate this question might be: *How much* willpower on a scale of 1 to 10 would be necessary for you to foil the corporate agendas of food production, conspiring with your time-honored genes pushing you to stock up for the next famine that some believe only the overweight will survive?

The estimated minority of adult Americans whose weight ranges from normal to thin require, we imagine, a willpower score of, say, 1 or 2, to out-maneuver these contravening forces. We're guessing, however, that overweight people will require much more (say a score of 7 to 10) to get the weight off and keep it off.

Could we guess that this might be true because (1) it is much more difficult to subject oneself to the pleasure deprivation of a weight loss regimen than to just stay as you are, and (2) non-overweight people are probably disproportionately more likely in the first place to have a higher rate of metabolism or other inborn advantage than their overweight counterparts? A persuasive reason, which *is* documented, not speculative, is that the neurobiological and endocrinological consequence of losing a chunk of weight initially is to mobilize the homeostasis-seeking brain's chemical tricks.

For example, leptin, a hormone put out into the bloodstream by fat cells under the direction of the hypothalamus, is secreted to decrease appetite ("wanting" food) and weight when the brain's watchdogs of homeostasis are saying "tsk, tsk, getting fatter." But when some weight has already *been lost*, the watchdog voices say "no, no, getting thinner—stop, stop!"

The brain then suppresses leptin release and substitutes secretion of chemicals that *stimulate* appetite and "wanting" food, through energy-level balancing strategies mounted by the hypothalamus in concert with other structures. So, in a nutshell, the more you lose, the more you want. The brain is continually moving your goal post.

In case you're thinking leptin might be a magic diet drug—sorry, it's been tried. It has worked very well for the (relatively small) population that has a

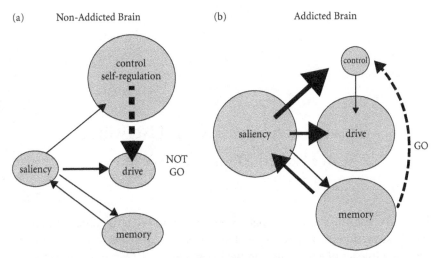

(a)   Non-Addicted Brain   (b)   Addicted Brain

FIGURE 22.1 *Model of brain circuits involved with addiction and obesity: reward/saliency, motivation/drive, memory/conditioning, and inhibitory control/emotional regulations. Disrupted activity in brain regions involved with inhibitory control/emotional regulation when coupled with enhanced activation of reward/saliency and memory/conditioning leads to enhanced activation of the motivational/drive circuit and the resultant compulsive behavior (drug taking or food ingestion) when the individual is exposed to the reinforcer (drug or food), conditioned cues, or a stressor. Note that circuits that regulate mood as well as internal awareness (interoception) are also likely to modulate the ability to exert control over incentive drives. (a) Healthy brain, (b) dysregulated brain. Modifi ed from Volkow, Fowler, and Wang, 2003.*

genetic mutation or other defect in leptin production or leptin receptors, but not for the vast majority of other overweight people with intact leptin factories.

I conclude with reproduction of a diagram first constructed by Volkow and colleagues in 2003, and still very relevant today (Volkow and Wang, 2003; Volkow, Wang, et al., 2012) Figure 22.1.

Some of the authors of studies reported in this book have expressed hope that advancing scientific knowledge about the biochemistry of obesity will ultimately lead to new and more effective remedies than are currently available. Certainly that is a more realistic possibility, in my view, than the giant redistribution of resources worldwide that would transfer resources from rich to poor countries, combined with widely disseminated scientific education to outwit the profit agendas of food and diet industries, two enormous changes that in the best of worlds could solve the problem.

23

Trauma and Stress: Neural Networks
By Elizabeth D'Amico, MSW, PhD

The awareness of a connection between trauma and brain function is not new. Freud's seduction theory, which he abandoned in response to criticism, recognized the impact of experience on the brain—in particular, traumatic experiences. Around the same period, there was some acknowledgment of what was known as *shell shock* in World War I veterans. It is only within the past several decades that the terminology has become slightly more precise, if not ideal, with the development of a specific diagnosis, posttraumatic stress disorder (PTSD).

This diagnostic category includes a range of traumatized individuals: physical and sexual abuse victims, survivors of natural disasters, veterans of wars, especially the growing number of identified veterans of Iraq and Afghanistan who present with the psychological consequences of their experiences. These categories of environmental factors contributing to PTSD are the best known, but many other situations can have similar effects on people of all ages. Shalev (1996) points out that part of the challenge of this single PTSD framework is that it includes a broad etiological spectrum ranging from unfortunate events such as motor vehicle accidents to horrific atrocities.

The task of adequately describing for social workers how traumatic events impact the human nervous system is daunting, especially when space is limited. Trauma is a huge topic in itself. We've selected a few aspects of trauma that seem essential for practitioners. However, we hope your appetite will be sufficiently whetted to explore further.

I am increasingly struck by the inadequacy of language to communicate concepts, particularly those related to the complexity of the human condition—and trauma is no exception. Working for many years as a clinical social worker, specializing in the often long-term treatment of those who have experienced a horrible loss, abuse, neglect, torture, and similar horrendous events, others and I have struggled with the semantics of this area of clinical specialty in trauma-related disorders. But perhaps we should start with a core concept related to trauma: stressors and stress.

The ability to deal with new, potentially dangerous situations is critical to survival. This capacity is built into specific brain circuits whose development is influenced by multiple experiences beginning early in life. Environmental stimuli that activate these circuits are often referred to as *stressors*, and stress reactions are the body's chemical and neural responses that promote adaptation (National Scientific Council on the Developing Child, 2005).

Shalev (1996), in a historical review, notes that authors of the third edition of the *Diagnostic and Statistical Manual of Mental Disorders* (APA, 1980), intended for the definition of the new diagnosis of PTSD to delineate extreme catastrophic or traumatic stress. A more recent edition of the *DSM* defines a traumatic event as "an experience that is threatening to oneself or a close person, accompanied by intense fear, horror, or helplessness" (APA, 1997). Thus there is a difference between *stress* and *traumatic stress*. The field of traumatic stress has developed independently from the preexisting field of stress and coping (Shalev, 1996), and there has been little overlap between the two.

Stress theory deals with immediate consequences of a mild to moderate stressor, proposing that intermediate- or long-term consequences are due to a failure to deal with the effect of the stressor. Therefore, Shalev argues that the use of the term *stress* for both "acute" and "chronic" conditions is problematic. Further, traumatic stress research tends to be retrospective, observational, and naturalistic whereas stress research is primarily experimental.

An individual's level of resilience or vulnerability to stress will depend on his or her innate neurobiological sensitivity that has interacted with previous experiences over time. As Perry and Szalavitz explain, stress—in appropriate measure—can make a system more functionally capable. However, when the stress overloads the individual, particularly his or her developing neuronal system, the stress becomes traumatic stress and a profoundly negative result can occur (2006). More on that shortly.

Yehuda (2009) reconceptualized PTSD as a disorder of stress response systems since it is not a normative response to extreme stressors. Only some of those experiencing trauma develop the disorder (Pace and Heim, 2011). Another paradigm for conceptualizing stress, particularly in children, divides stress into a continuum from positive to toxic (National Scientific Council on the Developing Child, 2005). Stressful events are viewed as beneficial, tolerable, or harmful depending on the level and length of time of physiological response that is provoked in the child. The level and length of response relate not only to the stressor itself but also to the child's prior history of *stress activation* as well as the degree of supportive relationships that exist in the environment. Positive or moderate, predictable stress makes the body stronger and more resilient. This is part of the normal developmental process.

Tolerable stress is the term used for stress responses that have the potential to negatively impact brain systems. Generally, these stressors occur for relatively short periods or are events that are mitigated by the involvement of supportive adults. In this way, even some otherwise major events, which might have become toxic stress, can have positive outcomes for the individual child. In this paradigm, toxic stress is the term used to refer to intense, frequent, and/or sustained activation of the body's stress management system.

Research supports that such stress responses not lessened by caring adults in the environment can have negative outcomes on the brain architecture. For example, in the extreme, toxic stress may result in the development of a smaller brain. Less extreme exposure to toxic stress can change the stress system so that it responds at lower thresholds to events that might not be stressful to others, thereby increasing the risk of stress-related physical and mental illness (National Scientific Council on the Developing Child, 2005, p. 1).

For some time, social workers having expertise in trauma assessment and treatment has seemed to place them among the elite of clinical specialists. It is a popular area of concentration and a needed one. Lifetime prevalence rates for exposure to traumatic events are estimated at 40–90% in the general population, with an estimated lifetime prevalence of PTSD of 7–12% (Kessler, Sonnega, Bromet, Hughes, and Nelson, 1995). For example, approximately 794,000 children were found to be victims of abuse and/or neglect in the United States in 2007, although many more children are probably subject to negative conditions (U.S. Department of Health and Human Services, 2009).

Like all specialties, trauma has a particular knowledge base. While social workers will always be needed, the major take-home message that neuroscience and the related fields of genetics and epigenetics have to teach us social workers about the impact of stress and traumatic stress is that the primary focus should be on early intervention, and, ideally, prevention. In other words, while there will always be important trauma assessment and treatment work, the more critical work is with children before the trauma, or at least intervening as rapidly as possible after the event. Although we'll touch on adult-related traumas, the primary theme in this chapter is developmental trauma—that is, the neural damage that occurs during childhood developmental periods and generally has lifelong consequences. Perry and Szalavitz (2006) remind us that "the same miraculous plasticity that allows young brains to quickly learn love and language, unfortunately, also makes them highly susceptible to negative experiences as well." And Stien and Kendall (2004) note that securely attached children are likely to have brains that are better balanced biochemically and better organized structurally than children raised in chaotic or abusive environments.

Why do we need neuroscience to work with PTSD sufferers? There are multiple reasons why social workers need to learn neuroscience related to trauma: symptom recognition and accurate diagnosis; client education around myriad related topics (e.g., psychopharmacology, manifestations of trauma on child development, intergenerational impact); need for public policy changes; appropriate and precise treatment selection relative to the specific manifested damage; consultation with related stakeholders (family, school personnel, and others in the child's community); and assistance with framing emotions or behavior within a developmental trauma context. Again, it is critical that human service workers grasp the dramatic impact that trauma has on human neurobiology if they are to work more actively toward its prevention, since we know that children are far more vulnerable to trauma than adults (Perry and Szalavitz, 2006; Pervanidou, 2008).

Perry and Szalavitz (2006) suggest that conservatively, about 40% of American children will experience at least one potentially traumatizing event before they are eighteen, such as death of a parent or sibling, ongoing abuse or neglect, serious accident, violent crime, natural disaster, or domestic violence. The Adverse Childhood Experiences Study, which reviewed retrospective reports of 17,337 adult HMO members, found that exposure to early abuse or adversity accounts for 50–78% of the "population attributable risk" for suicide attempts, drug abuse, alcoholism, and depression (Anda et al., 2006).

The research suggests that traumatic events in the developing child result in negative outcomes into adulthood, such as increased psychiatric difficulties, serious medical problems, and health risk behaviors (see for example Carpenter, Shattuck, Tyrka, Geracioti, and Price, 2011; Danese, Moffitt, Pariante, Ambler, Poulton, and Capsi, 2008; Watts-English, Fortson, Gibler, Hooper, and De Bellis, 2006). Felitti (2002) noted that common disorders in adults are likely to result from lack of recognition and remediation in childhood.

Certainly social workers will not be able to prevent all traumatic experiences. Rather, we hope that through increased neuroscientific knowledge about the potential impact of trauma on development, workers can be more critically attuned to situations and symptoms that allow for the mitigation of traumatic stress. Not all children who experience a traumatic event are doomed to develop severe symptomatology, and negative situations, once identified, should be addressed. In other words, once symptom identification occurs social workers need to focus on the broader system and the transaction between the child and environments (both toxic and remedial) to ensure change for the child. Lieberman and Van Horn suggest that the assessment and treatment of traumatic stress in young children must be geared to identifying and addressing environmental risk factors. "[C]hild development is best understood using an ecological-transactional model that encompasses the biologic characteristics of the child in the context of family, community, and cultural protective and risk factors. . . . Unless clinicians are alert to these findings, they might focus narrowly on the traumatized child's symptoms and miss the. . . . context that triggers and sustains these symptoms" (2009, pp. 708–709).

Also, it increasingly appears that adults who are vulnerable to trauma are likely to have had earlier traumatic experiences during development in childhood or adolescence.

The term *posttraumatic stress disorder* (PTSD) was first utilized in psychiatry in 1980 to designate clusters of symptoms seen in veterans returning from Vietnam. PTSD symptoms now are postulated to reflect changes in neurobiological systems and/or an inadequate adaptation of neurobiological systems in response to severe stress (Heim and Nemeroff, 2009). PTSD is a multidimensional disorder that may be comorbid with other symptoms or diagnoses (Pervanidou, 2008).

It was sometime after 1980 before there was recognition that children could exhibit similar responses to stressful events. In fact the *Diagnostic and Statistical Manual of Mental Disorders IV-TR* (2000) has not as of this time of writing distinguished the very real differences between children and adults in trauma sequelae, primarily because most research on trauma has been done on adults, although much work is now in progress in this area. Many children who do suffer from PTSD do not meet the current criteria, one indicator that the DSM-IV diagnosis PTSD is not particularly developmentally sensitive.

Children may manifest a range of symptoms that vary depending on the origins of the trauma as well as their own histories and genetic make-up. Symptoms may include one or more of the following: somatization; accentuation of typical fears; irritability; depression or sadness; impaired concentration and hyperactivity; dreams of being killed, reenacted play of the traumatic event (Stien and Kendall, 2004; Terr, 1990). There are active national field trials toward the creation of a developmental trauma disorder (van der Kolk, 2009). While the field has come light-years since 1980 relative to child trauma, it has a way to go.

Relationship of Trauma to Key Neural Structures, Systems, Neurotransmitters, and Neurons

The second half of this chapter provides introductory information on neural structures and systems, much of which relates to the current topic. In this section, we focus on a number of structures, functions, and neurotransmitters that have been identified through research as playing critical roles in stress response processes, both during a stressful or traumatic event and sometimes afterword as a residual impact on the neural system. These elements are described below, including both the function of the element as well as its particular relationship to the stress response.

DEVELOPMENT

The human brain can be divided into sections in various ways, depending on focus. Three critical parts of the brain (brain stem, limbic system, and cortex) develop in order from the simplest to the most complex, and from the inside out (Perry and Szalavitz, 2006; Stien and Kendall, 2004). The cortex develops last. Although its development may begin as early as the first year, maturation continues through adulthood. Brain growth explodes between birth (actually starting before birth) and age two, with some additional growth spurts thereafter. This knowledge is critical to understand trauma's impact on development.

Each process of overproduction of neural connections is followed by a "pruning" of unused connections, in response to the unique characteristics of the environment affecting and affected by that individual. Thus the relationship between the infant and caregiver is critical to developing and stabilizing the neural connections (Stien and Kendall, 2004). Developmental psychopathologists stress that we need to determine how persons respond to and interact with vulnerability and protective factors at multiple system levels (i.e., culture, community, family, and their transactions), and that diversity in developmental outcomes is typical (Stien and Kendall, 2004).

Cicchetti concurs. He writes that the route to either resilience or psychopathology is molded by a "complex matrix of the individual's level of biological and psychological organization, current experiences, active choices, the social context, timing of the adverse event(s) and experiences, and the developmental history of the individual" (2010, p. 145).

Hyperarousal and Dissociation

When we speak about the physiological stress response to trauma, we generally think of fight-or-flight response, or hyperarousal. This response has received the most research attention and appears to have the greatest negative outcomes at all points along the developmental continuum. An equally important stress response is the dissociative response. The body has different adaptive responses to danger. If an individual does not have the developmental capacity for fight or flight—that is, if he or she is too young or small, or is in a situation that otherwise precludes those options, the body may utilize a dissociative response.

These reactions to extreme stressors appear to be a function of primitive brain systems activating survival mechanisms, similar to hyperarousal. Contrary to the individual being revved up through the hypothalamic-pituitary-adrenal (HPA) axis and related systems as explained below, in dissociation the brain is preparing the body for injury. Heart rate and breathing are slowed down and a flood of endogenous opioids is released, creating a sense of disconnection, numbing, and lack of fear response and pain.

However, in most traumatic events, both dissociation and hyperarousal responses—fight and flight—become activated, one process modulating the other. If these patterns are activated long enough, the intensity, duration, or pattern of the trauma will produce "use-dependent" changes in the involved neural systems (Perry and Szalavitz, 2006). At this point, an individual shows dissociation symptoms with or without an apparent threat. We are most

familiar with the memory deficits associated with marked dissociation resulting from psychological disconnectedness, but it impacts multiple aspects of
the organism. Dissociation is on a continuum and can be a highly adaptive
and utilitarian response in stressful situations, whether for example, during
childhood trauma or battle combat as Stein et al. have said: "People growing
up in extremely neglectful or abusive homes habitually resort to dissociation—
not only defensively, but preemptively too. [For example], it becomes a way of
hosting aggression without acknowledging its toll" (Stein, 2007, p. 3).

STRUCTURES

Several structures comprise brain networks that process trauma. Among
these, the hippocampus, amygdala, and prefrontal cortical regions have shown
alterations in individuals with PTSD (Heim and Nemeroff, 2009).

   Thalamus. The thalamus is a gray matter structure that together with the
hypothalamus makes up a region called the *diencephalon.* The thalamus is
involved in sensory perception and movement, including sleep and awake
states of consciousness, through its connection to the cortex. Under stressful
conditions, those who experience traumatic events seem to develop impairments in the relaying of information from the thalamus to the cortex. This
impairment may distort the processing of incoming information, resulting
in some people attending more to the trauma-related stimuli, and some less
(Weiss, 2007).

   Hypothalamus. The hypothalamus, in concert with the pituitary gland,
is responsible for behaviors critical to survival. It maintains control over the
autonomic nervous system and endocrine system via the pituitary gland. The
pituitary and hypothalamus are linked to the adrenal gland in a feedback loop
known as the HPA axis, which plays a central role in trauma response (see
Stress Response Systems below).

   Hippocampus. The hippocampus is a gray matter structure of the limbic
system that is involved in declarative memory (conscious memories that can
be recalled, both factual knowledge and episodic personal events) and working memory (the ability to hold information necessary to complete complex
tasks such as reasoning, comprehension, and learning). It also controls stress
response and contextual aspects of fear conditioning (Heim and Nemeroff,
2009). The thalamus sends information to the hippocampus during a traumatic event and it is there that traumatic memories are created. Bremner et al.
(1999) found evidence that the hippocampi of those exposed to trauma have
lower activation and lower metabolism levels than those who have not had
such exposure, particularly during traumatic memories. Small hippocampal
volume appears to be related to deterioration or atrophy of neuronal processes
(such as decreased density of neurons, decreased branching of dendrites,

decreased growth of new neurons and degeneration at the neuron terminals) (Duman, Malberg, and Nakagawa, 2001). These deficits may correlate to symptoms such as avoidance and numbing as well as the inability to remember details of trauma, fragmenting of memory, dissociation, or total amnesia for an event (Weiss, 2007).

As with a number of areas of neuroscience and trauma, some data are unclear if not contradictory. For example, studies have found smaller hippocampal volumes in adults who suffered child maltreatment and subsequent trauma symptoms, suggesting that there may be an atrophying process that is related to the early stress but only manifests over time (Carrión et al., 2010). On the other hand, Gilbertson et al.'s (2002) combat-related study of PTSD suggests that having a smaller hippocampus may be a risk factor for the disorder, that is, a pre-existing vulnerability. (Could both be true?)

Amygdala. The amygdala is a limbic structure located within the temporal lobe. It consists of a mass of nuclei and is involved with many emotions and motivations, particularly those related to survival, or fight or flight. Thus, it is involved in the processing of stress, along with the prefrontal cortex and the hippocampus (Heim and Nemeroff, 2009). It combines information and sends it to subcortical structures and brain stem, which prompts physical responses (e.g., startle, a particular facial expression).

The amygdala also is responsible for which memories are stored and where they are stored. The amygdala gives input to the hypothalamus, which then triggers neuroendocrine and autonomic responses. Weiss (2007) noted that an overactive amygdala may be responsible for symptoms of hyperarousal such as exaggerated startle, irritability, anger outbursts, and hypervigilance. It might also be related to the re-experiencing of the original event when reminders of traumatic events trigger intense physiological and emotional reactions.

Prefrontal cortical region (neocortex). The prefrontal cortex is the most advanced and most recently developed region in the brain. It accounts for humans' capacity for complex cognitive processes. It is divided into a left and a right hemisphere by a bundle of nerves called the corpus callosum. It orchestrates much of language, imagination, abstract thought, and consciousness related to such functions as higher emotions, reasoning, spatial abilities, speech, visual processing, and many others.

Bremner (2002) found via neuroimaging studies that child victims of sexual abuse with PTSD had decreased volume in the prefrontal cortex. Symptoms such as numbing and dissociation may also be linked to neuronal deficits in the prefrontal cortex of traumatized children. Yang, Wu, Hsu, and Ker (2004) found associations with hypoactivation of the prefrontal cortex in children, adolescents, and adults with PTSD, especially during their active recollection of the trauma.

Corpus callosum. This is the primary "commissure" (or bundle of nerve fibers passing from one side to the other of the brain or spinal cord). It controls communication between the two hemispheres. Jackowski, de Araujo, de Lacerda, de Jesus Mari, and Kaufman (2009) cited two studies that reported decreased midbody and posterior corpus callosum area in children and adolescents with PTSD.

Mirror neurons. An increasing body of research supports the critical role of the caregiver relationship in the development of the prefrontal cortex. The role of a group of nerve cells called the mirror neurons is prominent in this development (e.g. Chersi, 2011; Perry and Szalavitz, 2006). These fronto-parietal neurons respond in synchrony with others' behavior, allowing humans to understand each others' experience through a form of neurological echo while observing each other (Ocampo and Kritikos, 2011; Perry and Szalavitz, 2006; Rizzolatti and Craighero as cited in Gerdes, Segal, Jackson, and Mullins, 2011).

Mirror neurons were discovered by a group of Italian neuroscientists (di Pellegrino, Fadiga, Fogassi, Callese, and Rizzolatti, 1992) who were studying motor behavior in macaque monkeys (Gerdes et al., 2011). Schore (1994) posits that the reciprocal interactions between infant and caregiver increase levels of dopamine, triggering a local growth spurt in the blood vessels, neurons, and glia of the prefrontal cortex especially in the early maturing right hemisphere.

The infant's sense of positive emotions from the caregiver elicits the release of opioid peptides, which activate dopamine neurons. Thus, an infant's emotional system is shaped and a variety of emotions are developed from a very early age. As Stien and Kendall explain, through sharing emotional states, designated as mirroring, babies use adults as extensions of themselves to reflect specific emotions and reinforce related behavior. The baby smiles, the mother smiles back or exclaims her delight or gives a smile and a hug. The baby's smiles are reinforced, and his or her emotions validated. In this way, the baby's emotional circuitry organizes itself, and the network of neurons dedicated to this particular emotion is strengthened. If, on the other hand, emotions are met with indifference or rejection, emotional and cognitive development is thwarted. Without adequate mirroring, circuits that integrate cognitive and emotional systems are unable to develop (Stien and Kendall, 2004).

In other words, primary sensory information from the caregiver is turned into similar patterns of neural activity in the infant, stimulating the same parts of the brain that the caregiver is using for her activities (Perry and Szalavitz, 2006).

Hormones/Neurotransmitters

Cortisol. Cortisol is the body's primary stress hormone, secreted by the adrenal gland. Individuals who have experienced chronic stress or trauma have brains that are frequently exposed to high levels of cortisol, resulting in their nervous systems becoming sensitive to psychologically threatening stimuli (Weiss, 2007).

Glutamate. The amino acid glutamate is also released during the stimulation of the adrenal gland. Glutamate contributes to extended synaptic connections among neurons, called long-term potentiation, or LTP. Carlson (2011, p. 341) defines LTP as a long-term increase in the excitability of a postsynaptic neuron to a particular synaptic input, caused by the high frequency activity of that input from the synapse. That is, some kind of action by something crossing the synapse is repeated multiple times. This bombardment by a particular input or message sensitizes that receiving (postsynaptic) neuron's excitability to that particular input, on a long-term basis. This is one way that memories are created. Memories of trauma are the source of anguish for people with PTSD.

Weiss (2007) comments on this creation of strong and vivid trauma memories that increase likelihood of recurrent dreams and other intrusive memories. In addition, if there is excitotoxicity (cell destruction due to excessive neural excitation), neural circuits may be damaged or destroyed, causing symptoms of avoidance, numbing, or complete dissociation or the inability to remember critical parts of the traumatic event (Weiss, 2007; Vermetten and Bremner, 2002).

Catecholamines. As has been discussed, trauma causes a number of changes to the brain, particularly to the developing brain, including to brain chemistry. It appears to contribute to markedly high levels of the catecholamines (epinephrine, norepinephrine, and dopamine) connected to some primary PTSD symptoms such as panic attacks, hypervigilance, exaggerated startle response, irritability, and intrusive thoughts and images (De Bellis, Baum et al., 1999).

Epinephrine. Epinephrine (also known as adrenaline) is a neurotransmitter that increases respiration, heart rate, metabolism, and certain cognitive activities. The state of hyperarousal induced by epinephrine may be useful in the short term, but those who have experienced extreme stress often display chronic central nervous system hyperarousal when exposed to trauma triggers (Bremner, 2005). Notably, van der Kolk (2003) observed that medications that decrease epinephrine generally reduce intrusive trauma memories, while those that increase arousal induce panic attacks or flashbacks.

Norepinephrine. Norepinephrine is another neurotransmitter that is active in arousal. It assists the system to remain alert and focused during periods of hyperarousal as well as seeming to attempt to balance the firing rate for central nervous system activity. The norepinephrine system is also vulnerable to becoming oversensitized through chronic activation, in which case the inhibitory function can be impaired (Weiss, 2007).

Dopamine. Dopamine has chemical similarities to adrenaline (epinephrine) in its messenger function. It is involved in brain processes that control movement, emotional response, and the ability to experience pleasure and pain. Research suggests that levels of dopamine are increased in the amygdala and prefrontal cortex by the presence of either acute or chronic stress (Vermetten and Bremner, 2002). Higher dopamine levels are associated with a variety of trauma-related symptoms such as feelings of depersonalization or derealization secondary to sensory processing problems, which are often seen in dissociative disorders. An abundance of this neurotransmitter can also contribute to hypervigilance and irritability (Weiss, 2007).

Serotonin. Serotonin is a well-known neurotransmitter and influences the frontal cortex during times of moderate stress by reducing anxiety and dysphoria. Extreme stress, though, appears to result in marked serotonin release in myriad brain regions which can ultimately cause serotonin depletion (Bremner, 2005; Matsumoto et al., 2005) Chronic serotonin activation can occur not only through repeated traumatic events but also through the ongoing reactivation of trauma memories. Decreased serotonin reduces an individual's ability to cope with additional stressors and may be related to typical PTSD symptoms of hyperarousal. Medications that make more serotonin available to the central nervous system (selective serotonin reuptake inhibitors, known as SSRIs) are thus particularly useful in assisting with arousal in response to stressful triggers (Weiss, 2007).

Stress Response Systems

At least two neural systems markedly affect stress reactions, arousal, physical and cognitive development, brain development, and emotion regulation (Watts-English, Fortson, Gibler, Hooper, and DeBellis, 2006). They are interrelated, such that difficulties in one system can lead to problems in the other. These stress systems are the *sympathetic-adrenomedullary (SAM) system* (or sympathetic nervous system) and the *hypothalamic-pituitary-adrenocortical (HPA) axis* (Taylor and Gonzaga, 2007). Both can manage the fight-or-flight response. Multiple papers from the literature document changes in both the SAM system and the HPA axis in PTSD sufferers (Pace and Heim, 2011).

Look at the sequential action map for stress and traumatic stress now, as you begin to read this account (color images K., Environmental Stressors Excite Neural Systems (phase 1), and L., Neural Systems Excite Body Action Systems (phase 2), and Negative Feedback Loop (phase 3)). Then refer to these representations of the three-phase process as needed while you read the steps in the process.

The SAM system is mediated primarily by epinephrine and norepinephrine. Messages from stressors in the environment are transmitted to the medulla in the brainstem, which sends neural messages to the adrenal medulla on top of the kidneys, directing it to release epinephrine and norepinephrine into the bloodstream. These transmitters are then dispersed around the body into specific tissues, where they direct receiving organs to dilate airways, increase blood pressure and heart rate, and make more energy sources such as glucose available (Taylor and Gonzaga, 2007).

The HPA Axis (sometimes referred to as the LHPA axis with L indicating *limbic*) is the primary biological stress response system (see, for example, Faravelli et al., 2010). In response to stress, it is the neural network that produces cortisol and then assists in feedback processes to curtail the stress response (Jackowski et al., 2009; Stien and Kendall, 2004). Chronic stress may result in the hypoactivation of the HPA axis as well as changes in the hormones of the axis (Pervanidou, 2008; Stien and Kendall, 2004).

Follow the indicators in color images K. and L. to see some of the workings of this process, as spelled out in the following steps.

Steps in the HPA process, with contributions from the SAM system:

1) An arousing event in the environment (or internal, such as pain or illness) activates sensory cells in the eyes, ears, skin, nose, and/or mouth.

2) Sensory neurons in the peripheral nervous system transmit these records of a sensory stimulus from the receiving cells to the spinal or cranial nerves, and thence to the *primary sensory cortex* in the brain. Whatever senses are engaged, records of different kinds of sensory stimulation (for example, warmth, pressure, or tickling, if the sense is touch) are then sent to the *sensory association cortex*.

3) In the sensory association cortex, these records are converted into perceptions of sight, sound, touch, smell, and/or taste, then transmitted to the hypothalamus. The amygdala is also an important link, and the hippocampus is involved as well in forming memories of the event. These structures send messages directly or indirectly to *effector systems* (systems that produce actions).

4) When the paraventricular nucleus of the hypothalamus receives the signal, it secretes a peptide called *corticotropin-releasing hormone (CRH)*, formerly known as *corticotropin-releasing factor (CRF)*, which is delivered to the nearby pituitary gland by tiny local blood vessels.

5) CRH stimulates the anterior lobe of the pituitary gland to produce adrenocorticotropic hormone (ACTH).

6) ACTH enters the general circulatory system (large blood vessels) and travels to the two adrenal glands, each located on top of one of the kidneys, where they stimulate the outer layer (*adrenal cortex*) to produce the hormones called *glucocorticoids*.

7) These glucocorticoids are released and dispatched all over the body via the circulatory system. Glucocorticoids (cortisol in humans,

and corticosterone in rats and mice) have receptors in cells of most peripheral tissues and in the brain, where these powerful chemicals initiate metabolic and neuromodulatory changes.

8) As the adrenal cortex is producing glucocorticoids, neurons in the *adrenal medulla* (inner section of adrenal gland) are producing their epinephrine and norepinephrine in response to messages by the sympathetic nervous system (SNS), specifically the SAM system mentioned above. These actions illustrate the interweaving of different functions to produce mutually enhancing effects.

9) Glucocorticoids themselves supply negative feedback to the HPA's production line, directly inhibiting pituitary ACTH secretion and CRH transcription (changes in the expression of brain CRH messenger RNA) (Aguilera, 2011). This activity goes beyond the scope of this book. This complex termination process involves many players: second messengers, metabolites, and additional hormones contribute to terminating the system's arousal action (Manzo, 2013). Although Chapter 8 on genetics and epigenetics does introduce this material, an in-depth analysis such as that of Aguilera (2011) is necessary to understand the process.

Glucocorticoids also have indirect effects on the CRH neuron by inhibiting stress-induced norepinephrine release from the paraventricular nucleus of the hypothalamus (Aguilera, 2011). Once secretion of CRH (corticotropin releasing hormone) and ACTH (adrenocorticotropic hormone) is inhibited, homeostasis is restored with respect to HPA arousal.

10) However, if stress-inducing events do not abate, the production cycle keeps repeating, eventually overriding the attempts of the negative feedback loop to reduce the secretion of more glucocorticoids. As these repetitions continue through time, at some unknown moment glucocorticoids around the body start to cause damage to body cells.

Several studies have found that children with histories of early-life trauma exhibited alterations in HPA activity. The varying results of these studies suggest that the effects of such early-life stress may differ, activated by multiple factors (Faravelli et al., 2010; Nemeroff, 2004; Neigh, Gillespie, and Nemeroff, 2009).

The two systems (HPA and SAM) account for both the protective effects and long-term harm of stress-managing systems (Taylor and Gonzaga, 2007). Under stressful conditions, these responses can have short-term benefits as they activate the body to respond to critical environmental stimuli and then allow for the return to homeostasis. However, repeated or recurrent stress responses can have implications for long-term health.

Large or ongoing doses of epinephrine and norepinephrine can suppress immune function, cause chronic increase in blood pressure, and provoke abnormal heart rhythms. Glucocorticoids have immunosuppressant effects, and stress-related increases in cortisol have been tied to an increased susceptibility to infectious disorders (Cohen et al., 2002; Taylor and Gonzaga, 2007).

Areas of inquiry. It is unclear whether certain neurobiological changes in PTSD are due to the consequences of the traumatic event and/or a correlate of PTSD, or, rather, are secondary to pre-existing vulnerability factors. Might the observed neurobiological changes in PTSD patients represent markers of neural risk to develop PTSD upon exposure to extreme stress, rather than markers of PTSD itself (Heim and Nemeroff, 2009)?

Several studies suggest that neuroendocrine dysregulation may be among the risk factors that predict development of PTSD under exposure to extreme stress (Pace and Heim, 2011). Charney has proposed an integrative model of resilience to extreme stress that centers on adaptive neurobiological factors impacting the stress response (2004). Matto and Strolin-Goltzman (2010) suggest that neuroprotective factors be included in existing social work resilience frameworks using risk/protective factor data, and that effectiveness of psychosocial interventions intended to promote neural reorganization and stronger neuroadaptive structures be assessed.

It will also be critical to identify both risk and resilience factors to assess an individual's potential for developing negative responses to extreme stress. In addition, increasing attention is being paid to the individual factors that may impact vulnerability to versus resilience against developing PTSD (such as genetic variations, gender, developmental exposure to stress) (Heim and Nemeroff, 2009).

Shalev (1996) suggested that much of PTSD research has been based on widely held but unproven assumptions that are important to explore. First, PTSD is often viewed as the eventual outcome for what begins as a normal response to an abnormal event. Shalev (ibid.) cites countervailing evidence that many experience relatively low-level events of traumatic exposure and yet develop significant PTSD, whereas the symptoms of some exposed to horrific trauma resolve over time. A related assumption is the concept that the response occurring at the time of the event will continue on to become chronic PTSD (Shalev, ibid.).

Gender difference is another area related to trauma outcomes that warrants additional attention. Mental health professionals have sometimes worked from anecdotal premises rather than research-based knowledge about gender. However, several scholars find the evidence persuasive that gender may have an impact on an individual's response to trauma (De Bellis and Keshavan, 2003; Weiss, 2007; Teicher et al., 1997). For example, over the past several decades, a number of trauma-related arenas (e.g., prevention, mental health, child welfare, victims' services) have focused on the increasing urgency of attending to the specific needs of females. One explanation is that significantly more females than males develop PTSD, with women's lifetime risk being twice that of men (Kessler et al., 2005).

However, neuroscience provides a more comprehensive picture. In fact, some studies suggest that males suffer more marked neural damage than females from extreme stress or trauma. For example, Teicher et al. (1997) found that the middle part of the corpus callosum was reduced in children with a history of maltreatment compared with psychiatric controls, with a more extreme effect on boys, who were also more likely to have smaller overall brain volume than did girls.

De Bellis, Keshavan et al. (1999) also found boys with PTSD to have significantly smaller corpora callosa than girls with similar symptoms. A study of 28 maltreated children and adolescents with PTSD found decreases in volume in several brain regions (intracranial, cerebral cortex, prefrontal cortex, prefrontal cortical white matter, and right temporal lobe) compared to matched controls (De Bellis et al., 2002) Larger ventricular volumes (spaces in the brain between structures, filled only with fluid) were found in boys with PTSD more than in girls. These findings supported the hypothesis that boys may be more vulnerable than girls to the impact of maltreatment-connected PTSD, even if the lifetime incidence of PTSD is greater in females (De Bellis and Keshavan, 2003).

There are variant theories about the reason for the greater risk for females developing PTSD. One theory is that women have a higher exposure over the life course to particular kinds of trauma such as such child sexual abuse and sexual assault (Pimlott-Kubiak and Cortina, 2003). Work by Breslau and others suggest the hypothesis that females are simply more likely to develop PTSD, and that this cannot be attributed to greater exposure to traumatic events (e.g., Breslau and Anthony, 2007; Breslau, Chilcoat, Kessler, Peterson, and Lucia, 1999).

Koenen and Widom (2009) note significant methodological challenges with many studies of child abuse victims that address gender questions. Many are retrospective, gender differences affect individuals' willingness to report certain abuse, and there is subject selection bias among many samples—all of which may influence the greater number of females in trauma studies. In addition, females overall are more likely than males to seek mental health services, but this fact does not necessarily suggest that they have greater symptomatology.

Developmental Sequelae of Traumatic Events, or Why Prevention Really Does Matter

An important goal of preventive intervention research is to identify specific periods in development when children may be able to benefit most from certain interventions (Cicchetti, 2010). There are sensitive periods for the development for particular capacities or windows of opportunity when the brain may be most available to certain experiences. An important example is that babies are predisposed to attach to caregivers. If the caregiver response is inconsistent or negative, the child's ability for healthy relationships may be permanently impaired.

The research is building that individuals who experience extreme stress or trauma early in life often manifest developmental consequences. The severity of these consequences depends on the timing of the event(s) as well as other factors. The argument for genetic vulnerability is underscored by the awareness that only a subset of children who experience negative events develop stress-related sequelae (Neigh et al., 2009).

These individuals—infants or children—have been hypothesized to develop pathophysiological alterations in the central nervous system that increase vulnerability to later stress, and predispose them to psychological and physical disorders. For example, early severe stress may elevate glucocorticoids and CHR, impacting vulnerable brain areas (Teicher, Andersen, Polcari, and Navalta, 2002). Also, the HPA axis influences endocrine systems that are critical for growth and development. Chronic changes to these systems as a result of stress may have irreversible effects on a child's growth and development (Charmandari, Tsigos, and Chrousos, 2005).

As observed earlier, the current DSM is imprecise relative to identifying the consequences of traumatic events in children and even adolescents. Clinicians and researchers have known for years that children do not manifest trauma the same way as adults and, sadly, this has resulted in many being misdiagnosed or not diagnosed, as well as the source of trauma going undetected. Certainly, some youth meet the criteria for PTSD, which has allowed them to be included in a number of studies. However, others present with some symptoms that appear to be linked to the stressor, but do not meet the PTSD profile. Studies have shown that even this more limited symptomatic response to stress can markedly impact children's functioning (Carrión, Weems, Ray, and Reiss, 2002). Those who don't meet full criteria are sometimes referred to as having posttraumatic stress symptoms (PTSS).

Lieberman and Van Horn (2009) urge practitioners to intervene actively with children, whether or not a formal diagnosis can be made, since the impact of traumatic events often derails normal acquisition of developmental skills with significant long-term consequences in a variety of domains. This derailment of typical developmental processes ranges from mild to disastrous neural-based changes in relationships, attention and impulsivity, and speech and language. Evidence suggests that these changes are likely to be lifelong.

Transgenerational effects of trauma. PTSD was long considered among the last of the mental health disorders to have primarily environmental etiologies. This view has been discredited. Growing evidence supports the transgenerational effects of trauma through various mechanisms affecting the mental health of the next generation. Parental PTSD is an established risk factor for childhood PTSD. It is likely that some of the effects are due to epigen-etic changes in the DNA (Meaney, Szyf, and Seckl, 2007). However, mothers' trauma symptom-related behavior is also likely to have an influence on chil-dren developing PTSD in a postnatal period. Thus, the genetic vulnerability may develop in relation to environmental contributions (Pervanidou, 2008). Pervanidou suggests that in utero effects are caused by fetal programming of the HPA axis that can contribute to offspring PTSD. Elevated glucocorticoid levels in pregnancy, induced by stress, impact fetal brain development as well as major organ development, and program the HPA axis (Neigh, Gillespie, and Nemeroff, 2009; Seckl, 2004). For example, mothers exposed to the World Trade Center attacks who developed PTSD demonstrated lower cortisol lev-els than those who were exposed but did not develop PTSD. Notably, lower cortisol levels were most evident in babies whose mothers were traumatized on September 11, 2001, in their third trimesters. Yet PTSD symptom severity in the entire sample was correlated with infant cortisol levels regardless of the trimester when the traumatic event took place (Yehuda et al., 2005).

Yehuda and colleagues published a number of studies related to chil-dren of Holocaust survivors. These outcomes support the environmental effects/epigenesis route of transmission, as the children of Holocaust survi-vors with PTSD reported to have suffered more emotional abuse and neglect than comparable children of parents without the disorder. Adult children of Holocaust survivors have also shown multiple alterations in HPA axis func-tion (Yehuda et al., 2002). To summarize, there is still much uncertainty about the precise mechanisms by which traumatization occurs, but if we continue to keep abreast of this area of research, we can be apprised of information to better understand and help families and individuals suffering from the conse-quences of traumatization.

24

🏛 Jason: Multiple Traumas, Social Work Interventions

By Elizabeth D'Amico, MSW, PhD

I met Jason in the early 1990s when I worked as a clinical worker on an inpatient child psychiatry unit just after finishing my MSW. There is no doubt that had I treated him today within a more informed neuroscience framework, his case would have been understood quite differently. Jason was only eight years old when he was admitted by his child protective service (CPS) worker and legal guardian, Marge. In the early 1990s, even private hospital stays for children were extended, allowing for comprehensive evaluations and history gathering, albeit in a restrictive setting, and thus I got to know a great deal about Jason's complex and all too common background.

Reason for admission. Jason was referred for admission by his foster parents and outpatient clinician due to his dangerous level of impulsivity and chronic aggression toward others in response to unclear antecedents. Jason was placed with caring, if overwhelmed, foster parents who were responsible for two other foster children plus two biological children. Two specific incidents that precipitated the hospitalization were his abrupt running out of the house into the street and almost being hit by a car, and, during a noisy family dinner, assaulting a younger foster brother by repeatedly striking him with a plate for unknown reasons. Since his functioning across almost all developmental domains was marginal, it was decided that a comprehensive inpatient evaluation was necessary, despite Jason having had a series of shorter hospitalizations for similar events.

Jason was a challenging child but, to his benefit, maintained a likeable quality that drew others to him. Despite periodic violent tantrums that at the extreme could eventually end in restraint (remember, this was the early 1990s) and more periodic verbal tirades, Jason had a smile that would break through when he appeared to feel comforted and a shy sense of humor that needed encouragement. He was artistic and had potential in a number of arenas that had not been developed.

Being likeable is not universally true of traumatized children, depending on a number of factors such as the degree, form, and timing of the stressors. Some children whose trauma occurs quite early in life may present as disconnected, or even cold, as a result of the particular neural damage that ensued.

Jason engaged with me via play, if only for fleeting moments when it appeared that he felt safe to do so, and generally his interaction of choice was playing war with little plastic army figures that on rare occasion he would engage in mock sexual activities. At other times, Jason would sit for a moment or two and then move frenetically from toy to toy. He constantly scanned his environment and rarely put his back to the door. Any unexpected noise would cause him to startle, resulting in a reaction from a jump to a screaming episode which could take some time to calm. This was more likely to occur on the unit where I observed him frequently appearing overwhelmed, seemingly by the degree of environmental stimulation. He presented somewhat like a child with attention deficit hyperactivity disorder (ADHD) but much more reactive.

Jason also at times had a "deer in the headlights" appearance. There was briefly a question as to whether he was suffering petit mal seizures which were quickly ruled out, and it was decided that he was presenting with more dissociative-like episodes in response to particular environmental stimuli, all of which were not clear.

Brief history. Jason was the oldest child born to his Caucasian mother, Anna, who was 18 at the time of his birth, and the only child to his parents, who were not married and together only briefly. Little information was available about the father except that he was 19, also Caucasian, and from a blue-collar background, known to be bright and an underachiever. Anna had been raised in a suburban New England town, the middle daughter of blue-collar parents who struggled with bills, depression, and alcoholism, generally providing structure and the basics for their children, if not always kindness. Anna left home at 17 and moved in with friends, and she continued a substance use pattern that had started in early adolescence. Her plan to finish high school vanished with her pregnancy with Jason. Although she tried to limit her substances during the nine months, she acknowledged that she was not entirely successful. Anna had two more children by other men in fairly rapid succession related to her drug use.

The next several years were ones of marginal living for Anna, baby Jason, and later his two siblings. For the first two years of Jason's life, Anna and Jason moved back with her parents, and Anna's mother did much of the caretaking for Jason, as Anna continued her lifestyle, despite some efforts to parent Jason and change her life course. For the next couple of years, Anna attempted to live on her own, or with friends. At some points, Jason and his siblings remained with their grandparents without Anna; at others, they lived with her. Suffice it to say, life was chaotic at best for the children. The child protective service caseworker, Marge, reported that there were dozens of reports to child protection related particularly to Jason but also to all three children, primarily for neglect. A few reports were made by a subsidized preschool Jason attended that found bruises on him. Ultimately it was determined that these were the result of his impulsivity rather than abuse. There were numerous instances when neighbors recognized that the three children (toddlers and infants) had been left alone while Anna went out. The time periods varied but seemingly were as long as 24 hours on one occasion. Since the apartment was an "open" door, it is unknown who was in and out when Anna wasn't there or what may have occurred in the presence of the children or to the children during those times.

Another report Anna herself called in which was an incident of four-year-old Jason's being sexually abused by an adolescent neighbor, which was confirmed. It was unclear how many incidents of abuse occurred but it was likely that these were ongoing occurrences. By the time Jason was five, the number and degree of CPS reports were such that the agency filed for his removal from his mother's custody. The grandparents agreed to take the two younger children, but the state would not allow them to take all three. Sadly, Jason—who was the most bonded to them—had to be placed in foster care.

By the time of the hospitalization when I met him, Jason was in his sixth foster placement since his removal from his mother, with several brief hospitalizations interspersed. Although the foster placements certainly varied in expertise and ability to manage an extremely challenging, complex young boy, even the most successful was only able to maintain Jason for six months before he disrupted, needing either hospital admission or another foster placement. Some event or series of events would engender the disruption: either an act of aggression toward some member of the family, or the foster parents tiring of his constant low frustration tolerance, tantrums, screaming, misinterpreting, attacking other children, using sexual language, not following directions, and related issues. It was as if they could not find a way to communicate with him or make him understand that he was safe. Although he had regular visits with his grandparents and siblings and somewhat less regular visits with his mother, these contacts did not seem to have an impact on his functioning— although he did reasonably well during the visits.

Brief developmental history. Jason was the result of an unplanned full-term pregnancy and normal vaginal delivery. There was no prenatal care until the sixth month and mother states she did not know she was pregnant until the fourth month. Mother acknowledges using some unspecified substances during pregnancy. Jason presented with some jaundice that resolved without issue. Birth weight was 5 pounds, 2 ounces. Grandmother reports that milestones were generally within normal limits although talking was slightly delayed and toilet training was not completely accomplished until age four and a half. No significant medical issues are reported. Jason is on the low end of normal limits for height and weight for his developmental age. There are no physiological indicators of genetic or chromosomal anomalies. Dental care is adequate. There has been no known exposure to lead.

Jason has not received any early intervention but was in preschool for approximately six months prior to starting kindergarten. In kindergarten, the teacher reported that he was unable to pay attention, did not attend or follow directions, was impulsive, highly reactive to other children, and easily over-stimulated by the environment, moving rapidly to a physical response.

Mental status exam. Jason presented as a thinly built Caucasian male who appeared somewhat younger than his stated age of eight years and two months. His grooming was adequate if a bit haphazard, as evidenced by his somewhat disheveled clothes. It was unclear whether his partly tied sneak-ers were due to inattentiveness or difficulty with the task itself. Activity level was moderate to high as Jason had difficulty sitting during the interview and frequently got up and walked around. Mood was dysphoric; affect varied from sad to irritable. Jason appeared mildly anxious. There were no obsessions or compulsions noted. Attention and frustration tolerance were fair to poor as Jason struggled to respond to questions without becoming irritated, continu-ally asking when he could leave. Jason displayed impulsivity as he frequently would get up and move about the room, pick up objects, asking if he could have them. Speech was normal in rate, tone, and cadence but content of speech was unusual for this child's age as it contained periodic obscenities and ref-erences to sexual content. There was apparent mild oppositionality noted as he was slow to respond to redirection but it was unclear to the interviewer whether this was a refusal of the request or a potential lack of understanding. No verbal or physical aggression was evidenced although it was reported by history. There was no frank evidence of hallucinations, delusions, or formal thought disorder. Intelligence was estimated to be in the average range with significant scatter. Tested intelligence placed Jason in the low average range overall with significantly higher capacity in the performance than verbal areas. It is unlikely that the full standard IQ score was a valid measurement of his true cognition, however, due to the impact of his psychiatric issues on the test-ing. (Note: due to his young age, there are limits to IQ validity.) Judgment and insight were fair to poor.

Brief neuroscience formulation. The stress response systems are among only a few neural systems that if poorly functioning can create dysfunction in all major areas of the brain (Perry and Szalavitz, 2006). It is likely that Jason's history of abuse, chronic early exposure to toxic, unpredictable stress, and potential genetic vulnerability to stress combined to create a number of his problematic symptoms.

Although it is unknown whether Jason's mother, Anna, met the diagnostic criteria for PTSD, it is probable that she experienced significant stress during the pregnancy with him. Research confirms that this may have impacted his brain and organ development but more specifically and critically the HPA axis. If Anna was then unable to be a consistent caregiver during early develop-ment, this would have caused another form of stress but also one that again impacts the HPA system through the elevation of glucocorticoids and CHR. Any mitigation of this stress was through the consistency and nurturing provided by Anna's parents, during Jason's critical developmental periods.

Conclusion

As Matto and Strolin-Goltzman aptly point out,

> The social work knowledge base of the next decade has potential to be supported by interdisciplinary scientific findings that inform advocacy efforts regarding health disparities, impart policy decisions, contribute to practitioner education/training, and facilitate more effective service-delivery decisions through new treatment developments and evaluation plans (2010, pp. 154-155).

My own view, in agreement with Matto and Strolin-Goltzman, is that social workers must become exquisitely well informed about the neuroscience of trauma so that they may be competent participants in the areas outlined above. The stakes are too high to allow this profession to remain but guests at the neuroscience table. We need to be assertive, active players who comprehend the rules, the stakes, and the neuroscientific operations that mediate traumatic stress.

PART IV

Substance Abuse and Addiction

DEFINITIONS, CONTRIBUTING FACTORS, AND INTERVENTIONS

25

Addiction: Definitions, Risk and Protective Factors

What is addiction? As with mental illness, definitions are strongly influenced by culture and at the same time deeply rooted in biology. Although the World Health Organization (1992) and the American Psychiatric Association (2000) have substituted the term *drug dependence*, the words *drug addiction* are still widely used today. Yet confusion spawned by the word *dependence* has led to pressure to return to *addiction* in the fifth edition of the *Diagnostic and Statistical Manual of Mental Disorder (DSM)* (Nutt, Lingford-Hughes, and Chick, 2012).

A recent analysis of definitions of addiction based on 52 studies of elements of addiction (Sussman and Sussman, 2011) includes five components: (1) engagement in the behavior to achieve appetitive effects, (2) preoccupation with the behavior, (3) temporary satiation, (4) loss of control, and (5) suffering negative consequences. The definition we have used in this book comprises four of the five: *compulsive, persistent seeking and using a substance or engaging in another behavior despite major adverse consequences for the individual and/or others, for the purpose of experiencing either intense pleasure or relief from an aversive state.* Substances of abuse and non–substance addictive behaviors act as positive reinforcers (giving a "rush" or euphoria) or as negative reinforcers (offering escape from or avoidance of withdrawal symptoms or painful emotional states). The definition we use applies unequivocably to nondrug situations, including not only nondrug consumables (food) but also behaviors such as gambling, shopping, or Internet gaming, when the four criteria of this definition are applied. Just enjoying gambling, shopping, or Internet gaming does not constitute "addiction" until it has reached the level of intensity described. The subject is still controversial, with some authors challenging the notion that the addictive experience goes beyond alcohol and other drugs (see for example Doweiko, 2012; Ziauddeen and Fletcher, 2013).

Addiction connotes a subjective state of urgent wanting. Addicted persons may maintain abstinence for long periods of time and remain addicted nevertheless (still with potential for relapse), for reasons we'll explain later.

What images does the word *addict* bring to mind? Perhaps a street person, unwashed, usually in the inner city, living outside the law, and dark-skinned?

The facts belie this stereotype. The vast majority of addicted Americans are Caucasians of all socioeconomic levels who are steady and frequent users of caffeine, alcohol, or nicotine—all legal and all, arguably, addictive. I concur with a widely but not universally held opinion that another kind of addiction is to the pleasure of food, and further that obesity/overweight, now epidemic in the United States, often results from relationships with food (in general or with a particular food) that meet the criteria for addiction used in this book (see above). The view that *addiction* is an apt and appropriate word as applied to compulsive overeating, like compulsive over-drinking or over-drugging, is supported by neuroscience research conducted by the director of the National Institute of Drug Abuse (NIDA) and several other leading neuroscientists (Volkow, Wang, Tomasi, and Baler, 2012), but others argue that more research is needed to confirm this view (Ziauddeen and Fletcher, 2013).

Another way of thinking about addiction is as a vulnerable individual's response to taking addictive substances with sufficient dose (enough of it), frequency (often enough), and chronicity (over a long enough period of time) to enter an addicted condition (Hyman, 1995).

Vulnerability is a very complicated state. The same individual can have different levels of vulnerability in different environments or life situations at different times in his or her life. For example, you may not be a vulnerable person most of the time, but when you lose your significant other or get fired from your job, you may become vulnerable to substance abuse or addiction.

How many of us can claim honestly that we're free of addiction? For example, I know I'm addicted to a substance—sugar (I can't conceive of a day without ice cream, cake, or pudding, and a fairly generous amount of it at that). Even bowls of cereal with heaps of sugar and saturated fat–free almond or soy milk take the edge off the craving. How am I different from poor homeless people addicted to crack of heroin? Answer: I've had a luckier roll of the dice in life, and my addiction is socially acceptable in the dominant culture.

My addiction, however, is similar to those of people addicted to crack or heroin with respect to the neurobiological process by which I became addicted, the eager seeking and compulsive use of a substance, and strong cravings to the point of obsession when the substance is withdrawn. Are there serious negative consequences? Though not visible to others, fairly often my body communicates unpleasant sensations related to overconsumption, and there are some ominous warnings. These substances contribute to chronic gastritis and inflammation that are known to predispose to stomach cancer, which I did contract and from which I was lucky enough to recover more than a decade ago.

Concepts related to addiction include tolerance, dependence, and sensitization. *Tolerance* refers to the loss of effect of a drug after repeated administration over a long time on a frequent schedule, so that more and more is needed to produce the same high. *Dependence* is defined as a state in which stopping a drug suddenly ("cold turkey") causes withdrawal sickness that is dramatically relieved by another dose of the same drug (Goldstein, 2001, pp. 88–90). Where does the term "cold turkey" come from? The gooseflesh symptom of withdrawal from opiates gave rise to that expression.

Sensitization is the opposite of tolerance. The drug's effect is enhanced rather than diminished with repeated use, which sometimes happens with a few particular drugs when taken rapidly and repeatedly such as cocaine (Goldstein, 2001). Sensitization refers to persistent hypersensitivity to a drug's effect in a person with a history of exposure to that drug (Cami and Farré, 2003).

From risk factors for addiction to a changed brain. In Part I, we defined risk and protective factors. Risk factors are biological or nonbiological variables in individuals and in environments, interacting through time, to cause or exacerbate problems of physical health, mental wellbeing, and social conditions. Protective factors are the converse of risk factors, acting to diminish problems in these areas. With respect to addiction, the more risk factors and the fewer protective factors we have, the more likely it is that we'll get hooked. These risk factors fall into the categories of individual vulnerability, environmental factors, and drug effects, which differ according to the drug (see Table 25.1).

TABLE 25.1 Risk Factors for Addiction

Individual vulnerability

(some aspects can change over time)
- genetic
- psychiatric condition
- chronic pain
- feeling stressed
- user goals (such as experimentation, escape).

Environmental factors

- drug availability—if you can't get it, you won't become addicted no matter how vulnerable you are
- peer-group pressure to use
- lack of behavioral alternatives to drug use (no opportunities for fun or satisfaction)
- settings in which drugs are used such as religious ceremonies, family holidays
- presence of conditioned cues (such as being at a place where you used to use frequently, or running into drug-using friends)

Drug effects (drugs differ)

- drug's addictiveness (some are highly addictive, such as cocaine; others are not very addictive, such as LSD)
- drug purity
- route of administration (for example, you'll get addicted to cocaine faster if you freebase than if you snort)
- dose
- frequency of use
- chronicity of use

26

Brain Structures and Systems Involved in Substance Abuse and Addiction

Brain structures referred to here have been described in Parts II and III. Systems of major importance are the *mesolimbic dopamine pathway*, also called the *pleasure pathway*, and the *mesocorticolimbic* system. These are not exclusive neural pathways. Numerous varying paths connect structures in these regions.

The mesolimbic dopamine pathway originates in neurons in the ventral tegmental area (VTA) of the midbrain (upper brainstem) (see color image D., Larger Inner Brain Structures and Cerebellum). The axons of these neurons transmit dopamine messages to the nucleus accumbens in the forebrain region of the *limbic system*. These travel routes, highways in the midst of a bustling crowded lively neural metropolis, are the scenes of celebration: pleasures, delights, discoveries, and fun. No wonder they are sometimes referred to as hedonic highways, sites of some well-known hedonic hotspots (see color image J. (1), Hedonic Hotspots).

The mesocorticolimbic system adds prefrontal cortex efforts—the "cortico" part—to limbic and brainstem activity. That is, it adds cognition to the dopamine pathways mix of drives and emotions—perhaps we can call it "enlightened passion," or maybe "passionate enlightenment?" The *substantia nigra* also dispatches dopamine to the basal ganglia rather than the nucleus accumbens (see color image D., Larger Inner Brain Structures and Cerebellum).

All drugs of abuse are believed to act by using at least one of these systems. The systems act in parallel (separately) and also in tandem (interactively) to mediate substance abuse, addictive behaviors, and the processes of becoming addicted.

The mesolimbic dopamine pathway may be the most important circuit involved in reward. In this system, a bundle of nerve fibers (axons) project from the VTA in the midbrain to the nucleus accumbens (NAc) where the limbic system overlaps with the forebrain (see color images J. (1), Hedonic Hotspots and M., Cocaine in Action). Opioid pathways also participate in reward by adding their actions to the effects of the actions of dopamine in the nucleus accumbens. The action of opiate drugs gives highs by inhibiting the natural dopamine inhibitors GABA (see color image N., Natural Opioids and

Opiate Drugs). Messages are often relayed through the amygdala and/or the hypothalamus as part of these circuits.

Another limbic structure involved in addiction is the hippocampus, a major actor in memory formation. The mesolimbic dopamine pathway has a role in creating privileged memories of highly rewarding novel stimuli. These memories cause addicts to have cravings and risk relapse even after years of abstinence. The limbic system plays a key role in determining what is salient enough to be remembered.

The mesocorticolimbic circuit projects from the prefrontal cortex to the region of the nucleus accumbens and the VTA, involving the anterior cingulate (mediates response inhibition and initiation), and the orbitofrontal cortex (mediates ability to evaluate future consequences and balance immediate rewards against long-term negative consequences).These structures are involved in the conscious experience of drug-taking, cravings, and compulsions (Cavedini, Riboldi, et al., 2002).

Basal ganglia structures, the caudate nucleus and the putamen (together called the striatum) are also involved. The hypothalamus, located near the limbic region and the basal ganglia, is activated when stress is contributing to addictive responses. The hypothalamus controls many hormones, including those that help the individual cope with stress, such as cortisol (see Chapter 35).

The prefrontal cortex, critical for higher cognitive functions such as executive planning, working memory, hypothesis generation, response inhibition, action initiation, and problem-solving, is also importantly involved in substance abuse and addiction. Some cognitive dysfunctions are seen fairly often in heavy users, such as poor appraisal of likely consequences of behavior, overvaluation of drug effects, difficulty making decisions, and poor response inhibition. Interactions between mesolimbic structures and prefrontal and other cortical structures mediate cognitive functions.

Color image F., Favorite Highways for Pleasure-Making Neurotransmitters, shows some of the neurotransmitters that carry out these processes related to reward and cognition. The arrows in color image F., Favorite Highways for Pleasure-Making Neurotransmitters, illustrate these regions. Please turn to color image F. here. The arrows help us visualize these regions.

Dopamine (DA) neurons originate in the VTA and project their axons *to* the nucleus accumbens, the amygdala, and structures in the region of the prefrontal cortex. Neurons processing glutamate (GLU), the major excitatory transmitter in the brain, send messages *from* the prefrontal cortex to the VTA and the nucleus accumbens.

Neurons processing GABA, the major inhibitory transmitter in the brain, send messages from the NAc to the prefrontal cortex and also act on the VTA and the nucleus accumbens. Opioid-processing neurons (OP on the diagram in color image F.) modulate GABA's inhibitory influence on the release of dopamine in the VTA and also affect the release of norepinephrine (NE) from the locus coeruleus. Serotonin neurons (5-HT) originate in the raphé nuclei and project to the VTA, the nucleus accumbens, and the striatum, where they modulate release of dopamine. These processes are described by Cami and Farré (2003).

These networks are very complicated, and it's not necessary to "master" this information in order to use it to help your clients. You do need a basic understanding of the ways some rewarding and cognitive events take place in relation to specific drugs such as alcohol, cocaine, opiates, and nicotine, and the ways that using drugs or engaging in addictive behaviors leads us to become addicted.

27

How Do We Become Addicted?

Chronic use of drugs causes long-lived molecular changes in the signaling properties of neurons. Depending on the drug and the circuits involved, these adaptations have different effects on behavior and different time-courses of initiation and decay (Hyman, 1995). With chronic drug use, three types of changes may take place in the brain centers that control somatic functions (body functions), rewards and pleasures, and emotional memories. We can see physical effects of drugs that affect somatic functions when the drug is withdrawn. We can't see the physical effects of drugs on reward and pleasure pathways in the brain or on emotional memories, but these effects are physical too. They are just as real, and just as physical, as common somatic effects of withdrawal from alcohol (e.g., tremor, hypertension, grand mal seizures, tachycardia, irritability, delusions, hallucinations); caffeine (e.g., headache, fatigue); or opiates (e.g., severe muscle cramps, bone ache, diarrhea, tearing, hypothermia or hyperthermia, insomnia, restlessness, nausea, gooseflesh).

Only a few drugs involve somatic dependence, but almost all drugs of abuse are believed to induce the other two kinds of changes in brain structures and functions. With respect to brain reward and pleasure pathways, changes both in micro-anatomic structures and chemical processes involve motivation and volition.

Motivational aspects of withdrawal are

- dysphoria: feeling sad, blue, down in the dumps;
- anhedonia: inability to experience pleasure or to enjoy things enjoyed in the past; and
- cravings: need to have the substance or do the behavior, *fast.*

The person suffering from these feelings experiences a change in behavioral priorities, so that getting the drug of abuse often becomes the most important goal in life.

Changes in emotional memories are a hallmark of addiction. During a lifetime, many memories are eventually lost through decay of memory traces in the brain. However, memories of powerful experiences remain. Cues evoke these memories of either intensely pleasurable experiences, leading to cravings in addiction, or intensely painful experiences, leading to traumatic flooding, as in posttraumatic stress disorder (PTSD). These memories are referred to as *privileged* memories because they take precedence both in affecting the individual's emotional state and in motivating behavior.

These latter two types of long-term changes—changes in structures and functions affecting motivation and volition, and changes in emotional memories—are actual physical effects in the brain that you cannot see. We used to distinguish between *physical* and *psychological* addiction by the presence or absence of somatic withdrawal, such as tremors, nausea, or muscle cramps. Now we know that all drugs of abuse produce actual physical changes in the brain. Even though many of the physical effects of drugs on the brain are not directly observable, they are just as real as tremors and muscle cramps.

How long do these brain changes last? Somatic withdrawal may last days, weeks, sometimes even longer. Motivational aspects of withdrawal may last from several weeks to months, even years. Emotional memories may last a lifetime—we may never shake them off. That is, once addicted, you may never "withdraw" from the memories of intense pleasure associated with a substance or a behavior. That's why Alcoholics Anonymous members with years of sobriety call themselves "recovering," not "recovered," alcoholics.

Each drug has its own special neurotransmitter. Drugs of abuse work in the brain through different neurotransmitter systems. Some drugs affect several transmitters through a chain of reactions. Table 27.1 shows some of the transmitters that are active with different drugs.

The complex neurobiological processes identified over the past decade that underlie these effects are reported in numerous sources (see, for example, Yang, Zheng, Wang et al., 2004; Thompson, Swant, Gosnell et al., 2004; Bolanos and Nestler, 2004; Wang, Gao, Zhang et al., 2003; National Institute on Drug Abuse (NIDA), 2004). A process referred to by Wang and colleagues was "abnormal engagement of long-term associative memory."

Current theories of addiction rely heavily on neurobiological evidence showing connections between addiction-related behaviors and neural

TABLE 27.1 Neurotransmitters That Are Active with Different Drugs

Drug	Neurotransmitter
Opiates/Heroin	Endorphins/enkephalins
Cocaine/Amphetamine	Dopamine
Nicotine	Acetylcholine
Alcohol	GABA, opioids, and others
Marijuana (cannabinoid)	THC receptor ligand anandamide
Hallucinogens	Serotonin
Caffeine	Adenosine

But.... most roads lead to dopamine highways.

structures and functions. These connections have been identified by imaging, biochemical analyses, genetic studies, and laboratory experiments.

It is widely agreed that all drugs of abuse act on dopamine systems either directly or indirectly. Determining the role of dopamine has been the predominant focus of addiction research during the past 20 years (Kalivas, 2004). Drug seeking and drug self-administering in humans and animals can be triggered either by direct exposure to drugs of abuse or by stressful events, both of which increase strength of excitatory synapses on mesolimbic dopamine neurons (Saal, Dong et al., 2003).

Moreover, it appears that other forms of addiction, such as compulsive gambling, also create feelings of pleasure, excitement, or satisfaction through dopamine pathways (Cami and Farré, 2003; Goudriaan, Oosterlaan et al., 2004; Ibanez, Blanco et al., 2003).

Behavioral addictions are increasingly being found to resemble substance addictions in many domains: natural history, phenomenology (how we perceive things, not what their inner essence may be), tolerance, comorbidity, overlapping genetic contribution, neurobiological mechanisms, and response to treatment) (Cami and Farré, 2003).

Addiction to nonconsumables (such as gambling, shopping/spending, internet games, some forms of sexuality), and a consumable nondrug, food, engages similar neurobiological structures and processes as addiction to alcohol and other drugs. This evidence supports the DSM-5 Task Force's proposed emended category of Addiction and Related Disorders, encompassing both substance abuse and nondrug addictions. This more-inclusive addiction category might be appropriate for nondrug addictions such as food, gambling, internet use, shopping/spending, or sexuality. In addicted states, one or more of these substances or behaviors has advanced from "Wow, that feels great!" to "Must have/must do no matter what the cost!"

When does experiencing pleasure cross the line into addiction? That depends on your definition of addiction (see Sussman and Sussman, 2011). Commonly used definitions often co-occur with the observer seeing the addicted person as having failed cognitively and emotionally to correctly evaluate the benefits and costs of continued use. Apparently, those who continue to seek the addictive object conclude, on an emotional level, that deprivation of that object would be more aversive than those (admittedly negative) consequences. This view raises the question as to whether the addicted person might ever be justified in his or her choice. Most of us professional helpers overwhelmingly support sobriety and drug-free choices—are there ever situations in which the addicted person's choice to continue using might be better for him or her on the pros/cons balance scale?

The concept of reward is central to most views of addiction. Several brain circuits, structures, and neurotransmitters are involved in the reward process. Dopamine has had front runner status in this regard for several decades, but other neurotransmitter systems (those that process serotonin, norepinephrine, opioids, GABA, and glutamate) also have important roles in the regulation of reward. Among neuroscientists, it has been widely accepted for some time that dopamine mediates the rewarding (reinforcing) properties of natural stimuli such as food and sex as well as drugs of abuse.

However, it appears that the relationship between dopamine and food or sex is more complex than was previously thought. Recent studies indicate that pleasure from food or sex (*hedonic response* in scientific terms) may continue in laboratory animals even when dopamine functions are suppressed. For some addictions, dopamine may promote effort to get and consume (food) or to perform an act (having sex) without mediating the reward process itself (another transmitter may be responsible for reward). Is dopamine the happy chemical? I vote for "often, yes, always, no" (Cannon and Bseikri, 2004; Salamone, Correa, Mingote et al., 2003; Berridge and Robinson, 2003; Wise, 2004; Hajnal et al., 2004; Giuliano and Allard, 2001; Paredes and Ågmo, 2004).

Cannon and Bseikri (2004), despite their own research showing that dopamine is not necessary for food pleasure in laboratory animals, conclude that there's reason to think it's important. In a recent review article on drug addiction, Cami and Farré state unequivocally, "Both natural rewards (food, drink, and sex) and addictive drugs stimulate the release of dopamine" (2003, p. 980). Studies have found the transmitter to be involved in drugs of abuse, gambling (Goudriaan et al.,2004), food (Wise, 2004; Hajnal et al., 2004), sex (Giuliano and Allard, 2001), pair-bond formation (Young, Lim et al., 2001), listening to music (Sutoo and Akiyama, 2004), seeing attractive faces (Kampe, Frith et al., 2001), video games (Koepp, Gunn et al., 1998), positive social interactions (Vandenschuren, Niesink et al., 1997; Hansen, Bergvall, and Nyiredi, 1993), and best of all, humor (Mobbs, Greicius et al., 2003).

Yes, humor is fun and feels good—is it surprising that Mobbs and colleagues, using fMRI (functional magnetic resonance imaging), found that humor activates the dopamine-processing pleasure pathway in the brain? To clarify the role of dopamine in reward, Cannon and Bseikri (2004), citing Mobbs et al., quip that scientific progress would be greatly expedited if we were all simply funnier. I agree. Next time you're late to work, might you try telling your boss that you were late because of a herniated hippocampus?

Other views of addiction expand existing theories of reward by separating its psychological components, based on processes that are related to each other but operate through different circuits. These are *learning* through the experience of using, *liking* that experience (pleasure that usually diminishes over time), and *wanting* to repeat it (Berridge and Robinson, 2003). These researchers believe that although liking often decreases over time, wanting often increases, continuing to be a powerful motivator even when using is no longer enjoyable. One common reason given by addicted persons is that they have to escape from intolerable effects of being in an addicted state. That is, they are in a sometimes desperate pursuit of negative reinforcement, defined as the response to avoiding or escaping from aversive stimuli (Miltenberger, 2012).

Goldstein and Volkow (2002) have expanded the focus on limbic subcortical structures to include structures in the frontal cortex using findings from neuroimaging studies. They found that the orbitofrontal and anterior cingulate cortices, regions neuroanatomically connected with limbic structures, are the frontal cortical areas most frequently implicated in drug addiction. These structures are activated in addicted subjects during intoxication, craving, and bingeing; deactivated during withdrawal; and also involved in higher-order cognitive and motivational functions. That is, addiction connotes cognitive and emotional processes, regulated by the frontal cortex, that result in overvaluing drug reinforcers, decreasing sensitivity to alternative reinforcers (that is, perceiving them as less desirable), and deficient inhibitory control for drug responses (Volkow, Fowler, and Wang, 2002). These changes in addiction, called *salience attribution* and *impaired response inhibition* respectively, expand traditional concepts of drug dependence that emphasize limbic system responses to pleasure and reward.

A related view cites evidence that compulsive drug use and its persistence arise from pathological usurpation of molecular mechanisms involved in memory (Hyman and Malenka, 2001), a process we spelled out earlier. This process characterizes the takeover of the addicted person's life so familiar to users, their families, and those of us who try to help them grapple with addiction.

Another theory proposes that specific brain reward and stress circuits become dysregulated during the development of alcohol dependence (Koob, 2003). Parts of the amygdala and the nucleus accumbens (a grouping called the *extended amygdala*) mediate multiple neurotransmitter systems that process GABA, opioid peptides, glutamate, serotonin, and dopamine. Withdrawal from drugs of abuse is associated with subjective negative affect, accompanied by action of stress hormones. This "toxic" effect of chronic drug use creates an ongoing state of vulnerability for relapse.

There is fast-growing evidence that the excitatory transmitter glutamate plays a central role in processes underlying the development and maintenance of addiction (Kalivas, 2004; Tzschentke and Schmidt, 2003). In the last five years, 3,718 articles using the two keywords "glutamate" and "addiction" have been listed in PubMed, with only 1,528 for all years together prior to March 2008 (date of search March 8, 2013). Glutamate dispatched from the prefrontal cortex to the nucleus accumbens appears to promote reinstatement of drug-seeking behavior. That is, glutamate maybe a major contributor to relapse. In particular, context-specific aspects of behavior (control over behavior by conditioned stimuli, such as cues like running into a drug-using companion or going down a street where a beloved bar is located), involve the transmission of glutamate.

The pace of finding new knowledge about the influence of genetics has also accelerated in recent years, culminating in the publication of the Human Genome Project reports in 2003 and the subsequent decade of research on the genetics of addiction (see for example Alia-Klein et al., 2011; Li, et al., 2011).

The roles of genes in addiction are elusive because substance abuse is a product of polygenetic action and is strongly influenced by environments through epigenetic systems in the brain (see Chapter 8). Data have been available for many years showing much higher risks for alcohol addiction in biological children of substance abusing parents adopted at birth into non–substance-abusing homes, than for adopted children without a family history of addiction (Schuckit, 1985). Specific genes and variants of genes (alleles) have been identified that either protect individuals from addiction by, for example, causing aversive effects from ingesting certain substances, or put individuals at risk for various types of substance abuse (Alia-Klein et al., 2011; Cami and Farré, 2003; Comings and Blum, 2000).

Hommer, Bjork, and Gilman (2011) compared evidence from PET and fMRI neuroimaging studies pertaining to two important hypotheses about how alterations in the brain's reward system (getting intense pleasure or almost no pleasure from rewards that give mild or moderate pleasure to typi-cal people) underlie addiction. The *impulsivity hypothesis* proposes that exces-sive sensitivity to reward combined with a failure of inhibition characterizes addiction. The *reward-deficiency hypothesis* postulates that a reduced response to nondrug rewards (for example, not getting the typical amount of pleasure and satisfaction from sensory enjoyment such as eating) leads people to seek drugs to compensate for this deprivation.

The PET studies of dopamine receptor density and dopamine release strongly supported the reward-deficiency hypothesis, whereas fMRI studies of goal-directed behavior supplied both support and contradiction for each of the hypotheses. The authors' view was that both the impulsivity and reward-deficiency hypotheses may contribute to addictive conditions (Hommer et al, 2011).

Alia-Klein and colleagues (2011) found that (1) individuals with cocaine use disorder had reductions in gray matter volume in the orbitofrontal (OFC), dorsolateral prefrontal (DLPFC) and temporal cortex, and hippocampus, compared to controls; (2) the reductions in the OFC were uniquely driven in cocaine users who had both a particular genotype (low MAO-A) and lifetime cocaine use, a gene/environment interaction; and (3) reduced gray matter in the DLPFC and hippocampus was driven by lifetime alcohol use in conjunc-tion with cocaine use. The study is the first to demonstrate the enhanced sen-sitivity of cocaine users who are low MAO-A carriers to gray matter loss in the OFC, indicating that this specific genotype may exacerbate the harmful effects of cocaine in the brain. Concurrent cocaine and chronic alcohol use was a major contributor to gray matter loss in the DLPFC and hippocampus, increasing impairments in executive function and learning that result from cocaine addiction. The interactive effects of genes and long-term use of a drug, and the potential harm of using certain drugs together (in this case cocaine + alcohol), are illustrated in this study.

The prominent role of neurobiology in serious medical, psychological, and social problems related to addiction has led to efforts to identify and use pharmacological agents (i.e., more drugs) to treat drug addiction. Let's briefly review the kinds of medications in use.

There are at least three types of drugs for treating addictions: agonists, antagonists, and aversive agents. *Agonists* bind with receptor molecules in a similar fashion to the drug of abuse and prevent withdrawal symptoms, but do not give the high of the drug of abuse. For example, methadone binds to opiate receptors in place of heroin, prevents heroin withdrawal, and takes away the craving for heroin. Nevertheless, the street marketability of some treatment drugs such as methadone suggests that they do give some kind of a high. Another problem with agonists is that they are also likely to be addictive, so the user substitutes one addiction for another. The advantages are that the person may be able to function (e.g., hold a job) better than when using the original drug, and that the prevention of withdrawal symptoms and cravings diminishes the need for criminal behavior to get money for the drug of abuse.

Antagonists bind with receptors in a different way from the drug of abuse (competitive binding at the receptor site). Taking the drug of abuse gives no high because the antagonist drug now occupies the receptors meant for the brain's own neurotransmitters. The craving, however, is not satisfied. For example, naltrexone binds to opioid receptors and blocks the effects of heroin, but does not remove the craving for heroin or other opiate drugs. Since the antagonist therapeutic drug now blocks the effect of the original drug, the user may just substitute a different drug of abuse for the original drug. Researchers are developing and testing new drugs that combine agonist and antagonist actions in the hope of remedying the limitations of each type of medication.

Aversive agents, such as disulfiram (Antabuse) for alcohol addiction, deter drug use by making you very sick if you use the drug while taking the medication. But there's a way around that too—want to get high? Just take a different drug that does not make you sick when combined with Antabuse. For that reason, probably, this medication has not been very successful except with people highly motivated to get sober.

28

Cultures of Therapy and the Recovery Boondoggle

So far we've been reviewing science-based knowledge about addictions and the psychology of substance use and addictive behaviors. Practitioners of healing, unfortunately, have too often disregarded science or repudiated it outright. Because these popular leaders of psychological movements are so influential, it's important to discuss the topic here at least briefly. Culturally based influences, including some antiscientific treatment cultures typically led by well-known gurus of recovery, have attracted a huge following among people who are unhappy for reasons that they may not understand and that make them vulnerable to zeal and dogma.

Recovery movement gurus like John Bradshaw (2005, 1988) and Charles Whitfield (2006, 1987) have often generalized from specific instances to include in the category of "addict" almost everyone with almost any kind of emotional or behavioral characteristic. The inescapable corollary is that all these people purportedly need treatment on the basis of replies to items on a questionnaire. While we believe the evidence supports a notion that almost everyone has a penchant for a substance or behavior that gives enough pleasure to cause something like cravings when it is unavailable, by no means do most people need treatment for this state of being. These psychology entrepreneurs have generated millions in revenue from unhappy people looking for answers through sale of their books, televised appearances, and attendance fees at workshops, "therapeutic" cruises, and resort vacations. A four-hour documentary by Ofra Bikel, *Divided Memories*, first aired on *Frontline* on April 4, 1994, and numerous published critiques by writers such as Elizabeth Loftus, Carol Tavris, and Wendy Kaminer have dramatized the dangers of these enterprises. Psychologist Michael Yapko has poked fun at these popular therapies (1994, pp. 144–146).

"I have a cartoon I sometimes show in my workshops. It shows a huge auditorium with a banner hanging on the wall that says 'Annual Convention of Adult Children of Normal Parents.' In this huge auditorium are scattered only a half-dozen attendees." Pathologizing common human emotional experiences has been the subject of critical appraisals in social work, not only from the strengths perspective, but also in the context of ecosystems and evidence-based approaches (see for example Chapters 4, 7, 9 and 39).

Popular psychology has expanded the usage of the word *addiction* to include women who "love too much" (have a pattern of attachments to hurtful partners), "workaholics" (who work too long and too hard), and "codependents" (significant others of addicted persons who supposedly *need* to have an addicted partner).

Some people in these groups can sometimes meet criteria for science-based definitions of addiction when they not only have overpowering cravings that they compulsively and repetitively seek to satisfy despite very adverse consequences, but also have shown similar patterns of brain functions on radiologic scans. In cases where compulsive work or repeated hurtful partners is found to resemble the process that has been identified for addictive drugs and gambling, that interpretation might be justified.

Here's an example that does seem to meet criteria for addiction as we've defined it. What about a middle-aged woman who has partnered for many years with a succession of men 15 to 30 years younger than her, having obsessive thoughts about them day and night, and emailing, texting, and calling them as they pull away, leading to anguishing rejection and profound suicidal depression? Is there something so rewarding about being with this particular man (whoever the current partner is), that well-known "high" of being in love with someone who often initially "comes on strong," that she continually tries unsuccessfully to reignite his early behavior as he increasingly pushes her away? This example is not meant to suggest that older women cannot have very satisfying long-term relationships with much younger men—many have and do. But in her case, does this history fit the definition of addiction as compulsively seeking either intense pleasure or escape from an aversive condition, despite serious adverse consequences? It is obvious that rejections and disappointments in love happen to lots of people, but what is different about this is repetition, over many years, of a particular behavior in pursuit of a love object that always leads to catastrophic emotional pain? However, even if a person who is "loving too much" may on occasion meet criteria for a definition of addiction, likely most do not.

With respect to the designation "workaholic," there are many possible alternative ways of framing the behavior of spending most of one's time working other than an addiction for which "recovery" is required. How about anxiety about not making enough money to meet expenses, or needing to compete with co-workers for approbation by the management in these times of layoffs, or (for a lucky few), deriving great fun or satisfaction from the work itself?

The concept of "co-dependency" in families with an addicted member (Whitfield, 1991) fails to consider the possibility that the attachment to an addicted loved one is because of that person's other qualities, *despite* the addiction and not *because of* it. In this case, the therapeutic issue is not to determine the partner's "co-dependency"—defining the partner of the addicted person as "sick"—but rather to weigh costs and benefits of the relationship as it is, and to consider strategies for bringing about change.

A body of published critiques of the co-dependency concept has noted its pejorative connotations, characterizing interpersonal behaviors as addictions or diseases, pathologizing women, promulgating a value-laden Anglo cultural narrative, and requiring partners of addicted persons to assume responsibility for their partner's addiction (Montgomery, 2001; Anderson, 1994; Collins, 1993; Inclan and Hernandez, 1992).

Although recent validation studies of instruments measuring problems and issues of family members have shown reliability and validity with respect to characteristics on the inventories (Dear, 2004), the designation "co-dependent" remains offensive. Studies that simply gather data about the kinds of challenges experienced by families with a member experiencing addiction, in the context of a stress and coping conceptual framework, can supply information that may help practitioners support families. Unlike the co-dependency frame, a stress and coping model normalizes and destigmatizes individuals and their behaviors (Hurcom, Copelle, and Orford, 2000).

The issue of *enabling* (well-meaning family or friends doing things that inadvertently support rather than discourage the addicted person's habit) is separate from the concept of co-dependency. Enabling does not by definition assume pathology in significant others (some friends, family, and providers, however not infrequently do attribute pathology when they think of enabling). Therefore the concept of enabling is an important target for educational efforts (Rotunda, West, and O'Farrell, 2004).

Enabling has been defined as "to supply with the means, knowledge, or opportunity; make able; make feasible or possible" (The Free Dictionary, 2012). Definitions that are inherently neutral can be applied in either a positive or negative way, so supplying the means or making feasible or possible can be carried out for purposes viewed as either "good" or "bad."

Before its debut in the substance abuse lexicon, *enabling* had a positive meaning in social work culture as a practice behavior by *workers* to facilitate and support their clients taking positive steps toward their goals. For example, "My client's goal is to enter a rehab program. The intervention plan is to enable him to apply for services and to make the arrangements needed for the care of his child."

Today, enabling has taken on a negative cast in relation to well-meaning family members or friends who usually have the best interests of their loved one at heart, but inadvertently support rather than discourage the addicted person's habit.

On the one hand, we can see enabling behaviors in light of the enormous pressure on loved ones to ease the user's pain as well as their own in the short term. Examples might be bailing the person out of jail, calling his or her workplace saying he or she has the flu and won't be in to work today, or cleaning up the vomit the drunk person left on the living room sofa—all behaviors that protect the person from having to experience some of the harsh consequences of the addictive behavior.

However, language on the part of some in the helping fields conveys the judgment that enabling behavior by significant others is blame-worthy. For example, take the label "chief enabler." "The chief enabler could be a parent, spouse, someone the addict works with. It is the person that protects the addicted person from the consequences of their addiction" (Blogspot.com, 2007, 2013).

How easy is it to "hear" the phrase as "chief culprit" when the phrase "chief enabler" is spoken? Does using the phrase "chief enabler" imply that the speaker (or writer) attributes the cause of the person's continuing addictive behavior to the family member or friend who engaged in enabling behaviors? Yes, that spouse or parent may make it less inconvenient for the user to use and thereby contribute to ongoing addictive behavior. But the language diminishes significant others in ways that vary from insensitive to outright disrespectful.

By contrast, in a spirit of acceptance, workers should strive to appreciate the experience family, friend, or co-worker may be having and be respectful of everyone involved in the situation. Significant others are struggling to find ways to survive what are often terrible circumstances and can be helped to reduce these behaviors by matter-of-fact explanations of how loving family members often may unintentionally slow the progress of the person with the addiction, even though that's the last thing they want to do. The in-depth assessment of Pat (Chapters 32 and 41–45) gives a classic example of a very loving and devoted mother who needs psychoeducation on how to support her daughter's recovery from an eating disorder.

Now, back to science.

29

Some Street Drugs—How They Can Get You Hooked

We'll look briefly at the actions of some classes of drugs. Let's start with *stimulants*.

Cocaine, amphetamine, and other stimulants produce euphoria and increase arousal, alertness, concentration, and motor activity. They also increase blood pressure and pulse rate and stimulate the release of stress hormones such as cortisol. With prolonged use, they can cause aggressive behavior, irritability, stereotyped behavior, and paranoia. In fact, people brought to emergency rooms in a state of acute psychosis are sometimes misdiagnosed as having schizophrenia when they are actually experiencing the effects of stimulant overdose. Stimulants not only affect dopamine neurons directly, but also act indirectly by altering the excitability of dopamine neurons through pathways that transmit norepinephrine and glutamate (Paladini, Mitchell, Williams et al., 2004).

Cocaine blocks the reuptake into the presynaptic neuron of three kinds of transmitters—dopamine, norepinephrine, and serotonin—by jumping on board the "shuttles" that carry transmitters back up into the sending neuron. The word shuttle is a metaphor for molecular structures, called transporters, that are embedded in the presynaptic membrane. Transporters pump neurotransmitters back into presynaptic neurons. Cocaine's main effect works through dopamine and dopamine transporters. As dopamine neurotransmitters float around in the synapse waiting to be reuptaken, cocaine grabs the slots on the shuttle away from them, and they're unable to be taken up into the presynaptic neuron—so there's a lot more dopamine left in the synapse than before the person had a hit of cocaine. That is, cocaine makes a direct hit on the dopamine pathways. Look at color image M., Cocaine in Action. The bundles of dopamine neurons that form the mesolimbic dopamine pathway extend from the ventral tegmental area (VTA) in the midbrain to the nucleus accumbens (NAc) in the limbic forebrain. The top half of the diagram shows the ordinary everyday dopamine neuron's neurobiological behavior. When you indulge in your usual pleasures, like eating a bagel with cream cheese or listening to music, dopamine neurons originating in the VTA squirt small amounts of dopamine into synapses where dopamine receptors are waiting on the dendrites of neurons in the nucleus accumbens. The dopamine's message is that the cream-cheesy bagel tastes yummy and the music has a groovy beat (or sweet lyrical melodies if that's what you prefer). If you're lucky, you get a lot of little shots during a typical day. The bagel and the music give you those little squirts.

Why is this food so enjoyable for most people while broccoli is not? Hyman (1995), referring to innate properties of consumables as the reason for the pleasure they evoke, notes that broccoli, unfortunately, does not emit chemicals that stimulate our dopamine production.

The lower half of the image then demonstrates what happens when you take a hit of cocaine. The cocaine blocks the normal reuptake from the synapse of some of the dopamine molecules into the presynaptic neuron. This means that a lot of dopamine is now available in the synapse to combine with the postsynaptic receptor molecules that are located on the surface of the receiving neuron. Now your synapses are flooded with your own dopamine. The dopamine is what gives you the rush. *You get high on your own dopamine!*

What happens when continuing floods of dopamine triggered by cocaine pound the dopamine system like a sledgehammer? The brain tries to adapt to this sledgehammering. After you've been using cocaine at a sufficient dose, often enough, over a long enough period of time, DNA (genetic material) is transcribed (read out to make a copy) as RNA, which is then imprinted on protein (see Chapter 8 for more detail about genetic material). This protein is a precursor of the neurotransmitter dynorphin, which tells neurons to cut down on dopamine production. The brain's adaptation to too much dopamine is to reduce the number of dopamine receptors, so the brain adapts to the effects of cocaine, and when you take the cocaine away, you're in an adapted state.

Now you're in trouble. You don't have enough dopamine receptors anymore, so you have symptoms of dysphoria (depression) and anhedonia (inability to experience pleasure). All this leads to cravings. You're much worse off than you were before you took the drug because you don't feel just a sort of normal blah, now you feel severe psychic pain. This psychic pain is neurobiological in origin. It comes from molecular changes in the brain brought about by genetic activity in response to drug use.

Recent research is giving evidence of cocaine-induced dysregulation of glutamate systems. Glutamate mechanisms are now recognized as underlying several clinical aspects of cocaine dependence, including euphoria, withdrawal, craving, and pleasure dysfunction (Dackis and O'Brien, 2003). Even denial that addictive actions are happening or that they are harmful, traditionally assumed to be purely psychological, appears to result in part from glutamate dysfunction in cortical regions.

Researchers reviewed 23 studies with 2066 participants to test the use of dopamine agonists in treating cocaine addiction (Amato et al. 2011). In the context that there was no pharmacological treatment of proven efficacy for cocaine dependence as of 2011, studies included randomized and controlled clinical trials comparing dopamine agonists alone or associated with psychosocial intervention or placebo, no treatment, or other pharmacological interventions.

Two authors independently assessed trial quality and extracted data. The results were not encouraging for dopamine agonists as treatments for cocaine addiction. Comparing any dopamine agonist versus placebo, placebo performed better for severity of dependence, depression, and abstinence at follow-up. The integrity of this evidence judged by a high-quality research method (GRADE), was moderate for judging efficacy of any dopamine agonist versus placebo, and moderate to high for comparing amantadine versus placebo and versus antidepressants (Amato et al., 2011). Thus, the authors had to conclude that evidence from randomized controlled trials does not support the use of dopamine agonists for treating cocaine dependence. Even the potential benefit of combining a dopamine agonist with a more potent psychosocial intervention, which was suggested by the previous Cochrane review (Soares 2003), was not supported (Amato et al., 2011).

Amphetamine makes a direct hit on dopamine systems as well, but it follows a different process. It causes vesicles storing dopamine to release dopamine faster into the synapse from the presynaptic neuron. It also inhibits reuptake of dopamine, norepinephrine, and serotonin by membrane transporters. The net result, again, is a lot more dopamine in the synapse available to combine with postsynaptic receptors. Once again, the rush comes from our own dopamine. Different mechanism, same effect. Like cocaine, amphetamine has been found to increase dopamine release in the nucleus accumbens (NAc) through a mechanism regulated by glutamate transmission from the prefrontal cortex (Ventura, Alcaro, Mandolesi et al., 2004).

In the case of "ecstasy" 3,4-methylenedioxy-methamphetamine (MDMA), a so-called "designer derivative" of amphetamine, the serotonin transporter is the main target (try pronouncing these 11 syllables-worth of designer euphoria, or 13 syllables if you include 3 and 4, (3,4-methylenedioxy-methamphetamine)). Ecstasy gives euphoria and increased empathy (called an *entactogenic* effect). Ecstasy and other designer derivatives of amphetamine can have toxic effects on dopamine and serotonin neurons. Acute intoxication with psychostimulants can cause cerebral hemorrhage, hyperthermia, heat stroke, panic, psychosis, or *serotonin syndrome* (altered mental state, neuromuscular abnormalities).

Methamphetamine (Meth) is a highly addictive psychostimulant drug whose abuse has reached epidemic proportions worldwide. Damage from methamphetamine use has been found to be even worse than previously thought (Gonzales et al., 2011; Thompson, Hayashi et al., 2004). In a study comparing 22 long-term users with 21 controls matched for age, the users had lost an average of 11% of tissue in the limbic system and were depressed, anxious, and unable to concentrate. The hippocampus, the brain's center for making new memories, had lost 8%, a deficit comparable to brain deficits in early Alzheimer's (Thompson, Hayashi et al., 2004).

Meth users have described a sudden rush of pleasure lasting for several minutes, followed by euphoria for 6 to 12 hours, the result of the drug causing the brain to release excessive amounts of dopamine. All drugs of abuse cause the release of dopamine directly or indirectly, but as Rawson and colleagues characterize it, "methamphetamine produces the mother of all dopamine releases" (Gonzales et al., 2011).

In animals, sex causes dopamine levels to jump from 100 to 200 units, cocaine causes them to jump to 350 units, and methamphetamine to about 1,250 units. This bombardment of pleasure is generated by approximately 12 times as much dopamine as you get from food, sex, and other normally rewarding activities—unlike anything you've ever felt. As with many drugs of abuse, when the drug wears off, profound depression sets in and users feel the need to keep taking the drug to avoid or escape from the crash.

The long-term consequences are grim. Over time, meth destroys dopamine receptors, preventing pleasure, and with possibly permanent damage to users' cognitive abilities. Chronic abuse can lead to psychotic behavior including paranoia, insomnia, anxiety, extreme aggression, delusions and hallucinations, and even death (Gonzales et al., 2012). Meth increases sexual desire and stamina, but decreases not only the user's performance but also his or her sexual desirability, because meth demolishes the user's good looks. It impairs judgment centers of the brain. According to Peter Staley, a former meth user turned anti-meth activist in New York, "You do things when you're on meth that you would never do sober." It leads to impotence and is known in some gay circles in New York as "crystal dick."

Because the long-term effects of cocaine and amphetamine products on users and their families are so devastating, it is fervently to be hoped that science will find effective treatments in the near future, until such time as efforts at prevention prevail.

Opiates. Opiate drugs such as heroin and morphine give euphoria, sedation, and calmness. However, with repeated use, tolerance and strong physical dependence occur. Overdose can cause fatal respiratory depression. Opiates' effects are produced through a chain of actions using the inhibitory neurotransmitter GABA (gamma-aminobutyric acid). Remember that neurons come in different sizes and shapes, and that each neuron can connect with many other neurons. Short neurons make connections with longer neurons. These interconnecting short neurons are called *interneurons.* There are lots of interneurons in the brain that transmit GABA. These inhibitory interneurons inhibit the action of receiving neurons. These are the neurons that just say no. Look at color image N., Natural Opioids, Synthesized Opiate Drugs. In the upper half of the page, you again see a dopamine neuron in its everyday state, giving common ordinary pleasures. The short GABA interneurons are keeping the dopamine neurons in check by sending inhibitory messages to receptors on the dopamine neurons' dendrites, balancing the messages these receiving neurons are getting at the same time from excitatory neurotransmitters. When the right amount of GABA is coming through, you get modest amounts of dopamine—just the right amount of dopamine to enjoy your bagel with cream cheese or your music.

But what happens when the GABA neurons stop squirting GABA onto the dopamine neurons? Not enough inhibitory messages? Right. The balance between excitatory and inhibitory messages is disrupted. The dopamine neuron gets overexcited and fires faster and faster. That's what happens when opiate drugs get into the system, shown lower on the graphic.

Opiates (like heroin and morphine) also, like GABA neurons, have inhibitory effects. Their axons form synapses with dendrites on GABA neurons. They inhibit the inhibitory GABA neurons (that's a double negative). Opiates say no to GABA neurons, so the GABA neurons *stop* saying no to the dopamine neurons. Did you notice in the diagram that the neurotransmitter molecules being sent from the GABA interneuron to the dopamine neuron have vanished? That's because the opiate drug has inhibited the GABA neuron, and the everyday restraint on dopamine release supplied by GABA is removed. Result: you get a flood of your own dopamine. The dopamine neurons have a field day!

Mannelli, Peindl, and Wu (2011) note the increase in opioid dependence (OD) despite widespread use of opioid agonist substitution, as with methadone, yet naltrexone, an opioid *antagonist*, has shown a "remarkable association of theoretical effectiveness and poor clinical utility in treating OD," with high rates of noncompliance and low acceptability among clients, even when somewhat modified by psychosocial interventions. By contrast, naltrexone has a very good record of effectively treating alcohol addiction. Mannelli and colleagues found several reports in their searches of significant reduction in opioid use and improved retention in treatment with naltrexone implants (long-term) and "depot" treatments (long-acting intramuscular injections), both used to improve compliance and to simplify the treatment procedures. Positive effects also can occur with combinations of naltrexone with selective serotonin reuptake inhibitors (SSRIs) and adrenergic, opioid, and GABA agonist medications. They caution that more research is needed on effectiveness and safety of these promising pilot stage treatments.

A substitution treatment for opioid abuse that appears to have promise is buprenorphine for the treatment of opiate-related conditions in primary care and family care outpatient settings (Ducharme, Fraser, and Gill, 2012). These reviewers found it feasible, safe, and effective. It is a partial μ-opioid agonist and κ-opioid antagonist with less abuse potential than methadone, and this review and update judges it at least equivalent to methadone and superior to clonidine for detoxification. For maintenance it performs better than placebo.

It has been received with much greater approval by adolescents with opiate drug issues than has methadone.

Alcohol is often referred to as *ethanol* in the research literature to identify it as the kind of alcohol you drink to have fun. We'll use the terms interchangeably here. Almost immediately after a couple of drinks (especially if you drink on an empty stomach), alcohol (ethanol) gives a buzz or even a little euphoria as the drug stimulates release of dopamine from mesolimbic dopamine neurons. Then you start to feel relaxed as well. It is now acting on receptors for GABA, an inhibitory transmitter, and potentiates (strengthens) GABA's action of making you relaxed, mellowed out, maybe a little silly.

But are you one of those people who reacts quite differently to alcohol? Do you get angry and aggressive? For many years, "mad drunks" were assumed, because of the disinhibiting effects of alcohol, to be releasing pent-up anger that they'd been suppressing. Now, however, we know that disinhibition— which allows us to express underlying feelings we were afraid to express when sober—is not the only explanation for why good-hearted Glenn has rages when he's drunk. Chemicals in the drink can actually create a rage in the brain that was not present before using the drug, because of the interaction between that person's limbic chemistry and the drug's properties.

It's possible that your friend Glenn, who's always so nice except when he's drunk, isn't covering anything up when he's sober—he's really nice, and he isn't the least bit angry. When he's drunk, though, he becomes nasty. He isn't just letting his "true colors" show—the chemistry in his brain has actually been altered by the drug.

Your other friend Beverly, however, also gets nasty when intoxicated—she's the wife of a misogynist and gets punished for being too assertive. In her case, that anger really was already present and really did come out because of the disinhibiting properties of the three martinis she had at your party (but who's counting? . . .).

Glenn and Beverly illustrate the great diversity of the brain's responses to environmental inputs. Gerald Edelman, Nobel laureate and neuroscientist, assures us that no two people, and no two experiences shared by those people, are ever exactly the same, even for identical twins and even from the day of birth (well, earlier, actually—situations *in utero* aren't identical either). This is so because epigenesis continuously creates differences in gene expression (Edelman, 2004).

Alcohol consumption changes concentrations of several neurotransmitters (dopamine, GABA, endogenous opioid peptides, serotonin, glutamate, and noradrenaline). These changes are associated with activation of reward centers in the brain, disinhibition, and "mellowing out." Dopamine and norepinephrine mechanisms, together with endogenous opioid peptides, are thought to play important roles in the reinforcing properties of alcohol through activation of positive reinforcement pathways. Alcohol potentiates GABA (causing relaxation) and stimulates release of dopamine from mesolimbic neurons (causing pleasure). It also reduces the firing rate of *pars reticulata* (PR) neurons, which are believed to have an inhibitory effect on dopamine neurons, so ethanol disinhibits the dopamine neurons through an indirect process. Low doses of ethanol produce significant enhancement of the release of dopamine in limbic structures in mice.

For more than a decade, three drugs have maintained their leadership status for treatment of alcohol addiction: naltrexone, acamprosate, and disulfiram (De Sousa, 2010). All three drugs have received both support and refutation from testing trials, and each has many meta-analyses to support its use. The most important factor in efficacy overall, according to De Sousa's review, has been the combination of psychosocial treatment with medication.

Naltrexone is an opioid receptor antagonist that blocks μ-opioid receptors. This action may produce its anti-relapse effects either by blocking opioids' reinforcing effects when alcohol is consumed by grabbing receptor slots on dendrites of GABA neurons away from the natural opioid transmitters or by diminishing conditioned expectation of these effects (Littleton and Zieglgansberger, 2003).

Naltrexone reduces heavy drinking by diminishing the rewarding neurobiological effects of alcohol. Its action is by reducing dopamine release from the ventral tegmental area (VTA) to the nucleus accumbens (NAc) when alcohol is consumed. Naltrexone alone has been shown to reduce heavy drinking rates in a smoking-cessation program (King, Cao, Vanier, and Wilcox 2009) and has been shown to improve cost-effectiveness of cognitive behavioral therapy in alcohol dependence (Walters, Connors, Feeney, and Young, 2009). Naltrexone also has a favorable safety profile.

Opioid peptide antagonists such as naltrexone decrease self-administration of ethanol by laboratory animals. Clinical trials have shown that these drugs can decrease relapse rates in detoxified outpatient alcoholics because dopamine-mediated rewards are reduced (Fuller and Gordis, 2001). Some recovering alcoholics report that naltrexone takes away their cravings for alcohol, even though these same opioid blockers *don't* take away cravings for opiate drugs. In fact, in the early 1900s, morphine, an opiate drug, was used to treat alcoholism. However, recent research has shown mixed results.

Naltrexone was no more effective than placebo in a large multisite study of veterans, almost all male, who had been severely addicted for decades (Krystal, Cramer, Krol et al., 2001). The lack of effectiveness for the population of alcohol-addicted older male veterans may differ from results for younger persons with shorter histories of use, involving more females, and in social environments more conducive to hope for the future. The psychosocial treatment in the veterans' study consisted only of outpatient counseling 1 hour per week for the first 16 weeks, then less often. Better results have been obtained when naltrexone is combined with much more intensive interpersonal treatments.

Thus, despite some negative results, tests of naltrexone as a treatment for alcohol addiction have shown frequent positive effects with a range of populations.

Acamprosate (calcium acetylhomotaurinate) has a chemical structure similar to the amino acid neurotransmitter GABA. As of 2001, it had been used to treat over 1.5 million patients since its introduction in 1989 and was prescribed in over 28 countries (Mason, 2001). It is believed to act by modulating glutamatergic hyperactivity that chronic alcohol use can create. Acute alcohol intake disrupts the normal balance between neuronal excitation and inhibition regulated by GABA, glutamate, and other receptor systems. This results in an exaggeration of the inhibitory processes.

The efficacy of acamprosate was found consistently as a 30 to 50% increase in nondrinking days, as well as decreased drinking days, with acamprosate compared to placebo. It has a favorable safety and tolerability profile, no abuse potential, and few side effects. Worldwide, naltrexone and acamprosate are cheaper than Disulfiram, and Disulfiram is not easily available in many nations (De Sousa, 2010).

Disulfiram (Antabuse) is an aversive therapy to deter alcohol use. It works by blocking oxidation of ingested alcohol and preventing its rapid metabolism. So when a person on disulfiram consumes even small amounts of alcohol, acetaldehyde, a product of alcohol metabolism, accumulates and causes tachycardia, hypotension, nausea, vomiting, and other symptoms (De Sousa, 2010).

Disulfiram is an old drug, much of whose former use was curtailed by the introduction of naltrexone and acamprosate. However, there is evidence of its effectiveness under various conditions. De Sousa in his review article (2010) appears to agree with addiction specialists who deplore the failures of providers to use it very often.

Combined naltrexone and acamprosate. A reason for combining naltrexone and acamprosate therapy in the management of alcohol dependence is that they act on different neurotransmitter systems (Mason, 2005). Clinical trials have shown that combination is better than acamprosate alone but not better than naltrexone alone. Numerous other medications have also been tried with some successes, so readers may want to read the De Sousa review (2010) to learn about possible additional interventions for their clients.

Nicotine. The World Health Organization (WHO, 2004) estimated that the global yearly death toll as a result of tobacco use is currently 6 million, a figure that includes exposure to secondhand smoke. This rate is expected to rise to 7 million by 2020 and to more than 8 million a year by 2030. It is predicted that by the end of the 21st century, tobacco will have killed one billion people. For every death caused by smoking, approximately 20 smokers are suffering from a smoking related disease (World No Tobacco Day 2011 celebrates WHO Framework Convention On Tobacco Control; WHO report on the global tobacco epidemic, 2008; World Lung Foundation and American Cancer Society, 2010).

Smoking harms nearly every organ of the body and dramatically reduces both quality of life and life expectancy. Smoking causes lung cancer, respiratory disease, and heart disease as well as numerous cancers in other organs including lip, mouth, throat, bladder, kidney, stomach, liver, and cervix. The 2010 U.S. Surgeon General report, *How Tobacco Smoke Causes Disease*, concludes that "there is no risk-free level of exposure to tobacco smoke, and there is no safe tobacco product" (U.S. Department of Health and Human Services, 2010).

Nicotine binds to receptors for the neurotransmitter acetylcholine, causing an increase in number and sensitivity of acetylcholine receptors. This process probably accounts for withdrawal symptoms when the drug is withheld, because there are now too many unfilled receptors. Nicotine produces reinforcing effects by acting on the nicotinic subtype of acetylcholine receptors located on dopamine neurons in the VTA, stimulating the release of dopamine to the nucleus accumbens (NAc) and the cerebral cortex. It may also sensitize nicotinic acetylcholine receptors located on glutamate terminals. It enhances glutamate's excitation of dopamine neurons and decreases GABA's inhibition of dopamine neurons, leading possibly to long-lasting heightened sensitivity of dopamine neurons (Pidoplichko, Noguchi et al., 2004).

Caffeine is an antagonist to a transmitter that blocks dopamine D1 receptors, called *adenosine*. It acts as another of those double negatives. Caffeine blocks the dopamine blocker, thereby enhancing dopamine levels. Caffeine induces dopamine-dependent behavioral arousal and enhances motor activity in rodents. It also activates norepinephrine-producing neurons. Prolonged use of caffeine can lead to physical dependence as evidenced by withdrawal symptoms during abstinence. Some tolerance occurs, but in most cases the effects of caffeine continue over time (Nehlig, 2000).

Addicott and Laurienti (2009) compared the effects of caffeine in an abstained versus a normal caffeinated state to determine whether the stimulant effects of caffeine can mostly be attributed to alleviating withdrawal, or whether caffeine can produce stimulant effects beyond the normal baseline. The results suggest that caffeine was most effective at improving mood and simple reaction time following 30 hours of abstention among moderate users. However, caffeine also provided some performance gains on more cognitively demanding tasks, when administered following usual daily caffeine consumption. This finding validates the common practice among daily caffeine users of loading caffeine before a particularly challenging mental activity.

Using autoradiography, a procedure that locates radioactive substances in slices of tissue, Nehlig and Boyet (2000) found that caffeine activated multiple systems: caudate nucleus, raphé nuclei, locus coeruleus, striatum, thalamus, ventral tegmental area (VTA), and amygdala. Caffeine was found to have no effect on mood in rested subjects, nor did it improve mood that was depressed due to lack of sleep (James and Gregg, 2004).

Brain imaging was used to measure blood volume in the frontal cortex during mental work, both with and without caffeine (Higashi, Sone, Ogawa et al., 2004). The volume of blood decreased during rest periods as a result of caffeine-induced constriction of the cerebral blood vessels but increased during mental work. However, volume increased equally with and without caffeine. Performance on complex mental tasks clearly improved. This improvement was not reflected in increased blood volume. The results indicate that caffeine activates neurons in several locations in the prefrontal cortex.

In an experiment with eight habitual coffee drinkers, neuroimaging demonstrated that placebo conditions can induce release of dopamine in the thalamus and the putamen at levels similar to those found with oral caffeine (Kaasinen, Aalto et al., 2004). This finding is consistent with other studies showing that placebo effects involve dopamine as well as endogenous opioids (Sher, 2003). So if I believed I was getting caffeine from a look-alike taste-alike stand-in for coffee, could I kick the habit and get the same results? Not likely—placebo effects are often powerful initially, but wear off after a while. Otherwise, maybe we'd have put the pharmaceutical industry out of business by now?

Marijuana, a cannabinoid, produces general euphoria, mild release from inhibition, and sometimes distortion of sensory perception, stimulation of appetite, drowsiness, relief from anxiety, and altered states of consciousness. Toxic effects include carcinogenesis and cognitive impairment, especially when used together with alcohol (Jacques, Zombek et al., 2004).

Cannabis has a long history of consumption both for recreational and medicinal uses. The main psychoactive constituent of marijuana, delta-9-tetrahydrocannabinol (THC), was identified in 1964 (Akirav, 2011).

Contrary to previous belief, cannabinoids are now known to trigger reinstatement of drug-seeking behavior in animals previously weaned from intravenous self-administration of drugs (Gardner, 2002). The preponderance of neurobiological studies indicates that cognitive impairments in users are probably reversible, but consequences of use in pregnancy have been serious, including long-lasting cognitive alterations in children whose mothers used marijuana during pregnancy (Mereu, Ferraro et al., 2003).

The psychoactive component of marijuana, delta 9-THC (delta 9-tetrahydrocannabinol), appears to stimulate dopamine neurons in the VTA by depressing GABA inhibitory inputs to these neurons (Szabo, Siemes, and Wallmichrath, 2002). Another desired effect may be the extinction of aversive memories, mediated by a part of the amygdala known to perform this function.

Research on this topic has recently proliferated, as it generates great excitement about the possibility of major relief from the pain of intrusive aversive memories in posttraumatic stress disorder (PTSD) sufferers or possibly the intensely euphoric memories of drug highs that torment the would-be recovery seekers (see for example Myers and Carlezon, 2010; Kamprath, Romo-Parra et al., 2011; Knoll, Muschamp et al., 2011). The numerous investigators are

researching potential different neurobiological avenues for solving such problems as extinguishing aversive memories while preserving others, requiring
agents that select in or out certain chemical substances or different levels of
intensity of memories. When definitive solutions are discovered, unknown
numbers of sufferers may capture days and nights unmarred by fears, tranquil-
ity, and joys that might have been obliterated before the treatment.

Cannabinoid agonists' value for multiple medical treatments is best known
with respect to nausea in cancer chemotherapy. Its use is also suggested to
stimulate appetite, reduce inflammatory pain, and reduce spasticity and tremor
in diseases characterized by motor impairment (multiple sclerosis, spinal cord
injury, Huntington's and Parkinson's diseases), as well as for glaucoma, bron-
chial asthma, and vasodilation that accompanies advanced cirrhosis (Pertwee
and Ross, 2002). Cichewicz (2004) reports that combining low doses of cannabinoids and opiates to treat acute and chronic pain appears promising, especially for pain that may be resistant to opiates alone.

Hallucinogens (psychedelics) powerfully alter perception, mood, and cognition. They are not known to produce dependence or addiction. Hallucinogens
stimulate the serotonin receptor 5-HT(2A), known to play an essential role
in cognitive processing and working memory (Nichols, 2004). Stimulation
of these receptors in turn leads to higher levels of glutamate in the cortical
regions. These drugs engage the thalamocortical circuits that are central to
altered states of consciousness (see Chapter 38) and imaging studies have
shown that hallucinogens increase prefrontal cortical metabolism.

The preceding brief review of several drugs raises a question of paramount
concern to persons with addictions, their loved ones, and those of us who
work to try to help them: Why do persons with addictions self-destruct? It's
because addiction usurps brain mechanisms that are prime movers in motivated behavior (Hyman, 1995). Addiction commandeers the parts of the brain
that control motivation and set behavioral priorities. The addict is only aware
of dysphoria and craving, and believes that everything would be okay with
just another hit or another drink. "If only I could get another hit off my crack
pipe, I'd be able to talk to you about treatment." The "strange" behavior of an
addicted person—who despite disasters from drug use, still sees the drug as
the most important thing in life—seems not so strange when we realize that
the person's brain is really changed.

Avram Goldstein, an early leader in the science of addiction and longtime
advocate for people with addictive disease, urged us to engage in a multi-
pronged political and economic attack on addiction. He emphasized the need
for knowledge to vanquish the usurper:

> What can science teach us about addictive drugs and addictive behavior?
> That requires a thorough analysis, drug by drug, of how each one acts and
> what harm each one does to users and to society. (Goldstein, 2001, p. 133)

How Do Psychosocial Interventions Work in the Context of a Changed Brain?

Interventions for substance abuse include support groups such as Alcholics Anonymous, Narcotics Anonymous, and Smoke Enders; cognitive-behavioral strategies; residential communities; other psychosocial interventions; and medication.

Like a person who has had a stroke, an addicted person has lost certain nerve cells but can recover some functions because other parts of the brain are sometimes able to take over what the damaged part used to do. Psychological, social, and contextual treatments support this process, acting as prostheses for the person's broken brain. By asking people to take responsibility for themselves, you're asking for other thinking parts of the brain and other emotional parts of the brain to do things the damaged part of the brain used to do. It doesn't make the changes go away. Problems are still there, especially long-term emotional memories that predispose people to relapse. But psychosocial treatments enlist other parts of the brain to act as bulwarks against these parts of the brain that want nothing more than to get another hit. Similar principles work in trauma as well. You can never get rid of the traumatic emotional memories, but you can get other parts of the brain to manage. You learn ways of suppressing and managing these memories, focusing on other things, and utilizing strategies to circumvent the force of those memories. But the memories are almost always still there.

Successful treatment requires that the addicted person eventually take personal responsibility for himself or herself, overcome denial, commit to sobriety, and take active steps to achieve it. Once a commitment is made, we can then provide ways of propping up the compromised brain. The same principles apply in most serious chronic diseases. The individual is asked to comply with treatment and to avoid behaviors that put him or her at high risk of relapse or of worsening the condition. For example, a person is at high risk for a heart attack because he or she is obese, has a family history of heart disease, smokes, and is a couch potato. Only he or she can actually change that situation by following the doctor's orders to lose weight, change eating habits, stop smoking, and exercise. The person with the disease must take responsibility for compliance. Just because you were unlucky enough to have been more at risk than some other people doesn't change the fact that only you can behave in ways that will perpetuate or discourage the condition.

Treat Drugs with Drugs? Is That Craziness?

Maybe so. But often it helps, in conjunction with psychosocial interventions. In each individual case, we need to ask (1) what are the risks of our proposed interventions, (2) what are the likely benefits of our proposed interventions, and (3) what are the possible risks of *not* doing the proposed interventions?

That third question (which is often sadly neglected) is really on target with respect to treating drug abuse with drugs. If we had a drug that could take away cravings and help the person stay clean or sober, and it was a cliffhanger between relapse and sobriety, wouldn't there be a risk attached to *not* giving that medication?

The state of medical treatments for addictions at the time of writing (2012) has been reviewed by Nutt, Lingford-Hughes, and Chick (2012). Table 31.1 below, reprinted from their article, presents three major drugs of abuse—heroin, alcohol, and nicotine—for which there are medical treatments falling into one of three general categories. The three types of treatments for addiction/dependence on alcohol/drugs are designated (1) *withdrawal* (stopping use of the drug), (2) *substitution* medication that has one or more of the pharmacological effects of the substance which are believed to be relevant to the addiction), and (3) *abstinence-promoting* therapy, respectively. Nutt and colleagues define abstinence promoters as medications that discourage drug use by reducing cravings or by aversion/deterrence. Example are buprenorphine for smoking, naltrexone or acamprosate for alcohol use, or disulfiram for alcohol abuse as an aversive agent. Different people define *abstinence* in different ways, sometimes as no use of any drug, and as abstinence from the drug of abuse substituted for by some other drug.

Substitutes can prevent withdrawal from the abused drug and can usually be started once a decision is made to stop using the abused drug. They can reduce craving and thus the desire to use the abused drug. Patients prefer substitution treatment and therefore are most likely to be compliant when this alternative is chosen, such as the substitution of methadone for heroin or the substitution of a nicotine patch for smoking cigarettes.

TABLE 31.1 Types of Treatment Medications and Other Medical Interventions for Three Drugs of Abuse

Medications	Other Interventions
Heroin	
Substitution	Needle exchange
Methadone	Foil (–> smoking not i.v.)
Buprenorphine	Citric acid
Prescribed heroin	Filters
Abstinence-promoter	
Naltrexone/nalmefene	
Alcohol	
Substitution	
Thiamine (B1), other vitamins	
(Sodium oxybate)	
Magnesium	
(Benzodiazepines)	
(Clomethiazole)	
(Baclofen)	
Aversion	
Disulfirametc	
Abstinence promoter—primary clinical effect	
Acamprosate	
(Baclofen)	
(Topiramate)	
Drinking regulators—primary clinical effect	
Naltrexone, Nalmefene	
Tobacco	
Substitution	
Varenicline	
Safer forms of nicotine	
Patch/gum/lozenge	
Nasal spray	
Electric cigarette	
Abstinence promoter	
Bupropion, Baclofen	

The drugs in () means putative mechanism though not yet proven.

Nutt DJ, Lingford-Hughes A, and Chick J (2012). Through a glass darkly: can we improve clarity about mechanism and aims of medications in drug and alcohol treatments? *Journal of Psychopharmacology* 26(2):199–204.

32

Assessing Pat: (Beginning) Food Struggles and Mental Challenges. A Young Woman and Her Family Respond to Co-occurring Conditions

The story that follows is about Pat, a young woman who appears to have food addiction in the context of mental health conditions. Pat's situation is presented as an account of progression from enjoying food as a child and teenager to an all-consuming preoccupation and challenge. Pat illustrates some of the struggles discussed in Chapters 25–31 above.

As with alcohol and other drugs, the process entails increasingly intense involvement with some specific kind of activity, as the person approaches and then enters an addicted state (see definitions of addiction, Chapter 25). For people in addicted states, the body's responses to using a particular substance or enacting a behavior are experienced as so pleasurable to the person, or so necessary for avoiding or escaping from aversive conditions, that this experience preempts smaller pleasures and life goals and aspirations the person had valued prior to becoming addicted.

As you read the report about Pat's and her parents' lives here in Part IV, you will probably observe that several of her psychological characteristics (behaviors, emotions, cognitions) are typical of persons addicted to or abusing substances as discussed earlier. You'll probably be able to recognize her relationship with food as an addiction, using criteria for addiction such as those used in this book (see Sussman and Sussman, 2011, for a review of differing criteria sets). Because Pat's food addiction happens in the context of complex interactions with mental health challenges, the assessment continues and is developed analytically in Part VI (Mental Health and Mental Illness) as a holistic analysis of the range of issues she faces. Pat and her social worker brainstormed together about the combination of interventions that each thought could probably help Pat the most, amplified in light of research-based knowledge they discover in database searches about her identified challenges.

Thus the knowledge in this section about an individual trapped in a food addiction (recorded in MEBA, Multisystem Evidence-Based Assessment, items 1–7, see Chapter 9) must be integrated into the systems-level assessment in Part VI. The overall evaluative components are documented (in MEBA items 8–12) as part of a comprehensive assessment of Pat in her family context.

This client and family ecosystems evaluation was written by a clinical social worker who decided to remain anonymous to protect the client's privacy and his own reputation in his local practice community.

At the end of the evaluation (Part VI), the social worker uses the data compiled in the history to present his assessment and explain what interventions he thought might be helpful. His agency does not use this protocol. The attending physician's brief discharge note is included. The social worker wrote the detailed report for these chapters, of course disguising the material, but the issues are those of the client and her family.

Discharge Note May 27, 2012. Bristol Community Mental Health Network

Pat W, a 27-year-old 98-pound Caucasian female, was admitted May 22nd, 2012, in acute crisis due to dehydration and electrolyte imbalance. She has a 12-year history of bulimia nervosa and intermittent anorexic episodes. This was her third hospitalization in a crisis condition over the 12-year period. She was hydrated intravenously and treated with cyproheptadine to stimulate weight gain. When vital signs were stabilized, she was discharged to outpatient care.

Evaluation and Recommendations by social worker GB

Pat W, May 27, 2012
Bristol Community Mental Health Network, Outpatient Clinic
MEBA items 1–7.

1. **Presenting problems and strengths; views of client, significant others, and worker**. Pat is a 27-year-old Caucasian woman who has suffered from eating disorders (bulimia and intermittent anorexia) since the age of 15. She has recently been admitted to the inpatient psychiatric unit at the Bristol Community Mental Health Center, a state-funded multiservice facility for psychiatric patients in a small industrial town in a midwestern state. This was her third hospitalization over the 12-year period since the inception of disordered eating behaviors. When Pat's 5-day length-of-stay allowed by her insurance for persons with her diagnosis elapsed, she was discharged to outpatient services.

The treatment staff is not in agreement about recommendations for ongoing care. Some members of the treatment staff view Pat's problem as stemming from failed attachment in childhood and ambivalent relationships with both parents. However, previous psychotherapy geared to working through these issues has failed. Pat, on the other hand, views her problem as inability to control insatiable urges to binge and purge. She is very cognizant that this problem is ruining her life, but feels helpless to do anything about it. She expresses the wish to be dead, but denies having formulated any specific plans for committing suicide.

Nevertheless, all three of her hospitalizations have occurred in response to life-threatening medical crises brought on by starving herself or intensive bingeing and vomiting. The fact that she has allowed herself to get into a dangerous physical condition on repeated occasions suggests at least passively suicidal behavior.

Pat has revealed other important facets of her view of the problem. She reports often not being able to feel the way other people do, sometimes even feeling detached from her body. "I see other people having fun and enjoying things and laughing. I just can't seem to feel anything." She has complained through the years of feeling "empty."

Pat does not accept professionals' views that she and her mother did not attach or bond properly, or that her conflicts with her father during adolescence were a major contributor to her emotional fragility. She sees her feelings of emptiness and sadness as something arising within herself that she cannot explain. She views her episodes of bingeing as temporary relief, time spans when she briefly feels happy, that she likens to a sunny island in the middle of a stormy sea.

2. What do the individual client and significant others want? Pat wants to be like everyone else, able to eat normally without the food cravings that have commandeered her life, without feeling empty, sad, and devoid of feelings; she wants to be free from anguish and to enjoy herself. Her parents' foremost desire is for her to be happy. They are heartbroken by her life-threatening Russian roulette eating behaviors and her despair. Her siblings are concerned, especially her brother.

3. History of the presenting problem(s). Pat was overweight most of her childhood and into adolescence. Some of her classmates referred to her as "Fatty Patty." At age 15, she was rejected by a boy she'd had a crush on for two years, and learned through the grapevine that he had told friends that he had no interest in Pat because she was fat. This experience was excruciating for her. She responded by intensive dieting, losing 60 pounds over the summer months by eating only "rabbit food" (her brother's term) and jogging several miles a day in the hot sun.

Her schoolmates responded approvingly to her new *persona* when school reopened in the fall. She was now slender and had dates for the first time, but still struggled with food. On Christmas Day, her mother, according to Pat, prepared all her favorite foods, and Pat stuffed herself. "My mom's cooking is awesome!" She looked at herself sideways in the mirror, saw a very distended belly, and believed this condition was permanent. All her suffering to lose weight, blown in one huge binge. It was at that moment it occurred to her that she could get rid of all the food by vomiting. She induced vomiting, and immediately felt an overwhelming sense of relief. She said she had found a "magic bullet." She began to eat voraciously again. She vomited more and more frequently.

In the ensuing 12 years, she meticulously counted calories and tried to eat no more than 900 per day, but also continued to binge and purge. She attended college, worked in department store sales, and had an active social life, but described herself as still being in a prison of deprivation, bingeing, and purging. Sometimes Ella, Pat's mother, would bake a bag of cookies and bring it with a gallon of milk to Pat at her apartment. Pat would eat the entire amount in one sitting, and then lie to her mother about who had eaten it.

Pat went to the extent of vomiting calorie-free soda, even though she knew this behavior was irrational since diet sodas would not make her fat. She usually hid her eating behaviors from her family, friends, her fiancé during a year-long engagement, and eventually therapists as well, whom she saw intermittently starting her sophomore year in college.

4. Client's current life situation and family history: family, work and school, health issues in family, economic security, religious involvement, social interaction outside family. Pat is the oldest of four, three girls and a boy, all of whom were overweight during their growing-up years. Pat did very well in school until the teen years, attended college for two years while working part time, then left to work full time. At the time of her recent hospital admission, she was working as manager of the women's clothing division of a department store, but had lost considerable work time just prior to the hospitalization. Pat and her brother, Freddie, are very close. Freddie has taken an active role in trying to connect Pat with sources of help and in supporting their parents through years of grief and stress with Pat's condition.

Pat lives in the town next to her parents' town. She is single, currently without a partner, but was engaged for about a year when she was 25 to Evan, who was nurturing, devoted to her, and willing to extend himself to help her overcome her eating compulsions. He himself had overcome obesity in high school and was very sympathetic to her fear of regaining lost weight.

To her family and friends, Evan seemed like a wonderful match for Pat. However, she broke their engagement. It appeared that Evan could not fill the emptiness that she was experiencing.

Pat's mother Ella was one of 12 children in a poor family, her father Edwin one of 5. Maternal and paternal grandparents worked in a local factory and eked out a living for their large families. Ella and Ed told the social worker they've been very happy together for 29 years, but have suffered greatly because of Pat's illness. Ella becomes tearful when recounting how she and Ed lie awake nights wondering what's happening with Pat. They brought many pictures of happy times when the children were young: Ed with Pat on his lap reading a picture book, Ed helping Pat learn to ride a bicycle, Ella baking cookies with Pat and her sister Joanne as small children, and family gatherings.

Ed continues to work in a small local factory, and Ella works part time in a drugstore. Ella and Ed attend a local Catholic church, as do their other two daughters. Pat, however, is no longer religious, but attends church to be with the family on major holidays. The parents live in a small house in the middle of their town, where they have been most of their married life. Ella is delighted with the comfort they are able to afford, which her family of origin could not: central heating and an indoor toilet.

The family socializes mostly with relatives, many of whom live nearby. Both Ella and Ed conveyed to the social worker a sense of family support, cohesion, and affection.

Apart from Ella's high blood pressure and Pat's moods and eating disorder, family members are in good health. Ella has been known to forego her blood pressure medicine at times when Pat was living at home and eating enormous amounts of food, because there wasn't enough money for both. When questioned about this, Ella said to the social worker, "Wouldn't any mother give up something for one of her children?"

5. Previous experiences with help. Pat first came to the attention of mental health professionals while in college. Her brother Freddie had suspected for some time that Pat was vomiting, and confronted her, but until Pat was hospitalized in medical crisis (life-threatening electrolyte imbalance), she had been unwilling to seek professional help. Her mother, in a family interview with a social worker, said she was shocked when she found out about Pat's bingeing and purging at the time of the first hospitalization. "I don't know why I never thought of that, it just didn't occur to me." Pat acknowledged in a moment of honesty that she is a talented actress and manages to fool almost everyone, most of the time, about her bingeing and purging.

Records from previous hospitalizations reported individual psychotherapy, milieu therapy on the unit, daily group therapy, and medication to promote hydration and appetite, but gave no information about the kind of therapy or its goals. After the longest hospitalization, which lasted three weeks, Pat appeared to her family to have given up the binge-purge behavior, but reverted some months later. Pat has been in and out of outpatient treatment over the past 12 years, but typically discontinues when her therapist becomes confrontational about her bingeing and purging, which she attempts to deny and conceal.

The Bristol Center's policy is to treat persons diagnosed with schizophrenia or bipolar disorder with medication, but to use pharmacotherapy only rarely with nonpsychotic illnesses. Insight-oriented therapy is emphasized for "internalizing" disorders (involving subjective internal states such as depression and anxiety). Behavior modification is the clinic's frontline intervention for "externalizing" disorders (involving disruptive behaviors typical of attention-deficit hyperactivity and intermittent explosive disorders). During this recent hospitalization, Pat was hydrated, fed intravenously, and treated with cyproheptadine to stimulate appetite, but no psychotropic medication was prescribed.

6. Family interactions and dynamics. Food has always been a central part of the family's life. Ella is of short stature but has been very overweight since childhood. "I grew up the hard way, we all worked very hard, and you had to get nourishment to keep up your strength." Ed grinned as he recounted how he fell in love with Ella on their first date, during which she cooked him a meal of roast beef, Yorkshire pudding, and fudge cake. Ella once decided to try to lose weight, but did not follow through.

Pat has helped her mother learn to read and write, and they appear to be very fond of each other. Ella says the other three children are "easygoing like me," enjoy life, and take things as they come.

Ed and Pat, however, are alike in that they are serious, perfectionistic, and Pat especially is easily upset. Ed reports that at age three, Pat already had to do everything perfectly. Her parents said she was not convinced when they tried to explain that she doesn't have to be "the best."

During her adolescence, Pat and her father had repeated conflicts over her social life. "I'm from the old school, but she just thought she could come and go as she pleased, and she wore those tight sweaters that showed everything." Ed believes that teenagers should do what their parents ask "because I say so." Pat responded to her father's injunctions about curfews, clothes, and other social issues by flouncing out the door on dates with boys whom Ed did not like. Pat had outbursts of rage, sometimes breaking dishes. These outbursts were often a response to what she perceived as irrational restrictions, but Pat also had outbursts of anger in relation to situations at school, and later, even occasionally in the workplace. Her episodes of intense anger, then, have been fairly pervasive rather than being limited to her relationship with her father. Ed and Ella say they've done a lot of soul-searching over the years. They wonder whether they might have caused Pat's illness.

7. **Environmental stressors and their impacts on family members and influence on family dynamics.** Pat does not identify major sources of environmental stress in her life except when she becomes too ill to work, causing anxiety about income. However, she has never been without money for long, because she has been very successful in department store work, is highly valued by her employer, and is not in the line of fire in times of retrenchment. For her parents, Pat's illness is the major source of stress, pain, and grief. Although they are of modest means, they feel fortunate to be so much better off than their families were as they were growing up. Ella takes her high blood pressure in stride, considering it a normal part of growing older. Although having to choose between buying food and medicine would be considered a major stress by most people, Ella does not seem too troubled about it. Her major distress is Pat's unhappiness. Pat as well as her parents have what they consider to be acceptable health insurance through their employers, except for medication. However, recent cutbacks are causing them some worry about how they will manage in the event one of them develops a major illness.

GB, Clinical Social Work
To be continued, Part VI

We've just read the problem statement and client and family history section of a psychosocial evaluation of Pat, considered fairly standard since the 1950s as it is even now (early 21st century) in the era of automated multiple choice case records. It encompasses views of individual client, significant others, and worker about the nature of the problem. So far (items 1–7) no analytic or formal assessment judgments have been proposed. Interpretive statements then, as now, were and are supposed to be presented separately from facts, after all the available client and family information has been organized and set forth.

The first seven items on our biopsychosocial assessment tool MEBA, (Multisystem Evidence-Based Assessment instrument) have been included in Part IV here in relation to substance abuse and addictions to illustrate a now popular but still controversial belief that non-alcohol/other-drugs addictions such as to food or gambling (1) are very real; (2) typically demonstrate neurobiological processes of pleasure experience and progression to an addicted state very similar to those pertaining strictly to chemical drugs; (3) inflict on users the similar kinds of intense craving, seeking, and compulsive using/enacting as do alcohol and other drugs, and (4) generate hardships and grief for the user and loved ones potentially as painful and disruptive as do consumed chemicals.

For example: have you ever met a person whose family income plummeted to bankruptcy levels as a result of a breadwinner's gambling? Or whose obese child suffered years of loneliness and rejection attributable to extreme overconsumption of fatty sugary foods? Emotional pain is often involved both for the person with an addictive behavior and for the people who love him or her.

The placement of Pat's story in Part IV was intended to convey the human responses that addictive behavior can ignite in users and family members, and to supply human information needed to identify issues accurately, assess competently, and intervene effectively. This is the first part of a comprehensive assessment of Pat's situation continued in Part VI. The remainder of the MEBA addresses the context of multiple systemic factors, drawing directly from items 1–7 and expanding the range and depth of knowledge. The finished record will include some of the micro-underpinnings (neurobiological) of intense and unstable emotions, dissociative episodes, feelings of emptiness, outbursts of anger, and the influence of macro socioeconomic environments, emphasizing contemporary economic and cultural climate as powerful forces.

With the information you now have about this family and about substance abuse and addiction, you should be able to determine whether Pat seems to have an addiction to food (assuming you accept the possibility that addiction to non-alcohol, non-other drugs could occur) and what positive and negative effects the family culture may have had on Pat and her parents.

The next steps in the helping process entail completing (in Part VI on mental health and mental illness) the MEBA instrument first presented in Chapter 9, then in items 1–7, and then remaining items 8–13 about Pat (Chapter 32). The analysis encompasses all levels of systems including neurobiological, and also demonstrates the incorporation of evidence-based knowledge acquired through systematic database searches, into client assessment and intervention planning.

PART V

Child and Adult Development

RECENT RESEARCH ON CRITICAL DEVELOPMENTAL TOPICS

I blush as I recall telling my first undergraduate class in 1954 that a rejecting mother could create an autistic child.

Jerome Kagan, 2003
Daniel and Amy Starch
Research Professor of Psychology Emeritus,
Harvard University

For more than a century, clinical investigators have focused on early life as a source of adult psychopathology. Early theories about psychic conflict and toxic parenting have been replaced by more recent formulations of complex interactions of genes and environment.

Tracy Bale, Tallie Baram, Alan Brown,
Jill Goldstein, Thomas Insel, Margaret McCarthy, Charles Nemeroff, Teresa
Reyes, Richard Simerly, Ezra Susser, and Eric Nestler, 2010
Early life programming and neurodevelopmental
disorders. *Biological Psychiatry* 68(4): 314–319.

The recent eruption of neuroscience into both academic culture and popular consciousness has taken place as the scope and focus of human developmental knowledge is being dramatically altered. Yet the 11 authors of the second quote above go on to note that a central idea continues: "Early life is a period of unique sensitivity during which experience confers enduring effects. The mechanisms for these effects remain almost as much a mystery today as they were a century ago" (Bale, Baram, et al., 2010, ibid).

In Part V, I review research on some of the issues pertinent to human development that appear critical for human service practitioners. Many important

topics have been omitted. These chapters should be understood as an introduction to some highlights of child and adult development, not only relevant
for human services practice but also—sometimes—just plain fun! (You never
did like science? Maybe you'll be surprised.)

Jerome Kagan (2003), arguably the preeminent developmental psychologist
of the second half of the 20th century, has summarized some of the conceptual
changes in developmental research during the period from the 1950s to the
early years of the 21st century. What was the situation in developmental psychology in the mid-20th century? To answer that question, Kagan's own brief
words, in the preamble above, perhaps could supply the most succinct possible
tweet or text message to students of developmental psychology in the second
decade of the 21st century.

Two schools of psychological thought dominated American psychology
during the decades of the mid-20th century: psychoanalytic and ego psychological theory, on the one hand, created and elaborated by Sigmund and Anna
Freud and their followers, and on the other, theories of respondent and operant conditioning in the tradition of John Watson, Ivan Pavlov, and B.F. Skinner.
Proponents of ego psychology and early behaviorism vehemently denounced
each other.

Adherents of psychoanalytic models claimed authoritative knowledge
about developmental psychology. Behaviorists made no such claim, limiting
their sphere of expertise to behaviors. Despite the marked differences between
them, however, they had one thing in common: adherence to relatively simple
basic assumptions and organizing constructs.

During the final four decades of the 20th century, systems theory advocates
asked the two schools of thought to account for influences from the world
beyond family, friends, and colleagues. Cultural diversity, economic forces,
political power, and organizational structures were recognized as critical influences on child and adult development.

There was no conflict between systems theory and neuroscience, because
the latter, as a relatively new systemic natural science, interfaced broadly with
social science systems structures and functions. The biology/psychology/social
science connection for human behavior in the social environment has been
known to social work and other helping professions for decades as "biopsychosocial." However, among human service professions except medical fields,
the biological member of the tripartite creature existed mostly in name only
until we became aware of neuroscience. (Medical specialties, however, also
often appeared lacking in some social areas.)

Some important conceptual advances relevant to human development
accompanied the increasing attention to neuroscience knowledge. The role of
temperament in development, first made popular by Thomas and Chess (1977),
was increasingly recognized. Our understanding of psychological phenomena
such as affiliation, bonding, and attachment advanced with new discoveries

about their neurobiological and genetic foundations, enabling investigators to "peer beyond the behavioral display to infer more fundamental processes, as the student of musical composition perceives the theme hidden in the surface improvisation" (Kagan, 2003, p. 3). Knowledge increased about the effects of stress, vulnerability, and resilience on children's development, mediated by invisible but powerful events in the brain. Interdisciplinary research uncovered important information about critical periods in development and the role of brain maturation in emotions and cognition. And explorers in the neuroscience of consciousness ventured into the frontiers of knowledge with intriguing insights and hypotheses about the emergence of mind/body connections in homo sapiens.

{ 33 }

Genes, Temperament, and Resilience

Genes. What do genes have to do with social behaviors? A relatively simple example from animal research in the mid-1990s is illustrative. Prairie and pine voles (small mouselike rodents) make a monogamous attachment to their mates, but montane and meadow voles, entirely similar animals except for a tiny segment of DNA (the genetic material deoxyribonucleic acid), do not. Insel and Hulihan (1995) discovered that this difference in behavior between species with otherwise similar genetic makeup arose from the DNA of a gene responsible for the distribution of receptors for the peptide neurotransmitter vasopressin in male prairie voles.

Here, specific brain structures (a segment of DNA and vasopressin receptors) affect physiological process by influencing activity of the neurotransmitter vasopressin to produce the behavior of having sex with only one mate! In female prairie voles, the peptide oxytocin rather than vasopressin is the monogamy neurotransmitter. Oxytocin is released by the female when she mates, an event that precedes monogamous pair-bonding.

What role did the voles' environments play in the emergence of the different species-typical behaviors? Montane voles, who lack this fragment of DNA, have multiple partners if the environmental condition permits—that is, if other willing and eager montane voles are available. (But if no other mates were available, wouldn't the montane vole settle for one partner rather than none?)

Why do the same peptides have such different effects in two closely related species? Receptors for arginine vasopressin (V1a) and oxytocin (OT) have markedly different locations across species (Insel, 2010; Insel and Shapiro, 1992). V1a receptors are highly concentrated in the ventral pallidum and OT receptors are expressed most heavily in the nucleus accumbens, both regions strongly associated with reward and reinforcement. In prairie voles, males and females pair-bond following mating. In montane voles, V1a and OT receptors are more heavily expressed in the lateral septum and amygdala, regions less associated with reward and reinforcement. It appears that neuropeptides are released in both species with mating, but that the neurobehavioral consequences of mating are different because the neuropeptides are activating different pathways. In pair-bonding, the act of mating is highly reinforcing and leads to attachment. In non-pair-bonding species, mating is missing those unforgettable highs, and therefore has no enduring effects (Young, Murphy, Young, and Hammock, 2005).

It was easy in the mid-1990s to view this bit of vole lore as intriguing but not to be taken seriously with respect to humans. The effects of socialization are obviously more complex in humans than in voles, such that the influence of one gene may be overridden by multiple environmental and cultural forces, not to mention the plethora of other genes that may also exert contravening influences on human development.

However, disputes about the relevance of simple animal models for complicated human beings take place in a larger arena of neuroscience learning. In anticipation of and following the publication of results from the Human Genome Project in 2003, a new wave of genetic research on connections between genes and human psychology gathered speed. Differences in human social behavior arising from seemingly tiny genetic variations are now widely studied by neuroscience, psychology, and related disciplines.

For example, several researchers have found associations between attachment-relevant behavior and gene variants influencing the neurotransmitters oxytocin, dopamine, serotonin, and their receptors, in adults and children (for detailed references, see Chen, Barth, Johnson, Gotlib and Johnson, 2011, in a recent review of advances in molecular genetics influencing human attachment).

The small variations in some of these transmitter-influencing genes are known as *polymorphisms*, defined as "the occurrence of different forms, stages, or types in individual organisms or in organisms of the same species, independent of sexual variations" (Free Online Dictionary, 2011). *Polymorphism* is a generic term referring to structures or shapes of organisms in general, including genes as one type of structure that has possible variants; *allele* is a term specific to variations in individual genes.

Polymorphisms in genes that help manufacture, transport, or metabolize neurotransmitters have been related to a variety of mental health outcomes, including psychiatric conditions, normal variations in stress reactivity, shyness, behavioral inhibition, social stress regulation, approach/withdrawal, and other behaviors and emotional traits.

The research of Chen and colleagues (2011) is part of a substantial literature on polymorphisms in human genes both for oxytocin and its receptors. These recent studies have found associations between attachment-related phenomena in adults and *oxytocin receptor genes* (OXTR genes). One of the alleles of OXTR has been linked to less-sensitive parenting behavior, higher stress reactivity, reduced social support seeking, and reduced amygdala activation when processing facial emotions. Other alleles of OXTR have been associated with insecure attachment in depressed adults, amygdala volume in both adults and adolescent girls, attachment anxiety in adult females, depression and anxiety symptoms in adolescent girls, and autism-spectrum traits in males, although some inconsistent findings were noted within some of the studies. Given the overwhelmingly positive effects of oxytocin on social behavior overall, it would appear that these alleles in oxytocin receptors must be a few bad apples! The OXTR research illustrates the burgeoning discoveries of contributions by genes to human psychology, far greater than many of us could have imagined a decade or two ago.

Oxytocin, a neuropeptide produced in the hypothalamus for its dual role as hormone and neurotransmitter, influences numerous social behaviors in mammals including mother–infant attachment, pair-bonding, social recognition, and social communication. Conversely, when either the transmitter oxytocin or its receptor is deactivated in mice (called "knockout" mice), these animals show severe deficits in social behavior (Insel, 1997; Winslow and Insel, 2002; Takayanagi et al., 2005; Lim and Young, 2006). For ethical reasons, it is not possible to suppress oxytocin in human research (no reason to believe that mice like it much either—such is the nature of using animals other than humans to further medical research).

Oxytocin plays multiple important roles in human social behavior. One study (Buchheim et al., 2009) found that intranasal administration of oxytocin increased the experience of attachment-related security in previously insecure adults. In another study, children with a history of institutionalization and social deprivation had lower levels of urinary oxytocin during an interactive episode with caregivers than did children without such a history (Wismer Fries et al., 2005). When a single dose of oxytocin was administered to typical adult populations intranasally, people focused more on the eyes of others, showed improved ability to infer mental states from this information, remembered emotional faces better, decreased negativity to offensive faces, increased recognition of positive social words, and for persons with autism, improved their social cognition in the area of social engagement (see Chen et al., 2011, citing multiple studies). A range of social stimuli are now known to be responsive to effects of oxytocin.

Results from a few of the many recent oxytocin and vasopressin studies widen the pool of existing neuropeptide knowledge—a bit like a series of concentric waves rolling out from the center where neuroscientists' latest contributions are dropped into the pool.

Temperament. One dimension of human behavior and development derived directly from genes has been called *temperament*. Temperament refers to a stable, biologically based profile of mood and behavior that emerges early in development. Our temperaments are emotional and behavioral responses that are typical of us and differentiate our own styles and natures from those of others. Temperament is programmed genetically but can sometimes be modified slightly through years of interactions with environments. Temperament tends to remain stable through time, even though behavioral repertoires and styles can be learned that do not come "naturally."

Temperament is powerful force in the entire spectrum of affiliation, bonding, and attachment. Some contemporary developmental psychologists restrict the definition to behavioral components only. For example, Zeanah and Fox define temperament a "behavioral style exhibited by infants or young children in response to a range of stimuli and contexts" (2004, p. 33). We are more persuaded by the view (following Kagan, 2003) that temperament comprises both mood *and* behavior and is a lifelong aspect of individuals rather than primarily a characteristic of infants and young children. The concept of temperament offers a possible explanation for the consistency of certain moods and behaviors through time.

Children's temperaments vary greatly. How many times have you heard mothers with more than one child say "They were as different as night and day from the minute they were born!"? As we shall see, these individual differences play a critical role in development.

On the basis of their famous longitudinal study, Thomas and Chess (1977) identified nine temperamental characteristics: activity level, eating and sleeping rhythms, tendencies to approach or withdraw in novel situations, adaptability to changes in routine, emotional intensity, responsiveness to stimuli, mood, persistence, and distractibility or soothability. They found that the temperamental characteristics of individual children showed considerable stability into adulthood over a 25-year period. The advances in knowledge about temperament made possible by neuroscience findings have led various scholars to revise this formulation of temperament, although the dimensions identified by Thomas and Chess overlap with many of the more recent definitions.

A central concept of many of the newer definitions is that any temperamental category implies specific anatomical structures and specific physiological processes coupled with a set of possible behaviors. Behaviors chosen from this set depend on inputs from the environment. That is, temperament confronts the environment and influences the individual's choices about how to respond to the environment.

A leading temperament scholar, Mary K. Rothbart, defined temperament as constitutionally based differences in reactivity and self-regulation (2011, 1989). *Reactivity* is the ease with which responses are aroused in four areas: motor (by action of muscles), affective (emotional), autonomic (pertaining to involuntary, automatic body functions), and endocrine (through hormone-secreting glands). When she speaks of *self-regulation*, she is referring to behaviors that modulate reactivity, such as approach, withdrawal, attack, inhibition, and self-soothing. As we saw in Chapter 8, genetically based characteristics shape the person by interacting with environmental inputs through complex adaptive systems over time. In Rothbart's model of temperament, individual differences in reactivity are present at birth—that is, they are strongly influenced by genetics. Self-regulation, on the other hand, emerges gradually from interaction between genetically based characteristics and the environment. Recent neural network research is now elucidating how these processes work (Rothbart, Sheese, Rosario, Rueda, and Posner, 2011).

An example of the interaction of temperament with environment came from the work of van den Boom (1994). She assessed infants' irritability at 15 days of age and then measured the babies' attachment to their mothers at one year of age using Ainsworth's Strange Situation Procedure (Ainsworth, Blehar, Waters, and Wall, 1978). Mothers were primarily of low socioeconomic status. Temperamentally irritable infants were far more likely to be classified as insecurely attached one-year-olds; non-irritable infants were more likely to be classified securely attached at one year. However, *parent sensitivity was not related to attachment status as measured by the Strange Situation procedure.* This finding suggested that genetic influences were more important determinants of attachment status at age one than was the quality of parental responsiveness.

In a second study, van den Boom repeated the measures, but only with temperamentally irritable infants. The infant-mother pairs were assigned to a treatment group and a control group. Control-group subjects received no intervention and were simply reassessed at one year. The mothers in the treatment group were visited at home and were given instruction about how to soothe their babies and how to play with them.

At one year follow-up, infants in the control group were much more likely to be classified insecurely attached, whereas infants in the treatment group were just as likely to be classified securely attached as the nonirritable infants in the first study. It appeared that infant temperamental irritability may affect the quality of mother–infant interactions. Irritable, hard-to-soothe infants behave in ways that push their mothers away. Thus, irritability may impede attachment by interacting with mothers' not knowing how to soothe their babies and/or the exhaustion and frustration involved in trying to care for an irritable baby. It appears that a negative feedback loop takes shape: irritable infants discourage mothers' attempts to cuddle, frustrated mothers withdraw, and the infants lose opportunities for attachment-promoting exchanges with the mother.

In a study of child fear and compliance, temperament/environment interactions were also important (Kochanska, 1993). Because individual differences in fear reactivity reflect the child's sensitivity to conditioned signals of punishment, very fearful children should be more sensitive to maternal demands for compliance than less fearful children. Indeed, mothers' directives elicited higher compliance in fearful children than in less fearful children. The child's temperament interacted with the mothers' management behaviors.

Behaviors related to cross-cultural differences in values and child-rearing attitudes were studied by Chen, Hastings, and colleagues (1998) using the Child-Rearing Practices Report scales. North Americans typically devalue temperamental behavioral inhibition to novel stimuli (limiting one's overt responses to the stimuli), but this is a valued characteristic in Chinese culture.

Chinese children showed more behavioral inhibition to novel stimuli than their Canadian counterparts. In almost all cases, the direction of the relationship between the children's behavioral inhibition and the mothers' child-rearing beliefs was reversed between the two groups. In the Chinese sample, children's behavioral inhibition correlated positively with mothers' acceptance and negatively with a punishment orientation. In the Canadian sample, children's behavioral inhibition correlated negatively with mothers' acceptance and positively with a punishment orientation. The study showed the effects of prevailing cultural beliefs and norms on interactions between mothers' beliefs and children's behavior.

Kagan (1994) identified two clusters of temperamental qualities that usually persist from infancy through adolescence. Inhibited children (about 10% of American two-year-olds) are described as shy, cautious, timid, watchful, and restrained. At the opposite end, uninhibited children (also about 10%) appear naturally sociable, bold, energetic, spontaneous, and friendly. The majority of children (80%) fall somewhere between these two extremes.

Kagan and his colleagues observed two temperamental dimensions in the second year with regard to response to unfamiliar events: excessive shyness versus sociability, and timidity versus boldness. The researchers found that these characteristics in toddlers were related to characteristics that the children exhibited as four-month-old infants, whom the researchers dubbed "high reactive" because the babies showed vigorous motor activity and distress in response to unfamiliar sights, sounds, and smells. In the second year, the "high-reactive" infants tended to become shy, fearful, and timid in response to unfamiliar events.

The other group of four-month-old infants ("low reactive") showed low levels of motor activity and little irritability in response to the same stimuli. These children were likely to become sociable and relatively fearless as toddlers.

The high-reactive children showed elevated levels of morning cortisol (a hormone produced by the body in response to challenge or stress), faster and less variable heart rates, and a pattern of right frontal activation on encephalograms (Kagan, Snidman, and Arcus, 1998). Kagan suspected that each temperamental type has a distinct neurochemistry that affects the excitability of the amygdala. Neurochemical profiles were thought to involve variation in the concentration of dopamine, norepinephrine, opioids, or GABA, or the distribution of receptors for these neurotransmitters. Kagan's hypothesis was that because GABA inhibits neural activity, infants who cannot regulate distress may have inadequate GABA function.[1]

Some of the children who had been classified as high or low reactive at 4 months were studied again at the age of 11 years using a three-hour battery of tests (McManis, Kagan, Snidman, and Woodward, 2002). A larger proportion of high than of low reactive children remained shy and subdued at age 11 years when presented with an unfamiliar stimulus, whereas a larger proportion of low than of high reactive 11-year-olds were sociable and emotionally spontaneous in the same unfamiliar situations.

The 11-year-olds classified as high-reactive infants showed greater electroencephalogram activation in the right parietal lobe than in the left at age 11 and, if they had also been classified as fearful in the second year, greater activation in the right frontal area. Together with other neurobiological measures, these observations suggested that levels of psychological reactivity are associated with greater neurophysiological activity in very specific brain regions, and that observed behavioral differences first observed and recorded at 4 months of age were still present (although not universally so) when the children were 11 years old (Kagan, 2003).

A powerful implication of this longitudinal evidence for temperament is that children's temperaments can actually shape their environments. Since temperament is typically stable over the developing years, the behaviors that express the particular temperament are repeated again and again, therefore eliciting similar patterns of responses over and over.

During the first decade of the 21st century, an unprecedented volume of neuroscience research has revealed extraordinary complexity in these processes, much of it not yet known at the time Kagan articulated his hypotheses. He continued to strongly support advances in neuroscience research, as he had before developmental psychology became immersed in this emerging science.

A child's development is influenced by millions of exchanges back and forth between the child and his or her environment. Cheerful, relaxed, or outgoing infants and children tend to elicit responses from their environments that differ from those elicited by tense, anxious, or irritable infants and children. The developing child is affected by the feedback from his or her environment and then responds to it, so that there is an ongoing pattern of reciprocal influence. It's important to remember that a child's development is shaped not by temperament alone nor by environment alone. The repeated interactions between children and their environments—environments in which primary caretakers are very important but by no means the only actors—are recorded in children's experiential memories and form the basis for emotional learning.

Some aspects of the developing child's constitutional make-up can be modified at the neurobiological level as a result of the environment's responses to the child's responses. Kagan found that the temperaments of children born fearful and inhibited usually remained stable throughout development, but that in a few cases, relaxed, low-key environments with especially sensitive mothers could lessen this inborn characteristic. In other words, environment can modify genetic effects. A heavy trip for mothers? Yes indeed.

But these findings should not lead us to conclude that most children can be remade by parenting. Although temperamental characteristics can sometimes be modified, they tend to be stable. Parents influence, but they can't determine. With more knowledge and better support, parents can enhance and enrich, but they can't remake. American culture is permeated with the belief that parents have the power to raise their children to become happy, well-adjusted adults.

The corollary of this belief is that adults who are unhappy must be the victims of parental failures somewhere along the way. Despite the fact that neither the belief nor its corollary is borne out by research evidence, the belief's continuing popularity, according to Kagan (1994), reflects the fondness of Americans for the idea of connectedness—that the past leads in lock-step fashion to the present.

Resilience. Not all individuals are harmed by early caretaker deprivation. Rhesus monkeys and beagles are harmed, but crab-eater monkeys and terriers aren't (Fuller and Clark, 1968). Genetic differences among species of monkeys and dogs apparently create temperamental characteristics that lead them to process the experience of caretaker deprivation in different ways. Humans exhibit these differences as well (Kagan, 1994).

Several studies have shown that psychological damage early in life is often reversible, and that the degree of long-term harm conferred on children by early deprivation may vary considerably with the child's temperament. Most notable are the longitudinal studies of Emmy Werner (1989), who followed more than 200 children on a Hawaiian island from birth through the age of 32. Some of the children reared in horrendous circumstances were doing well at age 32. Conversely, some children who appeared to have had every material and emotional advantage during childhood had emotional disturbances and/or tumultuous lives at age 32.

A growing body of research focuses on *resilience*, people's ability to withstand or bounce back from adverse events. Taken as a whole, recent research on child development and adult psychopathology discredits long-popular developmental theories which presuppose that progression is continuous through various psychological stages. According to such theories, in order to progress satisfactorily to the next stage of development, a child must "pass" the current level—no skipping allowed (Kagan, 1994).

With respect to advancing through the presumed stages, these theories use phrases such as "successfully navigate" or "resolve conflicts inherent in" or "achieve the tasks of" a particular stage in order to make a successful transition to the next stage. Does failure to negotiate developmental tasks associated with an oral, anal, or genital stage by the developing child turn into a personality conflict or a personality deficit, often repressed, that resurfaces in adulthood as a psychological disorder?

The evidence runs counter to this belief. Numerous instances of resilience illustrate the self-righting tendencies of the human species. For example, children adopted into American families after early rearing in East European orphanages showed markedly diverse outcomes. At the time of adoption,

A. Three Mauras in the Lagoon --Reflections on the Self

B. PET Scans of Adults without and with Attention-Deficit Hyperactivity Disorder (ADHD)

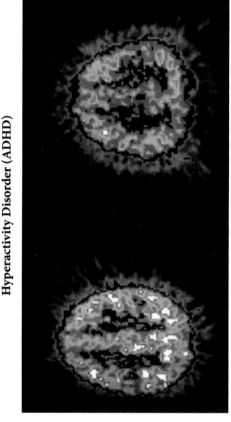

No ADHD

ADHD

Zametkin AJ, Nordahi TE, Gross M, King AC, Semple WE, Rumsey J, Hamburger S and Cohen RM (1990). Cerebral glucose metabolism in adults with hyperactivity of childhood onset. NEJM 323(20): 1361-1366.

C. Cerebral Cortex

Blue: prefrontal cortex plus premotor cortex
Beige: remainder of cortex with sensory locations

prefrontal cortex
(see color illustration E. for details)

premotor cortex

primary motor cortex
primary somatosensory cortex
(touch)

primary visual cortex
(hidden under skull)

primary auditory cortex

primary gustatory cortex

primary olfactory cortex

D. Larger Inner Brain Structures and Cerebellum

corpus callosum

caudate nucleus

thalamus

substantia nigra

midbrain

pons

BRAIN STEM

medulla

cere-bellum

spinal cord

hypothalamus

putamen

globus pallidus

nucleus accumbens

pituitary

VTA

mesolimbic dopamine pathway

amygdala

hippocampus

E. Team Players: Prefrontal Cortex and Inner Brain Structures

dorsolateral prefrontal cortex
(dlPFC)

mediolateral prefrontal cortex
(mlPFC)

anterior
cingulate
cortex
(ACC)

orbitofrontal cortex
(OFC)

insular
cortex
(IC or INS)

F. Favorite Highways for Pleasure-Making Neurotransmitters

mesolimbic dopamine pathway

mesocortical pathways

GLU = glutamate
DA = dopamine
5-HT = serotonin
NE = norepinephrine
OP = opioid
GABA = gamma-
    aminobutyric acid

cell
body
axon
terminal
buttons

G. Neuron on Stage

H. Neural Circuits for Eating

relays taste info to ventral postero-medial nucleus of thalamus

messages from stomach to visceral NTS that it's full or empty

messages from 10,000 taste buds to gustatory NTS in medulla

Hypoth

NAc

VTA

insular cortex (IC or INS)

orbitofrontal cortex (OFC)

Hypoth = hypothalamus
NAc = nucleus accumbens
VTA = ventral tegmental area

I. Neural Circuits for Eating: Zooming in on some Hypothalamus and Brainstem Contributors

J (1). Hedonic Hotspots and Their Many Collaborators in Pleasures

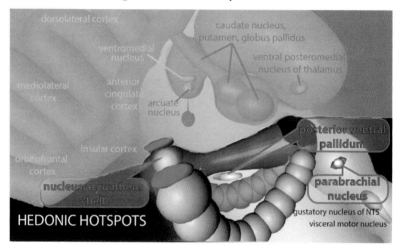

J (2). Sweet Taste, Bitter Taste

Positive reactions

Human newborns   *Orangutans*   *Rat*

Negative reactions

K. Environmental Stressors Excite Neural Systems (phase 1)

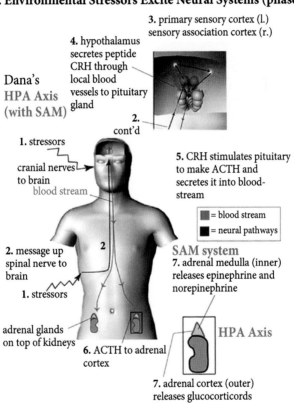

3. primary sensory cortex (l.)
sensory association cortex (r.)

4. hypothalamus
secretes peptide
CRH through
local blood
vessels to pituitary
gland

Dana's
HPA Axis
(with SAM)

2.
cont'd

1. stressors

cranial nerves
to brain
blood stream

5. CRH stimulates pituitary
to make ACTH and
secretes it into blood-
stream

■ = blood stream
■ = neural pathways

2. message up
spinal nerve to
brain

2

1. stressors

SAM system
7. adrenal medulla (inner)
releases epinephrine and
norepinephrine

adrenal glands
on top of kidneys

HPA Axis

6. ACTH to adrenal
cortex

7. adrenal cortex (outer)
releases glucocorticords

L. Environmental Stressors
Excite Neural Systems (Phases 2-3)

Neural System Excites Body Action Systems (phase 2)

8. Both HPA and SAM systems send their arousing chemicals around the body via bloodstream (glucocorticoids, norepinephrine and epinephrine).

 = bloodstream

= neural pathways

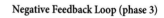

Negative Feedback Loop (phase 3)

9. Blood vessels and nerves carry messages back to brain structures themselves and give negative feedback to hypothalamus and pituitary. The messages order inhibition of CRH transcription and stress-induced release of norepinephrine. Now homeostasis is restored.

M. Cocaine in Action

Riding the Ecstasy and Despair Roller Coaster?

Dopamine neuron before a hit of cocaine

from VTA to nucleus accumbens

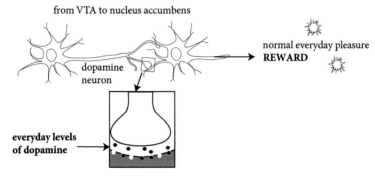

normal everyday pleasure
REWARD

dopamine
neuron

everyday levels
of dopamine

Dopamine neuron with a hit of cocaine

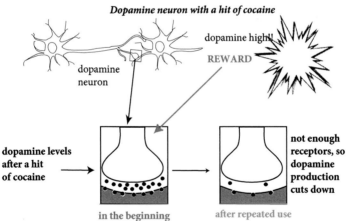

dopamine high!!
REWARD

dopamine
neuron

dopamine levels
after a hit
of cocaine

not enough
receptors, so
dopamine
production
cuts down

in the beginning   after repeated use

N. Natural Opioids, Synthesized Opiate Drugs

Inhibitory Interneuron Keeps the GABA Neuron in Check

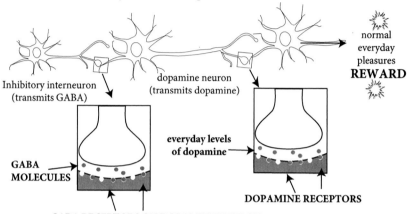

Inhibitory interneuron
(transmits GABA)

dopamine neuron
(transmits dopamine)

normal
everyday
pleasures
REWARD

everyday levels
of dopamine

**GABA
MOLECULES**

DOPAMINE RECEPTORS

GABA RECEPTORS ON DOPAMINE NEURON

Opiate Inhibits the Inhibitory Interneuron

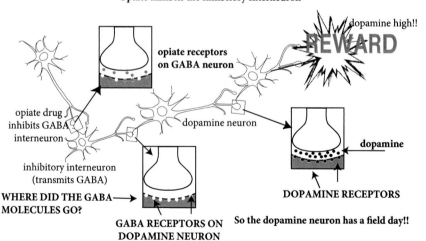

dopamine high!!

REWARD

opiate receptors
on GABA neuron

opiate drug
inhibits GABA
interneuron

dopamine neuron

dopamine

inhibitory interneuron
(transmits GABA)

DOPAMINE RECEPTORS

**WHERE DID THE GABA
MOLECULES GO?**

**GABA RECEPTORS ON
DOPAMINE NEURON**

So the dopamine neuron has a field day!!

Loss of brain volume associated with schizophrenia is clearly shown by magnetic resonance imaging (MRI) scans comparing the size of ventricles (butterfly-shaped, fluid-filled spaces in the midbrain) of identical twins, one of whom has schizophrenia (right). The ventricles of the twin with schizophrenia are larger. This suggests structural brain changes associated with the illness.

Source: Daniel Weinberger, MD, NIMH Clicnical Brain Disorders Branch

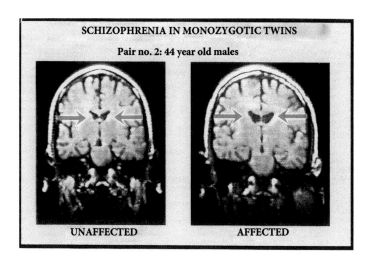

O. Schizophrenia: Monozygotic Twins, PET and MRI Scans

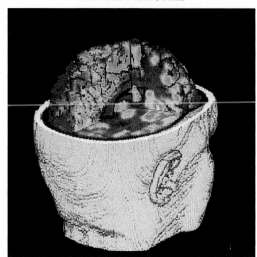

Combined 3-D PET and MRI scans show human brain activity (red structure at 4.00, just above ear) triggered by clozapine. This is a different pattern than is seen with traditional neuroleptics like haloperidol.

Source: John Hsiao, NIMH Experimental Therapeutics Branch

P. Obsessive-Compulsive and Depressive
   Conditions, PET Scans

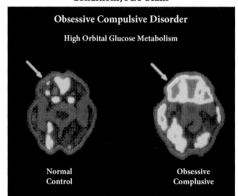

▲ PET (positron emission tomography) scans show increased brain metabolism (brighter colors), particularly in the frontal cortex, in the brain of a person with obsessive-compulsive disorder (OCD) juxtaposed with a brain of a person without OCD. This suggests altered brain function in people with OCD.

Source: Lewis Baxter, MD, University of Alabama

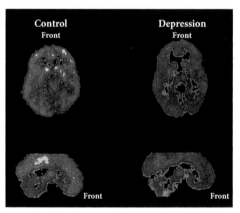

◀ PET (positron emission tomography) scans of the brain of a person without depression (L) and the brain of a person with depression (R) reveal reduced brain activity (darker colors) during depression, especially in the prefrontal cortex.

Source: Mark George, MD, NIMH Biological Psychiatry Branch

This material was made possible by the Campaign to End Discrimination Founding Sponsors: Abott Laboratories, Bristol-Myers Squibb Company, Eki Lily and Company, Janssen Pharmaceutica, Pfizer, Inc., Sandoz Pharmaceuticals, SmithKline Beecham, Wyeth-Ayerst Laboratories
In accordance with NAMI policy, acceptance of funds does not imply endorsement of any business practice or product.

For more information contact NAMI:
1 (800)950-6264

children were often cognitively impaired, had visual problems, sensory integration deficits, and language-processing difficulties that impeded cognitive
and emotional functioning. However, in one study of more than 200 children adopted into American families, as many as 60% made impressive leaps
forward in cognitive and emotional development during the years following
adoption. Another 20% continued to have serious deficits. The remaining 20%
(dubbed "resilient rascals") showed no ill effects from their institutionalization
(Groza, Ryan, and Cash, 2003; Talbot, 1998).

Observers agree that the child's age at the time of adoption is a critical
factor in the likelihood of normal development. Yet even children adopted
with major deficits and at older ages often show impressive developmental
catch-ups (Rutter, 1998). Another study concluded that all 46 adoptees from a
Romanian orphanage had been able to form some sort of attachment to their
adoptive parents (Talbot, 1998).

A study of resilience in 205 children from an urban community sample
assessed children in elementary school and then followed them for 10 years
(Masten, Hubbard, Gest et al., 1999). Outcomes of competence in late adolescence were examined in relation to adversity over time, preexisting competence, and psychosocial resources. Better intellectual functioning and
parenting resources were associated with good outcomes across competence
domains, even in the context of severe, chronic adversity. IQ and parenting
resources appeared to have a specific protective role with respect to antisocial
behavior.

The resilient adolescents had adequate competence across the three domains
of academics, conduct, and peer relations despite a history of high adversity.
They had much more in common with their low-adversity competent peers,
including average or better IQ, supportive parenting, and better psychological well-being, than with peers having high-adversity histories similar to their
own, who had few resources and high negative emotionality.

In a sample of middle-class and working-class families with normally
developing children and adolescents, Booth, Johnson, Granger, and colleagues
(2003) assessed the expression of testosterone-related problem behavior. In
adolescents, high levels of testosterone are related to stage of pubertal development and have been linked to problems with aggressivity, risk-taking, and
depression. The investigators found that increased problematic risk-taking
behavior and increased levels of depression were related to lower quality of
child–parent relationships. The higher the quality of child–parent relationships, the lower the amount of testosterone-related adjustment problems.

The authors present these findings as an example of the mediating influence
of psychosocial factors on a known biology-behavior connection. However,
alternative explanations fit equally well with an integrated biopsychosocial
model: could more positive child–parent relationships be a response to more
pleasant, unproblematic behaviors by the children rather than a stimulus for

them? Or could child–parent interactions form two different kinds of feed-back loops in which hormone-driven troublesome behavior was either ampli-fied or reduced in response to parental behaviors?

Granger and Kivlighan (2003) note that biological functions set the stage for behavioral adaptation to environmental challenge, and that environmental challenge, in turn, may affect fast-acting biological processes (such as hor-mone secretion) and slow-acting biological processes (such as gene expres-sion). Biological activities that facilitate a particular behavioral process may be either stimulated or attenuated by social forces. Once again, the theory of complex adaptive systems is invoked in developmental psychology as it inte-grates inborn temperament, biological processes, and social and environmen-tal forces.

34

Affiliation, Bonding, and Attachment

Affiliation is a precursor to bonding, which is another word for the process of becoming attached in humans and other animals. A simple model expresses this sequence:

Affiliation > Bonding > Attachment

In some species, attachment takes place very fast, immediately after birth, in a brief window of opportunity known as a *critical period*. The affiliation and bonding phases are collapsed into as little as a couple of hours. By contrast, the road to human attachment may be built slowly, advancing over time from affiliation through bonding over months or years. Friendly human associations may continue for years as affiliations or may become attachments, but in contrast to bonds (attachments), affiliations appear to not entail a sense of significant personal loss when those persons are no longer with us. When bonds are ruptured, we feel emotional loss.

We'll look at research pertaining to affiliation first, then bonding and attachment. In this book, we'll use the word *bond* interchangeably with *attachment* and the word *bonding* interchangeably with *attaching*. This way of defining the two concepts reflects that becoming either attached or bonded is a complex neurobiological and psychosocial process in which an individual develops strong positive emotion toward another person or a group. It is also common for a person to concurrently form a bond toward a group plus one or two special individuals within that group. Such groups exist all over the planet and are characterized by some distinct reason for being, such as a tribe in an uncentralized political system, an infantry combat group, a peer-support group for addiction, or a baseball team.

Affiliation has been defined as "to connect or associate oneself" (Merriam-Webster, 2011) and as "a positive, sometimes intimate, personal relationship" (Zimbardo and Formica, 1963). There are many definitions, some referring only to organizational affiliation. Our focus here is on individual interpersonal affiliation.

Illustrations of affiliative behaviors are an infant cooing to another person, little girls exchanging gossip, acquaintances chatting at the mall, or two adults flirting and dating. Affiliative behaviors are mediated by neurochemical systems that transmit monoamines (serotonin and dopamine) and neuropeptides (oxytocin, vasopressin, and the endorphins) interacting with sex and adrenal hormones.

Affiliation is fully developed only in birds and mammals. Deficits in affiliation among humans are prominent in autism and in some forms of schizophrenia, manifested by a decrease in separation distress, lack of reciprocal social interaction, and inability to form social bonds. Knowledge about the neurochemistry of affiliation is therefore important for finding routes to treat these disorders, apart from interest in affiliation as a defining feature of humanness.

Currently there appears to be a consensus among neuroscientists that affiliative and attachment processes are distributed in multiple regions of the brain, involving a few specific neurotransmitters mostly from the groups of neuropeptides and monoamines (Insel, 2010). To get a rough sense of the importance of different transmitters in the affiliation process, I reviewed the most recently published 100 out of a total of 381 abstracts (years 2008–2011), obtained by the following set of keywords: affiliation AND (oxytocin OR serotonin OR vasopressin OR dopamine OR endorphin*). In descending order, the neurotransmitters participating in affiliative processes in these 100 abstracts were: oxytocin, 53 abstracts; dopamine, 14; vasopressin, 12; serotonin, 11; and endorphins, 0. In addition, there were 2 abstracts involving corticotrophin releasing factor (CRF), and 1 each for norepinephrine and tyrosine hydroxylase (TH). That is, oxytocin was investigated more times than all of the others combined, and exceeded the next most studied (dopamine) by almost a factor of 4. In fact the three runners-up were virtually the same (14, 12, and 11 hits, respectively).

As early as 1992, oxytocin actions had been discovered that went far beyond its roles in childbirth (uterine contraction) and lactation (milk ejection)—roles known since the early 1900s. Oxytocin's involvement in social affiliation and attachment was now becoming a subject of fascination to neuroscience researchers and psychologists. Insel and Shapiro (1992) reported that recent research had revealed a more general role for oxytocin in modulating affiliative behavior in both sexes.

The news media began to take note. "A potent peptide prompts the urge to cuddle," proclaimed the *New York Times* (Angier, 1991, p. C1). This usually staid publication went on to rhapsodize about the neurotransmitter and hormone oxytocin.

> "New studies show an old hormone orchestrates many of life's pleasures and social interactions.... Just the potion for a bellicose world,".... In some cases, it acts as an aphrodisiac, inspiring males to seek females more ardently and females to invite their overtures more passionately. The hormone...helps stimulate the sensations of sexual arousal and climax. And after copulation, it acts as the proverbial cigarette, fostering a feeling of relaxed satisfaction.

It makes new mothers more likely to nurture their young and new fathers happier to help out around the nest. Even among those who are neither sex partners nor parents, the compound can spur an overwhelming urge to cuddle. (Angier, 1991).

Since this glowing endorsement marked the popular debut of oxytocin as a "social" neurotransmitter more than 20 years ago, knowledge about affiliation has advanced. The behavioral effects of oxytocin in 13 subjects with autism, a group of disorders characterized by deficits in social interaction, were studied by Andari, Duhamel and colleagues (2010). In a simulated ball game where participants interacted with fictitious partners, people with autism who had inhaled oxytocin showed stronger interactions with cooperative partners and reported feelings of trust and preference. While the subjects viewed pictures of faces, oxytocin selectively increased the duration that they gazed at the eyes, a region of the face that communicates social information. Thus, the study concluded that oxytocin increased their response to others and promoted social behavior and affect. This preliminary experimental treatment suggested a therapeutic potential of oxytocin through its action on a core dimension of autism.

To explore relationships among high neuropeptide levels, marital interaction, and wound healing, 37 married couples were engaged for a 24-hour stay in a hospital research unit where they volunteered to have small blister wounds created on their forearms. They then participated in a structured social support interaction task (Gouin et al., 2010). Blister sites were monitored daily after discharge to measure how quickly the wounds healed. Blood samples were drawn for analysis of oxytocin, vasopressin, and cytokine (a protein released by cells that influences interactions between cells).

Communication behaviors during the structured interaction task were more positive in subjects with higher oxytocin levels, and blister wounds in those in the upper oxytocin quartile healed faster than those of participants in lower oxytocin quartiles. Fewer negative communication behaviors were related to higher vasopressin levels. Moreover, experimental wounds of women in the upper vasopressin quartile healed faster than in the remainder of the sample. These data confirm and extend prior evidence implicating both oxytocin and vasopressin in couples' positive and negative communication behaviors, and also suggest further evidence of their role in an important health outcome, wound healing.

Almost 20 years after the *New York Times* celebrated this altogether lovable neurotransmitter, it was still the acknowledged favorite for promoting happy human connections. Lee, Macbeth, Pagani, and Young (2009) titled their article "Oxytocin: the Great Facilitator of Life!"

Grooming another individual is an important way that many animals, notably primates, affiliate. In fact, in many species this may be the predominant mode of socialization (Insel and Winslow, 1998; Dunbar, 1997). Although it may appear to human observers that a monkey energetically checking and combing another monkey's fur is trying to remove lice, grooming others is an important way of establishing alliances and reinforcing the dominance hierarchy, whether or not the groomed animal is infested. In fact, Dunbar (1997) suggests that this behavior is so important for social cohesion among primates that it represents a form of tactile "gossip"—that is, grooming may be the ape equivalent of conversations among customers and hairdressers at a salon.

Levels of serotonin metabolites (5-HIAA) have been positively correlated with time spent grooming and time spent in close proximity to other members of the social group and have been negatively correlated with aggression and impaired impulse control (Mehlman, Higley, Faucher et al, 1995). That is, the more 5-HIAA animals have, the more sociable and the less aggressive they are. The social meaning of grooming varies from species to species and is associated with social status and kinship.

Although grooming behavior appears simple, it's actually a complex social behavior with many possible different meanings, depending on how much time is spent, who receives it, relationship between groomed and groomer, and social status. In some species, dominants groom subordinates, in other species the reverse is true.

In an inventive study of the relationship between neurotransmitters and social behavior, Raleigh and colleagues (1991) removed the dominant male from each of 12 social groups of vervets (small African monkeys) and treated one of the remaining males with either a serotonin-enhancing drug or serotonin-reducing one. The design was a crossover study (that is, each treated male received each drug in two separate periods). In every instance, the male who had received the serotonin-enhancing drug became dominant, but when the same male received the serotonin-reducing drug, another male in the group became dominant. Of particular interest to us is that the males who achieved dominance didn't do so by aggression. Instead, they became influential in their groups by increasing affiliative behaviors, including grooming, with females.

Hormones are clearly important in affiliation. Mastripieri and Zehr (1998) administered the female sex hormone estrogen to female macaque monkeys whose ovaries had been removed. In response, the monkeys increased their handling of other monkeys' infants. Bardi French, Ramirez, and Brent (2004) report positive association of levels of female sex hormones and negative association of levels of cortisol with infant-directed behaviors in baboon mothers living in groups. Mothers who displayed more stress-related behaviors maintained less contact with their infants and had higher postpartum cortisol levels and lower postpartum female sex hormones levels than did other mothers.

An interesting finding was that mothers overall who had *higher* prepartum cortisol levels showed *higher* levels of infant-directed affiliative behaviors after their babies were born. Their cortisol levels dropped dramatically soon after the infant's birth (Bardi and colleagues, 2004; Bardi, Shimizu, Barrett, et al., 2003).

The reasons for these findings are not clear, but Bardi and colleagues note the importance of the whole endocrine (hormone) system as a functional unit with respect to enhancing maternal care in primates. If the high levels of cortisol persist for more than a brief period after birth, the negative effects of excessive cortisol over time set in (see Part III, Chapter 23).

Diet also can affect patterns of social and aggressive behavior of monkeys living in stable social groups (Simon, Kaplan, Hu, et al., 2004). Do you believe that soy products are "health foods"? In this experiment, diets rich in soy protein and other soy products were fed to 44 adult male macaque monkeys over a 15-month period. The soy-fed monkeys engaged in intense aggression 67% more often and submissive behavior 203% more often than monkeys receiving a usual monkey diet. The soy-fed monkeys also spent 68% less time in physical contact with other monkeys, 50% less time near other monkeys, and 30% more time alone.

The presumed reason for the marked effects of soy on affiliative and aggressive behavior was that soy-based foods bind with estrogen receptors and interact with estrogen-mediated responses. Estrogen produced by the processing of androgen (male hormone) facilitates typical male aggressive behavior.

Gillman, Rifas-Shiman, and colleagues (2008) examined 1,110 mother-child pairs in a prospective prebirth study to learn the risk of children being overweight at age three (Body Mass Index/BMI for age and sex > or = 95th percentile). During pregnancy, 9.8% of mothers smoked and 50% gained excessive weight. Four modifiable risk factors (levels of maternal smoking during pregnancy, gestational weight gain, breastfeeding duration, and infant sleep duration) together with covariates of maternal BMI and education, child race/ethnicity, and household income yielded estimated probabilities of overweight for each of the 16 combinations of the four risk factors.

At age three, 9.5% of the children were overweight with likelihood ranging from 0.06 among children exposed to favorable levels of all four risk factors, to 0.29 with adverse levels of all four. Healthful levels of four factors during early development predicted much lower probability of overweight at age three than adverse levels.

Using data from famine studies (Dutch Hunger Winter of 1959 and Chinese famines of 1961) prenatal undernutrition was found to double the risk of schizophrenia in adult life (Xu, Sun et al., 2009; Brown and Susser, 2008), possibly due to effects related to levels of nutrients and choline or folic acid during development (Zeisel, 2008; Steegers-Theunissen, Obermann-Borst et al., 2009). These studies consider epigenetic programming in schizophrenia risk by looking at prospective biomarkers such as nutrient deficiency that might predict vulnerability. Many other studies report long-term effects of epigenetic factors such as large-scale famines, maternal high-fat diets during pregnancy, and effects on dopamine functions of gestational protein deprivation.

The effects of environmental enrichment were studied in male mice to ascertain the relative roles of the physical and social components (Pietropaolo, Branchi, Cirulli et al., 2004). Mice five days old were randomly assigned to one of four different housing conditions for a period of five days: (1) alone in a cage, (2) with one other mouse in a cage, (3) alone in a physically enriched cage, and (4) with one other mouse in a physically enriched cage. As adults, 80 days after the exposure to physical enrichment environments, all mice were released into an open field. In the open, mice who had been housed with companions in the physically enriched environment showed more affiliative and less aggressive social interaction and more frequently became dominant. They also showed changes in growth-hormone levels. The combined physical and social enrichment appeared to increase brain plasticity (capacity for change) as well as the animals' ability to cope with social challenges.

In a novel experiment with human volunteers, Tse and Bond (2002) tested the effect of a selective serotonin reuptake inhibitor (SSRI), citalopram, on social behavior with an apartment mate and a stranger. Healthy volunteers (10 pairs) took part in a randomized double-blind crossover study in which subjects were given the drug for two weeks and a placebo for two weeks. That is, neither the subjects nor the investigators knew who was receiving the placebo nor who was receiving the medication at any given time. In each pair, one person (the subject) took the treatment, while the other (the apartment mate) did not. On the last day of each of the two treatment periods, the subjects socially interacted with a confederate (assisting the experimenter). The confederate behaved as a responsive person in a stranger/subject social interaction situation. After the interaction, the subjects played a game with the confederate that measures cooperative behavior and communication.

While on medication, subjects reduced the number of points they awarded themselves and sent more cooperative messages during the game. They also showed a dominant pattern of eye contact in the stranger/subject social interaction. They were rated as significantly less submissive by their apartment mates than when they were on placebo. The researchers concluded that the administration of a serotonin-enhancing drug can modify social status in different interactions and can increase affiliative behavior (Tse and Bond, 2002).

In another human experiment, 50 healthy men and women volunteers (criteria were no history of psychiatric diagnosis, psychotropic medication, or substance abuse) were randomly assigned to receive either placebo or paroxetine, an SSRI, for four weeks. Subjects worked in pairs to solve problems collaboratively, with new partners on each trial, one in each pair receiving placebo, the other medication. The study was blind (neither subjects nor experimenters knew who received the drug). Changes in cooperative and noncooperative behaviors were coded from the beginning to the end of the experiment.

Subjects receiving the medication showed a decrease in negative affect and an increase in affiliative and cooperative behaviors as compared with subjects receiving placebo. The degree of change correlated with measures of subjects' blood levels of the SSRI (Knutson, Wolkowitz, Cole et al., 1998).

There were numerous instances when social interaction dampened HPA-axis activity and improved health outcomes, but little information emerged about the underlying mechanisms through which social behavior can provide a buffer against stress-related disease. Data suggested that oxytocin is the physiological link between positive social interactions and suppression of HPA axis activity. Other studies suggested that increases in serotonin brought about by handling stressed rat pups may have prevented the increase of glucocorticoid receptors (Insel and Winslow, 1998). It appears that beneficial effects can be achieved through social or tactile behaviors by others that enhance these specific "happiness" transmitters.

Bonding. What is *bonding*? We usually think of it as forming connections with other creatures of a longer duration than simply a brief friendly encounter and of greater intensity or depth than long-term friendly associations.

Bonding requires a situation, environment, or condition in which bonding can take place, and individuals' temperamental capability to make bonds with other creatures. Most people need and form bonds with others, but a small minority of humans lack that capacity, presumably due to a genetic difference or developmental accident that is often considered a deficit in interpersonal need or ability.

Bonding is associated with words in addition to attachment and affiliation, such as attraction, affection, loyalty, unconditional love, needs fulfillment, gratitude, protectiveness—you can undoubtedly think of other important human states that you associate with bonding.

Pair-bonding (bonding between two individuals) can be sexual or nonsexual. We pair-bond with same-sex friends and opposite-sex friends, both with and without any perceived sexual component. We bond with our children, and they with us; sometimes we bond with other people's children. We bond with our pets. We bond with mentors and teachers. Bonding can also occur by an individual to a group. We even bond to performing artists, athletes, and political leaders whom we know well, because they spend many hours in our homes on TV and computer screens—and they don't know us at all!

Pair-bonding between couples and between parents and children involves hormones, neurotransmitters, and entire brain/body subsystems. These systems include microscopic and larger brain structures, pathways connecting these structures, and molecules of neurotransmitters and their cousin neuromodulators that transmit messages both chemically and electrically along pathways and across gaps between structures (synapses).

Oxytocin again comes into play in bonding. It's essential for sexual feelings, orgasm, nursing infants (letting down the milk), the urge to hold or care for other people's infants, levels of monogamy versus polygamy in some species, and—well, the overall urge to cuddle, as reported above. Pulitzer prize-winning science writer Natalie Angier (*New York Times*, January 22, 1991), evokes in the reader the scent of a magical potion—the type only the kindest, most loving fairies can bestow on human creatures and many other animals.

But oxytocin (mostly for females) and vasopressin (mostly for males) aren't myths, metaphors, or fantasies—they're real, measurable, hard science compounds, and almost all of us have them from birth to death. These chemicals promote positive feelings for others that emerge in the presence of positive reinforcement. *Positive reinforcement* itself is a pleasant feeling that takes place in a few locations in our brains (and the brains of many other creatures)—the pleasure centers or pleasure pathways of the brain (see Part III, Chapters 21 and 22). Freud always believed such centers existed but couldn't prove it; it turns out he was right. Decades after his death, technologies have enabled us to learn a great deal about the brain's virtuosity in transmitting pleasure messages.

Poor Freud—he would have been thrilled and excited to learn so much of what we now know by our sheer good luck to be alive in the decades of the brain! (In July 1990, President George H.W. Bush officially designated the years 1990 to 2000 the Decade of the Brain.) Throughout the history of the human species, unbeknownst to our grandparents, we would never have been able to enjoy anything without the actions of certain neurotransmitters and other chemical substances in our brain pleasure locations!

So whenever something about being with certain people makes us feel good (by activating those centers), we want to repeat those feelings (the definition of positive reinforcement). Those feeling-good or happy or satisfied or laughing or excited or exhilarating emotions are the building blocks of emotional bonds.

Moreover, shared suffering also creates emotional bonds between people. Some of our strongest bonds to others arise between ourselves and people who have been through something incredibly sad or life-threatening together with us, like military combat, death of a person we loved, victimization by some cruel and powerful person, or struggle for survival in an environmental catastrophe. Rescuers of people who have gone through any of these experiences also often become strongly and reciprocally bonded with individuals they've rescued. Bonding seems to be an inseparable part of the human condition.

So we see that the process of bonding requires certain life situations or external environmental forces interacting with structures and functions of human neural systems, physiological processes throughout the body, psychological events (emotions, cognitions, behaviors), and a panoply of neurochemicals including transmitters, enzymes, and hormones. What word and what three-word phrase, both widely accepted and used in social work, designate these highly complex interactions? (Hint: See Chapter 4.)

Attachment is a condition or state that in humans usually is an outgrowth of affiliation over some time. That is, affiliation can sometimes progress readily to attachment, sometimes slowly, and many human affiliations remain at that level, which we might call friendship, but not close friendship so much as a friendly mutual association in the absence of compelling emotional ties toward the persons or groups of people with whom we affiliate.

Psychology is replete with definitions for attachment as well as non-attachment, distorted attachment, and disrupted attachment. A great deal of concern has been chronicled when attachment in children appears lacking or to have been derailed.

The question of how effectively each of us "attaches" over our life spans is of particular interest to many middle-aged single (not partnered) people, especially women. The concept of male commitment phobia is quite prevalent in the popular press. However, academia appears to suspect that "commitment phobia" is a frivolous topic not worthy of serious study, considering the sparse scholarly output on this topic.

Schecter and Willheim (2009) note that the preponderance of research on attachment difficulties focuses on children raised in institutions. Studies of children adopted from Romanian orphanages have informed our understanding of reactive attachment disorders (RAD). Results from the Bucharest Early Intervention Project (BEIP), the first randomized, controlled trial of foster care as an intervention for institutionalized children, confirm and extend the previous findings on the negative sequelae of early institutional care on mental health, and underscore the benefit of early family placement for children living in institutions (Bos, Zeanah, Fox et al., 2011).

However, the diagnosis of reactive attachment disorder (RAD) (American Psychiatric Association, 2000) denoted a set of characteristics known to be associated with grossly pathogenic care. That is, by definition RAD is a disorder caused by the environment, in the same way that the diagnosis of posttraumatic stress disorder (PTSD) is defined by its association with an environmentally induced traumatic experience. Children meeting criteria for RAD show markedly disturbed, developmentally inappropriate social behavior either as extreme withdrawal and inhibition, or by its converse, indiscriminate sociability, such as excessive familiarity with strangers (American Psychiatric Association, 2000). This diagnosis overlaps poorly with categories of attachment security. (The DSM-5 separates these two very dissimilar manifestations into two different diagnoses) (Regier. Kuhl, and Kupfer, 2013).

The collective findings from the many studies of attachment forms cast doubt on the belief that humans only develop attachment bonds in critical periods of development (Boris and Zeanah, 2005). Romanian children initially assessed as nonattached developed attachment behaviors with their British adoptive parents when the new caregiving environment was typical (O'Connor et al., 1999, 2000).

British and Canadian adoption studies found no children meeting criteria for the withdrawn/inhibited subtype following adoption, across the spectrum of levels of their attachments to adoptive parents (Chisholm, 1998; O'Connor et al., 2003). Stovall and Dozier (2000) found that remediation of the emotionally withdrawn/inhibited subtype is possible in fostercare infants.

The only subtype of attachment dysfunction that appeared refractory to remediation overall was indiscriminate sociability. It appeared to persist regardless of child placement into adoptive homes, return to biological families, or continued institutionalization. Romanian children adopted by Canadians continued to exhibit indiscriminate friendliness both at 11 months and at 39 months post adoption, despite increases in attachment security with their caregiver during the same time frame (Chisholm, 1998; Chisholm and et al., 1995). Zeanah et al. (2000) conclude that the persistence of indiscriminate sociability in children adopted from institutions may be a long-term complication of early institutionalization.

Although the overall prevalence of RAD is extremely low (less than 1%) (Richters and Volkmar, 1994), as many as 38% of children in foster-care studies have been found to exhibit symptoms of RAD, and 40% of institutionalized Romanian children were found to meet criteria for RAD, with an additional 33% evidencing some features of RAD (Smyke et al., 2002; Zeanah , Scheeringa et al., 2004). These Romanian studies also suggest that the presentations of the two subtypes emotionally withdrawn/inhibited and indiscriminate/disinhibited may not be as mutually exclusive as initially thought, and as defined in DSM-IV-TR. Rather, institutionalized children may display features of both subtypes.

Boris and Zeanah (2005) stopped using the term "reactive attachment" and described the condition designated RAD as occurring in the context of deprivation or maltreatment such as persistent, severe parental neglect, or documented physical or psychological abuse. Schechter and Willheim (2010) have supported different nomenclature and conceptual underpinning from that of Boris and Zeanah that they believe more closely reflects developmental research into attachment. This model delineates three types of attachment disorders: (1) disorders of nonattachment, (2) secure-base distortions, and (3) disrupted attachment disorder. They note that one-person pathology (in a child) characterizes the first of these categories, whereas the second and third convey a two-person context in which pathology arises in a relationship with a specific object for the child's attachment.

According to this perspective, disorders of nonattachment described in the DSMs (Diagnostic and Statistical Manual of Mental Disorders) and the ICDs (International Classification of Diseases) are mostly characterized by the absence of any preferred attachment figure and any attachment behaviors directed toward such a figure. To meet criteria for the designation, non-attached children must have a mental age of at least 10 months and show no variability in attachment behaviors across relationships or contexts. Importantly, a proven history of pathogenic care should not be required for the diagnosis.

Children in the first of two subgroups of nonattachment, labeled emotionally withdrawn/inhibited, do not seek comfort from a preferred caregiver; do not respond or may even resist when comfort is offered; are not easily soothed; show limited or absent affection, cooperative interaction, response to the social overtures of others, or reliance on a preferred caregiver for assistance or reassurance; and often show disturbances in emotional regulation. This pattern has been found in populations of institutionalized children, neglected children, and children in foster care.

However, withdrawn and inhibited behavior also appears in early childhood depressive or anxiety disorders. Practitioners need to consider the possibility that hyper-arousal led to the inhibition (Schechter and Willheim, 2010). Another source of misdiagnosis is that institutionalization has been associated with a quasi-autistic disorder that looks similar to pervasive developmental disorder (PDD) as well as with the RAD emotionally withdrawn/inhibited subtype. Both conditions are characterized by lack of social responsivity.

While PDD has been found to occur in environments that are considered adequate, RAD is only found in conditions of extreme deprivation. Another important difference is that many of the children with institution-induced quasi-autism improve after placement in an adequate caregiving environment in ways that PDD children seldom do (Rutter, Kreppner, et al., 2007).

Children meeting criteria for the second subgroup of non-attachment, designated indiscriminate/disinhibited, lack the reticence young children typically show around strangers, to an opposite extreme of indiscriminate sociability toward unfamiliar adults. These children have been described as "attention seeking," "shallow," and "interpersonally superficial" (Boris and Zeanah, 2005). They seek comfort from unknown adults, protest when the strange adult leaves, and wander away from their caregiver without checking back. In a comparative study using an enactment called the "Stranger at the Door" procedure, institutionalized children were the most likely to go off with a stranger, children in foster care were at intermediate risk, and the least likely were the control children who belonged to neither group.

The indiscriminate sub-type has been found in children who have experienced frequent placement changes while in foster or institutional care (Tizard and Rees, 1974; Zeanah, Boris et al., 2000). "We have seen, for example, that institutionalized children placed into enlightened foster care, or internationally adopted by a new set of caregivers, can make substantive gains in developmental and relational domains. At the same time, plasticity has its limits such that so called "indiscriminate sociability" or "glomming on to strangers" does not improve or change substantially in the majority of cases" (Schechter and Willheim, 2009).

Secure-base distortions, the second major category of attachment disorders in the Schechter and Willheim definition, has not been well validated according to Boris and Zeanah (2005). It pertains to an existing attachment relationship. Subtypes of secure-base distortions were attachment disorder with: self-endangerment, clinging/inhibited exploration, vigilance/hyper-compliance, and role reversal. Boris and Zeanah (2005) note that the subtypes for secure base distortions are remarkably similar to behaviors described by Ichise, Vines et al. (2006) among peer-reared primates who did form attach-ment bonds, but problematic ones.

The third category for attachment disorders, disrupted attachment dis-orders, addresses the sudden and/or prolonged loss of an important attach-ment figure during early childhood, with a sequence of protest, despair, and detachment first described in 1989 by James and Joyce Robertson (Lieberman, Compton et al., 2003).

Moreover, in more recent work with a Romanian orphanage sample, Zeanah, Smyke, and colleagues (2005) have pointed out that traditional mea-sures of attachment behavior such as the strange situation procedure, among other measures, are ill suited to assess relational behavior in children who have never discriminated a preferred attachment figure due to institutional care.

What are we to conclude from this puzzling collection of studies and opin-ions? Clearly there's plenty of room for disagreement. Reports of untested and even dangerous interventions for purported attachment disorders indicate a need for caution in work with children believed to be suffering from failures of attachment (Mercer, 2013).

Nevertheless, numerous interventions developed recently to address dis-turbances of child–parent attachment have proven helpful in the past decade (for a review, see Schechter and Willheim, 2009). We describe one such study (Lieberman, Van Horn, and Ghosh Ippen, 2005) and briefly refer to several others.

Lieberman, Van Horn, and Ghosh Ippen (2005) studied 39 girls and 36 boys ages three to five and their mothers. Each child had been referred because of concerns about his or her behavior or the mother's parenting after the child witnessed or overheard marital violence. Family court made the most referrals (40%), domestic violence service providers made 12%, with remaining refer-rals, each less than 10%, coming from medical providers, preschools, child protective services, other agencies, former clients, and self-referrals. A core component of the treatment was child–parent psychotherapy (CPP).

A criterion for inclusion was that the perpetrator not live in the home. Mother–child dyads were excluded in the case of documented abuse of the target child by the mother or current maternal substance abuse, homelessness, mental retardation, or psychosis, or children with mental retardation or autis-tic spectrum disorder.

Participant children were ethnically diverse: more than one-third were of mixed ethnicity (predominantly Latino/white), 28% were Latino, 14.7% were African American, 9.3% were white, 6.7% were Asian, and 2.6% were other. Mothers' ethnicity was much lower for the mixed ethnicity category. Mean maternal education was 12.51 years (SD = 3.96), and mean monthly family income $1,817 (SD = $1,460; range $417-$8,333). Public assistance was received by 23% of the families, and 41% had incomes below the federal poverty line.

Most families had experienced pervasive violence in addition to marital violence. Maternal childhood trauma as reported by mothers included witnessing marital violence (48%), physical abuse (49%), sexual molestation (42%), and the sudden/traumatic death of someone close (44%). The children had experienced exposure to community violence (46.7%), physical abuse (18.7%), sexual abuse (14.7%), or both (4%). During the study, 33.3% of the mothers reported new traumas that affected the dyad, and 17.3% of the mothers reported either returning to a violent partner or entering a new violent relationship.

Mother–child dyads were randomly assigned to either the CPP (child–parent psychotherapy) treatment group or to a comparison group receiving monthly case management by an experienced doctoral degree–level clinician, together with referrals for individual treatment in the community for mother and child. Mothers received $30 for the intake and $40 for the outcome assessment, with all aspects of the assessments and interventions in Spanish, as appropriate. Most quantitative measures of children's improvements involved parental report because self-report measures were not available for preschoolers.

The findings support CPP efficacy for preschoolers exposed to marital violence. Children randomly assigned to CPP improved significantly more than children receiving case management plus treatment as usual in the community, both in decreased total behavior problems and decreased trauma symptoms. They were also significantly less likely to be diagnosed with traumatic stress disorder after treatment. The authors attribute these findings to CPP's focus on fostering child mental health *by promoting a relational process* in which increased maternal responsiveness to the child's developmental needs strengthens the child's trust in the mother's capacity to provide protective care (emphasis added).

Mothers receiving CPP showed significantly fewer PTSD avoidance symptoms at the end of treatment than comparison group mothers. The authors attribute these results to consistent attention during treatment to the construction of a joint trauma narrative between the child and the mother:

> They noted that when treatment began, many mothers did not speak about the marital violence with their children for fear of damaging them or because they believed that the children were too young to notice it. Workers dispelled these misperceptions. The children's own vivid depictions through words and play of the violence they had witnessed helped their mothers process these experiences within the protective frame of treatment. (Lieberman, Van Horn, and Gosh Ippen, 2005). The authors believed that mothers' frequent expression of surprise at their children's clear

recollections of the violence clearly indicated the importance of these joint sessions for mother–child communication.

Mothers in both groups overall had fewer PTSD symptoms and less global psychiatric distress at outcome, with treatment group mothers slightly more improved. Yet CPP does not target adult symptoms for intervention, whereas all of the mothers in the comparison group received individual services from a skilled case-management clinician, with individual therapy for 73% of the mothers. The finding that these interventions did not result in improved outcomes for comparison-group mothers relative to the treatment group supports the conclusion that emphasizing the child–mother relationship as an agent of psychological health helps both young children and their mothers. The authors believed the mothers in the treatment group may have found effective ways of processing their own traumatic stress by speaking about the trauma during the joint sessions and helping their children with emotional regulation and correcting misperceptions.

Limitations of this study included reliance mostly on maternal report for major outcome variables and lack of longer-term outcome data. Thus, it was not known whether the initial positive effects would be sustained through the child's development. A strength of the study was generalizability due to a diverse ethnic and socioeconomic sample recruited from the community rather than from battered women's shelters. In our view, its most compelling contribution was the evidence that including the mother as an integral partner in the treatment of preschoolers' traumatic stress symptoms was more beneficial to both mother and child than traditional practice. The traditional method of professional therapy treats mothers alone combined with play therapy for the child, also by himself or herself. The concept of parents as partners has been well known for more than two decades, but, as considerable research on parent–professional collaboration has shown, it has too often been neglected by therapists (see for example Johnson, Cournoyer, and Fisher, 1994; Johnson and colleagues, 2001). Several other recent studies also report success with mother–child joint treatment, video feedback of live interactions, and other interventions.

Minding the Baby is a relationship-based weekly home-visiting program for young high-risk and first-time mothers—many with a history of trauma—that uses the reflective functioning component of certain infant–parent psychotherapy models. Outcomes from this program have shown increases in maternal reflective functioning, decreases in maternal depression and PTSD symptoms, and no children exhibiting disorganized attachment (Slade, Grienenberger, Bernbach, Levy, and Locker, 2005).

In an effort to increase infant security of attachment in maltreating families, Cicchetti, Rogosch, and Toth (2006), using a modified version of infant--parent psychotherapy (IPP), report an intervention emphasizing increasing sensitive maternal responsivity by clarifying distorted maternal attachment representations. Rates of secure attachment increased from 3.1% at baseline to 60.7% at follow-up.

Dozier and colleagues (2005) have developed an evidence-based intervention for very young children in foster-care called *Attachment and Biobehavioral Catch-Up (ABC)*. ABC is a manualized ten-session training program for foster parents and in a controlled trial has been found to be associated with lowered cortisol values and fewer behavioral problems as reported by foster parents.

The Tulane–Jefferson Parish Human Services Authority (Louisiana) Infant Team has partnered with child welfare, judicial, educational, and health-care systems to provide intensive services to abused and neglected children younger than 48 months of age who are placed in foster care. Comprehensive interventions for birth families—including parent–child therapy, medication management, and assistance with housing— give families a range of services in a single setting and make it possible for the court to obtain assessments and progress reports from a single source. No formal outcome study was available, but the program was successful in reducing very young children's rate of risk for a subsequent incidence of maltreatment by up to 68% (Child Welfare League of America, 2003).

Finally, in Romania, Zeanah, Smyke et al. (2005) have described interventions for children with profound disorders of non-attachment. Children who entered the Budapest Early Intervention Program (BEIP), a foster-care placement program with attachment and development sensitized families, demonstrated substantial reduction or remission of emotionally withdrawn/inhibited symptoms. Children living in institutions but enrolled in both RAD subtypes groups are compared to the institutional care-as-usual group.

Child welfare literature has long noted that negative attributions to children are often made by parents who may have abused, often partially through ignorance about realistic expectations for child behaviors. False beliefs by parents can magnify the real and widespread challenges to parenting, resulting in harmful behaviors toward the child. As an example of cognitively oriented interventions, videotape feedback to traumatized mothers helped them changed their minds about their toddlers, supporting positive maternal attributions (Schechter, Myers et al., 2006).

35

Stress and Vulnerability

Stress. Several disciplines have contributed knowledge about the effects of stress on physical health, psychological well-being, and human development. People of all ages have varying vulnerability to stress and varying capacities to emerge from periods of stress relatively unscathed (resilience).

We know that egregious and long-term physical or emotional abuse in humans is associated with posttraumatic stress disorder (PTSD), depression, and cognitive and emotional deficits. We now have a wealth of evidence about the neurobiological underpinnings of these effects. The connections between emotional neglect and these outcomes are less well documented in research literature, but few observers doubt that they exist. Preliminary data suggest that severe emotional neglect (notably deprivation of caregiver–infant interactions over time) may cause abnormal metabolism in a part of the temporal lobe thought to be involved in social functioning. PET scans of eight children reared from infancy in Romanian orphanages until their adoption into American families showed these abnormalities.

Although data to control for possible confounding variables were limited, such brain changes are believed to account for the difficulties some neglected children show in relating to people, despite extended periods in nurturing adoptive homes (Chugani, reported by Talbot, 1998). Some of these orphanages have been observed to provide almost no tactile or emotional stimulation between caregivers and children even when the facilities were found to be clean, well supplied with toys, and offering adequately nutritious meals.

However, mild, moderate, or intermittent stressful events have not been demonstrated to lead to emotional disorders (except, perhaps, in uniquely sensitive individuals). By contrast, chronic or extreme trauma, stress, or deprivation are well-documented precursors to symptoms of psychiatric disorders.

Traumatic experiences have measurable effects on certain physiological indicators. Particular hormones, the glucocorticoids, are known to be central

---

To be read in conjunction with Chapters 23 and 24, which supply extensive information about stress, trauma, and traumatic stress. A prototype of a stress neural network engaging several locations in the human brain and body is presented. The brief information in this Chapter 35 supplements the more detailed and in-depth neuroscience and social science knowledge in Chapters 23 and 24.

in the mediation of stress. Glucocorticoids produced by the adrenal glands (located on the kidneys), together with some of the monoamine neurotransmitters (dopamine, norepinephrine), comprise a frontline defense for mammals experiencing stressful conditions (Meaney, Diorio, Francis, et al., 1996). These substances mobilize the production and distribution of energy during stress through a feedback loop between the brain, the adrenal gland, and the external environment, known as the *hypothalamic-pituitary-adrenal axis (HPA)*.

HPA responses are genetically programmed but can be altered by early environmental events (Alves, Akbari, Anderson, et al., 1997). Prolonged bombardment of the human organism by these substances early in development can alter neurochemistry sufficiently to effect long-term changes in neurons and brain systems.

Glucocorticoids are so named because of their profound effects on glucose metabolism. Glucocorticoids break down protein and convert it to glucose, help to make fats available for energy, increase blood flow, and stimulate behavioral responsiveness. They decrease the sensitivity of the gonads (reproductive glands) to luteinizing hormone (LH), thereby suppressing the secretion of sex hormones. Although glucocorticoids are essential for survival in the short term, the adverse health effects of long-term stress are legion: high blood pressure, suppression of the immune system, damage to muscle tissue, infertility, inhibition of growth, slowed healing from injury, and brain damage (Carlson, 2001).

Almost every cell in the body contains glucocorticoid receptors, so most of the body is affected by these hormones. When glucocorticoids are doing their stress-related work, there may be undesirable side effects. For example, male physician hospital residents showed severely depressed blood levels of testosterone, due most likely to their stressful work schedules, a response thought to be engineered by glucocorticoids (Singer and Zumoff, 1992).

The work of the HPA axis is possibly the most researched example in the behavioral sciences of the complex adaptive networks that manage human psychology. In Part III, Chapter 23, we trace the steps that take place each time the system mediates stress-inducing influences from the external environment. These steps can help us understand the concept of complex adaptive systems by illustrating how one such system actually works (see color images K. and L. in color insert).

The importance of the actions of the HPA can hardly be overestimated. Hans Selye, a leading scholar of stress, suggested that most of the harmful effects of stress were the result of prolonged bombardment of the organism by glucocorticoids (Selye, 1976). His hypothesis later proved correct.

The early postnatal environment can contribute substantially to the development of stable differences in HPA responsiveness to stressful stimuli. Animals exposed to physical trauma, the administration of endotoxins (substances that make animals sick, such as salmonella), or maternal separation showed increased HPA response to stress. These early effects can have delete-rious effects later in life, especially in individuals genetically predisposed to stress-sensitive disorders such as anxiety, depression, and Tourette syndrome (Meaney, 2001; Alves, Akbari, Anderson, et al., 1997).

Evidence suggests that glucocorticoids acting through glucocorticoid receptors in the central nervous system may operate as lifelong organizing sig-nals activated before birth and continuing to the end of life. When too many glucocorticoids bombard our neurons in old age, nerve cell death may be hastened (Fuxe, Diaz et al., 1996). Overall, glucocorticoid receptors partici-pate in neuronal plasticity (the capacity of neurons for change) from fetal and postnatal life to the onset of adult life and aging (Cintra, Bhatnagar, Chadi, et al., 1994). Stress can also change developmental programming prenatally. Glucocorticoid receptors affect the regulation of the HPA axis during fetal development and can produce long-lasting changes in dopamine communica-tion in the striatum and changes in serotonin communication in the brainstem (Slotkin, Barnes, McCook, and Seidler, 1996; Fuxe, Diaz, Cintra, et al., 1996). Stress-induced increases in maternal glucocorticoids may be a mechanism by which prenatal stress impairs the development of the adult offspring's gluco-corticoid response (Barbazanges, Piazza, LeMoal, and Maccari, 1996).

What environmental factors might diminish stress? Infant rats whose moth-ers engaged in frequent licking and grooming behaviors developed into adult rats showing smaller HPA responses to stress and decreased fearfulness in novel situations (Caldji, Diorio, and Meaney, 2000; Liu, Diorio, Tannenbaum, Caldji, et al., 1997). Enriching rat environments also positively affected devel-opment. Rats housed in groups with ample opportunities to explore new objects and to interact socially increased their brain weight and cortical thick-ness and produced more new synapses, more complex dendritic branching, and more new blood vessels than did their less privileged peers (Black, 1998).

There's other good news. Environmental stimulation through postna-tal handling or enriched environment can sometimes undo early damage. Specifically, in experiments with rats, impaired avoidance acquisition in adult-hood caused by inadequate stimulation in early life was reversed by environ-mental enrichment (Escorihuela, Tobena, and Fernandez-Teruel, 1994). Either short periods of infantile handling or stimulation, or the administration of a drug that enhances GABAA receptor action, attenuated the adverse conse-quences of stress by decreasing HPA responsivity to stress (Meaney, Diorio, Francis, et al., 1996; Patchev, Montkowsi, Rouskova, et al., 1997).

As stress and traumas pummel developing individuals and increase the risk of physical and mental disorders, biological and environmental protective fac-tors fight back. The contest between risk factors and protective factors con-tinues from conception to the end of life. (Did you ever think of your body as the arena for a mighty, never-ending contest among risk factors and protective factors?)

A major stressor for most young animals is the loss of, or separation from, caretakers, in particular a caretaker to whom the animal has formed an attachment. Human children and other young alike react with sadness, anger, apathy, and/or withdrawal to a parent's death, absence through separation, or emotional unavailability. Rhesus monkeys, deprived of contact with caretakers in infancy, show seriously deviant social behavior in later life (Harlow, 1958; Suomi and Harlow, 1972). So do some dogs (beagles) (Fuller and Clark, 1968).

The transmission of atypical neurochemistry from stressed mothers to their fetuses obviously involves a biochemical process. On the other hand, the death or prolonged absence of a parent is clearly an environmental condition. In both the biological and the environmental conditions, the involvement of the child's HPA axis over an extended time is a hazard to development. In the case of parental emotional unavailability, not uncommon when the caretaker suffers a mental illness or severe addiction, environmental stress on the child is cycled through the HPA axis and can subject the child to the long-term adverse effects of glucocorticoid overload, as reported above.

Maternal depression has been associated with changes in infants and children. Newborns whose mothers were depressed either before or after birth, or both, had elevated cortisol and norepinephrine levels, lower dopamine levels, and greater relative right frontal EEG asymmetry. Not surprisingly, effects on newborns appeared to arise more from prepartum than immediate postpartum maternal depression (Diego, Field, Hernandez-Reif et al., 2004). Ongoing maternal depression through the child's early years has been shown to exert small but significant effects on children's cognitive and emotional development (Beck, 1998).

Studies have shown that the role of maternal depression in the child's physiological and emotional distress is not unidirectional. It can act through different routes: (1) The mother suffers depression during the pregnancy, causing the child to be born with compromised HPA function (a physiological route of transmission). (2) The mother is depressed for reasons unrelated to characteristics of her child, but because of depression, she fails to transmit enough positive sensory and affective energy to the baby (through talking, smiling, making eye contact, cuddling), a psychosocial contributor to the baby's distress. (3) The mother's depression is a reaction to aspects of the baby, such as irritability, illness, or prematurity (a psychosocial contributor to the mothers' depression). (4) Gene(s) predisposing the mother to depression have been transmitted from the mother to the child (a genetic explanation). (5) Any or all of the above effects may be taking place simultaneously as interactive psychosocial and neurobiological events.

One remedy for lack of sensory inputs to infants that when a mother is depressed appears to be breastfeeding. multisensory experience—all five senses are involved. Since fits of these sensory experiences can be offered even by emot mothers, breastfeeding might relieve some negative effects of stress-induced glucocorticoids on the infant.

Jones, McFall, and Diego (2004) looked at the association between breast-feeding, physiological measures of infants, and the ways mothers and infants related to each other. In this study, 78 mothers and their infants participated; 31 of the mothers were depressed. Positive effects of breastfeeding were confirmed by the study. Depressed mothers who had stable breastfeeding patterns were less likely to have highly reactive infants. Infants of depressed mothers who breastfed did not show the frontal asymmetry patterns reported in previous studies. Moreover, breastfeeding stability, even in depressed mothers, was related to more positive mother–infant interactions. These findings suggested that promoting and supporting breastfeeding could enhance a positive feedback loop between infants and depressed mothers.

It should go without saying that treating the mother's depression should be a top priority goal, for her own well-being as well as for that of her child. However, it would probably be necessary not to use medications during breastfeeding since the child would receive it through the milk. Providers to mother and child would need to navigate this challenge in some way that might not be optimal, such as choosing the quickest possible help for the mother and foregoing breastfeeding, or relying on nonpharmaceutical interventions in a situation where severity of the mother's depression called for medication.

The sense of touch has been used explicitly as a therapeutic intervention with several different populations. Regular touching has shown beneficial effects on the physical well-being, development, and emotional states of infants as well as older persons. Infants born to HIV-positive mothers were given three 15-minute massages daily for 10 days. These babies showed superior performance on almost every Brazelton newborn cluster score and had a greater daily weight gain than control-group infants (Scafidi and Field, 1996). Touch appears to be an entry point into the HPA-axis feedforward and feedback loops. We return to touch as a health-promoting behavior in Part VII, Multiple Routes to the Quality of Life.

The question of separation has concerned many a parent entering or reentering the labor market, whether by necessity or by choice. In particular, parents have struggled with the decision to entrust a child to group care by strangers. Issues of concern to the parents include the following: *Will my child be safe? Will these teachers find time for her with so many other children to attend to? Is this a high-quality daycare center? How will the quality of care compare with what I can give at home? How will she feel and behave in a large group of children? Is the group care environment kind and gentle enough for her? What bad reactions is she likely to have? How will spending long days in care affect my child?*

A second set of questions lurks behind the first. *Am I being selfish? Will my* ' *feel rejected? Am I really rejecting her? Will my family disapprove? Will my child be maladjusted later? Am I really doing this just to get out of the house and be with people? Am I a bad parent for foisting my kid on babysitters? Am I abandoning my child?*

Many parents have observed that being dropped off at daycare stresses their children, causing the parents in turn to feel stressed (see for example, Brotman, Gouley et al., 2007).

During the early years of life, children's needs for social skills shift from very limited to extensive, as they are increasingly required to interact with adults and peers in sophisticated ways (Johnson, Christie, and Yawkey, 1999). In full-day center-based child-care settings, children must learn to navigate a complex social and cognitive environment with many same-age peers. It appears that children respond physiologically to this challenging environment with increased cortisol production.

Cortisol is a glucocorticoid manufactured by the adrenal cortex. Cortisol levels typically rise in stressful or challenging situations. Each of the studies focuses on one or two aspects of the complex influences of the daycare experience on children's development. When all the studies are taken together, the many relevant variables that are reported show promise in advancing our knowledge about the various influences. To answer the question *Is this good for my child?* meaningfully, however, we must look at the interaction between the many important variables that function in the family's complex adaptive systems (see Chapter 8).

One of the studies assessed children's stress levels by taking samples of saliva and measuring the hormone cortisol at 10:00 a.m. and 4:00 p.m. from children in the daycare center, from the same children on days they stayed home, and also from a comparison group of children being cared for at home (Watamura, Donzella, Alwin, and Gunnar, 2003). Among children cared for at home, 71% of infants and 64% of toddlers showed decreases in cortisol levels from a high in the morning to the low in the afternoon, following the natural cycle of cortisol production. In the fulltime daycare centers, however, cortisol levels rose in the afternoon rather than lowering in 35% of infants and 71% of toddlers. What might this disparity mean?

Several possible explanations have been suggested. First, children's stress responses to full-time center-based child care differ, and these differences are associated with emotional tendencies that may precede their entry into care (Crockenberg, 2003). That is, temperament appears to affect the level of stress a child experiences. Children described by teachers as more socially fearful showed larger cortisol increases (Watamura et al., 2003). Temperamentally fearful children apparently show greater stress responses to center-based care where considerably more social interaction takes place than in the secluded environment at home.

Second, the quality of center-based child care does affect stress levels of children as measured in their cortisol levels. Preschoolers produced larger rises in cortisol when the daycare was judged to be of lower quality. However, many other risk and protective factors interact to impact the child.

Third, differences in children's aggression, independent of the quality of caregiving both at home and in the center, are associated with the amount of time spent in care. The more hours spent in daycare, the higher the cortisol levels and the greater the aggression. Yet the effect was quite small statistically. It appears that only some children, not all, are negatively affected by longer hours in group care (National Institute of Child Health and Human Development, 2004).

Several research groups have studied connections between early experience in center-based daycare, HPA activity, and behavioral outcomes. The researchers tested interventions intended to prevent maladjustment in children at high risk for emotional or behavioral disorders.

As part of a ten-year study, Brotman, Gouley et al. (2007) assessed the effects of a prevention program for low-income urban preschoolers at high familial risk for conduct problems. Low cortisol levels have been related to conduct problems and antisocial behavior. The researchers evaluated effects of the prevention effort on affective and behavioral regulation as well as on physiology. Ninety-two preschool-age siblings of youths adjudicated for delinquent acts and their families participated. The experimental group of 47 children and families received multiple interventions: 22 weekly, 90-minute concurrent groups for parents and preschoolers, 30 minutes of guided parent–preschooler interactions, 10 biweekly 90-minute home visits, and up to 6 additional family visits provided during the 6- to 8-month period of intervention.

Using a videotape modeling intervention, parent groups were encouraged to use nonharsh, consistent, and appropriate disciplinary strategies, less criticism, and positive reinforcement and play interactions to promote children's social competence. In the children's groups, leaders taught social skills, reinforced positive behaviors, and provided consequences for negative behaviors. After the separate groups, parents and children participated in guided parent–preschooler activities with leaders coaching parents to use specific parenting skills and modeling and reinforcing effective parenting strategies. Home visits were designed to help parents implement skills at home.

Children's reactions to a challenging "ecologically relevant" peer situation were assessed prior to and after the peer experience. The test situation required the children to enter a classroom where all the other children were already playing with each other. The situation was deemed ecologically relevant because it is an instance of a real life social challenge.

Experimental (intervention) and control children completed the task in the same way, and their behavior was rated by trained observers who did not know whether the child was in the intervention condition or control condition. Intervention children entered the peer situation and played more interactively than control children, both by more engaging social behaviors and by an absence of withdrawal behaviors.

The cortisol levels of intervention children increased prior to entry into the challenge situation and then declined after the peer entry situation to home resting cortisol levels. Control children, however, did not show rising cortisol in the challenge situation.

Does this mean that intervention children were more stressed than control children in this situation? Apparently so—but cortisol increases were involuntary responses to challenge situations that help people cope. These children did so—by engaging. It appears that their HPA axes gave them the impetus they needed to succeed. The control children appeared not to have experienced as much arousal, but rather continued to avoid engagement. This finding illustrates that rises in cortisol are not inherently bad—they help people meet challenges, and become harmful only if the level of arousal continues for too long a period.

In a program designed to address the needs of preschool-aged foster children, called Early Intervention Foster Care (EIFC), Fisher and colleagues investigated whether improved behavior was matched by changes in neural systems involved in stress regulation, specifically the HPA axis. Using the foster-care setting as the milieu for therapeutic intervention, program staff members actively engaged foster parents as therapeutic agents. Parents were trained to use consistent, non-abusive discipline, high levels of positive reinforcement, and close monitoring and supervision of the child. In a pilot study and a more recent large-scale randomized clinical trial, results indicate that children in the intervention group showed significantly less disruptive behavior and less dysregulation in HPA axis activity than did children in the control group (Fisher, personal communication; Fisher, Gunnar, Chamberlain, and Reid, 2000; Fisher and Chamberlain, 2000; Fisher, Ellis, and Chamberlain, 1999). These results provided optimistic, albeit preliminary, evidence that neural systems affected by early stress may be responsive to environmental changes in early childhood.

Findings from studies by Fisher and colleagues and Brotman and colleagues suggest that environmental factors, operating at key points in development, may shape affective and behavioral regulation in human children, with corresponding changes in HPA axis function—exactly the process of biological and psychosocial interactions framed by the complex adaptive systems model (see Chapter 8).

Several interesting questions arise. Do changes in patterns of behavior and cortisol levels that occur in specific contexts endure over time? What additional factors such as temperament, age, previous experience with group settings, and cognitive appraisals, affect outcomes? What physiological indicators beside cortisol levels might be needed to confirm the findings? What are the roles of individual differences when children in the same context respond differently?

Do the patterns shown by relations among behavior, cortisol levels and context confer risk or resilience? Are rises in cortisol in the group contexts harmful, or are they positive adaptive responses to the cognitive and social challenges of group care? Will the early challenge in social engagement simply make it easier for children to adjust later to school, with corresponding declines in cortisol levels?

What about the danger of elevated cortisol associated with mild repeated stress related to center-based daycare? Is there evidence of any harm to developing brains? Hopefully not, because the daily experience of producing mild elevations in cortisol at child care did not appear to produce a permanent change in daytime cortisol rhythm. The children reverted to normal rhythms on days when they were not in child care. The most likely consequence is that daily increases in cortisol may contribute to the heightened susceptibility to illness that is well documented among toddlers in child care. Cortisol is known to dampen activity of the immune system, increasing the likelihood that exposure to viruses will produce illness.

Negative impacts on social or cognitive development seem unlikely, given the overwhelming evidence from studies of center-based child care showing that these settings, when they are of good quality, stimulate cognitive and social development (Watamura et al., 2003). However, the impacts of lower quality child care on development are unclear. There is some evidence that long hours in child care may be associated with increased externalizing behavior, especially in the case of center-based child care (Belsky, Weinraub, Owen, and Kelly, 2001). Nonetheless, without knowing whether cortisol levels that rise over the child-care day do confer long-term harm on developing neural systems, it's obviously wise to assess the factors that contribute to the child's stress and consider whether and how they can be modified. This inquiry may be particularly important for temperamentally fearful children who may be susceptible to larger increases in cortisol over the child-care day.

Newcombe (2003) identifies limitations of the studies due to omission of potentially important variables. Variables of interest are sometimes artificially isolated from other variables that actually operate in the context, so that some of the situations studied may be ones that do not exist in the real world. For example, amount of time in child care as a contributor to cortisol elevations was studied by controlling for family income and maternal depression. However, use of child care is also closely linked with maternal employment, which increases family income and decreases maternal depression. These variables (family income and maternal depression) in turn are linked to children's socioemotional adjustment. Therefore failure to include these variables in the analysis may give inaccurate estimates of real life effects.

Newcombe's insights underscore the need not only for prospective longitudinal studies, but also for the incorporation of models that trace interactive effects of several variables through time. In addition, future studies will continue to require interdisciplinary input, to carry out comprehensive assessment of complex biopsychosocial phenomena by measuring physiological, neurobiological, behavioral, and environmental processes within a developmental systems model. Furthermore, experimental manipulations of the kind evaluated in the studies we've reviewed are necessary to evaluate causal relations between the environment, child HPA axis function, and later behavior. If research on preventive measures continues to show that these interventions can improve outcomes, as preliminary results indicate, then it may teach us how to interrupt negative feedback loops and initiate positive sequences in their place.

36

Critical Periods in Child Development

ARE WE LIKE KONRAD LORENZ'S GOSLINGS?

The concept of critical periods in development is not new. In the 1950s, the ethologist Konrad Lorenz delighted scholars of behavior with pictures of goslings toddling and swimming after him. They had adopted him as their mother. Newly hatched goslings experience a critical period for attachment during the first few hours after breaking out of their shells. They follow the first moving creature that they see and hear, a phenomenon called *imprinting*. Having seen and heard Lorenz before any other creatures, the goslings preferred him to a goose mother!

Once imprinting occurs, it is irreversible. During the first week of life, infant rats develop a lifelong preference associated with the odor of their mother's nipples. However, if goslings are not exposed to an appropriate stimulus during this short time period, they never form typical parent–child relationships.

Oxytocin speeds up the conditioning process for maternal odor cues, and blocking oxytocin delays the conditioning process (Nelson and Pankepp, 1996). For birds, early imprinting plays a role in social development and later sexual preferences. And the bonding process works in the opposite direction as well. Animal parents also form bonds with their young at critical, often very short, time periods. Ewes imprint on the scent of their own lamb for a period of two to four hours after giving birth. After this time, they rebuff approaches by other lambs.

Critical periods are windows of opportunity for learning skills. Once a given time period has passed, the nervous system often becomes refractory to further experience, and the process of learning a skill that formerly came naturally becomes slow and difficult. If we knew when and how these critical periods occur, we could target our efforts to take advantage of them. The periods are limited to specific times and to particular species. They are not times of generally enhanced learning.

Songbirds learn their songs mostly during the first two months after hatching. The juvenile male bird listens to the song of a nearby adult male, memorizes it, and then matches his own song to the memorized model through auditory feedback. Exposure to other songs after the sensory acquisition period does not affect this learning. The bird vocally mimics only those songs heard during the sensitive period. Birds retain this skill for months or longer even without further vocal practice. Juvenile males need to hear the male model's song only 10 to 20 times to be able to reproduce it months later. And when young birds are presented with tapes of songs of many bird species, juveniles mimic the songs of their own species. That is, the birds are innately predisposed to learn the songs of their species (Purves et al., 2001). Do humans also have innate predispositions to learn certain things? We know that's the case—some of us learn math easily; others of us pick up tennis in a couple of sessions on the court.

However, in human brain development, critical periods are the exception, not the rule. Thompson and Nelson (2001) prefer to call these "sensitive" rather than "critical" periods, because the periods for developing complex behaviors such as human language are much longer and less well delimited. The example of goslings, which have a critical period lasting only a few hours to form attachment to a parent, is not characteristic of humans. In humans, the process of child–parent attachment is far more complex and is not yet well understood. We do know that the process can extend for years.

We also know that brain development is nonlinear. That is, it doesn't progress in a straight, uphill direction. In most species, including humans, brain maturation involves phases during which there's a flurry of activity, followed by phases in which activity diminishes.

Brain development continues throughout life. Although it is certainly true, as the Birth-to-Three movement proclaimed, that the period from birth to age three is a critical time for brain development, so is the prenatal period, and so are the years from four to adolescence. In adulthood the process continues, albeit at a slower rate. We can still learn in our eighties and nineties, and each time we learn something, a miniscule change takes place in a structure in our brain.

A few years ago, media coverage of neuroscience discoveries about child brain development drew widespread attention and aroused consternation. Television gurus admonished parents to stimulate their children in every possible way to promote brain development. Otherwise, these alarmists cautioned, the children might be left behind on the long road to admission into Harvard or Princeton. Parents scrambled to talk more to their babies in the crib and in utero, and Zell Miller, then governor of Georgia, decided to send parents of every newborn in the state a classical music CD. The so-called "Mozart effect" had caught the imagination of the popular press.

Although sensory stimulation of young children is believed to be very important in promoting development, some scientists became concerned. Where was the attention to the potential and often actual damage to children's brains from prenatal malnutrition, poor health care, viral infections and other maternal illness, exposure to toxic substances through environmental contaminants, alcohol and other drugs, and chronic maternal stress? The child's brain in gestation and during the early postnatal years has been shown to be extremely vulnerable to these hazards, yet the relevant knowledge from research, decades old, was being virtually ignored by policy-makers and media gurus. Where was public concern about creating safe and healthy environments for all of America's children? Thus far, politicians have failed to answer these questions.

Do adult brains make new neurons? Contrary to prevailing belief at the end of the 20th century, neuroscientists have discovered that new neurons do grow postnatally. This revolutionary discovery in the 1990s offers hope for recovery from brain injuries and illnesses. Although the new neurons have been found only in a few specific brain regions, more may be discovered. Even if not, the coming of age of stem-cell research may at some time in the future give us more generic tools to create new neurons and brain structures lost through illness or injury (Gould, 2007).

The current consensus among neuroscientists is that adult neurogenesis occurs in two main areas of the brain: the subgranular zone (SGZ) of the dentate gyrus (DG) of the hippocampus, where new neurons are produced and have been associated with learning, memory, and mood disorders; and the subventricular zone (SVZ) of the olfactory bulb (OB), where newborn cells give rise to neurons related to olfaction.

In the rodent brain, there are also recent reports of adult neurogenesis in the neocortex, striatum, amygdala, substantia nigra, and a few other areas. However, studies in healthy humans have suggested that neocortical neurogenesis is restricted to the perinatal period or, if not, that the contribution of adult-born neurons to the total cortical population is extremely small and undetectable. In rodents, at the end of a four-week period, the surviving new neurons mature and are integrated into the circuitry (Sierra, Encinas, and Maletic-Savatic, 2011).

However, it has long been known that neurons alone do not make things happen; connections are needed for various brain activities to occur. We've studied these connections through the functions of synapses (Chapters 11–16). At birth, there are relatively few connections between neurons compared with later in life. Over the first years of life, many connections are made, and then some are eliminated. Molecular changes take place when pathways are used that result in the hardwiring of some connections and the elimination of others. By adolescence, pathways that have been used repeatedly are hardwired, whereas processes that haven't reached a certain threshold of use are eliminated (use it or lose it).

Before birth, more neurons are produced than we need. After birth, connections proliferate richly for eight or nine years. This rapid formation of synaptic connections is followed by pruning of dendrites and elimination of many connections. The entire process of connection-building and pruning extends from infancy into adolescence. Even in the early teens, density of synapses can exceed that found in human adults.

Neurons in creatures raised in an enriched environment may be better protected from elimination and may form more connections. For example, mice reared in an environment enriched with toys, running wheels, and other interesting things had a thicker cerebral cortex than mice reared in a more limited environment. The enriched mice showed not only more connections, but also more neurons (Volkmar and Greenough, 1972).

Patterns of development are a complex sequence of modulating events. Critical periods of change during the first ten years of life give us opportunities to retain and increase the efficiency of connections through repeated use, and to eliminate connections that aren't used. This is nature's way of fine-tuning neuronal circuits. Ongoing and repeated interactions between the human organism and the environment sculpt unique individual neuronal architecture (Chugani, 1997).

Figure 36.1 shows levels of human neural activity in the cerebral cortex at different ages as measured by rates of glucose metabolism. Metabolic rates in various cortical regions can be identified using PET scan.

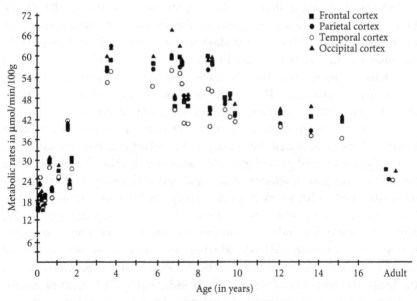

FIGURE 36.1 Levels of cortical activity from birth to adulhood. *Absolute values of local cerebral metabolic rates for glucose in cortical brain regions, plotted as a function of age in normal infants and children, and corresponding adult values.*

Source: Harry T. Chugani (1997). Neuroimaging of developmental nonlinearity and developmental pathologies. In *Developmental Neuroimaging: Mapping the Development of Brain and Behavior*, RW Thatcher, GR Lyon, J Rumsey, and N Krasnegor, Eds. San Diego: Academic Press, p. 190. Reprinted by permission of the author and of Academic Press.

The different symbols on the graph indicate different regions of the human cortex (frontal, parietal, temporal, and occipital). The graph shows that the developmental pattern is similar for the four regions. Since 95% of the glucose employed by the brain is used for connections, not for neuron cell bodies, PET scans can be used to estimate the number of synaptic connections present at different periods in development.

As the graph shows, the number of connections in the cerebral cortex increases dramatically in the first years after birth. Glucose values are about 30% lower at birth than adult rates and increase rapidly to reach adult values by the second year. By the third year, these values exceed adult values. By about 4 years of age, a plateau is reached that extends to 8 to 10 years of age. The peak level is more than twice adult levels. There appears to be a transient phase during child development when the brain requires more nutrients to support its activities than do adult brains. Thereafter, glucose values gradually decline and reach adult values by about 16 to 18 years. That is, changes in patterns of connections, as indicated by levels of glucose metabolism, are almost completed by mid-adolescence. The environment influences which connections are to be kept and which eliminated. Although we can't determine how neurons are shaped before birth, we can have some influence on the final connections that are made between neurons after birth.

Patterns of glucose utilization at birth differ markedly from adult patterns. In newborns, the most active regions are the sensory and motor cortices, the brain stem (region of the brain leading to the spinal cord), and parts of the thalamus and the cerebellum (see Figure 36.1). The cerebral cortex is not yet very active, although the cingulate cortex and the hippocampus are already busy regulating emotions. These patterns of glucose metabolism in newborns are in keeping with their relatively limited behavioral repertoires.

By 3 months, more regions are active. Several connections that mediate behavior have been added. For example, the infant can now track visually and can reach for and grab objects. At 7 to 9 months, the frontal cortex has become active. This development is associated with recognition of danger, often observed in babies as *stranger anxiety*. In his cross-cultural studies, Kagan (1994) observed that in all cultures, infants develop stranger anxiety around the age of 8 months. Recent neurobiological research offers an explanation of why 8-month-old Susie, who used to love everyone, now screams at the nicest ladies! The frontal cortex is the latest structure to become active in the brain. The sequence of maturation, as indicated by PET scans of glucose metabolism, correlates well with the behavioral development that we observe in children.

The human pattern of a rapid demand for glucose followed by a gradual decline also occurs in cats and rhesus monkeys. For example, the critical period in cats for the primary visual cortex is 3 weeks to 180 days, when puberty takes place. As in human brains, the cat's brain wiring slows down in adolescence.

Examples of cognitive functions that are wired in the early years include language and the ability to play a musical instrument. When a child learns a stringed instrument before the age of 12, the representation of the left hand (which plays the different notes) is expanded on the right cortex. Children learn a second language without accent and with fluent grammar until the age of 7 or 8. After that, we can still learn new languages, but it may be hard for us to fool you into thinking we're natives—language-learning ability usually declines even with a lot of practice. However, we do know one person who came to the United States from Italy at the age of 15 knowing no English and speaks flawlessly and without accent five decades later.

Visual systems are subject to even more dramatic restrictions as they develop. Depriving an animal of normal visual experience during a short period after birth irreversibly changes neuronal connections. The animal may remain blind for life (Hubel and Wiesel, 1970). Although the neural basis of critical periods has been most studied in visual systems, similar phenomena occur in auditory, olfactory (pertaining to smell), and somatosensory systems as well.

Feral children (children raised in the wilderness without human parenting) learn language if they are captured before age 10, but not if they are captured later. Children who sustain brain injuries can usually recover up to age 10, because new connections continue to be laid down to compensate for damaged connections.

An entire hemisphere can be removed before age 10 because of uncontrollable seizures, yet the child may acquire normal speech and a normal IQ. The ability to form new connections is called *plasticity* of the brain. Between ages 10 and 12, there is less recovery, and for adults there is even less. The window starts to close around age 10.

What do these findings mean for emotional development? Research on critical periods in emotional development is still limited. A few clues are available in studies of specific situations. For example, developmental specialists have wondered whether common fears in children and adults are the result of aversive conditioning (learned through unpleasant experiences) or innate "evolutionary-relevant" mechanisms for promoting survival. A particularly contentious debate revolved around separation anxiety: Do mothers or other environmental factors create it, or does it arise from children's inborn constitutions?

In a series of prospective longitudinal studies, Poulton and associates studied several common fears of heights, water, and separation from parents (Poulton, Milne, Craske, and Menzies, 2001). They found that fears of heights and water were primarily evolutionary-relevant, largely unrelated to a history of direct aversive conditioning. That is, these fears develop through natural selection to help the species avoid death by falling or drowning.

In order to answer the question with respect to separation anxiety, Poulton and his colleagues needed to ascertain whether known mechanisms for aversive learning—specific fear-generating events, modeling of fear by others, or transmission of frightening information—could account for separation anxiety at different developmental periods. They studied a variety of separation experiences from birth through age 18 (including loss of a parent through death or separation) and related these to measures of separation anxiety at ages 3, 11, and 18.

Certain planned separations in early to mid-childhood were modestly associated with lower levels of separation anxiety at later ages. Apparently, the children got used (were habituated) to being apart from their families through the experience of brief separations. Events at age 3 were not related to later separation anxiety, but at age 9, the child's vicarious learning (mother expressed fear of going out alone or being alone; teachers rated mothers as separation anxious or over-protective) showed a small relationship to separation anxiety at age 11.

This "modeling" effect (the child perceives the mother's fears, assumes her fears are founded in reality, and becomes fearful himself or herself) was the strongest evidence of learned separation anxiety. Yet it accounted for only 1.8% of the variance in separation anxiety scores at age 11 (that is, 98.2% of the variance was due to other factors). Furthermore, it wasn't possible to tell whether the mother's fear was in fact a modeling effect or a genetic effect. And the effect disappeared when the multiple regression equation was adjusted for the number of variables. Death of a parent between the age of 11 and 18 and lower socioeconomic status were positively associated with separation anxiety at age 18, but each of these variables contributed only about 1% of the variance.

The investigators expected that children's hospitalizations would contribute to separation anxiety, because that kind of separation is unpredictable and often entails pain. However, just the reverse was true. Child hospitalizations before the age of 9 correlated inversely with separation anxiety at age 18. That is, more overnight stays in hospitals during childhood were related to less separation anxiety at age 18, suggesting an "inoculation" effect. At ages 11 and 18, females reported more separation anxiety symptoms than males, a finding consistent with previous research. However, given the very small percentage of variance attributable to any of the predictors, it was not surprising that no variables remained significant when adjustment was made for the number of variables in the equation.

Overall, the findings were consistent with the "nonassociative" theory of fear acquisition; separation anxiety does not arise from associations with childhood experiences but instead is inborn and is an evolutionary-relevant fear. However, even though separation anxiety is inborn, it can be modified by experiences such as planned separations or hospitalizations (reducing the level of separation anxiety), or by death of a parent or low socioeconomic status (increasing the level of separation anxiety).

In a study of cognitive development among infants with low birth weight, the relationship between zinc deficiency and cognitive development was explored (Bhatnagar and Taneja, 2001). Although we don't know the exact mechanisms by which zinc acts, the premise of the study was that zinc is essential for neurogenesis (formation of neurons), neuronal migration (travel from the neural tube to their final sites in the brain during gestation), and synaptogenesis (formation of synapses). Studies in animals have shown that zinc deficiency during the time of rapid brain growth appears to decrease cognitive activity, increase emotional behavior, and impair memory and the capacity to learn. Low maternal intakes of zinc during pregnancy and lactation were associated with less focused attention in newborns and decreased motor function at 6 months of age.

Zinc supplementation resulted in better motor development and more playfulness in infants with low birth weight and increased vigor and activity in infants and toddlers. As I write, knowledge about critical periods in human emotional development is progressing slowly. Research using imaging with children is restricted because PET and SPECT scans use radioactive substances, and fMRI, although not involving radioactivity, is not feasible for small children who cannot hold still for long periods of time. A well-developed inventory of critical or sensitive periods in human development continues to be a part of the research agenda for developmental researchers.

37

Tyrone: ADHD, Genes, Environmental Stressors, and Family Coping

Tyrone is a six-year-old boy referred to a child mental health clinic by a social worker in Special Services in a suburban school. Tyrone jumps out of his seat, talks out of turn, picks fights with other children, does not listen, is disrespectful and rude to adults and children, yells and sometimes hits when frustrated. The school's consulting psychiatrist has ruled out bipolar disorder and advised Special Services that Tyrone meets criteria for a diagnosis of attention-deficit hyperactivity disorder (ADHD).

He is the second of three sons of Will and Edith M. Will is in the sales department of a large insurance company. Edith was a nurse, but is now at home full time. According to Will and Edith, Tyrone's brothers, ages eight and three, pose no special problems. Tyrone is in the first grade, reads and does arithmetic at his grade level. He is very bright (WISC Full Scale IQ is 132).

Will and Edith are African American and recently bought a small house in an ethnically mixed middle class neighborhood. Will is the elder of two children of middle-class parents. Edith is one of six children of urban working-class parents. Both have close ties to families of origin. Most family members are in a large city two hours away from their new home. Will's work has required several moves around the country. The longest time the family has stayed in one location has been two years. Edith thinks that Will could get a good job in a permanent location if he were more aggressive. Will is skeptical that such jobs are available.

Tyrone was the product of an uncomplicated pregnancy and an uneventful delivery. According to Will and Edith, he was a difficult baby, cried much more than either of the other two children, and woke often during the night. At about one year of age he became a head banger, which Edith says upset her greatly, but this behavior ceased after a few months. Tyrone attended nursery school at age four, but the school asked his parents to withdraw him after six weeks because of his unruly behavior. Will recalls an incident in which he was outside the classroom waiting to pick Tyrone up. Tyrone came out, saw a mother of another child, ran up to her, and kicked her in the shins. Will was mortified and reports he hit Tyrone on the behind and yelled, "Tyrone, why did you do that?" Tyrone said he didn't know.

Tyrone attended kindergarten part of the next year, but then the family moved. Because the school year was almost over, he was not re-enrolled in school until the following year. The kindergarten teacher had expressed concern about Tyrone's behavior and referred him for evaluation, but because of the move, it was not completed.

Edith remembers that one of her brothers as a child was a "mild version" of Tyrone. She is very close to her mother, a widow, who is ill with diabetes and hypertension. Edith had been upset by the frequent moves and at having to be far away. She had expected to see her mother often when they moved to their new home, but Will's and the children's schedules have made this difficult.

Edith and Will agree that they got along very well until Tyrone was about three, and his out-of-control behavior became a constant challenge. Before that, they hoped Tyrone's behavior was just the "terrible twos" and would diminish. They acknowledge that they fight a good deal, almost always around Tyrone. Each feels the other handles him the wrong way. Will advocates spanking, Edith opposes it.

Nevertheless, she says she is so frustrated that she also hits Tyrone, although she doesn't think it does any good. Will criticizes her for giving in to his tantrums, which Edith admits she does because she is too tired to hold out indefinitely. Tyrone has tremendous energy, is still going strong at 9 p.m., by which time Will and Edith are exhausted. Some relatives of both Edith and Will have expressed disapproval of their handling of Tyrone ("Maybe he just needs a little more loving," or "A good swat on the rear might help, don't you think?").

Assessment

FAMILY DYNAMICS

I began by reviewing current research on etiology and treatment of ADHD, then used tools described in Chapter 9 to do a risk factor/protective factor analysis, as well as an animated expanded ecomap showing chains of effects that emanate from the disability itself. The tendency among practitioners is sometimes to note areas of conflict and stress among child, family, teachers, and other involved persons (conflicts that are obvious in Tyrone's record) and then mistakenly attribute the cause of the child's problems to parental discord and inept parenting.

Current research emphasizes that impulsive disinhibited behaviors of ADHD, such as interrupting, picking fights, noncompliance with adult requests, and disregard for the rights of others, arise from a biological dysfunction in specific regions of the brain. These behaviors then produce strong psychosocial repercussions which often evolve into an escalating negative feedback loop (see, for example, Caplan and Hall-McCorquodale, 1985; Bale, Baram et al., 2010; Cournoyer and Johnson, 1994; and Johnson, Cournoyer, Fisher et al., 2001).

Data were assembled from Tyrone's record onto instruments using the tools described in Chapter 9:

1. *EPICBIOL*, a risk factor/protective factor matrix and acronym for data categories Economic, Political, Interpersonal, Cultural, Biological, Internal/Mental, Organizational, and Luck.
2. *Multisystem Evidence-Based Assessment* protocol (MEBA) (used here for Tyrone, but demonstrated and discussed in detail in Part VI in relation to an adult client, Pat).
3. *Database searches for scientifically credible research.*

Also used were two visual screening tools, the genogram and the ecomap, widely utilized during the past two-three decades (see for example Jolly et al., 1980; Hartman, 1983; Mattaini, 1999). I have continued the development of the ecomap by animations that show sequences of interactional processes visually. Our instruments in Chapter 9 elicit all the information verbally that is typically depicted in genograms and ecomaps, but visual representations add a multisensory dimension that can augment interest and comprehension.

1. *Relevant family medical history*:
   maternal grandmother's illnesses, maternal uncle's "mild version" of Tyrone's characteristics (can be taken from a genogram).

2. *Known or probable aversive exchanges:*

   Within the nuclear family
   Between the two parents
   Between each parent and Tyrone
   Between the family and external systems
   Between each parent and members of extended families on both sides (the vignette does not specify which family members)
   Between Tyrone and peers
   Possible (no data): aversive exchanges between the parents and school personnel?
   Even in the absence of overt conflict, parents usually feel anxious and under scrutiny by professionals when their child is troublesome
   Possible (no data): frequent punishment of Tyrone in school because of his disruptive behaviors? A common response of overloaded teachers who must meet needs of many children at once.

3. *Arenas for conflict*:

   Tyrone's clashes with teachers, peers, and parents (no information about siblings)
   Parents' disagreement about handling Tyrone's behavior
   Edith's unhappiness with Will's job
   Critical remarks by members of extended families about Edith's and Will's child-rearing practices with Tyrone

4. *Stresses, problems, and needs underlying the aversive exchanges (risk factors)*

Disruptive and aggressive behaviors by Tyrone

Disruption for at least the parents and Tyrone (no information about the siblings) arising from frequent moves due to Will's job

Separation of nuclear family from extended family supports

Attributions of Tyrone's bad behavior to parental deficits (by the parents themselves, extended family members, and probably some of the school personnel)

Lack of child care due to Tyrone's behavior, leading to

- Lack of respite for Edith
- Loss of work outside the home
- Financial stresses due to need for Edith to be available for Tyrone
- Family life is mostly punishing for parents because of constant management needs of Tyrone (not much opportunity for family to enjoy time together)
- Little opportunity for parents to have fun as a couple
- Lack of services (so far) provided by the school to meet Tyrone's special needs

5. *Strengths, resources, assets (protective factors)*

Parents well educated, have marketable skills

Will appears to have a well -paying job

Parents report getting along very well before Tyrone's difficulties surfaced

Apparent lack of difficulties with the two other children

Closeness to extended families

Parents' apparent commitment to helping Tyrone

Tyrone's condition probably treatable

Sufficient family resources to get help for Tyrone when specific needs for help are identified

Research on conditions like Tyrone's showing effective interventions are available (see discussion of search skills, Chapter 9)

Support to parents from the church

Support and advocacy groups for parents available in the community (middle class suburban).

Probably strong parental bonds with Tyrone, not obvious in vignette due to focus on problems

Our assessment is that a negative feedback loop has been set off and perpetuated by Tyrone's neurobiological disability, rather than by bad parenting or parental disagreement. There is no evidence that the parents' conflicts were active prior to the emergence of the challenges Tyrone suffers. It is typical for children like Tyrone to generate conflict, frustration, anger, and finger pointing, because no parental interventions are successful in changing the behavior. Nothing works.

Therefore, parents blame themselves and each other for their child's behavior, and other people blame one or both parents, in the absence of education about the real nature of his disability. Professionals unfamiliar with the research often reinforce misconceptions held by the parents and the extended family. For example, they may respond to failure of psychosocial interventions to diminish the troublesome behaviors by recommending more intensive applications of the same psychosocial interventions that have not worked. This approach is dictated by the belief that Tyrone's behaviors are responses to environmental inputs, not to an underlying brain disorder. Had Tyrone's behaviors been less severe, albeit still biological in origin, behavior modification training for parents and teachers might have been sufficient.

However, research indicates that for this degree of severity (major difficulties in social and behavioral functioning across settings), behavioral treatment alone is seldom adequate.

Possible Interventions

1. *Worker self-education.* The professional begins by educating herself or himself through searches of PubMed and government education/ research/advocacy websites specializing in the questions the worker needs to answer. In this situation. Websites of the Child Psychiatry branch of the National Institutes of Mental Health (NIMH) and the American Academy of Child and Adolescent Psychiatry (AACAP) would be good places to begin. Starting keywords: (attention-deficit hyperactivity disorder OR ADHD), effectiveness, etiology, (outbursts OR loss of control OR disinhibition OR aggressive). Additional keywords: age, gender, ethnicity, family history, any co-occurring illnesses or challenges, family situations or external environmental situations that might amplify difficulties within the child.

   I would also be interested in finding out what characteristics in Tyrone led the consulting psychiatrist to rule out bipolar disorder. Symptoms of the two different conditions are so similar that it is often very difficult for clinicians to distinguish them. In addition, it should go without saying that workers' self-education includes getting information about resources and entitlements for children and families as well as about local access routes to these resources.

2. *Education of family and child,* as appropriate for age and level of sophistication. First, explore with family and child (separately or together, according to worker's and family's best judgment) what each knows about the condition or problem. Misconceptions are the rule rather than the exception. Once the professional has familiarized himself or herself about current research on etiology and interventions, he or she can share this information with parents. Parents, not the child, usually make the decision about what action to take. Although the child's preferences should be factored in,

it may make sense to see parents without him or her and lay out the alternative intervention options, with potential benefits and risks/side effects of each. The choice of no treatment should be included as one option with the possible benefits and risks also made explicit.

3. *Websites of the National Institute of Mental Health (NIMH) and the American Academy of Child and Adolescent Psychiatry (AACAP) have materials for families. Parents should also be referred to scientific databases* if they want this information. Most of us can learn a lot from abstracts on research about a condition, even if we don't understand all the technical information, and parents are no exception. The worker's educational role includes answering parents' questions about the information they have gleaned from different sources, and facilitating the parents' processing of the information. The worker could offer to help parents get started with a search right there in the office that they can continue at home, or in their local library.

4. *Supportive exploration of feelings of the child and of the parents* (separately or together). Parents and children often (but not always) want the opportunity to talk about their feelings with respect to the child's difficulties. A helpful approach is to normalize the feelings that they may have by saying "lots of kids [parents] feel embarrassed [ashamed, scared, etc.] about getting into fights [getting sent to the principal's office, having to take meds, etc.]," or whatever the specific issue may be. It's important, though, not to push parents (or children) to talk about their feelings if they don't want to. Conveying an attitude of respect for clients is critical to a positive relationship, including respecting their wish to keep their feelings private.

5. *Medication evaluation.* Explore parents' beliefs about and attitudes toward medication. Refer the child for a consultation with a child psychiatrist or other child psychiatric expert, focusing on the question of whether medication is advisable, which medication, and what likely effect it might have. Be prepared to respond to parents' questions about the dangers of stimulants for ADHD children and the likelihood of improvement with behavioral and other nonmedication interventions and to direct parents to specific sources of information, because general Internet information is not subject to quality control and can be misleading, even dangerous. Families often are fearful of medication and prefer to try behavioral approaches. However, in cases as severe as Tyrone's, behavior modification in the absence of medication has seldom been found to be more than marginally helpful. Once the issue of medication has been addressed, behavioral strategies could be useful as adjunct treatment (see Advice on managing ADHD behaviors, below).

6. *Referral to parent support group.* Try to learn from the parents what they know about such groups, and whether one or both would like to try going to a meeting or talking on the phone with a parent experienced in the system. Many parents have found the support and expertise of other parents "life-saving."

7. *Advice on managing ADHD behaviors.* Characteristics that are common for a child's disability, for example, getting upset over transitions, are part of the knowledge that a worker needs in order to be helpful to the family.

This specific characteristic requires management strategies involving changing antecedent conditions. Many other more generic behaviors, such as poor listening or interrupting, are well suited to operant behavior modification approaches. The worker asks parents for details about the child's troublesome behaviors and suggests that they choose a single behavior to work on first. Behavioral treatment must usually start with a limited goal and scope in order to make progress. Acting as a behavior management consultant requires knowledge and experience. If you've had no behavioral training, you should probably refer the family to someone who has this expertise specifically for behavior management skills with a special needs child for whom common wisdom and consistent discipline are necessary but not sufficient.

8. *Advocacy for services and entitlements.* The worker shares what he or she knows about resources for the child and the family (services, financial, or other support). If families appear interested, the worker should facilitate a referral or at least provide the family with phone numbers of services.

9. *Ongoing collaboration with the family and the school.* A frequent obstacle to successful treatment is lack of follow-up after referral. Someone needs to be responsible for monitoring progress, which means being in contact with the parents and all providers of services, as well as being available to the parents by phone in order to respond to any concerns they may have. This mechanism should be set up at an initial team meeting that will include the parents, Special Services at the school, Tyrone's classroom teacher, and the clinic social worker. At this conference, a written agreement is needed to spell out who will do what, and by what dates. All participants will sign and will receive a copy of the agreement. If Tyrone is put on a trial of medication, there must be a plan in place for parents and teacher to keep records of his response on a daily basis. The length of time needed to judge whether the medication is effective, and whether the dose should be modified or a different medication substituted, will be decided upon at the initial meeting, along with contingency plans that depend on Tyrone's response. The monitoring role, often taken by a social worker, is critical to the success of the intervention plan.

Expected Benefits from Interventions

TYRONE

Lessened impulsivity, disinhibition, and aggressive behavior
Improved listening, compliance
More positive feedback from others (parents, teachers, peers)

EDITH AND WILL

Less blame/shame/stigma
Greater understanding of Tyrone
More acceptance of themselves and each other
Better management of Tyrone's behaviors
Reduced level of exhaustion

SIBLINGS

Calmer parents
Reduced conflict in the home
Possibly more parental time and attention available

Possible Adverse Effects from Interventions

Medication side effects (side effects of psychostimulants are seldom serious)
Loss of appetite
Remedy: give medication at times other than before meals
Trouble sleeping
Remedy: avoid late afternoon/evening medication
Appears lethargic
Remedy: reduce dose or try a different medication
Child experiences stigma at school by having to go to school nurse for medication
Remedies:
Single extended release dose, if effective
Support group for children in the school setting
Child stashes meds and sells or gives them to peers (usually not an issue with younger children).
Remedies:
Keep meds locked up and supervise administration
"Process" with child, that is, talk with the child about the behavior, explore child's ideas, explain why the behavior is a problem
Set up rules and consequences for infractions

Possible Adverse Effects of no Treatment

Disruptive behaviors continue, rejection of child by teachers and peers is compounded
As child grows older, increased likelihood of poor self-esteem, depression, substance abuse, antisocial behavior, dropping out of school.
Family life continues at chronic high-stress levels, parents drained both emotionally and physically so have reduced resources for positive parenting of all the children.

38

Consciousness: An Evolutionary Perspective

We [consider] consciousness as a biological phenomenon,
one that is a product of both evolution and development...
[It] can address and even dispose of several concerns articulated
by philosophers of mind...does not require metaphysical proposals,
mathematical reduction, or 'strange physics.' [and] can be explained
biologically in terms of patterns of neural activity.

Gerald M. Edelman, Joseph A. Gally,
and Bernard J. Baars (2011)
Biology of consciousness,
Frontiers of Psychology 2:4
The Neurosciences Institute, San Diego, CA.

Undoubtedly, some may take offense at the words of Gerald Edelman and colleagues, whose words some may read as diminishing the spiritual dimensions of life while egotistically claiming superior knowledge. However, Edelman's views are presented in this book because they offer possibly the most plausible ideas from a neuroscience perspective on consciousness, a subject at the cusp of the religion-science debate. Edelman, a Nobel Laureate in medicine, has long enjoyed a worldwide reputation as a neuroscientist, and many colleagues admire his work on consciousness.

For centuries, consciousness has fascinated philosophers, theologians, biologists, psychologists, and ordinary people. In Edelman's words (2004), "Consciousness is the guarantor of all we hold to be human and precious. Its permanent loss is considered equivalent to death, even if the body persists in its vital signs."

The concept has been widely debated, but there's still little consensus about what consciousness really is. Dictionary definitions don't reflect the concept's complexity nor the controversy that surrounds it. For example, Webster's designated it as "the quality or state of being aware, especially of something within oneself" (*Merriam-Webster*, 1988, p. 279). Although this definition is intuitively appealing, scholarly literature on consciousness suggests that it's inadequate.

Philosopher John Searle defines consciousness as "inner, qualitative, subjective states and processes of sentience or awareness.... [It] begins when we wake in the morning from a dreamless sleep and continues until we fall asleep again, die, go into a coma, or otherwise become "unconscious" (2000, p. 559). Examples are feeling pain, seeing an object, feeling anxious, solving a cross-word puzzle, trying to remember a phone number, arguing about politics, or wishing to be somewhere else (Searle, 2000).

Some authors equate consciousness with being aware that we're conscious, others with sensing ourselves as actors, agents, doers (the technical expression is having "a sense of agency"). Primary consciousness (the state of being mentally aware of things in the world, characteristic of many animal species) has been distinguished from higher-order consciousness, which involves the ability to be conscious of being conscious, to recognize one's own acts and affections, to have a social concept of the self, to re-create past experiences, and to form future intentions (Edelman, 2004).

Higher-order consciousness requires at least semantic ability (ability to assign meaning to a symbol). Linguistic ability requires mastery of a whole system of symbols and mastery of a grammar. Chimpanzees have semantic but not linguistic ability; they appear to have the ability to be conscious (Edelman, 2004).

Most scholars seem to agree that consciousness differs from other neurobiological phenomena in that it is inherently subjective—it is experienced in the first person. The essence of the person's experience of consciousness cannot be captured simply by measuring and describing the neurobiological correlates of that experience. Yet identifying these neurobiological characteristics is a part of any scientific understanding, assuming we acknowledge that this information cannot convey subjective experience.

In this regard, saying "I am conscious" is different from saying "I'm angry" or "I'm scared" (emotional states) or "I don't know how to solve this algebra problem" (cognitive condition). Those specific emotional or cognitive states can often be related to particular neurobiologic structures, chemicals, and systems such as the amygdala, adrenaline, or the HPA axis.

Consciousness, by contrast, is a more global state that appears to involve several brain systems. For this reason, it has been very difficult to visualize, much less demonstrate empirically, just which brain structures and systems participate in consciousness. Today, beliefs about consciousness fall into two broad categories: scientific ("of, relating to, or exhibiting, the methods or principles of science") (*Merriam-Webster*, 1988, p 1051) and metaphysical ("of, or relating to, the transcendent or to a reality beyond what is perceptible to the senses") (Ibid., p. 746). The scientific view holds that consciousness occurs in the form of brain functions performed by brain structures, even if we cannot specify what those functions and structures are. The metaphysical view asserts that consciousness transcends scientific principles.

The metaphysical view is in the tradition of René Descartes, who addressed the mind/body problem in the 17th century. Every person was a *res cogitans* (thinking thing), a unified rational acting entity in control of a body. However, according to Descartes, this thinking director-of-the-body was not subject to the laws of physics. Rather, it was nonmaterial and nonphysical, like the soul (Haldane and Ross, 1975).

Few scientists today still accept the notion that a thinking mind can exist devoid of a physical basis. Some humanities scholars such as Searle and philosopher Daniel Dennett endorse the scientific view as emphatically as do leading neuroscientists. However, the dualistic, dichotomous view considered in Chapter 4 has had a pervasive influence on academia as well as popular culture. Since the purpose of this book is to explore knowledge that integrates the biological with psychological and social components rather than separating the three spheres, readers wishing to learn more about the dualistic metaphysical perspective will probably want to look beyond this book.

Edelman has devised a model for the neurobiology of consciousness (2011, 2004), sparking animated dialogue both within and outside the scientific community. This chapter introduces Edelman's model, which he calls the *theory of neuronal group selection (TNGS)*. There isn't sufficient space to explore several models of consciousness in this book, so we've chosen the model that seems to have most excited scientists and nonscientists alike in the early 21st century. (The following discussion assumes that you're familiar with fundamentals of neuroscience presented in Parts II, III, and IV.)

Edelman first proposed TNGS in 1978 and has elaborated it since then. It appears to be the most comprehensive model to date and has received support from numerous leading neuroscientists, including Antonio Damasio, Oliver Sacks (neurologist known to the public through his books and the movie *Awakenings*), and Francis Crick, one of the scientists awarded the Nobel Prize in 1962 for the discovery of the double helix (Rothstein, 2004; Crick and Koch, 2003). Kim Dawson (2004) has extended Edelman's work in the area of time as a facet of consciousness. These scholars of neuroscience agree that the model is consistent with most of the relevant scientific evidence and offers a plausible explanation for consciousness. Data that could validate the model in its entirety are not yet available, however, so at the present time the TNGS awaits full validation.

Edelman's theory of consciousness encompasses some fundamental questions. How can the brain produce coherent activities such as speech, work, play, and social interaction that take place in a conscious state? How is it possible that 100 billion or more different nerve cells, acting in different parts of the brain, at different speeds, and in compliance with multiple sets of rules and procedures governing interacting body systems—how, in the context of such complexity, can the brain impose order rather than being overrun by chaos? Neuroscientists have been contemplating this mystery for some time and have named it the *binding problem*. To understand the neural basis for consciousness, a solution to the binding problem is required.

Edelman proposes that the workings of consciousness, and the coherence of brain activity despite its complexity, lie in the brain's developmental history and innate characteristics; in its presumed capability to self-organize through a process he and others call *reentry*; in the actions of at least three major brain systems; and in a selection process consisting of three overlapping steps. I'll review these topics to familiarize readers with some of the central concepts of TNGS; however, "complete" understanding eludes not only nonscientists today, but even some bona fide neuroscientists.

This chapter departs from the rest of the book in that it focuses on a theory that has only partially been demonstrated through research. Although the theory is consistent with neuroscience research over the past two decades, the actual mechanisms by which consciousness takes place have not been demonstrated empirically as of the time of writing. The theoretical material that follows is challenging but fascinating. It is at the cutting edge of neuroscience explorations in the early 21st century. Critics can argue that TNGS is not critical for human service practitioners to know, and I agree. It's included for readers who would like to expand their horizons and stimulate their thinking further.

The brain's developmental history and innate characteristics. In the brain, where's the master plan, and where's the executive director for this master plan? It would certainly seem that there must be one. Did you know that every attribute of a falling red ball is processed in a different location in the brain? In the case of the ball, there is color (red), shape (round), texture (rubbery), and movement (falling). There can be up to 30 different locations simultaneously processing different characteristics of a perceived object, yet we see only a single entity. We have a perception of an integrated object, the falling-red-ball. Surely there must be a brain equivalent of an air traffic controller directing the operation of the master plan.

Wrong, says Edelman. The coherence and integration that seem so amazing are achieved by quite different mechanisms. The brain develops from an embryonic structure called a neural tube. Precursor cells to neurons and glia (the cells that provide support to neurons) move to their final destinations in the brain, making various layers and patterns. As these precursor cells in the developing fetus differentiate into neurons and migrate to their final destinations in the brain, many die. Stronger cells survive and create new connections; weaker cells die off. Edelman likens brain development to evolution of the species. In fact, he designates the mechanisms of brain development "Neural Darwinism." The brain's power comes from natural selection acting in complex environments over eons. As in evolution of the species, there's no superordinate brain region or executive program binding the color, form, texture, and movement of an object into a coherent perception.

Structures and functions in the brain respond at any given moment in time to the demands of the situation at that time—not according to a blueprint drawn by a long-term planning committee and not overseen by a president's cabinet of ministers. In the process of evolution, species do not arise according to a preset program, and neither do our brains. Unlike computers, which execute programs that consist of logical steps following specific rules and procedures (algorithms), brains evolve through natural selection. Brains of higher-level animals construct patterned responses to events that are full of novelty. This behavior is unlike that of computers, which follow formal rules accompanied by explicit unambiguous instructions.

The brain is characterized by variation, versatility, and degeneracy. The concepts of variation and versatility are relatively easy to understand. We have many different kinds of neurons (at least 200) and many more brain cells than we need. So our brains are rich in numbers of cells and connections, variety, and patterns of cell movement.

Different individuals have different genetic influences, different epigenetic sequences (see Chapter 8), different bodily responses, and different histories in varying environments. The result is enormous variation at the levels of neuronal chemistry, network structure, synaptic strengths, timing of responses, memories, and motivational patterns. This variation endows the brain with versatility. The brain can choose which neuron or circuit will best respond to any unforeseen (environmental) input, and activate that structure. This incredible diversity of material from which to select means that there's a lot of waste—cells and connections that end up not being used. However, this extravagance gives the brain remarkable resilience and potential for evolution. No brain event ever happens the same way twice. This astonishing variation in the human brain probably has contributed mightily to its reputation as the most complex entity in the known universe, and to the fascination its secrets hold for creative young and old minds today.

That's where degeneracy comes in. Most of us think of degeneracy in its common usage, defined as a state "characterized by deterioration" or the condition of a "morally degraded person" (Morris, 1975, p. 347). But scientific meaning of the word is entirely different: "taking on several discrete or distinct values or states" (Morris, 1975). Edelman's definition is "the ability of structurally different elements of a system to perform the same function or yield the same output" (2004, p. 154).

Degeneracy accounts for the fact that when a certain gene is "knocked out" of a laboratory animal for experimental purposes, 30% of the animals show no changes in the phenotype (observable characteristic) created by that gene. This is not because the gene wasn't really knocked out, but because degeneracy allows the brain to call up other different brain functions to produce the same effect.

As neurons develop, they form parallel groups, and they begin to fire in synchrony. This synchronous firing within bands of nerve fibers leads to hardwiring (neurons that fire together, wire together). These bands of fibers (sometimes called *nuclei*, the plural of *nucleus*) are thought to make up the larger systems within the brain that work together to create the phenomenon of consciousness.

How does this happen? Once neurons have migrated to their final destinations in the brain, they grow dendrites and axons, growth that is guided by physical and chemical factors (for a detailed explanation of early brain development, see Carlson, 2001, pp. 73-76).

Axons form branches at their end. Each branch finds a vacant place on the membrane of an "appropriate" postsynaptic cell, grows a terminal button, and establishes a synaptic connection. "Appropriate" refers to a particular type of postsynaptic neuron, or even a different part of a neuron, appearing to secrete a specific chemical that attracts specific chemicals of axons (Carlson, 2001, p. 75). The chemical signals that the cells exchange to tell one another to establish synaptic connections are being discovered on an ongoing basis by researchers.

When a presynaptic neuron establishes a connection, it receives a signal from the postsynaptic cell that allows it to survive. About 50% of neurons do not succeed in finding vacant spaces of the right type on neurons that they can connect to, and they die. Once synaptic connections have been made, they can either become stronger or weaker. If a presynaptic neuron fires before an adjacent postsynaptic neuron fires, the connection—that is, the synapse—becomes stronger. If the time sequence is reversed, that is, if the postsynaptic neuron fires before the presynaptic neuron, the connection becomes weaker. So some connections become stronger and thrive, others become weaker. Connections that continue to weaken eventually die.

The phase of neuronal group formation is crucial to solving the binding problem. During the early establishment of brain structures, sets of interconnected neurons are existing side by side, but don't have much to do with each other—they happen to be hanging out, but not interacting. Variations in the patterns of connections among growing neurons form repertoires in each brain area composed of millions of variant circuits or neuronal groups. These variations arise at the level of synapses, because neurons that have fired together during embryonic and fetal stages of development have wired together.

When moments of synchrony between neurons begin to occur by accident, connections are made, and the more often these events are repeated, the stronger they become. Populations of synapses can become stronger or weaker. Here's how Edelman explained it to me (personal communication, 2004): Neurons are like musicians in a string quartet. Three of the four are playing a classical quartet from the eighteenth century (say, Haydn), while the fourth member, at the same time, is playing something hip and modern. Every so often, by chance, the deviant player and the Haydn players happen to hit an accented beat at the same moment. These occasional moments of synchrony form a connection. Both sides begin to play a bit more like the other, and the longer they play together, the stronger their connections and the more they play in sync. By the dress rehearsal, they are playing in almost perfect synchrony, but it's a new composition that integrates Haydn, Rock, and Rap.

Because the brain, unlike computers, is not logical, its central organizing principle is *reentry*. Reentry governs the space and time coordination among multiple networks in the brain. For example, the components of the falling red ball (movement, color, shape) are coordinated by the different brain regions involved communicating directly with each other through reentry. Let's summarize principles central to the theory of neuronal group selection (TNGS) that we've considered so far.

1. The brain was not created by design. There was no master plan, and there is no overseer in the brain setting rules and making connections. The brain's power comes from natural selection acting in complex environments over eons of time. Like individuals who compete with each other for survival, brain cells also compete with each other for survival.
2. The brain has an extraordinary amount of variation.
3. The brain is characterized by degeneracy, not efficiency or parsimony. In the brain there is always more going on than seems necessary, more randomness, and more variation than in any system designed by humans. Degeneracy allows parts of the brain to "choose" other parts to connect to, flexibly responding through epigenetic mechanisms to demands created by input from the environment (see Chapter 8 for a discussion of epigenesis).
4. Parallel group formation is one of the keys to the functions of neural systems that allow different, separate neural systems to communicate with each other and to function in synchrony.

Reentry is pivotal to the TNGS. Reentry is a dynamic ongoing process of signaling back and forth across parallel fibers. These fibers are reciprocal, that is, they go in both directions between one neuron system and another. This process results in binding and is the basis for the emergence of consciousness. Reentry allows coherent, synchronized events to occur in the brain (Edelman, 2004, p. 174).

Reentry coordinates the activities of different brain areas in space and time. It binds neuron activities that are taking place at distances away from each other into circuits capable of coherent output. That is, reentry solves the binding problem. Through reentry, color, orientation, and movement of a visual object can be integrated. No overarching map is necessary to coordinate these activities. These attributes communicate directly with each other through reentry and are thus able to coordinate their messages so that we perceive a single entity in one time and one place.

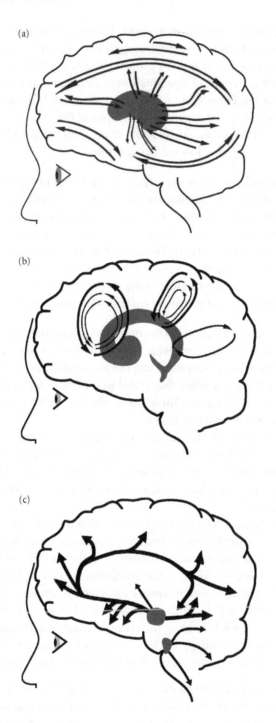

FIGURE 38.1

Source: Adapted from Gerald Edelman, 2004, *Wider than the Sky*, New Haven: Yale University Press, Figure 3. Printed with permission.

Actions of three major brain systems. I stated earlier that three principal neural systems come into play, according to Edelman, in the creation of consciousness. Consciousness is not a property of a single brain location or neuronal type, but the result of dynamic interactions among widely distributed groups of neurons. Figures 38.1a, 38.1b, and 38.1c sketch these three systems, clearly demonstrating the expansive geography of the systems.

Adapted from Gerald Edelman, 2004, *Wider than the Sky*, New Haven: Yale University Press, Figure 3. Printed with permission.

1. The *thalamocortical circuits* (Figure 38.1a) consist of tightly connected groups of neurons reaching both locally and across distances to form rich reciprocal connections between the thalamus and the cortex. The thalamus governs the levels of conscious states by regulating the amount of cortical activity. The content of conscious activity depends on which of the various cortical areas are active—is it motor, visual, auditory, tactile, one or more of the specific cognitive functions emanating from the prefrontal cortex, or some combination?

The thalamus is in the center of the brain and is essential for conscious function, even though it's only somewhat larger than the last bone in our thumbs. All nerves from sensory receptors except those conducting olfactory messages connect to the thalamus when they travel to the brain, through specific clusters of neurons called nuclei. These nuclei should not be confused with the generic concept of the nucleus of cells.

Postsynaptic neurons in each specific thalamic nucleus then project to axons that connect to particular areas of the cortex. The cortex receives messages from the thalamus, but there are also reciprocal axonal fibers that go back from the cortex to the thalamus. These reciprocal connections abound within the cortex.

Specific thalamic nuclei do not connect directly with any of the others. However, their activity is coordinated by a structure surrounding the thalamus called the reticular nucleus, which connects to the specific nuclei and which can inhibit their activity. The reticular nucleus acts as a switch or gate controlling the level of transmission of sensory messages. It "decides" how to balance nucleus A's level of activity with nucleus B's level of activity, perhaps allowing one to increase while holding the other constant. Another set of thalamic nuclei called the intralaminar nuclei is suspected of being essential for consciousness in that it sets appropriate thresholds or levels of cortical response.

2. The *basal ganglia* (Figure 38.1b) are composed of loops of circuits whose neurons produce the inhibitory neurotransmitter GABA. These GABA neurons are in series with each other within the loops, so inhibitory GABA molecules are dispatched from the axon of one GABA neuron and picked up by the dendrites of the next GABA

neuron in line. The action of those transmitters is to inhibit the inhibitory action of the second GABA neuron. The second GABA neuron now dispatches less GABA to the third neuron in the chain. That means it inhibits the third neuron less, so the third neuron becomes more excited. Thus we see that inhibitory neurons and neurotransmitters not only inhibit other neurons directly, but can also indirectly excite other neurons one step removed from them. That's the double negative effect we discussed in more detail in Chapter 29 on drug actions.

3. *Value systems* are widely spread out ascending projections of several systems, each of which processes a specific neurotransmitter (Figure 38.1c). Value systems govern the threshold of activity of other neural structures. They generate motivation to survive and behaviors to carry out survival-directed activities such as the four Fs: feeding, fighting, fleeing, and fornicating. The use of the word "value" here appears to mean "priority." The agendas of these circuits take priority over other possible brain actions that might not be crucial to survival. We saw sketches of the two value systems that produce and transmit dopamine and serotonin respectively in Part II, Chapter 14, Figure 14.1a and 14.1b.

Value systems of neurons originate in lower regions of the brain, travel upward throughout almost all brain regions, spread out, and communicate widely throughout the brain. They behave like leaky garden hoses, spraying neurotransmitters into the far reaches of the brain. Each system of neurons specializes in a specific neurotransmitter and carries out various functions around the brain that utilize that specific transmitter. These systems specialize in dopamine, serotonin, norepinephrine, and several other transmitters. In order to promote the organism's survival, these value systems confer constraints on what other systems can do.

The many bundles of nerve fibers that form circuits in the thalamocortical circuits, the basal ganglia, and the value systems share information without going to any command-and-control center, overseer, or stage director. These circuits often travel in parallel routes, on paths within the brain that may be circular or unidirectional. Often they pass through gating stations that regulate their output, such as the reticular nucleus. This is reentry, the means by which they coordinate their activities. The selection process that comprises the TNGS is made up of three overlapping steps:

1. *Developmental selection during early brain formation involves epigenetic variations* (see Chapter 8). As neurons form connections, patterns are formed in each brain area consisting of millions of variant circuits or neuronal groups. The variations arise at the level of synapses. According to Edelman, during embryonic and fetal stages of

development neurons begin to fire together and as they do, they wire together.

2. *Experiential selection overlaps with the first phase of selection and also continues after major neuroanatomy is built.* It creates large variations in synaptic strengths resulting from variations in environmental input. These synaptic modifications are subject to constraints of the value systems referred to above, systems of neurons geared to promotion of the individual's survival.

3. *Reentry.* During development, large numbers of reciprocal connections are established both locally and over long distances. These reciprocal neurons transmit signals around the circuits that make up the three major brain systems involved in consciousness: the thalamocortical circuits, the basal ganglia, and the value systems, depicted in Figures 38.1a, 38.1b, and 38.1c.

Are you still wondering how all of this works to make possible the phenomenon of human consciousness? So am I. Perhaps definitive evidence will be unearthed one of these days—filling in today's gaps of uncertainty that prevail. When the science of consciousness is finally confirmed and validated, perhaps neuroscientists will find a way to help the rest of us understand the foundations of this empire of human experience.

Mental Health and Mental Illness: Medical Conventions, Recent Research, from Assessment to Intervention Planning

Part VI on neuroscience and mental illness begins with an unlikely topic, some ideological and political environments within which we work (Chapter 39). The premise is that practitioners give the best services when we understand the environments in which we are embedded. The focus is on the influence of current mental health environments and how we as nonpsychiatrists may be shaped by these environments. (We do not discuss managed care here as it has been scrutinized and discussed in the literature by several disciplines for about two decades.)

The rest of Part VI explores one common example of a diagnosis, borderline personality disorder (BPD), and presents an in-depth assessment of a woman who meets criteria for that diagnosis. Chapters 40 to 45 convey the kinds of information needed for high quality assessment, where to access it, and how to apply it in practice as multisystemic and evidence-based biopsychosocial assessment and intervention planning.

Chapter 40 presents information that is responsive to the question "What is borderline personality disorder (BPD)"? Definitions, categorical and dimensional approaches, boundaries of the diagnosis vis-à-vis other diagnoses, epidemiology, insights of some leading researcher/clinician scholars, environmental contributions to borderline conditions, and roles of families are considered.

Chapter 41 illustrates ways that neuroscience can inform us about borderline conditions. Chapter 42 is a review and analysis of aspects of BPD as experienced by Pat, the client introduced in Part IV and continued here. She meets criteria for BPD as well as for severe bulimia nervosa, intermittent episodes of anorexia nervosa, and chronic dysthymia (depressed mood) punctuated by episodes of major depressive disorder. In addition, she has intermittent symptoms of depersonalization and feelings of emptiness, but does not meet criteria for the dissociative identity disorder diagnosis. Her feelings of emptiness appear in Linehan's (1993B) dimension of "dysregulation of the self." Over and above her multiple mental health issues, her bulimia history meets criteria for a food addiction (see Part IV, Chapter 25), so she falls into the group meeting criteria for "co-occurring" mental health and addiction diagnoses, once called the "dually diagnosed."

As we go to press, we still do not know what provision the APA (2013) has made to recognize the concept of food addiction in the DSM-5, but we consider food addiction here since it conforms with the set of criteria for addiction used in this book, which in turn are derived from research findings.

Chapter 43 reviews research on medications used to treat borderline challenges, and Chapter 44 reviews evidence about major behavioral and psychosocial interventions that have been widely used with BPD. Finally, in Chapter 45, the second half of Pat's assessment using the Multisystem Evidence-Based Assessment (MEBA) is presented, integrating assessment and intervention planning related to both mental health and addictive struggles (see Chapter 9 for a detailed explanation of MEBA).

People meeting criteria for the DSM-IV-TR BPD diagnosis (APA, 2000) have been seen at some times by most social workers in their careers in a range of fields of practice—anything from mental health to family counseling to child welfare to school social work, various forms of violence, substance abuse and addiction, and other areas of practice.

We often feel challenged by these clients due to characteristics such as intense hostile-dependent feelings toward the practitioner, over-idealization of the worker alternating with rageful disappointment, suicidal or otherwise violent behaviors, impulsivity, recklessness, and the tendency to terminate treatment abruptly and prematurely when painful issues arise (Stone, 1994; Sadock and Sadock, 2003). Pat may not fit the standard profile of a person diagnosed with borderline personality, but she meets DSM BPD criteria as of April 2013 and does have the common BPD challenges of a serious addiction with behavioral dysregulation, depression, and intense moods.

Information for Pat's MEBA includes knowledge reported in Part III on pleasure and obesity, Part IV on addictions, and Chapters 39 to 44 on mental health issues in Part VI. One way to help prepare yourself for competency in a changing practice world is to replicate and complete MEBA, together with the client systems data collection tool for MEBA item 9 (the EPICBIOL).

Your subject can be either an active client, or a nonclient whom you know well, such as a relative, friend, co-worker, or neighbor (or yourself). A part of the in-depth knowledge that you seek will come from searches in scientific and research databases, especially PubMed, the premier medical and psychiatric resource that currently lists more than 22 million publications (NIH, 2013). Step-by-step skills in evidence-based searching are presented in this book in Chapter 9.

You might be surprised by the willingness of potential nonclient subjects to help you out (he or she will be doing this to support *you*, not the other way around). However, the person will probably get something out of it as well, at the very least some quality time with an interested and caring listener who sincerely wants to hear in detail about his or her concerns, aspirations, and everyday realities. Part of the task involves learning about some of the likely neurobiological processes that are associated with the person's major concerns or challenges. MEBA items 9 through 12 and Chapter 9 on search skills indicate how to go about this. To the extent that it is appropriate, doing these searches together with a client is desirable (on one computer, or two when the subject is tech-savvy). Collaborative learning can be very satisfying for both client and worker.

For practitioners already employed in the field, including those with many years of experience, the principle of lifetime learning endorsed by many human service graduate and undergraduate progams probably holds now more than ever before. Neuroscience knowledge of emotions, behaviors, and cognitions—that is, human psychology—has become a thundering water-fall flooding the plains where practice traditions have held sway for several generations.

Is this metaphor too melodramatic? I think so! Changes of this nature are more likely to trickle and infiltrate than gush. But the changes in developmental and clinical knowledge described by Bale, Baram, Brown et al. (2010, introductory citation, Part V) can be expected to have a long-term impact over, say, ten years, of at least equal magnitude overall to that of roaring, overflowing high waters happening within a time frame of a few days or weeks.

The core of this change? According to Bale and colleagues, "Early theories about psychic conflict and toxic parenting have been replaced by more recent formulations of complex interactions of genes and environment" (Bale et al., 2010, p. 314). These advances in mental health knowledge and practice were in process even before 1999, when they were described and advocated in the mental health report of the Surgeon General of the United States (Health and Human Services, 1999), in a collaborative undertaking by many of the country's leading mental health scholars.

The research literature on BPD is voluminous, as is the case for all the most prevalent mental and addictive conditions. I restricted my searches to aspects that are most critical in Pat's life.

39

Entering the Era of the DSM-5:
Sea Change in Practice Ideologies?

The Director of the National Institute of Mental Health (NIMH) has thrown down the gauntlet for the disciplines popularly known today as the "helping professions."

> This is an extraordinary moment in the science of mental disorders. Indeed, it is difficult to find a precedent in medicine for what is beginning to happen in psychiatry. The intellectual basis of psychiatry is shifting, from reliance on psychological principles and theory to research findings and understanding the brain through neuroscience. The basis of diagnosis is likely to be completely reformulated to consider biological information.... such as genetics and imaging data.
> Thomas R Insel (2009), Director, National Institute of Mental Health.
> Disruptive insights in psychiatry: transforming a clinical discipline.
> *Journal of Clinical Investigation* 119(4): 700–705.

The focus in this chapter is to bring to readers' attention what amounts to an upheaval in professional understanding of mental health and mental illness in the first and second decades of the millennium. Academic lingo might dub these changed beliefs and perspectives a "new paradigm" for psychological conditions referred to in psychiatry as "disorders."

For several decades, the medical discipline of psychiatry has framed the language and conventions used by several mental health-oriented disciplines including social work that serve people with emotional, behavioral, and cognitive challenges. This language and these conventions are embodied in the successive versions of the *Diagnostic and Statistical Manual of Mental Disorders*, referred to henceforth as the DSMs, published by the American Psychiatric Association (APA) since the 1950s. [Note: The American Psychiatric Association and the American Psychological Association have the same acronym, APA. In this book, APA refers to the former, and the latter will be written out.]

The DSMs have long been social work's primer for conferring psychiatric diagnoses that are congruent with the usual practices in mental health professional communities in America. Efforts by social work to broaden psychiatric

diagnosis with instruments providing more detailed environmental information, notably Person-in-Environment (PIE), were met with enthusiasm by
many in social work and are credited by some for bringing about the expan-
sion of environmental items on Axis IV of the DSMs (Karls and Wandrei, 1994;
Karls and O'Keefe, 2008; Ramsey, 2011). However, Ramsey has noted that PIE
has fallen short of the widespread use its proponents had hoped for.

Nevertheless, social work models and possibly some models from other
helping professions have usually been deficient in neuroscience knowledge for
practice, now widely recognized as essential by most of the scientific community and beginning to be acknowledged in social work practice and education.
It would appear that integrating biological and medical science with psychosocial and systems analysis would be required to remedy deficits in both psychiatry and social work.

Insel's 2009 prediction, cited above, that the basis of diagnosis is likely to be
"completely reformulated to consider biological information" responds to an
all-important question in psychiatry, framed two years earlier by his predecessor
as Director of the National Institute of Mental Health, Steven E. Hyman (2007).

> To date, the diagnosis of mental disorders has been based on clinical
> observation, specifically: the identification of symptoms that tend to cluster
> together, the timing of the symptoms' appearance, and their tendency to
> resolve, recur or become chronic. The Diagnostic and Statistical Manual
> of Mental Disorders and the International Classification of Disease, the
> manuals that specify these diagnoses and the criteria for making them, are
> currently undergoing revision. *It is thus timely to ask whether neuroscience
> has progressed to the point that the next editions of these manuals can usefully
> incorporate information about brain structure and function* (emphasis
> added).

If the answer to Hyman's question is yes—that is, if the APA recently thought
this change should begin implementation immediately rather than waiting for
some undetermined time in the future—then how did the organization plan
to make this happen?[1]

I noted in Parts I and II that not only Hyman but also two Nobel Laureates
in science have called the human brain the most complex entity in the known
universe (see Chapter 2, citations for Hyman (1997), Edelman (2004), and
Kandel (2011). As early as 1986, a popular book on the human brain entitled
The Three-Pound Universe expressed a similar view of the enormity of the
brain's role in human life (Hooper and Teresi, 1986). These thinkers suggest
a compelling question: can we really transform the time-honored providers'
guide to *mental disorders*—clusters of client characteristics assigned a diagnostic name and number—into a compendium of *brain events linked inextri-
cably to every emotion, behavior, and cognition*?

These brain events happen when interconnecting networks of neuronal structures generate chemical reactions and electrical charges to dispatch messages to millions of receptors around the brain and the body. These interconnections will be compiled into a map, called the Human Connectome, now hailed by numerous neuroscientists as the new Holy Grail of neuroscience knowledge (see Chapter 19; Seung, 2012).

Its predecessor the Human Genome, published in 2003 after more than a decade of work by a large number of scientists, now seems like child's play in comparison. The Connectome, as a map of neural structures, pathways, and networks of the brain, should be able to supply scientists with much of the brain side of brain-behavior connections, and on the other side, social and behavioral sciences can contribute knowledge about emotions, behaviors, and cognitions—our psychological events—that must be redefined to map accurately to their underlying neurobiological structures, functions, and networks (Kober, Feldman-Barrett, Joseph, et al., 2008).

The new technology that can put these components together has been advancing rapidly (Seung, 2012), and large-scale research to support construction of a human connectome is now receiving federal grant money (see Part III, Chapter 19). One of the major rationales by neuroscientists and medical specialists for linking neural underpinnings to specific psychological events is to develop capacities to remedy particular psychological malfunctions directly at their biological sources.

In answer to his own question as to whether the development of neuroscience is *ready* to be incorporated into official diagnostic mental health manuals after decades-long reliance on clusters of symptoms, Hyman wrote (2007):

> The term "mental disorders" is an unfortunate anachronism, one retained from a time when these disorders were not universally understood to reflect abnormalities of brain structure, connectivity or function (emphasis added). Although the central role of the brain in these disorders is no longer in doubt, the identification of the precise neural abnormalities that underlie the different mental disorders has stubbornly defied investigative efforts.

He continues:

> The substantial gaps in our knowledge of the neurobiology that underlies mental disorders derive in large part from the difficulty of characterizing the circuitry and mechanisms that underlie higher brain function, the complexity of the genetic and developmental underpinnings of normal and abnormal behavioural variation . . .

If that were the end of the story, we might say "Oh what the heck, let's just go on as we have been—an embellished version of the old DSM-IV-TR should be just fine."

But it wasn't the final word. Hyman concludes:

Yet excessive pessimism is not warranted.... neuroscience provides much that is relevant and useful—even if it currently falls short of providing a basis for individual diagnoses. Indeed, I will argue that neurobiological information can, along with clinical observations and family and genetic studies, help to shape a reconsideration of the important aspects of the DSM system. Moreover, the *DSM-V should be structured to allow the incorporation of well-replicated findings from neuroscience and genetics as they emerge—* without forcing us to wait a decade or more for the DSM-VI. (emphasis added)

Why not? Implicit in this statement is the belief that incremental incorporation of emerging neuroscience knowledge into future editions of psychiatric diagnosis and treatment manuals can be carried out to make the diagnosis more congruent with science, without unduly disrupting the work of the diagnosers.

If the physical incorporation into the DSM-5 of neuroscience findings would be too cumbersome, might it be possible for a committee representing research divisions of major government institutions—such as the National Institute of Mental Health (NIMH), the National Institute of Drug Abuse (NIDA), the National Institute of Alcohol Abuse and Alcoholism (NIAAA), the US Public Health Service (PHS), the US Department of Health and Human Services (HHS), the National Institute on Aging (NIA), the Children's Defense Fund (CDF), and undoubtedly numerous others—to provide a staff person to receive and compile these contributions in the agency's areas of specialization, and funnel them on a continuous basis to a central research and publication unit? To make them available to all sectors of mental health communities, they could be posted and continuously updated on a dedicated public website.

But what's the catch? Some DSM users would undoubtedly be happy and excited. But would others want to read the new research entries as they steadily poured in from the multidisciplinary research community? Or would typical reactions be "too time-consuming, distracting, we have to get the work *done*, most of that research won't apply to my clients, only the academics hanging in their labs have time for all that..." And journals as well as government agencies often need all the revenue they can raise. So who would bear the costs?

Yes, that's the way many practitioners probably will feel. So how could the planners of this campaign entice them? Ask them to check off areas of their practice interests and put them on list of their choice set up by fields of practice? And what rewards for participation could be offered?

Voices for replacing categories with dimensions, either among personality disorders or in the entire DSM, were given some credence by the APA's policy-makers during the years of work by the DSM-5 Task Force. Some of its leaders proposed a combined dimensional/categorical system intended to benefit from the advantages of both (APA, 2012). The Task Force provided multiple opportunities for input from the lay, practitioner, and academic public during the development of the document, ending in the summer of 2012. Finalizing the document was then carried out by the APA until final membership approval in December 2012. As of that time, the organization was still receiving empassioned critiques from observers and resignations of protest by members of the DSM-5 Task Force (Frances, 2012).

Multiple deficiencies in the categorical DSM-IV-TR system have been noted by an increasing number of critics both within and outside psychiatry (see for example Frances, 2012; Hyman, 2007; Brubeck, 1999; Kirk and Kutchins, 1992; Wakefield, 1992; Gunderson, 2009, 2010; Gottesman and Gould, 2003). Criticisms include excessive reappearance of the same or similar criteria in multiple diagnostic categories, no defined boundaries or cut-off points between "normal" and "disordered" personality, lack of method for weighting criteria differently as is the practice in the DSM-IV with major depressive disorder and posttraumatic stress disorder (PTSD), giving each diagnostic criterion a value of 1, no matter what the relative importance of each, by summing the total number of qualifying criteria (e.g., at least five out of nine for the borderline personality disorder diagnosis), too much heterogeneity among criteria such that two patients getting the BPD diagnosis might overlap on as few as only one criterion, need for an algorithm that moves the diagnosis away from clusters of observable symptoms toward underlying phenomena that more closely resemble the genetic template, doubt about the stability over time of a person's status with respect to criteria (type, level of intensity), and finally, inadequate scientific foundation (Samuel and Widiger, 2010; Clark, 2007; Widiger and Mullins-Sweatt, 2009).

The APA acknowledged in its text of DSM-IV-TR that "an alternative to the categorical approach is the dimensional perspective that personality disorders represent maladaptive variants of personality traits that merge imperceptibly into normality and into one another" (APA, 2000, p. 689).

Samuel and Widiger (2010) tested the discriminant validity of personality disorder criteria in the DSM-IV-TR in comparison with characteristics of the dimensional Five Factor Model of Personality (FFM) (McCrae and Costa, 2003; McCrae, Costa, Martin et al., 2004). The FFM consists of five dimensions on a continuum between high and low on each dimension, together with a range of single traits, integrated into a hierarchical structure. The FFM performed better than the DSM-IV-TR with respect to discriminant validity, that is, the ability of the instrument to identify specific characteristics of different personalities that "discriminate" them from each other and from typical ("normal") personalities.

All of the above being said, the DSM-IV-TR borderline personality diagnosis (APA, 2000) has shown substantial empirical evidence of validity and clinical utility (Gunderson, 2009; Johansen, Karterud et al., 2004; Sanislow, (…) et al., 2002). The DSMs are the usual choice for diagnosis when insurance reimbursement is sought, since most health insurance plans, private and public, have relied on them for years.

Activists who want to see the changes contemplated by scholars like Insel and Hyman actually happen, need to organize! Surely they can come up with strategies to engage reluctant colleagues in the excitement of learning amazing new knowledge? Could new knowledge about emotional brains or counterintuitive truths actually be fun?

Since much work is still needed to identify matches of specified pathways with particular traits, states, behaviors, emotions and cognitions, and at the risk of underestimating the speed and production of the best minds in the world, many of whom are engaged in this endeavor, my own guess is that we still have substantial time to assess and intervene until the finished product is disrobed.

The work of Kober and colleagues (2008) took a critical step in the advance toward the envisioned human connectome (Seung, 2012). The goal of the Human Connectome Project is to build a "network map" that will shed light on the anatomical and functional connectivity within the healthy human brain, as well as to produce a body of data that will facilitate research into brain disorders (National Institutes of Health (NIH), 2010). The knowledge to be gained certainly will advance the pool of knowledge with respect to behavioral pharmacology.

A sign that the Human Connectome Project has gained great momentum was President Barack Obama's recognition in his State of the Union address February 12, 2013, that the realization of the Connectome will be a momentous event. He placed the Connectome project as an advance in the trajectory that produced the Human Genome in 2003, a map of the genes in the human body. Now the structures, functions, circuits and networks in the "most complicated entity in the known universe" are the subject of this mammoth research construction (see references to SE Hyman, E Kandel, and G Edelman independently the brain as "most complex entity...").

Early steps in the Connectome construction process include (1) discovering and naming an individual structure performing an individual function in the brain; (2) showing that the target of this function by this structure is a specific emotion or behavior; and (3) demonstrating how this fragment of brain action connects, on increasingly complex levels, with more and more other structures and more and more other pathways to carry out its tasks.

Now we're discovering that psychological events typically have one or more *neural networks*, performing increasingly complex functions in collaboration with multiple other structures and networks, to generate multiple emotions, cognitions, or behaviors.

Kober and colleagues (2008) updated a quantitative meta-analysis of 162 neuroimaging studies of emotion using a novel multi-level approach called *kernel-based*. They focused on identifying brain regions that were *consistently activated in emotional tasks*. The two larger areas where this was the case were

the prefrontal cortex and the "subcortical" (beneath the cortical exterior surfaces of the brain, and deep in the center of the brain). Subcortical structures
included the amygdala, ventral striatum (with nucleus accumbens), thalamus,
hypothalamus, and periaqueductal gray matter, mostly in what's considered
the "limbic loop."

The investigators used specialized tools to identify functional groups that
co-activated with another such group to be able to tabulate the occurrence
of co-activated brain regions across studies. These analyses identified six distributed functional groups, including medial and lateral frontal groups, two
posterior cortical groups, and paralimbic and core limbic/brainstem groups.
*These functional groups provide information on potential organization of brain
regions into large-scale networks.* As I noted above, the groups did not lend
themselves to names of familiar emotional category labels such as anger, joy,
or fear.

Why? Because the authors are seeking to represent emotional experiences
as they take place in the brain, not in the groupings of dictionary-based emotions that characterize our global feelings at a given moment but do not conform with known scientific operations.

Does all this mean that we'll have to jettison our popular set of instances
of human experience we call "emotions"? Probably not any time soon. When
we consider "anger" or "fear" or other common emotions, we seldom care
whether our labels are congruent with labels of the functions in the brain.
Using our common language, whatever it may be, we quickly conjure up
images of someone who is "mad as hell," "happy as a clam," or "scared out
of his wits." The fantasy Connectome of the future—its developers hope and
expect—will sometime find convergence with common universal human
experiences.

Researchers, on the other hand, must be very specific about how they define
emotions as taking place in the human brain versus common dictionary definitions. When an emotion is being studied, these definitions must be specified
and made equivalent, otherwise there is little scientific basis for drawing inferences about brain-behavior connections.

Meanwhile, the diverse issues faced by people who meet criteria for BPD
and their loved ones will still require a range of multisystem interventions tai-
lored to the needs of each individual and family as best we can. This will be
the case whether you are treating a collection of targets (under a categorical
diagnosis) or separate targets now identified as single dimensions.

Gunderson (2009, 2010), Hyman (2007), and others emphasize the large
gap between today's scientific knowledge and what would be required for a
full-scale overhaul of the new DSM edition to attach its diagnostic param-
eters to underlying neuroscientific structures and functions. Gunderson
(2010) advocated caution in the short run about doing this for the fifth edition, because the DSM-IV, although entirely based on symptom clusters and

not neurobiological entities, has been developed to a point where it is familiar and relatively easy for clinicians to use and is supported in its chosen arena (categorical description) by reliability and validity measures. It works, for now, despite glitches and inequities.

Readers will be their own judges of how best to use contemporary tools to augment our clients' quality of life in the context of mental health political, financial, and ideological environments.

Postscript:

As an afterword to the preceding discussion of the political and sociocultural environment at the present time (June 2013), I want to add, now that DSM-5 has been made public, that although publication schedules are too advanced to include detailed application of DSM-5 criteria to Pat's situation, a cursory comparison of DSM-IV and DSM-5 assessments of Pat do not indicate to me (HCJ), any likely major differences either in the assessment or the intervention planning process with Pat that we recommend in this book.

A major schism within the psychiatric community was enacted as policy a few weeks prior to this final post-script, when the National Institute of Mental Health, the source of much of today's leading research on mental health, declared that it could not use the DSM-5 in its future work because the manual's categories lack scientific evidence. Thomas R Insel, Director of NIMH, stated April 29th, 2013 on his blog:

While DSM has been described as a "Bible" for the field, it is, at best, a dictionary, ... each edition has ensured that clinicians use the same terms in the same ways. The weakness is its lack of validity. . . . Indeed, symptom-based diagnosis, once common in other areas of medicine, has been largely replaced in the past half century as we have understood that symptoms alone rarely indicate the best choice of treatment.

Note

1 As a caution to readers about what information can be offered in this book with regard to the DSM-5, lack of access to the approved DSM-5 until its official release in May 2013 has forestalled attempts by mental health educators, writers, and practitioners, including myself, to reflect on and analyze the approved changes and their likely effects in advance of implementation. We regret this lack, but after release there will undoubtedly be no shortage of published responses!

What Is Borderline Personality Disorder?

Borderline personality disorder has moved from being a psychoanalytic colloquialism for untreatable neurotics to becoming a valid diagnosis with significant heritability and with *specific and effective psychotherapeutic treatments* (emphasis added)....Two major findings have greatly affected the borderline construct, one showing that *the disorder is significantly heritable* and the other that *it has an unexpectedly good prognosis*....Torgersen and colleagues' finding of a 69% heritability abruptly invalidated the many theories about borderline personality disorder's etiology that had focused exclusively on environmental causes. It established borderline personality disorder's credentials as a "brain disease.

John Gunderson, MD, 2009
Borderline Personality Disorder: Ontogeny of a Diagnosis
American Journal of Psychiatry 66(5): 530–539.

What is borderline personality disorder? Neurobiological knowledge will figure prominently in answers to this question. People who meet criteria for a borderline personality disorder (BPD) are heterogeneous; many different combinations of BPD characteristics can lead to a BPD diagnosis (Distel, Willemsen Lighardt, et al., 2010). Therefore it should not be surprising that answers to this question have been the subject of controversy within psychiatry for some time, and probably will continue to be in the era of the *Diagnostic and Statistical Manual of Mental Disorders*, 5th edition (DSM-5).

Neurobiological dysfunctions are hallmarks of BPD. It is important to distinguish the terms *neurological* and *neurobiological*. All psychological phenomena have neurobiological underpinnings, whereas the term *neurologic* designates specific subtypes of neurobiological functions or processes that are diagnosed and treated by the specialty of neurology rather than psychiatry (Schmahl et al., 2002). These distinctions are becoming increasingly fuzzy as knowledge about the neurobiology of psychiatric disorders advances, but they are rooted in medical tradition.

The National Institute of Mental Health (NIMH, 2013) has paraphrased the criteria for BPD diagnosis set forth in the "old" DSM-IV-TR (APA, 2000) in which a person must show an enduring pattern of behavior including at least five criteria:

- extreme emotional reactions to real or imagined abandonment;
- pattern of intense stormy relationships;
- distorted unstable self-image;
- impulsive and often dangerous behaviors such as spending sprees, unsafe sex, substance abuse, reckless driving, and binge eating; recurring suicidal behaviors or threats;
- intense and changeable moods;
- chronic feelings of emptiness and/or boredom;
- inappropriate, intense anger or problems controlling anger; and
- stress-related paranoid thoughts or severe dissociative symptoms (such as feeling cut off from oneself, observing oneself from outside the body, or losing touch with reality).

BPD scholars frame diagnosis in varying ways, roughly centered around either diagnostic categories (as in the DSMs) or around emotional and behavioral dimensions (see for example Linehan, 1993A, 1993B). Marsha Linehan, recipient of the 2012 American Psychological Foundation (APF) Gold Medal Award for Life Achievement in the Application of Psychology, is well known as the creator of dialectical behavior therapy (DBT), designed initially for treating borderline conditions. Linehan characterizes DBT as the integration of what appears to be two mutually exclusive components: "radical acceptance" of oneself *just the way one is*, while at the same time working to change one's behavior and/or cognitions.

She conceives of borderline personality as five dimensions of a core disorder, *psychic dysregulation*:

1. *Emotional dysregulation* (highly reactive emotional responses including episodes of depression, anxiety, irritability, or anger);
2. *Interpersonal dysregulation*, characterized by fear of abandonment and chaotic, intense, difficult relationships;
3. *Behavioral dysregulation* (extreme impulsivity seen in profligate spending, sex, binge eating, self-mutilation, reckless driving, or suicidal attempts);
4. *Cognitive dysregulation* (brief nonpsychotic depersonalization, delusion, or dissociation); and
5. *Dysregulation of the self* (feelings of emptiness or problems with self-identity) (Linehan, 1993A, B).

Michael Stone (2006), long-time scholar of BPD, summarizes major features of BPD as cognitive-perceptual, affect dysregulation, and impulsive/behavioral dyscontrol.

The McLean Study of Adult Development (MSAD), a ten-year longitudinal study, found that half of the 24 symptoms of BPD they identified fit a description of acute symptoms and the other half could be called temperamental symptoms. Acute symptoms remit relatively rapidly, are the best markers for BPD, and are often the main reason for expensive psychiatric treatments such as inpatient stays and day programs. Temperamental symptoms, on the other hand, remit slowly, are not specific to BPD, and give evidence of ongoing psychosocial impairment (Zanarini, Frankenberg et al., 2010).

Zanarini and colleagues (1998, 2008) believe there are two key features of BPD: intense inner pain that persons with BPD live with on a chronic basis, consisting of both dysphoric affects (e.g., *I feel grief-stricken, I feel completely panicked*) and distorted cognitions (e.g., *like I'm being tortured, like I am damaged beyond repair*) that are specific to BPD. Zittel and Westen (2005) strongly support this view in a community study of borderline personality disorder patients. They were found to have more distress, emotion dysregulation, and overall intense psychological pain compared to the DSM-IV descriptive criteria for BPD.

The second key feature is the effort that borderline patients make both to hide this pain and to express it. Examples are self-mutilation and help-seeking suicide threats and gestures. Substance abuse, promiscuity, and disordered eating are also common and also destructive in nature. The least derogatory way to refer to these strategies might be "outmoded survival strategies" (Zanarini et al., 1998).

Additional characteristics of BPD emphasized by some mental health professionals include intolerance of aloneness, low levels of emotional awareness, inability to coordinate positive and negative feelings, poor accuracy in recognizing facial expressions of emotion, and intense responses to negative emotions (Levine, Marziali, and Hood, 1997; Gunderson, 1996).

What causes the intense inner pain of people meeting criteria for BPD? Why do they handle it in such a self-defeating manner? Zanarini (2008) notes that she and her colleagues had assumed that only serious adversity, such as childhood abuse and neglect, could have resulted in the intense inner pain that both characterizes and distinguishes borderline patients from those in other diagnostic groups. These authors' views have changed. They now believe that many borderline patients are so temperamentally vulnerable that much more subtle experiences can engender this excruciating pain.

Zanarini (2008) characterizes this temperament as *hyperbolic*. Borderline patients insist that others such as family members, spouses, and mental health professionals "recognize and acknowledge" the intensity of their pain. Statements such as, "I am in the worst pain since the history of the world began" are heard fairly often, conveying the sense of isolation and alienation the person with BPD often experiences. Why do borderline patients rely on such counterproductive interpersonal strategies? Zanarini's response is that there's no clear answer and not much if any data to support any answer.

She suggests a three-step approach to lessening this intense pain (Zanarini, 2008). First, help the sufferer find a way to lessen his or her subjective but severe inner pain, often highly disabling. Second, help the person find a way to be more straightforward and direct in expressing his or her wishes or needs. Third, help him or her find a way to be more future oriented and less obsessed with the past and its litany of disappointments. With respect to Linehan's term *validation*, Zanarini concludes:

> [Validation is] an essential aspect of efforts to help lessen the pain of BPD. Patients need to feel that someone understands their pain and is neither frightened nor disgusted by it. This type of acceptance can come from a therapist. It can also come from a friend or a romantic partner. However, this ability to listen and empathize can be distorted in non-useful or even destructive ways. Some companions in the process of acceptance of what can seem like unending pain can begin to convey an acceptance of the patient's "theory of the case" or the maladaptive ways that the patient has handled his or her pain. This is less than fortunate as it interferes with a borderline patient's ability to forgive both him- or herself and those who have disappointed and/or frustrated him or her.... Experience suggests that therapy is best thought of as being adjunctive to life and not a substitute for it. This thinking goes against what many mental health professionals believe... (Zanarini, 2008).

She emphasizes the "reparative" properties of adult life as a major supportive influence for people suffering with aspects of BPD, and most of the rest of us as well.

The borders of borderline personality. Symptoms and defining characteristics of BPD overlap with symptoms of several DSM-IV-TR diagnoses, including other personality disorders, Axis I conditions of major depression, dysthymia, and the spectrum of bipolar disorders, substance abuse, eating, anxiety disorders, and disorders of dissociation and depersonalization (APA, 2000).

Many persons with BPD have symptoms characteristic of bipolar, cyclothymic, and unipolar affective disorders. It's sometimes difficult to distinguish ultrarapid-cycling forms of bipolar disorder, in which people are morose or irritable and have mood swings, from BPD (Akiskal, 1996). *Substance abuse* also occurs commonly with BPD. Several studies highlight overlaps between *dissociative* phenomena and BPD (Schmahl, McGlashan, and Bremner, 2002; Zanarini, Ruser, Frankenburg et al., 2000; Kemperman, Russ, and Shearin, 1997).

Epidemiology. Borderline personality disorder (BPD) is a common psychiatric condition affecting 1.6% of community adults in the United States, about 19% of adult psychiatric inpatients, and 11% of adult psychiatric outpatients

(Gunderson, Zanarini, Choi-Kane et al., 2011; Lenzenweger, Lane, Loranger, and Kessler, 2007).

In studies using semi-structured diagnostic interviews, approximately half of patients with an Axis I diagnosis also had a personality disorder. Thus, personality disorders are among the most common groups seen by psychiatrists, especially BPD (Zimmerman, Chelminski, and Young, 2008). These authors note the importance of diagnosing co-occuring personality disorders in psychiatric patients with an Axis I disorder. Co-occurrence with a personality disorder is associated with more negative outcomes of some Axis I conditions.

The estimate that females qualify for the BPD diagnosis twice as often as males is questionable, since males with BPD are often in jail and remain undiagnosed (Cowdry, 1997). Meta-analyses reported by McGilloway, Hall, Lee, and Bhui (2010) showed lower prevalence of personality disorders among black than white groups (p < 0.026) but no differences between Asian or Hispanic groups and white groups. It was not clear to these authors (McGilloway et al., 2010) whether the findings indicate neglect of BPD diagnosis among black persons or an actual lower prevalence.

Etiology of BPD. Research indicates that no matter which diagnostic criteria are used, borderline personality is the outcome of a heterogeneous developmental course involving interacting biological and environmental risk and protective factors. The components appear to be biological vulnerability (predisposition for affective instability, impulsivity or harmful addictive behaviors, or other borderline characteristics) interacting in about half the diagnosed BPD group with a childhood history of lack of validation, loss, abuse, or other unidentified environmental inputs (Cowdry, 1997; Linehan, 1993A, B). About half of BPD sufferers have no history of these adverse environmental inputs in childhood, supporting the views of Zanarini and her colleagues that the force of disabling inborn vulnerabilities can result in the BPD outcome despite all the efforts of kind and concerned parents.

Environmental contributors to BPD characteristics. Linehan (1993A, B) identifies a specific kind of environment, which she calls "invalidating," that interacts with biological factors (genetic, intrauterine, or physical trauma at an early age, especially head trauma) to give rise to BPD. Invalidating environments convey the message that our responses to life situations are invalid, inappropriate, or incorrect. In such environments, all problems are viewed as motivational in origin: "If only you were to try harder, the problem would be solved." Typically such environments tell children to "calm down."

However, it is very difficult for such children to calm down. These environments fail to recognize the biologically based emotional vulnerability and overly sensitive responses that may lie behind children's inhibitions, irritability, or frequent crying in infancy.

Paris (1997) disputes the belief that adult psychopathology arises primarily from environmental factors, because personality traits are heritable, children are often resilient to the long-term effects of trauma, most studies of trauma in personality disordered persons suffer from retrospective designs, and only a minority of patients with severe personality disorders report major childhood trauma.

According to Paris, the effects of trauma in the personality disorders can therefore be better understood in the context of gene-environment interactions (i.e., epigenetic factors). Interaction is key, because many biologically vulnerable persons do not develop BPD, and many persons with histories of childhood trauma or loss do not develop BPD. When a child has a biological vulnerability, it might be possible to prevent a later onset of BPD by recognizing the vulnerability early, supporting parents, and educating them about the child's special, idiosyncratic needs. These vulnerable children require parenting efforts different from and/or greater than the ordinary parenting behaviors that succeed with typical children.

Role of the family. Until the 1980s (and unfortunately sometimes even today) parents of persons with BPD were assumed by professionals to have caused their children's disorders (see Chapter 4). In an early review, Gunderson and Englund (1981) found little evidence to support the literature's messages that parents are culpable. They suggested that the tendency of persons with BPD and their therapists to see the mothers as "bad" may be a function of the splitting mechanisms so frequently used by persons with BPD. They might, in fact, be projecting nonexistent negative behaviors or affects onto their mothers in the process of reconstructing their pasts.

Many practitioners were oblivious to the evidence and continued to conduct psychotherapy based on an assumption of parental culpability. A few other scholars in the early eighties, however, concurred with Gunderson and Englund. Palombo (1983) observed that persons with BPD experience the world as hostile and chaotic, often convinced that their caretakers have failed to provide a benign environment:

> Whether or not the parents did fail, [they] were most likely helpless to provide an environment [that could] meet the child's special needs. Because the child's needs were not met, the most responsive, caring parents may be perceived as failures from the child's perspective...Yet neglectful parents raising a competent, well-endowed child might be experienced as loving and responsible. [The person with BPD] could, and often does, pin the blame for his suffering on those around him. From his perspective, they are the causes of it. Since [the parents] are perceived as powerful and mighty, the child believes that such powerful people could have prevented his suffering. This belief becomes the source of myths about the terrible things that parents did to the child, even though the parents may have tried mightily to help the child. (Palombo, 1983, pp. 335–336)

In their study, Gunderson and Englund (1981) had expected to find empirical support for the beliefs prevailing in the late 1970s that family psychopathology for persons with BPD was characterized by overinvolved, separation-resistant, dependency-generating mothers. Instead, they found that parental under-involvement was much more common.

Neglectful parenting was also implicated in a study by Zanarini and colleagues (1997). In comparison with people with other personality disorders, three family environmental factors were significant predictors of a borderline diagnosis: sexual abuse by a male noncaregiver, emotional denial by a male caregiver, and inconsistent treatment by a female caregiver. The results suggested that sexual abuse was neither a necessary nor a sufficient condition for the development of BPD and that other childhood experiences, particularly neglect by caretakers of both genders, represent significant risk factors. However, since the majority of children who experience any of these risk factors do not develop BPD, other variables clearly must be present to account for the later development of BPD.

Gunderson, Berkowitz, and Ruiz-Sancho (1997) caution us against one-sided assessment of BPD. Much of the early literature about the families of borderline patients derived solely from reports provided by the borderline patients and rarely included the families' perspectives. "When you consider that borderline patients are by nature often devaluative and that they often find on entering treatment that devaluing past caretakers—past treaters as well as families—is a way to ignite the ambitions and enthusiasm of the new candidates for becoming their caretakers, it is disturbing in retrospect that we have not been more suspicious about their accounts of their families" (Gunderson et al., 1997, p. 451).

Natural course and prognosis. BPD is a chronic disorder into middle age, by which time the majority of persons formerly diagnosed with BPD no longer meet the criteria (Gunderson, Stout, et al., 2011). In several studies, mean Global Assessment Scale scores were in the normal range by middle age, and most former patients were working and had a social life. However, recent studies have also shown that although many of the defining characteristics of BPD attenuate and are no longer in the diagnosable range, difficulties with psychosocial interactions continue.

A set of studies comprised the 10-Year Longitudinal Collaborative Study of Borderline Personality Disorder (Gunderson, Stout, et al., 2011). Within the group, a subgroup of researchers led by Mary Zanarini (2010) focused on psychosocial functioning over the ten-year course, as contrasted with what the Gunderson group defined as psychopathology of the BPD diagnosis.

However, the psychosocial functioning subdivision of the study was itself divided into "social" and "vocational/employment" types of psychosocial functioning. It is striking that more than 90% of the persons reported as still having psychosocial functioning problems close to the end of the ten years were showing poor *vocational* but *not poor social* performance (Zanarini, Frankenburg, Reich, and Fitzmaurice 2010). That is, most impairments classified as "psychosocial" involved performance on jobs or inability to get jobs, not lacking friends or a social life.

Although about 10% of persons with BPD commit suicide by the 15th year of posttreatment follow-up, for the majority of those with BPD who survive, long-term prognosis appears to be fairly good (Paris, 1993; Paris, Zweig et al., 2004). What treatment could account for this apparently favorable outcome (assuming you agree that the 10% who suicide can be separated from the 90% who are survivors)? Actually, it's unclear how often improvement is due to treatment at all; it may occur as a natural course of BPD. To the extent that treatment during crisis periods can deter suicide, however, it would be essential to buy time by intensive support for BPD sufferers ("holding") until the risk of suicide has passed (Waldinger, 1987; Buie and Adler, 1982). Holding is usually a metaphor, since it does not ordinarily mean actual sustained physical embracing, hugging, or holding the client's hand (although therapists may sometimes do this). It refers to worker behaviors communicating that he or she is a stable, reliable person who cares about the client, is consistently supportive, and weathers the emotional and behavioral storms of the person with BPD (Waldinger, 1987; Buie and Adler, 1982).

It would be interesting to know how many of the posttreatment suicides are carried out by "graduates" from long-term intensive therapies and to what extent planned periodic follow-up with former treaters is associated with lower rates of suicide. The 10% suicide rate sounds unacceptably large to me, so of course the question remains: What could any of the programs working with these clients, whose pain was so extreme as to succeed in killing themselves, have done over the post-treatment years to prevent this outcome?

What Can Today's Neuroscience Tell Us About Mental Conditions?

BORDERLINE PERSONALITY AS A CASE IN POINT

Heritability versus environmental etiology. Contrary to the expectations of long-time borderline treaters, studies have shown the borderline personality disorder as defined by the DSM-IV-TR (APA, 2000) to be strongly heritable (Gunderson, 2009). In a study of 92 monozygotic and 129 dizygotic twin pairs, Torgersen et al. (2000) found an overall heritability of 0.69 for borderline personality disorder (BPD). That is, on average, genetics appear to explain more than two-thirds of the borderline personality diagnosis. High levels of genetic influence were also found for emotional and behavioral variables of affective instability, impulsivity, and self-injurious behavior.

As noted in Chapter 40, John Gunderson, a former believer in psychodynamic views of parental culpability for BPD and psychiatric conditions in general (see Chapter 4), bluntly states that the genetic findings of Torgersen and colleagues "abruptly invalidated the many theories about borderline personality disorder's etiology that had focused exclusively on environmental causes (Gunderson, 2009).

With respect to core characteristics of BPD, Gunderson et al. (2011) also report elevated levels of affective, behavioral, and interpersonal sectors in two studies of relatives of persons with BPD, as well as heritability estimates ranging from 31% to 49% for affective instability, cognitive, and impulsivity traits (see for example Distel, Willemsen, Ligthart et al., 2010). Affective instability and self-injurious behavior had previously been identified as having a strong genetic basis by Livesley, Jang, Jackson, and Vernon (1993), whose research also showed genetic underpinning of identity problems.

Close relatives of persons with BPD also have a higher prevalence than average of major depression and substance-use disorders (Sadock and Sadock, 2003). However, studies differ in estimates of the proportion of first-degree relatives of people with BPD who themselves meet criteria for BPD itself, ranging from negligible to as high as 23% (Dahl, 1994; Torgersen et al., 2000). Since BPD is comprised of a fairly heterogeneous set of elements combined into one overall diagnostic category, the result of lower numbers of first-degree relatives meeting the requisite *five* criteria for the BPD diagnosis, as compared with higher rates of overlap with various *single* criteria each relative may share with the person with BPD, make sense.

Distel, Willemsen, Ligthart et al. (2010) utilized data based on 5,533 twins and 1,202 siblings from the Netherlands, Belgium, and Australia to estimate heritability of four main features of BPD (affective instability, identity problems, negative relationships, and self-harm) on the PAI-BOR, a self-report questionnaire. Correlations among the scales were best explained by a genetic common pathway model in which the heritability of the latent BPD factor was 51%.

With respect to eating disorders, genetic studies on twins and families suggest substantial genetic influence for anorexia nervosa and bulimia nervosa. Candidate gene studies have initially focused on the serotonergic and other central neurotransmitter systems and on genes involved in body weight regulation. However, confirming evidence is needed (Scherag, Hebebrand, and Hinney 2010).

Grilo, Pagano and colleagues (2012) prospectively studied the natural course of bulimia nervosa (BN) and eating disorder not-otherwise-specified (EDNOS) and tested for the effects of stressful life events (SLE) on relapse after remission from these eating disorders. Female patients with BN ($N = 35$) or EDNOS ($N = 82$) were prospectively followed for 72 months using structured interviews performed at baseline, 6- and 12-months, and then yearly thereafter. Overall probability of relapse was 43% with no difference between the groups in time to relapse. Negative stressful life events significantly predicted eating disorder relapse, with elevated work and social stressors the significant predictors. Co-occurring psychiatric disorders, eating disorder duration, and variable time courses in personality disorder status did not significantly predict relapse. Higher work and social stress emerged as significant warning signs for triggering relapse.

Carpenter, Tomko, Trull, and Boomsa (2012) have reviewed recent gene-environment studies relevant to the borderline personality phenotype as an entity, as well as studies focusing on components of the diagnostic category including impulsivity, emotional sensitivity, suicidal behavior, aggression and anger. Carpenter et al. (2012) go beyond the now widely accepted view that BPD develops through gene-by-environment interactions (GxE). In addition to GxE influences seen in the studies, they note the action of *gene-environment correlations* (rGE) model for borderline personality traits and a range of adverse life events. The simpler GxE conditions are still just as much at work, but in addition, those at risk for BPD are also at increased risk for *exposure to environments that may trigger BPD*. This perspective incorporates an insight of Jerome Kagan (1994) that children with difficult behaviors contribute to development of their own environments by evoking a different set of reactions from caretakers, teachers, and peers than do outgoing, comfortable children, whose inborn temperaments generate positive behaviors that elicit positive responses from others.

While the latter observation is referring strictly to environmental responses generated by the child, the rGxE model displays a double whammy effect of children who are genetically vulnerable, have characteristics that negatively impact their environments to arouse unfavorable responses, and *also* often have parents (1) with similar vulnerabilities that (2) negatively influence their parenting behaviors over and above provocation by the child. One implication is that risk computation for BPD should incorporate both GxE and the added risk (rGxE) from afflicted biological parents, if the biological parents are raising the child.

However, this calculation may facilitate prejudicial attributions to parents, who despite serious deficits may be loving and responsible parents, or can become that with training and support from providers. It should go without saying that practitioners should take cognizance of their own expectations, and evaluate the observable parent–child interactions in a context of acceptance of child and parent alike, negative behaviors notwithstanding.

Connecting neuroscience knowledge with a real person. We'll look at a few of the behaviors, emotions, and cognitions comprising NIMH's interpretation of the DSM-IV BPD criteria. As I review neuroscience information that begins to help scientists explain psychology in terms of the physical structures, processes/functions, pathways, and networks that govern human brain function, the focus will be on assessing Pat. When we unearth information to solve practice challenges, usually it doesn't include every aspect of the subject matter, mostly just those aspects that pertain to the specific client or groups of clients we're trying to help. If I'm an administrator, organizer, or policy planner, it will apply either to a particular population or to a specific issue across multiple populations.

This approach to assessment and intervention planning applies to one of the two main types of searches proposed in Chapter 9: the individualized set of searches for the benefit of my particular individual client, client family, group, or constituency.

The purpose of the other main type of search is to learn as much as I can, generally, about a given subject. In this general search, I'm not targeting a specific individual or group or population to find an immediate solution to a current challenge—time is usually limited when that's the case—but rather I'm surfing PubMed to become really well informed and up to date about some aspect of the mind or the brain or a detour the brain is leading me to . . . I do it fairly often, actually. It's fun no matter what, and every once in awhile I find a sparkling tiny rock flashing in the sun—something so brilliant or counter-intuitive or priceless that I know I have discovered a gem.

{ 42 }

👪 Neuroscience with Social Science Can Give Us Insights about Pat

If you haven't recently done so, you should read Pat's and her family's history (Chapter 32, Part IV) before you go any farther. The analysis that follows here assumes knowledge of the details of Pat's problem formulation and history presented in Part IV (MEBA items 1 through 7), without which readers are unlikely to derive benefit from the analysis below.

Here are Pat's most powerful challenges in my view.

1. ***Binge eating and vomiting*** are included in diagnostic criteria sets under the general descriptor *impulsivity*. Impulsivity as a defining characteristic of BPD has been endorsed by the APA (DSM-IV-TR 2000), National Institute of Mental Health (NIMH) (2013), and in Marsha Linehan's dimensional inventory (1993A, B), that is, by BPD scholars across the philosophical spectrum. Linehan includes it under behavioral dysregulation, which she equates with "extreme impulsivity."

Long and widely considered to be a core feature of BPD, impulsivity—quickness to act on urges such as abusing substances, binge eating, spending wildly, having aggressive outbursts—is often but not always defined as a deficit in the inhibition of response (Schmahl, McGlashan, and Bremner, 2002). These authors view BPD as a compilation of dimensions, each with its own neurobiological underpinnings, with impulsivity a defining BPD dimension. The medial prefrontal cortex regulates impulse control and inhibition of responses to external stimuli (Schmahl et al., 2002).

Impulsivity is a major constitutional predisposition in BPD, regardless of whether there is a history of trauma (Schmahl et al., 2002). The serotonin system is prominent in impulsivity (Markovitz, 2004; Paris, Zweig-Frank, Kin et al., 2004; Schmahl et al., 2002).

Various forms of impulsive behavior have also been associated with platelet monoamine oxidase activity (Brown, Goodwin, et al., 1979; Linnoila, Virkkunen, et al., 1983). Using blood platelet measures of serotonin and monoamine oxidase activity to assess monoamine functions, Verkes, Pijl, and colleagues (1996) found that people with bulimia could be subdivided into two groups: those with and those without BPD. Persons with bulimia *and* BPD resembled suicide attempters with BPD *without* bulimia by showing levels of impulsivity, anger, and biochemical characteristics as high as those of suicide attempters meeting criteria for BPD. This finding from almost two decades ago seems important because it suggests that persons meeting criteria for BPD and bulimia together have underlying levels of negative affect possibly as profound as those having BPD who are suicidal.

With respect to the term *impulsivity*, Smith, Fischer, et al. (2007) argue that it encompasses a wide range of traits, not a single unidimensional personality characteristic. My own understanding of Pat is consistent with that view. I substitute the word *compulsive* to describe Pat's bulimia nervosa, because she often eats and then vomits in a calculated, pre-planned manner, rather than as a quick, unthinking action. She engages in time-consuming rituals (counting calories, measuring food portions) and obsessive thinking about eating over extended periods of time, usually considered symptoms of anxiety. In addition to being chronically depressed (dysthymic), she is also anxious about regaining past lost weight. What is most striking to me, consistent with research in this area, is the enormous salience that she attributes to food rewards, overshadowing any other possibly pleasurable activity. Rather than just stuffing herself on an "impulse," her life appears to revolve around her daily eating plans.

Pat's bulimia defines her life. If the word *urge* is substituted for *impulsivity*, the quick or sudden connotation of impulsivity is minimized and Pat's eating behaviors can be more accurately characterized. Stone (2006) refers to a characteristic as "impulsivity/behavioral dyscontrol," two expressions of which the latter but not the former seems to describe Pat. In an assessment of Pat, I would use the descriptors *urge* and *behavioral dyscontrol* as central features of her severe and debilitating bulimia rather than of impulsivity.

Much of the recent research on challenged eating focuses on obesity. Pat has not been obese for a long time, but she experienced the social consequence of being obese as so excruciating that it has controlled her life. Levels of dopamine shown in recent imaging studies of dopamine function in drug addiction, eating disorders, and obesity have shown the critical roles that dopamine often plays in these conditions (Broft, Berner, Martinez, and Walsh, 2012; Volkow, Wang, Fowler, Tomasi, and Baler, 2012b; Wang et al., 2009, 2011).

These writings underscore the importance of compromised ability to experience pleasure as a major motivator of relapse in drug use or weight loss efforts. This effect may well apply to Pat. She does not appear to get much pleasure in daily life and activities, yet at the same time experiences enormous salience to contemplated pleasures of eating. If you remember from Part IV, persons who are addicted tend to undervalue other ordinary pleasures, for such reasons such as diminution of numbers of dopamine receptors taking place in the process of addiction (an automatic compensatory mechanism by the body seeking homeostasis), or overestimation of rewards of the addiction object and devaluation of other rewards (as part of cognitive distortions that arise in the addicted state).

After the initial periods of getting a rush from ingesting/inhaling/injecting, one of two opposite long-term outcomes can set in. If tolerance rises, persons in addicted states find that their favorite drugs or foods give less and less of the pleasure than they did at first. However, the converse effect, sensitization to a target of addiction in which the pleasure of use increases, can happen instead. It's possible that sensitization has influenced Pat's perceptions of the pleasures of taste, which would explain her unremitting longings for food at the top of her priorities. She has never to our knowledge discussed binge eating as an escape from or relief of aversive states, only the deliciousness of her mother's cooking (lots of butter, cream, and other fats). That is not to say that she doesn't also binge to alleviate aversive states.

Striatal dopamine (DA) is a key neurotransmitter in the neurobiological regulation of both food and drug rewards. DA is released by neurons originating in the ventral tegmental area and substantia nigra, and these neurons project to dorsal striatum (caudate and putamen), nucleus accumbens in the ventromedial striatum, and prefrontal and other cortical regions (Volkow, Wang, and Baler, 2011).

DA projections to these various subregions are thought to play somewhat distinct roles. Dorsolateral striatal circuits appear to mediate aspects of habitual reward processing (Volkow, Wang, and Baler, 2011; Berridge, 2009). Nucleus accumbens DA, however, in response to a novel reward (food, sex with a new partner, or other reward), appears to be involved in learning associated with the reward, including the conferral of salience of that reward, the association of the pleasure of that reward ("liking") with desire ("wanting"), and the learning of behaviors ("remembering") associated with repeating the acquisition of that reward. Repeated increases in levels of DA (from repeated exposure to rewards) may serve to mediate the shifting of attentional bias towards cues associated with reward. Additionally, striatal DA appears to shift over time, to occur more predominantly in response to conditioned cues rather than to the reward itself.

"Non-natural" rewards (drugs of abuse) release extremely large amounts of DA in reward-related circuits, conferring a "better than expected" signal, and stimulating over-learning of behaviors, cues, and desire related to these nonnatural rewards (Broft et al., 2012). Once the user becomes addicted, neuroimaging studies have consistently shown *low levels of ventral and/or dorsal striatal dopamine and low striatal levels of dopamine type 2 (D2) receptors.* This progression is true for both drugs (nonnatural) and food ("natural," although it would probably be easy to demonstrate that most of what we eat is not in its original natural state). In any case, food addiction is now widely acknowledged as a "legitimate" addiction.

According to Volkow, Wang, Fowler, and Telang (2012), both drug addiction and obesity are conditions in which the saliency value of one type of reward (drugs or food) is greatly enhanced relative to and at the expense of others. Both drugs and food have powerful reinforcing effects—partly mediated by dopamine increases in the limbic system—that could overwhelm the brain's homeostatic control mechanisms.

Results from brain-imaging discoveries are uncovering common features between these two conditions and are identifying overlapping brain circuits. It appears that both obese and drug-addicted individuals suffer from impairments in dopaminergic pathways that regulate neuronal systems associated with reward sensitivity/salience, incentive motivation/drive, conditioning (memory/learning), and impulse control (behavioral inhibition/emotional regulation/executive function) (Volkow, Wang, Fowler, and Telang, 2012; Volkow, Wang, Tomasi and Baler, 2012; Wang et al., 2009, 2011 to summarize, incentive salience of the object of addiction increases as strength of the control mechanism decreases).

Two other circuits, mood regulation and interoception (awareness of inner events) are also involved in modulating the propensity to eat or take drugs, but were deemed less critical and omitted from the model by Volkow, Wang, and colleagues.

The researchers posit that the disruption of these four circuits results in enhancing value of one type of reinforcer (drugs for the drug abuser and high-density food for the obese individual) at the expense of other reinforcers, which is a consequence of conditioned learning and resetting reward thresholds from stimulation by drugs (drug abuser/addict) or high-density food (obese individual) in vulnerable individuals.

The reward/saliency circuit is mediated in part through the nucleus accumbens, ventral pallidum, medial orbitofrontal cortex, and hypothalamus, modulating responses to both positive and negative reinforcement, a process believed to result in the undervaluing of stimuli that usually motivate non-addicted persons. Both positive rewards and potential negatively reinforcing consequences have lower saliency in an addicted state.

When the inhibitory control/emotional regulation circuit is impaired as well, which often is the case, inhibition from using the object of desire is disempowered. These processes are mediated in part through the dorsolateral prefrontal cortex (DLPFC), cingulate gyrus, and lateral orbitofrontal cortex.

When the memory/conditioning/habits circuit (mediated through the hippocampus, amygdala, and dorsal striatum) calls up memories of repeated pleasurable use, new linked memories are created including conditioned positive reinforcers such as smells or TV images conditioned to the drug (e.g., the smell of cigarettes) or the food (e.g., seeing food on TV or sniffing aromas from your kitchen). These stimuli trigger automatic responses that frequently drive relapse in persons addicted to drugs or food, even in those who are strongly motivated to stop taking drugs or to lose weight.

The motivation/drive and action circuit is involved (mediated through the orbitofrontal cortex, dorsal striatum and supplementary motor cortices), both in executing the act and in inhibiting it. Its actions are dependent on the information from the reward/saliency, memory/conditioning, and inhibitory control and emotional reactivity circuits. When the value of a reward is enhanced owing to previous conditioning, its motivating power is increased. When at the same time the inhibitory control circuit is disrupted, reflex actions in the absence of cognitive control can take place, and using/eating is likely to be triggered as a reflex action. (see Figure 22.1)

Volkow, Wang, Fowler, Logan et al., (2002), note that this set of circumstances may sometimes explain why drug-addicted subjects report not being aware of having taken a drug, why obese people find controlling their food intake so difficult, and why users/eaters report compulsive use even when use/consumption is no longer perceived as pleasurable.

With respect to the neuroscience of obesity, most nonspecialists are unlikely to be well versed in some of the forces that impel persons to binge or overeat, become overweight, and engage in bulimic and anorexic behaviors, so providers to clients with this issue, like helpers for Pat and her family, and authors like myself, need this knowledge to assess competently.

2. *Intense and changeable moods*. Here, Linehan's BPD dimension *emotional dysregulation* (1993A, B) most accurately describes Pat's moods: "highly reactive emotional responses including episodes of depression, anxiety, irritability, or anger."

Pat's moods are certainly intense, but do not appear highly changeable. Most of the time they are in the dysthymic range and intermittently at the severe depression level (MDD).

A reason for difference between depression and other characteristics is thought to be that depression reflects both low serotonergic function and low reward sensitivity (Carver, Johnson, and Joorman, 2008). A person with low reward sensitivity does not get as much enjoyment or satisfaction from a given experience, be it sex, eating a favorite food, or laughter, as do typical persons. Low reward sensitivity may be an important cause of *anhedonia* (inability to experience pleasure). Anhedonia is an insidious experience, in that it can take away the will to live ("I have nothing to live for").

Researchers believe that gray matter deficiencies may mediate the dysregulation of affect and impulse in BPD. Using voxel-based morphometry, Soloff and colleagues (2008) compared 34 persons with BPD to 30 healthy control subjects. Compared with healthy controls, BPD subjects had significant bilateral reductions in gray matter concentrations in the ventral cingulate gyrus, anterior cingulate gyrus, prefrontal cortex, medial temporal cortex, and medial temporal lobe including the amygdala, at varying levels. Differences in amounts of gray matter depend on control variables such as gender and levels of depression.

Gray matter is a major component of the central nervous system. In living tissue, gray matter actually has a gray-brown color, which comes from capillary blood vessels and neuronal cell bodies. Gray matter consists of neuronal cell bodies, dendrites and unmyelinated axons, glial cells, and capillaries. Gray matter contains neural cell bodies, in contrast to white matter, which does not. White matter mostly contains myelinated axon tracts, with myelin the source of the whiteness.

Minzenberg, Fan, and colleagues (2008) found frontolimbic dysfunction in BPD that involved gross structural changes in gray matter in cortical and subcortical limbic regions. These *structural* changes in gray matter took place in conjunction with altered *functional* activation of emotional stimuli. Exaggerated responses to emotional stimuli in the amygdala and impaired responses in the anterior cingulate cortex (ACC) were noted, a pattern that is similar to that seen in animal models of stress responses and depression, where *hypertrophic* changes in the amygdala (nontumor enlargement of an organ or a tissue as a result of an increase in the size of cells, not the number of cells), and *atrophic* changes in the ACC (wasting or decrease in size of a body organ, tissue, or part) were observed.

3. ***Recurring suicidal behaviors or threats***. Pat expresses wishes to be dead but denies having figured out ways to kill herself. Rather than proactive suicidal acts, her suicidal tendencies are passive in that she neglects to stop the dangerous behaviors or to ask for help before she gets herself into a situation of lethal danger due to dehydration and electrolyte imbalance. This behavior suggests that she often or even usually suffers from dysphoria—negative moods—such that accidental dying is not her greatest fear.

For Pat, the greatest danger she seems to experience most of the time is the threat of gaining back the lost weight and becoming fat once again, probably because of anguishing conditioned emotional memories of the rejection she experienced at age 15. The pain of this memory seems to be so motivating that it overwhelms other memories. Although we only know of three instances in her 12 years of illness of passively suicidal behaviors, we guess that there may have been more not reported because she herself, or someone who was with her, took some action that prevented her from going "over the cliff."

Pat's style of *self-injurious behavior* (SIB) does not fit the common understanding of SIB in BPD as an act that inflicts physical pain in typical people (such as cutting or burning). Acts of SIB are often associated with relief of intense sadness or other painful emotional states (Schmahl et al., 2002).

Many persons with BPD, in the usual type of SIB, report having felt no pain when performing the act, suggesting some kind of cutting off of feeling in part of the body system, or possibly profuse secretion of natural opioids that suppress pain. There is agreement that the self-destructive behaviors often engaged in by people with BPD are very effective in alleviating psychic pain, especially anxiety and anger. These behaviors are also effective in managing the environment, for example by getting others to admit the person with BPD to a hospital or otherwise to express concern and caring (Linehan, 1993A, B).

Pat's life-threatening behavior does have the consequence of admission to a hospital. However, from what I know about Pat, it sounds more like self-neglect commonly seen in depression than an intentional SIB.

4. and 5. *Chronic feelings of emptiness and dissociation,* as reported by Pat, are certainly of concern and warrant investigation. Linehan (1993A, B) designates feelings of emptiness as dysregulation of the self, and the NIMH version of the DSM-IV lists "chronic feelings of emptiness and/or boredom" as one of nine possible criteria for BPD. I searched PubMed for connections between feelings of emptiness and neurobiological process but was unable to find any clearcut evidence on this question.

Dissociation, on the other hand, is a psychobiological mechanism often seen in BPD in which specific, anxiety-provoking thoughts, emotions, or physical sensations are cut off from the individual's psychological whole. Examples are feeling cut off from the world around or observing the self from outside the body. Neurobiological correlates of dissociative experience are addressed in Chapter 23 in the discussion of traumatic stress.

However, these issues appear not to be causing Pat the kind of intense pain or threats to survival related to the first three characteristics (binge eating and vomiting, intense moods, and recurring brushes with death). Once her redesigned intervention plan focusing on the first three issues has made initial progress, exploration of emptiness and dissociation with her providers would be important.

6. *Interpersonal stress.* This term refers to stormy, tumultuous, or chaotic relationships and interpersonal conflicts often related in some way to fear of abandonment. It is viewed as another core dimension of BPD. Precursors to this characteristic appear to be related to a protracted developmental history of stress (such as chronic neglect, invalidation by important adults, or repeated abuse), or to a single intense period or episode (such as war combat or a violent assault). Single episodes or periods occur more frequently in cases of post-traumatic stress disorder, whereas protracted developmental history of stress is more characteristic of persons with BPD.

Interpersonal sensitivity in multiple regressions of potential predictor variables for the borderline diagnosis in one study was the only significant predictor of the diagnosis (Figueroa, Silk, Huth et al., 1997). These authors postulated that at least in some cases, interpersonal sensitivity may be the inborn constitutional condition with which environmental forces (such as traumatic events) interact to lead to BPD. That is, biologically based interpersonal sensitivity makes such individuals especially vulnerable to trauma.

I do not see evidence that interpersonal stress is one of Pat's challenges, nor that the traumas in the list above of common traumatic experiences are part of her early history. Her teenage conflicts with her father appear to be highly cultural and intergenerational in nature and were no longer a major issue after she moved to her own apartment while attending college.

The first truly traumatic experience she is known to have had was rejection by a long-fantasied male love object, a fellow student at her high school, when she was 15. Many typical teenagers (and of course older persons as well) suffer intensely from unreciprocated longings for a particular romantic object. What is different about Pat, I suspect, is how profoundly vulnerable she was to this experience, such that it created long-lived scars and fears.

Borderline Characteristics: Medications

Evidence is accruing rapidly that specific neurochemical abnormalities underlie atypical borderline personality disorder characteristics (BPD) (Hyman, 2007; Insel, 2009; Gunderson et al., 2011). Because inclusion criteria for a DSM diagnosis of BPD in current and recent DSM editions are heterogeneous, there is wide variation in brain chemistry and functions among people who meet criteria for the BPD diagnosis.

It is well documented that high percentages of people who meet criteria for BPD now take psychotropic medications (Zanarini, 2008). Since particular neurochemistries are associated with specific psychological functions, well-trained prescribers try to match emotional, behavioral, and cognitive symptoms with pharmacological products. This should not falsely convey the idea that accurate maps are already available for most networks that process human emotions. Since we usually try to do our best with what we have, the "best" often entails educated guesses in conjunction with clinical trials and preliminary studies about what medications may have been effective for similar symptoms (and, of course, show good evidence of safety).

Zanarini (2004, 2008) and Markovitz (2004) reviewed medications in use as of the early 21st century. Zanarini found that most of the medications studied in double-blind placebo-controlled trials were efficacious. She disputes the view that polypharmacy recommended by some BPD scholars is necessary, given that some individual drugs positively influence multiple troublesome characteristics of BPD. In addition, she believes choice of medications should be guided by tolerability and safety more than by symptom targeting. Markovitz (2004) noted disagreement about this issue among leading researchers, but virtually all agree that medications are important and effective for BPD. Most were useful to treat symptoms of two core dimensions of BPD, emotional dysregulation and impulsive aggression.

Since my earliest review of BPD (Johnson, 1988), views about the role of medication in BPD have changed from endorsement by only a small minority of mental health providers to widespread belief that medications are major interventions for persons meeting criteria for BPD (Markovitz, 2004). Although effective medications are often found by trial and error, advances in knowledge about underlying neurobiological functions and structures that mediate dimensions of BPD are helping providers use medications more accurately. I will not repeat here the descriptions of numerous medications recently tested, released, and used in practice to improve functioning. Readers are referred to current studies reported in PubMed for information about the efficacy of a specific drug for various emotional, behavioral, or cognitive challenges. These may also be presented in comparative reviews of different drugs within a class or across classes of medications.

The operative questions to answer using database searches include the following: What medications work for what specific problems, needs, or challenges, and how does each class of drugs work? In what populations? With what beneficial and negative effects? Under what conditions? Once the appropriateness of the choice of drug is established, the next decisions have to do with doses and timing. However, answers to these questions are still frequently piecemeal, with fragments of good information for a particular client's diverse needs. Service providers are advised to check with "watchdog" agencies who publish ongoing detailed critical reviews of a large number of drugs. Among these are numerous psychotropic medications; nonprescribing providers and licensed prescribers alike must keep abreast of these developments and also inform the clients about this knowledge. Both workers and clients must be prepared to actively seek knowledge about medications and other drugs so they can raise questions with prescribers. Unfortunately, prescribing professionals too often appear to be unaware of these warning studies (Wolfe, 2013).

Before a decision is made with respect to an individual client or a cohort of clients, it's really imperative for frontline practitioners and administrators to do targeted searches. The alternative, short of pure guesswork, is to ask the opinion of an agency consultant or other generalist psychiatrist or nurse practitioner (NP). However, their opinions typically derive from general psychiatric knowledge, often inadequate when psychiatric specialty expertise is needed. I ask students to ask themselves, "Would I be satisfied enough with this person's level of knowledge of this complicated issue to follow his/her advice to medicate my own child (or parent or partner or close friend)?" If you answer yourself with a "no" or "I don't know—I need more information about him/her," should you accord your client the same effort to get information as you would for one of your own loved ones?

Selective serotonin reuptake inhibitors (SSRIs) and serotonin norepinephrine reuptake inhibitors (SNRIs) have been widely used for treatment of depression, impulsivity, and aggression in persons with borderline personality disorder, based on findings from 10 open studies and 3 double-blind placebo-controlled studies (Markovitz, 2004; Zanarini, 2008). Because placebo-controlled studies of SSRIs have proven inconclusive due to the large response to placebo, a larger-scale study was needed to distinguish drug effects from placebo effects (Rinne, van den Brink, Wouters and Van Dyke, 2002). These authors carried out the largest and most comprehensive double-blind, placebo-controlled, randomized study as of 2002 of the effects of an SSRI for the treatment of moderately severe BPD in 38 women using the SSRI fluvoxamine. The authors measured rapid mood shift, impulsivity, and aggression. Fluvoxamine produced a strong and long-lasting reduction in rapid mood shifts that were not helped by placebo, but had no more effect than placebo on impulsivity and aggression. That is, two of the most important characteristics of BPD challenges did not appear to be very responsive to fluvoxamine. The only way to test whether in the long run it can induce greater improvement than placebo is to continue the treatments over a long period, increasing the likelihood that placebo will cease to have an effect.

However, it has also been demonstrated that impulsivity and aggression can be attenuated with other serotonin-increasing treatments. Researchers have succeeded in reducing aggression and normalizing prefrontal cortex metabolism in ten persons with borderline personality disorder using fluoxetine (New, Buchsbaum, et al., 2004). PET scans verified that improvements as measured on the Overt Aggression Scale were accompanied by significant increases in metabolic rates in two specific regions of the prefrontal cortex (Brodmann areas 11 and 12). It is not known whether the difference in these studies in response to fluvoxamine and fluoxetine, both serotonin reuptake inhibitors, with respect to aggression, is due to differences between the two drugs or some other factors.

For individuals with frequent psychotic-like symptoms, *atypical antipsychotics* have shown the following effects. Olanzapine benefited BPD clients with self-injurious behavior and other BPD symptoms except for depression, which was not alleviated. Clozapine recipients showed decreases in self-injury and hostility and improved social adaptability. Risperidone reduced impulsive-aggressive behavior and was associated with a 13-point improvement on the Global Assessment of Functioning (GAF) scale. Quetiapine was helpful for self-injurious behavior. These antipsychotic medications were clearly useful for some BPD symptoms, but not effective for treating depression in persons with BPD (see Markovitz, 2004, and Zanarini, 2004, for more detailed analysis of these studies). Clients typically take a combination of medications, since no single drug is effective for every type of symptom. Weight gain is often a problem with these antipsychotics.

Medications that have been helpful with various aspects of BPD include *opioid antagonists, modafinil,* and *omega-3 fatty acids.* Naltrexone, an opioid antagonist used successfully with some individuals addicted to alcohol or opiates, led to a cessation of self-injurious behavior for 32 weeks in an open trial (Griengl, Sendera, and Dantendorf, 2001). Modafinil, used to treat people with narcolepsy (falling asleep suddenly in the middle of the day), was given to 12 clinically depressed people with BPD who experienced lethargy. A third of the group showed marked improvement, a third moderate improvement, and a third little to no improvement in sleepiness (Markovitz and Wagner,

2003). Omega-3 fatty acids were given to women in a double-blind placebo controlled trial and are thought to be helpful to some individuals with aggression and impulsivity, but statistical improvement by the women receiving the supplement did not differ from improvement with placebo. Both groups showed substantial declines in aggression and depression (Zanarini and Frankenburg, 2003).

Several neurotransmitters and neuromodulators (brain chemicals that modify neurotransmission without meeting all the criteria for neurotransmitters) are involved in regulation of eating behavior in animals and have been implicated in symptoms such as depression and anxiety in humans with eating disorders (Mauri, Rudelli, Somaschini et al., 1996).

Other studies pertaining to neurobiological underpinnings of BPD have tested relationships between BPD and hormonal responses (Steinberg et al., 1997); BPD and sleep disorders (Akiskal, Judd, Gillin et al., 1997); association between platelet monoamine oxidase activity and stable personality traits such as impulsiveness, monotony avoidance, and aggressiveness (Stalenheim et al., 1997); and a possible neural basis for the phenomenon of "splitting" so often observed in persons with BPD (Muller, 1992). Splitting refers to seeing some people as all good and others as all bad, and idealizing the former while vilifying the latter.

In general, Cowdry (1997) observed that psychotropic medications in treatment of BDP occasionally result in marked improvement, but more often served to modulate affect (observed emotion) enough to make daily experiences somewhat less disruptive. In most cases, medication is only one weapon in an arsenal of individual and group interventions to help persons with BPD develop coping skills. Stone (2006) reports that psychopharmacology is often used adjunctively to help control target symptoms (shorter-term challenges), in conjunction with various psychotherapeutic approaches needed to effect progress on longterm personality issues.

What can we make of this complicated, confusing information? Schmahl and colleagues conclude that the complex symptoms of BPD are best understood as a combination of alterations in different neurobiological systems (2002, p. 81). Each person with BPD must be assessed to identify the unique combination of features that may be responsive to different kinds of interventions for this particular individual—that is, the essence of a dimensional approach.

Empirical evidence leads to the conclusion that BPD is an outcome arrived at by interactions between a vulnerable (hyperbolic) temperament, a traumatic childhood (broadly defined), and/or a triggering event or series of events (Zanarini and Frankenburg, 2003). In a particular situation, any one of these three conditions may contribute most strongly, and not all three will always apply, inasmuch as approximately half of BPD sufferers have no history of trauma, invalidation, or significant loss.

Delayed responses to severe psychological trauma (seen in symptoms of posttraumatic stress disorder (PTSD)) present paradoxical symptoms: continuing elevation of epinephrine and norepinephrine response mediating anger and fear, together often with *normal* levels of hypothalamic-pituitary-adrenal (HPA) axis activity (Henry, 1997). A normal level of HPA axis activity is counterintuitive; we would expect it to be elevated in response to trauma along with elevated epinephrine/norepinephrine (see Chapter 23 on Stress and Traumatic Stress).

Re-experiencing the trauma and the arousal may be associated with dysfunction of the locus coeruleus, amygdala, and hippocampal systems. In addition, dissociation of the connections between the right and left hemispheres may account for the alexithymia (lack of awareness of one's emotions or moods) and failure of the cortisol response that often follows severe psychological trauma (Henry, 1997). In this condition, it appears that the right hemisphere no longer fully contributes to integrated cerebral function. Children with damage to the right hemisphere lose critical social skills, whereas adults lose a sense of relatedness and familiarity.

{ 44 }

Borderline Characteristics:
Non-pharmacological Interventions

Noting that nonpharmacological interventions for borderline personality disorder (BPD) are subsumed under the three categories of cognitive-behavioral,
psychodynamic, or supportive, Michael Stone (2006) states that agreement
among these otherwise quite different therapeutic approaches is virtually universal with respect to a *hierarchical progression of interventions related to the
level of seriousness* of each issue:

1. Pay attention to suicidal and self-mutilative behaviors.
2. Deal with any threats to interrupt therapy prematurely.
3. Address nonsuicidal symptoms such as (mild to moderate)
   depression, substance abuse, panic and other anxiety manifestations,
   or dissociation.
4. Work on personality issues such as "inappropriate anger, abrasive-
   ness, manipulativeness, demandingness, jealousy, all-or-none thinking and extreme attitudes (idealization/devaluation)" (Stone, p. 15).
5. Be alert to any signs of withholding, dishonesty, or antisocial tendencies. These have an adverse effect on prognosis.
6. Finally, attend to milder symptoms such as social anxiety or lability
   of mood.

Ideally, the person with borderline challenges graduates to better functioning after acute management issues have been resolved. Individual and group
therapies now take center stage, pursuing goals such as psychic integration,
skills training, and fostering long-range goals of friendship, partnering, and
work (Stone, p. 15).

As of the early 21st century, studies of treatment effectiveness emphasized medication; variants of cognitive-behavioral therapy, notably dialectical behavior therapy (DBT) and related methods; and the value of "holding"
actions by therapists. In addition to client-related behaviors, social workers
must engage in systems-oriented work to ensure that clients are best served by
mental health and other service systems. The practice situation described in
Chapter 6 (Jenny's Rages) is one illustration of the need for systems-oriented

action by practitioners. In fact, all the client material in the book at least suggests a need for systems work in tandem with up-to-date evidence-based assessment and intervention planning.

With respect to individually targeted interventions, emphasis has shifted from insight-oriented reflective therapies, widely used during the 1980s, to skills training targeted on the most common difficulties of persons with BPD, such as intense anger, self-destructive acts, excessive drug use, binge eating and purging, or reckless spending (Springer and Silk, 1996). Treatment components (inpatient or outpatient) may involve some combination of individual and group psychoeducation, behavioral strategies and skills training (such as anger management, relapse prevention, social skills training), medication, peer support groups, family psychoeducation and support, cognitive therapy, supportive counseling, environmental changes, and advocacy. BPD is a chronic condition and requires a wide range of interventive options in a model emphasizing ongoing availability and intermittent active intervention (Springer and Silk, 1996; Linehan, 1993A, B; Gunderson et al., 1997).

In addition, specific problem behaviors of persons with BPD arising from mood or impulse control dysfunctions are targets of treatment. Psychoeducation and cognitive-behavioral approaches are first-line interventions (Linehan, 1993A, B; Gunderson et al., 1997). Insight-oriented psychodynamic psychotherapy appears to have been effective mostly for a relatively small subgroup of persons with BPD who are generally likable by others, motivated, psychologically minded, focused, free of overwhelming impulsivity and substance craving, and without a history of "grotesquely destructive" early environments (Stone, 1987). However, impulsivity and/or cravings are among the defining characteristics of BPD, requiring structured, behaviorally oriented interventions to help persons with BPD control impulses that threaten their ability to maintain jobs or intimate relationships.

Psychoeducation for persons with BPD and their family members is essential, as information is empowering (Gunderson et al., 1997). The questions *Why am I this way?* or *Why is my family member this way?* are salient preoccupation even if not articulated. Palombo (1983) referred to the BPD sufferer's "maddening sense of inadequacy at coping with an imperfectly understood environment" (p. 331). To help people with BPD understand their own internal reactions as well as the effects of inputs from the environment, workers can give information about the role of biological factors in specific aspects of the person's borderline illness and about the ways in which the environment may interact with biological vulnerabilities to cause symptoms and suffering.

For example, when the person with BPD has a history of attention-deficit hyperactivity disorder (ADHD), head injury, or other neurological dysfunction, it is helpful to say "You know, your ADHD [head injury, epilepsy] seems to have the effect of making you fly off the handle easily" ["get distracted," "say things you're sorry for," "look for excitement all the time"]. When the client expresses sadness or hopelessness, the worker can point out that the client seems to have an (inborn) tendency toward depression that interacts with stressful life events.

It is often useful to suggest readings that can help persons with BPD understand their own vulnerabilities and explain treatment options. In addition to information about the connections between troublesome aspects of the person's reactions and inborn temperamental conditions, broad-based psychoeducation also includes information about the condition; benefits and risks of medications, side effects, and signs that the medication requires adjustment (larger or smaller doses, or a different medication); alternative treatment options; and information about financial assistance, health benefits, community resources, employment assistance, support groups, and respite care.

Teaching skills. The dual nature of dialectical behavior therapy (DBT)—behavioral skills training and development of mindfulness—has continued for many years to hold the position of gold standard for persons meeting criteria for BPD. It has been successful with an increasing number of other challenges as well. The "dialectic" highlights the paradoxical goals of treatment involving total acceptance of ourselves as we are, yet at the same time working seriously to change some of our behaviors, emotions, and/or cognitions. Work to change ourselves requires mastery of certain skills that are core curricula in DBT.

DBT was originally developed to treat women with BPD who are chronically parasuicidal (engage in self-mutilation such as cutting their skin, but do not wish to die). DBT has been adopted in numerous state departments of mental health as the treatment of choice for BPD, in conjunction with medication targeted on the individual's (typically biologically based) vulnerabilities.

A decade after the first randomized controlled trial of DBT, it remained the only outpatient psychotherapy with demonstrated efficacy for women with BPD (Robins and Chapman, 2004). DBT has shown success in reducing self-destructive behaviors in people with BPD, reducing hospital admissions, and improving social adjustment (Robins and Chapman, 2004).

Linehan (1993A, B) explains that standard cognitive-behavioral therapy, like psychodynamic therapy, has a change orientation: it strives to change behavior through learning and experience. Where these therapies fail, according to Linehan, the failure is often due to an apparent lack of acceptance of clients *as they are.* Treatment based on the goal of change alone may reinforce clients' inability to accept themselves unless an acceptance-as-you-are component is added.

DBT begins with a posture of total acceptance (called *radical acceptance*) borrowed from Eastern religions such as Zen. The word *dialectical* refers to the resolution of polarity and tension between opposites. Persons with BPD must accept themselves as they are and simultaneously try to change. Intervention is geared toward a balance involving supportive acceptance combined with change strategies. The treatment is behavioral because it focuses on skills training, collaborative problem-solving, contingency clarification and management, and the observable present, and is directive.

Individual visits with a therapist and weekly group sessions (some programs schedule groups more frequently) follow a manualized set of steps. First, the therapist and client must reach a collaborative agreement focusing on suicidal or other self-harming behaviors. Will the person with BPD agree to stop doing these things? Before other issues can be addressed, the individual must be willing to agree to stop hurting or threatening to hurt herself or himself.

The social worker engages with the client in active problem-solving, responds with warmth and flexibility, and validates the patient's emotional and cognitive responses. For example, the worker recognizes that the client's coping behaviors (such as cutting, burning, or attempting suicide) have been very effective or functional for that person by supplying predictable relief from pain. Treatment focuses on figuring out ways to avoid or escape from pain other than hurting oneself.

The worker frequently expresses sympathy for the client's intense pain and sense of desperation, creating a validating environment while conveying a matter-of-fact attitude about current and previous self-destructive behaviors (Linehan, 1993A, B). The worker reframes suicidal and other dysfunctional behaviors as part of the client's learned problem-solving repertoire and tries to focus the counseling process on positive problem solving. In individual and group sessions, workers teach emotional regulation, interpersonal skills, tolerance of emotional pain, and self-management skills. They openly reinforce desired behaviors to promote progress by maintaining contingencies that shape adaptive behaviors and extinguish self-destructive behaviors. They emphasize building and maintaining a positive, interpersonal, collaborative relationship using roles of teacher, consultant, and cheerleader.

Linehan and others have emphasized setting clear limits on workers' availability to give help and thus conveying various messages about which we can speculate. For example, does it teach BPD clients to recognize that their treaters have personal rights to pursue other facets of their own lives, away from their roles as supporters of clients' needs? Or that the person's need for contact with the treatment agency or for chemical relief of emotional pain may feel compelling, but that the person is actually strong enough to survive the denial of immediate comfort?

Different programs diverge in their philosophy about limits. Some programs emphasize availability as demonstration of caring, by, for example, offering 24/7 availability with help lines, home phone number of therapist, and postcards while the therapist is on vacation. In the absence of clear-cut positive or negative effects of such strategies, we guess that since persons meeting criteria for BPD can actually differ greatly from each other, they may require a variety of approaches or may do well with varying levels of structure and discipline versus constantly available help. Is it possible that individual therapist beliefs about this issue, and the skills they've developed to implement their beliefs, may influence what they do well and with what kind of client?

Since its introduction as a treatment targeted on parasuicidal women with BPD, DBT has been used for several other populations. In order to locate other diagnoses for which DBT has been used, a PubMed search to exclude BPD used key words (dialectical behavior therapy) NOT (borderline personality OR bpd). Numerous conditions or characteristics were returned among a total of 78 hits. My findings were similar to those of Robins and Chapman (2004), that is, that DBT has shown effectiveness or promise with persons with substance use disorders, suicidal adolescents, depressed elderly persons, inmates in correctional settings, persons with eating disorders, and adults with ADHD.

In a comparison of DBT and a nonbehavioral "treatment by experts" (TBE) for persons meeting criteria for borderline personality, well-known practitioners in DBT were nominated by community mental health leaders to do the comparison group treatment for persons meeting criteria for borderline personality. Both groups showed significant improvement overall with comparable rates of suicide. However, women in the DBT group had a significantly lower frequency of serious suicide *attempts* and use of emergency room and inpatient services, and they experienced less than half the rate of treatment dropouts from the initially assigned therapists of women in the TBE group (Linehan, Comtois, Brown et al., 2002).

Because their psychic pain is extreme, people with BPD may engage repeatedly in self-destructive behavior as they learn that it reduces emotional pain. It is not yet known how this mechanism works. Studies have compared persons with BPD who experience physical pain during self-injury with those who do not. Those reporting no physical pain show low electroencephalogram activity and more mechanisms of dissociation during self-injurious behavior than those who report feeling pain. Even during self-reported states of calmness, persons with BPD show a lower perception of physical pain than healthy controls.

DBT as developed by Linehan and her followers would seem to offer aspects of the holding environment in addition to its other features. Advocates of the holding environment believe that healing occurs not through interpretation, but by being a stable, consistent, caring, nonpunitive person who survives the client's rage and destructive impulses and is steadfast in serving this holding function (Waldinger, 1987, p. 270). According to this view, experiential factors are more important than psychological interpretations. Buie and Adler (1982) advocated implementing the holding function through such supports as hospitalization when needed, extra appointments, phone calls between sessions, provision of vacation addresses, and postcards sent to the client while on vacation.

Linehan, however, recommends setting firm limits on the worker's availability, but emphasizes a worker posture of reliability, stability, and consistent support. Persons with BPD typically move from crisis to crisis, so following a behavioral treatment plan may be difficult, especially if this plan involves teaching skills that are not obviously related to the current crisis and that do not promise immediate relief. Therefore, behaviorally oriented workers have developed psychoeducational group treatment modules using group process to teach specific behavioral, cognitive, and emotional skills.

Group therapy as part of a multimodal treatment package has been rated as highly effective by inpatients with BPD, although psychodynamically oriented group approaches do not appear to have demonstrated effectiveness (Leszcz, Yalom, and Norden, 1986; Linehan, Armstrong, Suarez et al., 1991).

Psychiatric rehabilitation models address the long-term and chronic nature of BPD by providing a validating environment, the opportunity to enhance skills, and a mechanism to accept input from families. Specific skills are taught, such as learning to accurately label one's own emotions, general problem-solving skills, and skills to enhance self-esteem and deal with anger as spelled out in Linehan's DBT (Links, 1993). Hospitalization in acute psychiatric settings is viewed as not very desirable, as it may be too emotionally stimulating and not validating. Other settings must be found, such as a community agency or a work environment, that mesh with the patient's characteristics and that can create a sense of validation.

Day treatment or *partial hospitalization* can sometimes bridge the gap between hospitalization and outpatient treatment for people with BPD who need more intensive care than outpatient individual and group therapy. Miller (1995) describes four characteristics of successful programming in a day setting for persons with BPD: affect facilitation, holding without over-containing, ensuring client safety, and providing focused time-limited treatment (three weeks in Miller's program).

However, all settings short of round-the-clock supervised hospitalization entail considerable risk of suicide. Suicide also occurs even on locked units, but less frequently than in part time community care. On locked units, patients at high risk for suicide are monitored with 15-minute observations around the clock—even this cautious procedure has failed to prevent suicide in a few cases.

To address the suicide risks, DBT therapists emphasize taking a strong position that they cannot save clients from themselves; only the individuals can ensure their own safety (Linehan, 1993A, B; Miller, 1995). Some practitioners and scholars of BPD argue that hospitals take away responsibility for individual self-care in persons with BPD by removing "sharps" and other implements of suicide, a view that fits with current managed care practices of quick discharge to out-of-hospital care. As with any treatment, there are undoubtedly clients for whom this policy works, others who may be casualties through suicide who conceivably might not have died in long-term hospital treatment.

Work with families of persons with BPD. Psychoeducation and family support groups have emerged as interventions of choice in work with families of persons with BPD (Gunderson et al., 1997). Research on BPD suggests that average or "good enough" mothering may be insufficient to protect a child with neurobiological vulnerabilities from developing borderline characteristics. Conversely, resilient children at high risk due to traumatic environments may grow into well-functioning, successful adults. A borderline outcome may be the cumulative result of interactive biological vulnerabilities and life stresses, with or without parental inadequacies.

The blame/shame stigma now beginning to dissipate for other major psychiatric disorders, such as schizophrenia and bipolar disorder, has been slower to diminish for BPD. This is probably because persons with BPD seldom have signs of psychosis, but frequently exhibit irritating or upsetting behaviors. In the absence of evidence to the contrary, parents are often assumed to be at fault when their children grow up with problematic characteristics.

Parents of persons with BPD need to be educated that BPD is a neurobiological disorder, not retribution for toxic parenting. They need the support of others in similar situations to break down their sense of stigma, self-blame, and hopelessness, and they need training in ways to cope with behaviors typical of BPD. As Gunderson has pointed out, parents should be viewed as collaborators in the treatment process, not objects of therapy (Gunderson et al., 1997).

Implications for Social Work Practice

How does this new expanded knowledge fit with our roles as case managers, therapists, family consultants, patient and family advocates, and social and political activists? All the contemporary approaches mentioned above fall within the purview of social work practice and fit with a complex adaptive systems approach. Even with respect to psychotropic medication, social workers perform all critical functions except for writing prescriptions, doing medical evaluations, and interpreting laboratory reports. Before we intervene, it is imperative that we familiarize ourselves with current research-based knowledge about characteristics and etiologies of BPD, what interventions are effective for what types of BPD clients, and under what conditions they are effective. Without valid knowledge about the diverse forms and different underlying characteristics of BPD, and without training in skills targeted at troublesome or dangerous characteristics of the condition, there is little reason to expect that our treatments will become more effective.

Research suggests that if we can prevent suicide in the crisis phase of the illness, individuals have a good chance at a satisfying life later. However, the recovery process is usually very slow and gradual. We should have a reasonable expectation that the condition will be chronic for an extended time and that relapses are to be expected. Meanwhile, until the risk of suicide is diminished, intensive therapeutic efforts are needed. At the same time, we can remind ourselves and our clients with BPD that tools of self-destruction are always available in the community, that we cannot save them, and that ultimately only they can choose to stay safe. The natural course of BPD, gradual diminution of symptoms over a period of years, underscores the need for ongoing structure and monitoring in the community and for short-term protected environments (hospitals or some other kind of safe haven) where clients can stay until the immediate threat of suicide has passed.

Currently, such services have been or are being canceled in the context of widespread economic illness. Social workers must vigorously advocate in the political sphere as well as on an individual basis.

Skills necessary to work with persons with BPD and their families are teachable and learnable. However, it appears that training in these skills is seldom available in bachelors' and masters' level social work programs, even when the program designates itself "clinical." To get solid training in behavioral and mindfulness skills typical of dialectical behavior therapy students usually must get it elsewhere. In our view, generic social work skills simply are not adequate to address the specific challenges of work related to this painful and sometimes dangerous condition.

Some other practice approaches have adopted methods similar to DBT that integrate *behavioral methods* with *mindfulness training*. Acceptance and commitment therapy (Hayes et al., 2006), mindfulness-based cognitive and behavioral therapy (Segal et al., 2002), and related therapies are becoming increasingly popular. The studies found are too numerous to list here, but readers who have an interest in challenges in any area of mental health should do their own searches to learn more about effective and not-so-effective interventions.

In conclusion, I propose some core skills for conducting DBT and related programs from a social work perspective, drawing on some of the principles that guide DBT (in addition, of course, to the specific training required for DBT practitioners).

1. Provide psychoeducation to a person with specific challenges and his or her family about the relevant issues, in language easily understood by the particular client system. Workers explain knowledge from neuroscience and genetics about the role of these variables in the person's probable vulnerability to develop and deal with the challenge under discussion. The individual and family are encouraged to ask questions about how this situation may arise and what its likely course may be. If the worker is familiar with up-to-date research relevant to these questions, he/she can share this information with client systems, including a caveat that research findings usually convey probabilities, not certainties.

   The worker recounts findings from the most up-to-date research and gives clients web links so they can read about it themselves. In my experience, clients often appreciate the worker teaching them in his or her office to search reliable websites and abstracts coming up in scientific database searches (notably PubMed from the National Institutes of Health, http://www.ncbi.nlm.nih.gov/pubmed).

It is critical for individual and group therapists to have knowledge about the underlying biological forces that are often decisive in a person's tumultuous life. Without this knowledge, many people assume by default that toxic influences in the environment, very often one or both parents, are responsible for their own or a loved one's suffering—a view that has unfairly caused anguish in parents of persons with mental challenges for many decades (Johnson, Cournoyer, Fisher et al., 2001). Sadly, it has also reinforced the tendency of the person with the mental condition to blame his or her parents, alienating children from parents rather than conveying the message of neuroscience that these are no-fault diseases.

2. Clearly specify and enforce the conditions under which client and practitioner will work together, especially the boundaries of treatment and the behaviors that will ensure the person can continue in the program, both individual and group components.

3. Engage or create a validating environment, especially by finding or developing such an environment for the client in the community. Environments that can validate contribute to helping people accept themselves as they are, while at the same time actively supporting change.

4. If you have the competency yourself, teach cognitive-behavioral skills for impulse control, anger management, relapse prevention, and/or self-soothing, for which groups are particularly well suited, and conduct individual sessions that can facilitate working on these skills and problem-solving in relation to the most salient issues for that individual. If you don't have the skills, you should become knowledgeable about such resources in your geographic area so clients and families can access them somewhere.

5. With respect to medication, practitioners must keep up with current information so they can share this information with clients and their families. Together with clients and family members, workers should carefully monitor the client's responses to a medication and report to the prescribing professional when necessary. Workers do not need to memorize drug information, as it changes often, but they should become adept at doing computer searches on PubMed and finding watchdog organizations of psychoactive drugs to obtain state-of-the-art information about drug safety, side effects, and effectiveness of a particular medication being considered for or already in use by a client.

Because these searches can be done on the Internet with only a minimal expenditure of time, technology has made keeping up with current knowledge infinitely easier than it was only a few years ago. The easiest method is to get online access at home to databases such as PubMed, or if not feasible, in public or college libraries.

6. Finally, skills in advocacy and political action are required for social workers to join with other activist groups fighting to make services available to thousands of service consumers and their families. At the time of writing, the gap between these goals for service delivery and the reality of their availability is great. All of the above should be available to clients on an as-needed basis, not only for crisis management but also to provide the continuity of a relationship with that consistent, caring person who has been a stable reliable creator of a "holding" environment.

These skills are the same as those I advocated earlier (Johnson, 1999a, pp. 451–452), except for one aspect that has changed significantly. Advances in electronic databases have made information about neurobiological aspects, brain-behavior connections, and effectiveness of biological and many other kinds of interventions so much easier to access. Once we learn the relatively simple skills of accessing and synthesizing relevant research abstracts online, state-of-the art knowledge and interventions to help our own clients are now only a few clicks of the mouse away.

This technology now makes it possible for workers, therapists, administrators, clients, family members, and advocates *to go straight to the top experts around the world and retrieve knowledge pertaining to almost any condition or challenge.* Want biological and environmental risk and protective factors (for assessment)? Research-based estimates of the relative effectiveness of possible interventions (for intervention planning)? Want it right now? Without leaving home, if you have the Internet? And MOLES will come out of their subterranean tunnels at a moment's notice to help you.

As we said in Chapter 9, this methodological filtering strategy spelled out by Gibbs is a not a very time-consuming tool, is easy to learn, and increases exponentially the ease and speed with which searches can yield methodologically sound studies (see Search Skills for Digging Up Evidence with Help from MOLES, Chapter 9). Yes, you'll still need to compile the research results in a coherent fashion and explain why one type of practice seems more promising to you than others—that does take time. But hours and hours of searching for likely methodologically trustworthy studies are now unnecessary.

👪 Assessing Pat (Completion): Analysis and Intervention Planning

THOUGHTS OF DEATH, BORDERLINE DIMENSIONS, AND OBSESSIVE-COMPULSIVE TRAITS IN A PERSON WITH EATING CHALLENGES

Part VI is intended to demonstrate well-planned and executed assessment and intervention planning. The Multisystem Evidence-Based Assessment instrument (MEBA) is used with a person with both mental and addictive challenges and her family. Here we complete the assessment of Pat, age 27, begun in Chapter 32 with MEBA Items 1–7. In this chapter, the assessment and intervention planning are reported as MEBA Items 8–13. Taken together, these two parts reported by an experienced social worker incorporate systems factors, research information including relevant neurobiology, issues experienced by Pat as pressing, and a collaboratively developed intervention plan. The MEBA is a biopsychosocial instrument in which behavioral neuroscience is integrated as an equal status actor in the biopsychosocial triad.

Two types of skills (multisystem analysis and evidence-based searches) were presented in Part I, Chapter 9. The first seven items on Pat's assessment protocol (Chapter 32) are for use in almost any kind of setting or field of practice. The last six items build on the data reported in the first seven items, to zoom in on in-depth, science-guided assessment of individuals with moderate to severe mental, emotional, or interpersonal challenges and their families, in the context of larger environments. These last six items (8–13) are also relevant for many human service situations in addition to mental health settings, since behavioral, emotional, or cognitive issues are endemic to any age and to many populations receiving diverse types of services. Information obtained to be responsive to items 8–13 can guide practitioners in addictions, child welfare, forensic, school-based, work-related, and other fields of practice.

As noted earlier, the complete MEBA was written by a social work specialist in mental health who decided to remain anonymous to protect the client's privacy and his own reputation in his local practice community. The evaluation follows the guidelines for multisystem assessment as presented in MEBA

(Chapter 9), uses EPICBIOL information for MEBA item 9, and incorporates neuroscience research relevant to some prominent dimensions of Pat's psychological profile. At the end of the evaluation, the social worker uses the data compiled in the history to present his assessment and explain what interventions he thought might help Pat.

His agency does not use this protocol. The hospital attending physician's brief discharge note to the provider outpatient service is a preface to the first seven items in Part IV and is repeated here to set the context for items 8–13. Needless to say, the material is carefully disguised, but the issues are those of the real client and her family.

Discharge Note May 27th, 2012. Bristol Community
Mental Health Network

Pat W, a 27-year-old 98-pound Caucasian female, was admitted May 22, 2012, in acute crisis due to dehydration and electrolyte imbalance. She has a 12-year history of bulimia nervosa and intermittent anorexic episodes. This was her third hospitalization in a crisis condition over the 12-year period. She was hydrated intravenously and treated with cyproheptadine to stimulate weight gain. When vital signs were stabilized, she was discharged to outpatient care.

Evaluation and Recommendations by social
worker GB (MEBA Items 8–13).
Pat W, May 27, 2012. Bristol Community Mental Health Center, Outpatient Clinic.

8. Cultural influences on the client and family members; worker's subculture; organizational subculture of agencies providing services.
   Cultural influences on the family.

Societal promulgation of thinness as a requirement for attractiveness, through social media, television, and social institutions.
Importance of food in this family.
Belief (Ella's) that providing abundant food is an essential of loving parenthood—to limit this supply is not loving.
Rural poverty background.
Roman Catholic religion.
Generational differences in attitudes toward sex, roles of parents in adolescent decision-making.

Worker and agency subcultures.
The agency subculture, that is, its beliefs about etiology and treatment, were summarized earlier. My own views as Pat's social worker are somewhat different from those of my agency, because I was trained in a teaching hospital where research was used to inform assessment and intervention. That's seldom the case at Bristol. My colleagues

occasionally go to workshops and retreats led by big names in the field, but usually these are pop psychology gurus. I know I sound like a snob, but sometimes I get upset that staff make decisions about clients' lives by quoting some well known therapist ("Dr S says....") without ever going to see what current research says. How do they know that this particular client's problems are comparable to the situations the gurus presented in their workshops? Or even that the gurus have kept up with research in their areas of expertise?

I've wondered whether these gurus cherry-pick their cases for presentation but mislead their audiences by not mentioning the less successful outcomes. Where I was trained, you had to defend your treatment recommendations by referring to research.

9. Environmental and individual risk factors and protective factors: data gathered with EPICBIOL.

Risk factors
Pat's temperament: tense, anxious, volatile, easily angered, perfectionistic, obsessive.
Ella's belief that eating a lot and being fat is "okay," as it was for her in her youth when survival needs took precedence over vanity and the adverse health effects of obesity were not yet widely disseminated by the media.
Ella's wish to express love to Pat by giving her large amounts of delicious home-cooked food (a risk factor in this situation, but would be a protective factor in another family).
Media images of slender glamorous women, mixed with intensive corporate advertising to promote sale of junk foods.
Cultural differences between Ella and Ed's generation and the high-tech media culture that has shaped their children's values and beliefs.
Worker and agency subcultures. I guess I'd have to say that the agency's lack of attention to research is a risk factor.
In relation to Pat's temperament as a risk factor, I use the word *impulsivity* with the caveat that her bulimia—intense cravings for food and her struggle to maintain moderation but repeatedly failing—seem more compulsive than impulsive (see explanation in Chapter 40).

Protective factors
Pat's intelligence.
Pat's competence at her job.
Ella and Ed's love for Pat.
Ella and Ed's devotion to each other and support for each other.
Freddie's concern and help for Pat and their parents.
Stable long-term residence near family.
Health of Ed, Pat's siblings.

Potential protective factors: Practice interventions yet to be tried
Educating parents, Pat, siblings about Pat's issues.
Well-monitored trials of medication for Pat.
Biopsychosocial therapy for Pat, specifically dialectical behavioral therapy (DBT).
Support/psychoeducation group for family members.

Exploring possible state or federal government medical assistance.

Some of these protective factors will only happen if I succeed in connecting Pat with an out-patient facility that will give her a trial of meds and DBT, neither of which has been tried yet.

10. Neuroscience research on emotions, behaviors, and cognitions that characterize BPD and are likely underpinnings to Pat's struggles.

Here we discuss aspects of the borderline diagnosis itself and components (criterion behaviors, emotions, cognitive states). For most of us, I think, this is the most difficult part of the assessment because we're not trained in neuroscience or any of the "hard" sciences for that matter.

As I look at Pat's risk and protective factors juxtaposed to borderline criteria, the following aspects come to mind: Pat's temperamental characteristics of "tense, anxious, volatile, easily angered" (aptly designated "hyperbolic" by Mary Zanarini et al., 1998) clearly fit with emotional dysregulation; behavioral dysregulation (behaviors deemed impulsive and often dangerous—that is, binge eating, vomiting, eating almost nothing at times); recurring suicidal behaviors or threats. She admits to sometimes thinking death would be the only way out of her pain; she has allowed herself at least three times to get into a lethal danger zone; she has intense negative moods; she states she has a chronic sense of emptiness; sometimes she appears to have intense, possibly inappropriate anger; and she describes some dissociative symptoms such as not having feelings she sees everyone else having.

In my view, her really painful, debilitating challenges are, first, her constant cravings for food with compulsive and obsessive food-related behaviors and thoughts, and second, her underlying "negative affectivity," sometimes mild to moderate (dysthymia with anxiety) and sometimes intense and crippling (intermittent major depression, in which a sense of hopelessness prevails). But I think the pain is almost always there. She appears to be in an almost continuous state of pain. There's a desperate quality of not believing that this pain can ever be lifted so she can have satisfaction in life.

Her obsessive and compulsive behaviors she uses most of the time to stave off anxiety about eating and episodes of bingeing don't work for her—the cravings are too intense. Her obvious tumultuous experience with bulimia may be distracting us from the likely core of her misery, chronic feelings of worry, anger, and frustration, for no apparent reason except her inborn temperament. Zanarini (2008) has highlighted this aspect of BPD, noting that temperamental symptoms tend to fall into two groups. The first group involves chronic feelings of dysthymia, such as anger or loneliness/emptiness and hyper-reactivity to even minor stimuli. The second group involves interpersonal symptoms that reflect abandonment or dependency issues, such as intolerance of aloneness. Pat clearly falls into the first of the two groups but not the second.

Perfectionistic, obsessive traits are not typically prominent in BPD, although the symptom of perfectionism was reported among young children who later developed BPD, as was true for Pat. Pat's adult obsessive and compulsive traits look more like the profile of "anxious, fearful" than the "dysregulated, intense, emotional" profile of BPD, which in most other ways fits her well. However, it's not unusual to have signs of mixed psychological profiles from more than one personality disorder. The visible intensity of her emotions, however, eclipses these expressions of anxiety.

When I think about cravings, a third profile, addiction, comes to mind. What motivates a person to crave something so much, so much of the time, when not in the actual moments of sensory pleasure? The returns of some of my recent searches I ran with Pat in mind may give us some clues. The areas of attention include Pat's major issues in my view: binge eating/vomiting (food addiction), emotional dysregulation, thoughts of death, underlying depression, feelings of emptiness, and dissociative moments. In addition, she has motivational states that facilitate addictive behaviors (see Part III on pleasure and Part IV on substance abuse and addictions).

11. Interventions known to induce change in visible psychological characteristics and/or underlying neurobiological states.

My preliminary assessment. I disagree with the Bristol Center's not using psychotropic medication in Pat's case. I also disagree with the view that optimal treatment for Pat is to help her gain insight into her longings for intimacy and attention, and her feelings of emptiness at not having these. From Pat's descriptions of her previous therapies, it sounds as though that has already been tried, once for at least two years. Pat doesn't think it helped her at all, although she says she tried to respond to her therapist's efforts. This exploration involves looking back into her childhood at presumed painful lacks in the attachment bond between herself and her mother. I concur with Pat's own view that she and her mother are strongly bonded. Pat's problems are undoubtedly exacerbated by her mother's plying her with food, and that's an area where her family needs education, but I don't believe the cause is attachment failure in childhood and adolescence. Rather, Pat's hyperbolic temperament, the roles of food in her family, and media-driven culture, interacting through time, are more likely the source of her ongoing misery.

I pulled up abstracts on effectiveness of treatments that addressed several of Pat's characteristics: binge eating, vomiting, obsessive thinking about food, compulsive and impulsive eating, depression, and feelings of depersonalization. All of these characteristics except maybe depersonalization are sometimes associated with inadequate levels of the neurotransmitter serotonin. Selective serotonin reuptake inhibitors (SSRIs) and serotonin norepinephrine reuptake inhibitors (SNRIs) have been successful in treating depression, obsessive-compulsive symptoms, and bulimia, even when the person with bulimia isn't depressed.

In Pat's case, though, she seems to have had an underlying depressed mood for many years. She's one of those people with bulimia who has a pervasive sense of missing something in life, of longing for something to fill an empty emotional hole. That's despite the fact that if we look at her risk and protective factors, she has plenty in the protective column—intelligence, good looks, two parents who love her and a brother who does as well, opportunity to go to college, and, from the time she lost 60 pounds at age 15 to the present, ongoing success in attracting boys/men, success at the workplace where her employers recognize her value, an extended family... certainly not a history that could create chronic dysthymia and intermittent major depression.

It seems to make sense for her to have a solid trial with either an SSRI or an SNRI. That would be for the prescribing physician to decide. *My job is to raise the questions* [emphasis added]. Maybe if the doc doesn't seem familiar with some of the recent research, I could give him the folder of abstracts, without seeming too offensive. I'd say something like "I know how busy you are, but perhaps you'd like to take a look at these abstracts I just pulled up."

With respect to psychological therapy, studies of the outcome of dialectical behavior therapy strongly suggest it could help Pat. I believe she should engage in it on an outpatient basis over an extended period of time, maybe a year. Other psychotherapies don't seem to have worked on any long-term basis. Pat has not had DBT, and DBT has the support in the abstracts for the view that for Pat, a combination of DBT and medication may be the best choice for interventions. I hope these supports will lift her mood, and take the edge off her cravings and feelings of tumult, and give her the incentive to pursue sources of enjoyment in her life.

I was very interested to find that a full DBT program was evaluated in a pilot study of seven women with both BPD and eating disorder (Palmer et al., 2003). The women received the full DBT program. "Full" included weekly individual therapy, weekly skills training group, out-of-hours telephone contact by experienced clinicians who received the approved intensive training program in DBT, and who participate in an ongoing biweekly consultation group for therapists. The authors point out that one of the strengths of DBT is the clear supportive framework that it supplies for patients and clinicians alike. In this pilot program, unlike many treatment programs for eating disorders, there were no dropouts. All patients seemed to benefit, and most were neither eating disordered nor self-harming at follow-up. This was a small pilot study and clearly larger, more systematic evaluations will give more information, and it certainly is resource-intensive and therefore expensive to mount. But the program showed considerable promise for helping this population that suffers so intensely.

12. **Environmental Interventions.** Pat agrees with me that her family needs support and education about the illness, like all families with loved ones who have a psychiatric illness. I'd like them to attend a family support group for family members of persons with eating disorders or borderline personality disorder, whichever one we manage to find in this area. I might even have to start such a group if there is none.

The most needed macro-level environmental change effort that I see is to educate the practice community about the new opportunities for help that neuroscience and practice research, working together, can make possible. Given that so many providers have spent their professional lives doing things the "old" way, that is a daunting prospect. My first effort in that direction is contributing this analysis of the assessment and intervention planning with Pat.

13. **Client preferences.** I've explored Pat's preferences for treatment following her discharge. She feels desperate and hopeless and is willing to try anything that she hasn't already tried that might help. I'm in a difficult position, because I want to connect her with what I think can help her the most, but my views are at odds with those of my

agency administrators. I've been looking into outpatient treatments that are offered within any kind of reasonable distance from where Pat lives. The closest facility is 60 miles away, but it uses medication for a wide range of conditions and it also has a small DBT program. My view is that it would be well worth Pat's time to do that driving, which she'd probably have to do twice a week, once for group and once for individual therapy. It looks as though her insurance will cover it. She'll have to decide.

GB, MSW. Bristol Community Mental Health Center, Outpatient Clinic

Final comment (HCJ): From my point of view, GB's work with Pat exemplifies the best of clinical social work practice. He has done his homework, as practiced in his MSW field placement in a major teaching hospital psychiatric service. Although his knowledge of neuroscience is modest, he used the tools (fundamentals of brain-behavior connections and skills in searching scholarly databases) to give Pat the best possible help. He continues to learn in his everyday practice, and is excited and happy with his journey of continuous discovery.

{ PART VII }

Multiple Routes to Quality of Life

RECENT RESEARCH ON SUPPORTS FOR LIVING

By Jill V. Haga, Elizabeth D'Amico, and
Harriette C. Johnson

46

Authenticity in Therapeutic Alternatives

HOW CAN I TELL THE BEST NATURAL
TREATMENTS FROM SNAKE OIL?

Did you know you can beat stress, lift your mood, fight memory
loss, sharpen your intellect, and function better than ever simply
by elevating your heart rate and breaking a sweat? The evidence
is incontrovertible... that exercise is truly our best defense against
everything from depression to ADD to addiction to aggression
to menopause to Alzheimer's.

(Advertisement for Spark: The Revolutionary New Science of
Exercise and the Brain by John Ratey (2008). Amazon.com (2013).)

Does this promotional blurb from amazon.com surprise you? Of course not—
isn't this typical American-speak these days? Just another rhapsodic endorsement, no doubt.

We saw a similar review in Part V, this time by a journalist, not a publishimg
company. Pertaining to a magic potion which, when we find out what it does,
most of us want more of, this peptide neurotransmitter doubling as hormone,
was heralded by Natalie Angier, 1991, then science writer for the *New York
Times*. Before and since then, there have been numerous scientific studies that
justify her celebration of this joy-infusing brain chemical, oxytocin.

Reader: But the study cited above—the superpowers of exercise—isn't it just
an unabashed sales pitch for *SPARK*? It reads like thousands of advertisements
that spill out of websites all the time. Surely you don't expect me to believe this?

Author: Well, that's an interesting question. Is there really evidence to con-
vince both you and me that exercise can confer all these benefits? Although
Ratey (2008) exhorts us to view exercise as a "medicine", could these claims be
just a lot of hype to sell the book?

As another example, there's brain-derived neurotrophic factor (BDNF), a
protein dubbed "Miracle-Gro for the brain" (Gabriel, 2010, citing Ratey, 2008).
When it's sprinkled on neurons in a petri dish, BDNF has been observed to
cause brain cells to sprout the structural branches required for learning—sort
of like fertilizer for the brain. BDNF also serves as janitor for our brain cells

by cleaning up waste and repairing cell damage, keeping existing brain cells healthy and stimulating new cells to grow (Ratey, 2008). Should we start a regimen for ourselves and our loved ones of cultivating our own ingrown BDNF? Actually, according to Gabriel (2010), to get more BDNF, all it takes is aerobic exercise!

This section (Part VII) looks at information that might help us find some answers to the veracity questions (VQs). Multiple routes to quality of life include not only traditional medicine but also complementary and alternative medicines (CAM) and other behaviors and practices usually considered part of everyday life, such as productive work and exercise.

Complementary medicine refers to conventional medicine and alternative therapies used together (Gant, Been, Gioia, and Seabury, 2009). *Alternative* therapies are those used instead of traditional medical approaches and make up CAM's unique categories, interventions seldom mentioned under traditional medicine, which could also be described as "Alternative Medicines With and Without Traditional Medicine" or, more accurately, as "Alternative Health-and-Happiness-Promoting Interventions With and Without Traditional Medicine."

Integrative medicine (IM), an increasingly common approach, is the most current designation for combining and integrating conventional and alternative therapies (Eisenberg, 2012). Alternatives can theoretically be combined with many or even most of the conventional treatments.

However, the social work profession supports an integrated, holistic approach to assessment and intervention (bio-psycho-social-cultural-spiritual). This wide net encompasses not only traditional medicine and the various categories of complementary and alternative medicines (see below), but also a third category for consideration that we'll call "none-of-the-above" opportunities for enhancing quality of life. For example, although not typically considered to be under the CAM rubric, exercise is a "natural" behavior demonstrated in a very large number of studies to enhance human physiology, contribute substantially to recovery from a wide range of illnesses and injuries, and, most recently, to confer *psychological benefits*. For the many people who in recent years have had no doubt about the inseparability of body and mind, the plethora of findings showing psychological benefits from exercise—enhancement of our emotions, cognitions, and behaviors—will come as no surprise.

47

Traditional, Alternative, and Integrative Medicine, Plus None of the Above: How Can They Elevate Our Emotions, Cognitions, and Behaviors?

This discussion revolves around issues of quality of emotional and mental life: can some of the strongest tools for promoting wellbeing be identified and practiced by social workers and other service providers? If so, how?

In their international comparative study of the social contexts of well-being, Helliwell and Putnam (2004) and Helliwell et al. (2010) report from their extensive reviews of "happiness" literature that among the most powerful predictors of happiness or "subjective well-being" are *genetic make-up* and *personality factors*, such as optimism and self-esteem; strong social support from family and friends; freedom in making life choices; and low levels of corruption..

Allen Frances, Chair of the Task Force for the DSM-IV (*Diagnostic and Statistical Manual of Mental Disorders*, 4th ed.) that guided mental health practices from 1994 to 2013, states (2012) that authors have a propensity to overvalue their own areas of specialization (his less-than-flattering evaluation of his colleagues in psychiatry). Let's assume that the assertion by Frances is at least partially true for many specializations both within and outside of psychiatry. If this assertion *is* often true, economist Helliwell's and political scientist Putnam's 2004 statement that biological factors are among the strongest predictors of subjectively perceived well-being sounds credible, given that these scholars of macro social sciences state that despite focusing their own work is on social contexts, they in no way discount the importance of volumes of research attesting to the power of biology to influence well-being. The findings from the later study by Helliwell and colleagues (2010) confirm the importance of social support, freedom of choice, and low levels of corruption—the salience of social support and freedom of choice should not surprise human services practitioners, but the inclusion of low levels of corruption as one of the critical influences on social well-being was a new concept to me (HCJ).

Helliwell comments wryly that economists too often tend to equate happiness with having money. Money improves subjective well-being up to the point of relative security at middle-class or upper middle class levels, but above that, it seldom make us happier (Helliwell and Putnam, 2004)–except perhaps for the multimillionaires and billionaires who have much more than they could ever possibly spend on themselves and their loved ones, and yet seem to experience highs with every successive financial coup. Who comes to your mind? Jack Abramoff and Donald Trump come to mine, but there are hundreds of thousands of human beings around the globe aspiring to amass comparable fortunes.

Alternative and complementary interventions (see roster by the National Center for Complementary and Alternative Medicine (NCCAM), www. nih.gov/about/almanac/organization/NCCAM.htm)

Social work is the discipline providing the largest share of credentialed professional mental health and related services. Our view, which we state without proof, is that social workers need to be grounded in the complementary and alternative medicine (CAM) literature: the science of what has been proven to be effective, an understanding of promising practices, and an awareness of the potential risks of this little regulated arena (Gant et al., 2009).

Social workers have variant roles relative to CAM including, but not limited to, educators about the domains of practice; referral to and advocates for services; and practitioners of selective therapies. Henderson (2000) reported that almost 80% of a sample of 321 National Association of Social Workers clinical and direct service members either used CAM methods themselves or referred their clients to CAM services.

Although there is no universal categorization of CAM, the National Center for Complementary and Alternative Medicine (NCCAM) offers a useful classification system that divides CAM treatments into five categories:

- *alternative medical systems* (e.g., acupuncture, homeopathy, naturopathy, traditional Chinese medicine);
- *mind-body interventions* (e.g., biofeedback, relaxation, meditation, hypnotherapy, yoga);
- *biologically based treatments* (e.g., special diets, hormones, herbal products);
- *manipulative and body-based methods* (e.g., massage therapy, chiropractic medicine); and
- *energy therapies* (e.g., Reiki, qigong) (NCCAM, 2011).

NCCAM also references movement therapies (e.g., Pilates, Rolfing, and Feldenkrais method) and practices of traditional healers. Typically, prayer to improve one's own or someone else's health, also an alternative approach to healing, is *not* included within CAM (Sevilla-Dedieu et al., 2010).

Yoga is another example of a body-based approach. Yoga appears particularly beneficial for individuals suffering from chronic low back pain. In a study of 80 low back pain patients (half intervention, half control), pain, anxiety and depression decreased after only seven days, and yoga was more beneficial than physiotherapy for increasing spinal mobility (Tekur et al., 2012). Outcomes were measured via several inventories and rating scales, such as the Beck Depression Inventory (BDI); the State-Trait Anxiety Inventory (STAI); and the Numerical Rating Scale (NRS) for pain (Tekur et al., 2012).

Use of CAM therapies has increased in the United States and beyond (Gant et al., 2009; McLaughlin, Adams, Sibbritt, and Lui, 2012). Historically, some approaches long have been recognized as effective by other cultures, but have taken considerable time to be accepted in Western practice. For example, lithium salts from mineral water springs in early Rome and Greece were prescribed for manic episodes by the fifth century BC physician Aurelianus. Lithium has a strong record of effectiveness in treating bipolar disorder, but has been available in America only since 1970, when it was approved by the US Food and Drug Administration for manic illness (Mitchell and Hadzi-Pavlovic, 2000)—a tragedy for individuals with bipolar disorder and their families, who suffered intensely during the many years when American mental health professions offered no effective help. Many practitioners can cite clients, family, or friends who presented with bipolar disorder, then called *manic-depressive illness*, before recent acceptance of a remedy found in a natural source 2,500 years ago. Lithium's recognition by conventional medicine came too late to spare these persons and their families years of suffering.

Interest in approaches to health and well-being outside the purview of conventional Western medicine appears to have snowballed in the past two decades, as demonstrated in a 2007 National Health Interview Survey (American adults) by the Centers for Disease Control's (CDC) National Center for Health Statistics, and by a recent flurry of scholarly publication (Barnes, Bloom, and Nahin, 2008). The 2007 survey includes the first national data review of CAM use by children under 18 years (Barnes et al., 2008).

The CDC's 2007 report showed that the number of adults using CAM therapy had risen to 38.3% of all respondents to the survey (23,393 completed interviews with sample adults) when prayer specifically for health reasons was excluded from the definition. Among CAM users, chiropractic care was reported by 49.2% of the adults surveyed; 47.4% reported using massage therapy. The report further stated that 44% ($14.8 billion) of all out of pocket health-related costs ($22.0 billion total costs in 2007) was spent on "nonvitamin, nonmineral products" such as DHEA, fish oils, glucosamine, melatonin, and probiotics (Barnes et al., 2008). We were not able to get information about the numbers of private health insurance companies and public medical programs and reimbursements that currently cover CAMs.

According to the survey, CAM use in the United States varies by gender, race, geographic region, health insurance status, lifetime cigarette use, lifetime alcohol use, record of hospitalization, and other variables. CAM has most often been used to treat back pain or back problems, head or chest colds, neck pain or neck problems, joint pain or stiffness, and anxiety or depression.

Among adults age 18 or over who used CAM, 54.9% said they believed that CAM combined with conventional medical treatments (integrative medicine or IM) would help. Most adults who had used CAM did so within the 12-month period prior to the survey (Barnes, Bloom, and Nahin, 2008).

Approaches are used with varying frequency for different targeted symptoms or disorders and diverse populations. Effectiveness is hard to measure because there are so many possible symptoms, populations, ages, family statuses, cultures, possible illnesses, and other relevant variables, requiring extremely large samples in order to include these variables. For example, some methods are preferred for end-of-life care (e.g., touch therapies, aromatherapies, hypnotherapy), but the particular form of illness may range from a cancer to a neurological disorder to kidney failure to a dementia-related presentation (Wootton and Sparber, 2003).

The variant levels of acceptance of alternative approaches among conventional medical practitioners at times contribute to competing if not dangerous situations. Although evidence of the efficacy of herbal preparations in treating psychiatric conditions is growing, translating the results of efficacy studies into effective treatments for patients has been hampered by the chemical complexity of the products, the lack of standardization of commonly available preparations, and the paucity of well-controlled studies (Ravven et al., 2011).

One study found that 15% of psychiatric patients were taking herbal medicines to treat their symptoms, but none of them had communicated this information to their doctors, creating a dangerous potential for drug-herb interactions (Matthews, Camacho, Lawson, and Dimsdale, 2003). Another study suggested that few CAM users informed their physicians prior to utilizing such approaches, and only about 40% of them shared the information after the intervention (Thomas, Jones, Evans, and Leslie, 2012). Like other treatments, alternative approaches can have positive and negative effects, and it is imperative that patients and physicians alike be aware of these dangers.

It appears that among certain groups, the increased use of alternative approaches is associated with perceived discrimination, both in and beyond the health-care system (Shippee, Schafer, and Ferraro, 2012). The authors found that "the experience of racial discrimination among Black people is associated with greater use of alternative means of health care, as a way to cope with the barriers they experience in institutional settings in the United States" (2012, p. 1155).

Although the CAM body of literature is still small in comparison to that of traditional medicine, psychiatry, and psychology, it has grown exponentially during the last two decades (Integrative Medicine Advisory Council, 2012). Only a handful of scholarly articles on any of these topics were listed in major databases before 1990. Published works in this area have typically relied mostly on anecdotal accounts, but more recently, the growing interest in these approaches has been paralleled by an increase in the CAM literature that is research based (Integrative Medicine Advisory Council, 2012).

Challenges remain. It appears from extensive review that in order to justify generalized claims of effectiveness, the majority of studies need larger samples, longer duration, and replication (e.g., Furlan et al., 2012; Leach and Gillham, 2011; Lietman, 2012; and Moraska et al., 2010). Generally, the developing literature continues to suggest that various practices show potential, some promise, or great promise. At the same time, the healing professions have begun to take a broader view of therapeutic strategies and the need for research evaluation. There is reason to be optimistic that this upward trend will continue.

As in traditional medicine, studies of effectiveness of various treatments are problematic when they are published only in journals advocating the method being studied, authored solely by practitioners of that method or approach, and/or the research does not meet the highest standards. We caution readers to consider the sources of the results reported. As with any claims of effectiveness, published research studies must have used design, data collection, and data analysis methods consistent with reliability, validity, and if possible, generalizability.

Given the breadth of CAM and IM therapies, it is impossible to provide a comprehensive review of each approach. However, it seems important to describe samples of the treatments, research support for the practice, and illustrations of their relationship to neuroscience. We use the NCCAM categories noted above as the primary framework for discussing a number of practices.

Alternative Medical Systems

Alternative medical systems can be stand-alone treatment (e.g., acupuncture) or broad approaches that overlap with a number of the other categories. For example, naturopathy is a form of primary-care medicine that mixes healing traditions with scientific advances and research (Fleming and Gutknecht, 2010). Naturopathic treatment approaches include diet and nutrition, botanical medicine, physical medicine, hydrotherapy, behavioral alteration, pharmaceuticals, homeopathy and minor surgery. Naturopathic physicians (NDs) train as primary care physicians in doctoral-level naturopathic medical schools. The ND license is increasingly recognized, including by 15 US states (Fleming et al., 2010).

Mind–Body Interventions

Relaxation, meditation, and hypnotherapy have histories of use for addressing biological and psychological distress. Biofeedback is a more recent approach.

Neuroimaging studies have demonstrated that executive functioning is impacted under stressful conditions. Those with histories of marked stress, such as presenting with posttraumatic stress disorder (PTSD), often cannot attend to their internal sensations and perceptions without becoming overwhelmed (van der Kolk, 2006). They also frequently have negative body images. Although there is anecdotal evidence of the utility of mind body approaches, there has been limited scientific study of the effect.

Lazar and colleagues utilized fMRI imaging to investigate the use of meditation (sustained mindful attention to internal and external stimulation) with PTSD symptoms (Lazar, Kerr, Wasserman et al., 2005). They found that the brain areas of meditation subjects engaged with attention, interoception (sensitivity to stimuli originating inside of the body) and sensory processing are thicker in those with extensive insight meditation experience, than in matched control systems. Lazar and colleagues (2005) surmised, through magnetic imaging studies, that meditation adherents, through formal practice, increased their ability to face daily stressful events. Moreover, these linkages between sensory- and emotion-processing cortices are centrally involved in adaptive decision making (Lazar, Kerr, Wasserman et al., 2005). This premise remains correlational rather than causal, and further research is required to test the idea.

Biologically Based Treatments

The literature on herbal interventions is voluminous and, as might be anticipated, the majority of the writing is from non-Western nations and cultures. Although most address beneficial aspects of "natural" remedies, there is increasing research around the potential adverse effects of these approaches. There is also much literature on possible benefits of changing diet to address medical, emotional, and developmental difficulties. While there is evidence that diet changes often precede improved functions, it is not always clear whether the diet change is affecting the targeted condition per se, or that other factors may be lessening the symptoms. Either way, benefit is welcome, but dearth of evidence of condition-specific diet interventions so far suggests that marshalling such evidence is a challenge.

Diet therapies have become particularly popular for addressing the symptoms of particular disorders. For example, there is increasing interest in the impact on autism spectrum disorders, although the reasons for the improvement may vary. For example, Knivsberg, Reichelt, and Nodland (2001) found that by eliminating foods containing gluten (wheat, oats, rye, and barley) and casein (dairy), autistic children showed decreases in autistic behaviors and improvements in communication and social skills, with a reappearance of autistic behaviors when the diet was broken.

Others report that at least some children *diagnosed* with autism actually have neurological symptoms caused by undiagnosed celiac disease and that the apparent autism symptoms resolve once a gluten-free diet is introduced (Genuis and Bouchard, 2010). The symptoms were the result of absorption problems and nutritional insufficiency secondary to celiac disease. Relatedly, it appears that a "leaky gut" (or intestinal permeability—IPT) is significantly more prevalent among those with autism (36.7% of sample) or their first-degree relatives (21.2% of sample) compared with typical (normal) subjects (4.8%). This information supports the benefits of a restricted diet in allaying gastrointestinal symptoms accompanied by psychological challenges (de Magistris et al., 2010).

Manipulative and Body-Based Treatments

Touch as a route to well-being has a long history in Eastern philosophies (Bonadonna and Ramita, 2002). Central to these philosophical perspectives of touch are concepts that person and environment are a single entity, that energy flows between them, and that a delicate balance of energy is necessary for healthy functioning. Diseases and disorders arise when the flow of energy is compromised by pathogens or stress. Massage and touch therapies help bring equilibrium back to the energy flow and thus return the person to good health (Bonadonna and Ramita, 2002). Touch therapies are sometimes viewed within the body-based treatment category and sometimes in the energy category; like other CAM interventions, they can be classified in more than one way.

The positive effects of touch have been demonstrated in myriad studies that suggest that a planned use of touching as a therapeutic strategy may benefit infants, children, and adults experiencing a range of difficult life circumstances (see for example Moyer, Rounds, and Hannum, 2004; Weze and Leathard, 2004).These findings raise an interesting question: Is touch alone, even in the absence of increased emotional responsiveness by caretakers, an effective psychotherapeutic technique? If so, it could be that even caretakers whose psychological states impair their abilities to respond proactively, or caretakers beleaguered with job demands (such as being responsible for large numbers of elderly persons in long-term care facilities), can be taught to enhance the well-being of those they care for with frequent and regular touch.

Western medicine is beginning to implement touch-related treatments for a range of conditions. A 2010 review of the literature related to massage therapy's impact on stress-reactive physiological measures noted multiple findings across 25 studies (Moraska, Pollini, Boulanger, Brooks, and Teitlebaum, 2010). First, reductions in salivary cortisol and heart rate were consistently demonstrated after single treatments, although sustained reductions were not supported. The data were insufficient for clear findings related to the effect of multiple session massage on cortisol or catecholamines. Some evidence was documented on the positive impact on diastolic blood pressure. The reviewers noted that, despite progress, there remains insufficient rigorous evidence to offer a clear understanding of the effect of massage therapy on numerous physiological domains (Moraska et al., 2010).

Given the potential for positive outcomes and often the avoidance of adverse side effects, the use of touch warrants much more study as a therapeutic technique, including longitudinal outcome studies of extended use of touch therapies with humans.

Exercise as CAM therapies

Exercise under the CAM rubric focuses on "movement" therapies such as Pilates, Rolfing, and the Feldenkrais method. We address exercise as a general activity later, under the none-of-the-above category, since most kinds of exercise don't fall within the CAM classification.

Energy Therapies

Reiki, an ancient form of Japanese healing, is considered an energy or biofield therapy. Although it is broadly used to address both physical and psychological symptoms, there is limited and conflicting evidence of its effectiveness. VanderVaart, Gijsen, de Wildt, and Koren (2009) did a systemic review of 12 studies of Reiki. Nine found significant therapeutic effect from the Reiki intervention, but 11 of the 12 studies were rated "poor" on methodological quality. Baldwin and colleagues (2010) completed a separate review of 26 Reiki studies. Of these, only 12 were done with a robust design with clear outcomes. Out of the 12, 2 demonstrated no support for Reiki's benefit as a healing modality, five had some support, and 5 lent strong evidence for Reiki as a healing intervention that produced such outcomes as relaxation, pain relief, decreased anxiety, and cognitive clarity (Baldwin, Vitale, Brownell, Scicinski, Kearns, and Rand, 2010).

Another review looked at 66 studies of several biofield therapies (e.g., Reiki, therapeutic touch, and healing touch) (Jain and Mills, 2010). The studies were found to be generally of medium quality, meeting at least minimum requirements for validity. The studies found strong evidence for decreasing pain intensity in pain cohorts and moderate support for decreasing pain in cancer or hospitalized patients. There was "equivocal evidence" for the interventions' impact on both fatigue and quality of life for cancer patients, moderate evidence for reducing behavioral problems in dementia patients, and decreasing anxiety in cardiovascular patients (Jain et al., 2010).

A review of eight studies of energy healing for cancer patients found that none of the studies had a sufficient "N" or appropriate design to allow for conclusions regarding efficacy or effectiveness (Agdal, Hjelmborg, and Johannessen, 2011). These authors argue for more vigorous research around the potential of diverse approaches.

Natural healers and spirituality. Interventions within the spirituality arena are perhaps the most difficult to evaluate scientifically and, indeed, there is limited evidence in this area (see for example Cadge, 2012; Lucchetti, Lucchetti, Bassi, and Nobre, 2011; Masters and Spielmans, 2007; Rath, 2009). In the literature, "religion" and "spirituality" are often used interchangeably, although there is not always agreement that they are the same. For the purposes of this discussion, no strict delineation is made. Most reviewed studies address prayer, although there is some literature regarding other religious/spiritual practices such as laying on of hands, spirit release therapy, magnetized water, and spirit education (Lucchetti, Lucchetti, Bassi, and Nobre, 2011).

As Cadge notes, despite the fact that many Americans (and others) believe that through faith, prayer can influence well-being, there is a need for empirical evidence (Cadge, 2012). In 2004, a *New York Times* front-page piece featured this headline: "Can Prayers Heal? Critics Say Studies Go Past Science's Reach" (Carey, 2004). Despite debate on whether religion/spirituality's impact should be an area for study, researchers continue to pursue prayer as a possible therapeutic behavior. Double-blind clinical studies of prayer, including intercessory prayer, have increased markedly over the past two decades, published not only in alternative journals but also in mainline medical journals. This increase resulted from some studies with modest positive findings for prayer, but also the wider increase of similar interventions—for example, meditation, tai-chi, and yoga—raising the issue of "natural" versus "supernatural" division (Cadge, 2012).

As might be expected, many of the studies that found a correlation between the use of prayer and improved well-being were completed in areas with relatively high levels of religiosity, use of prayer, and church attendance (Hollywell and Walker, 2009). Chida, Steptoe, and Powell (2009) completed a meta-analysis of studies examining the possible protective factor of religiosity/spirituality and mortality. They examined 69 prospective studies that looked at the impact of use of prayer for healthy populations and 22 studies that considered the impact on diseased populations. Overall, the studies found that religiosity/spirituality was associated with decreased mortality in healthy groups but not among diseased cohorts.

For all of these types of interventions (traditional, alternative, integrative, or complementary medicine or none of the above), a single psychological event often illustrates a perfect fit between fundamental neuroscientific events and behavioral principles. Such an event (or "stimulus" in behavioral terminology) may activate pleasure circuits such as the mesolimbic dopamine pathway (thus conferring positive reinforcement); diminish pain and memories of pain by activating neural circuits that oppose negative emotionality and/or sensations of pain (conferring negative reinforcement); or induce a sense of calm by activating circuits that produce and disperse endogenous (natural, inborn) opioids, often resulting in feeling "mellow" (positive reinforcement) and/or less anxious (negative reinforcement). The opioids also have a role in amplifying pleasure within the dopamine circuits, heightening pleasure (positive reinforcement).

The proposed neurobiological explanation for "motivational opposition"—that is, diminishing pain and memories of pain by activating neural circuits that oppose negative emotionality (Koob and Le Moal, 2008; Koob and Zorrilla, 2010)—was advanced in relation to addiction. However, it draws our attention to a more general principle we should probably increase in our work—to lessen life's unhappiness in general by finding ways to activate circuits of pleasure and reward. These moments can give admittedly short-term but usually much needed relief from distress. In addition to giving intermittent moments of relief, respite, or even fun to people whose lives are beset with unhappy circumstances, these experiences convey messages of hope that are stored in memory even if not consciously recognized. Thinking up such actions is limited only by our creativity, in the context of situational constraint.

48

None of the Above: Exercise as a Major Example[1]

Exercise

Exercise is now emerging in psychological literature as a potentially powerful antidote to anxiety and depression. It has long been known to medically oriented practitioners as a critically important activity for maintaining health and for fostering recovery in people with cardiovascular, musculoskeletal, and many other diseases (see, for example, Häuser, Klose, Langhorst et al., 2010; Kamioka, Tsutani, Mutoh et al., 2011).

We're using exercise as our example of a none-of-the-above route to quality of life (emphasizing its psychological aspects) because it applies to almost everyone everywhere, it has been researched widely across disciplines, and new evidence of more and more areas of benefit from exercise to humans as well as other creatures continues to accrue. What new incentives can we find to overcome our inclinations to start that exercise program tomorrow rather than when the weather gets better or the semester is over?

Before we delve into the value of exercise to combat depression, let's look at the example of the much-touted "runners' high." It shouldn't be surprising that several natural chemicals in our brains, resembling drugs of pleasure and abuse in chemical structure and function, sometimes *act* like drugs of pleasure when stimulated by "none-of-the-above" behaviors and cognitions (see Part IV on Substance Abuse and Addictions). Alas, this particular example is a tease—only about one out of 20 runners actually get that high (Linden, 2011). In my running days, I was among the disappointed other 19 whose only major pleasure from running was feeling so good when the day's run was over.

The runners' high has been attributed to two neurotransmitters, endorphins (doubling as a peptide hormone and neurotransmitter in the opioid family) and serotonin (a monoamine). Both of these (elevated levels of serotonin and raised endorphin concentrations) are mentioned as neurobiology-based benefits of exercise, as for example in the four-decade review of depression and exercise by Helmich and colleagues (2010).

To get a sense for effects of exercise on mental health, we first looked at its effects on health in general, of which mental health is a subspecialty. We searched relationships between exercise and health overall. The keywords (*exercise* and *health*), with no limits on type of article, elicited 101,503 responses from PubMed as of August 28, 2012. When limiting all hits to Research and Review articles only was stipulated, the total response number declined to 85,988 articles, still 84.7% of the returns for exercise and health without this requirement. This large proportion of research-based articles should not be surprising given that both keywords—exercise, health—lend themselves to quantitative measurements related to known physiological functions, increasing the likelihood of a credible evidence base.

When a publication date limit of "last 5 years" was added to Research and Review, 41,760 hits were returned, equal to about half of the 85,988 total hits with Research and Review limits alone. That is, about half of all Research and Review articles on exercise and health were published during the most recent five years, with all the remaining articles over several prior decades.

The magnitude of the entire body of publications gives a sense of the enormity of the topic of exercise among health issues.

The keywords (*exercise* and *mental health*) drew 27,836 hits with no limits, 23,190 hits when limited to Research and Review articles, and when a publication date limit of "last 5 years" was added to Research and Review, 10,729 hits were returned. In all three conditions the ratios of mental health and exercise hits to general health and exercise hits were about $\frac{1}{4}^2$, suggesting that the subject of mental health and exercise mirrors overall health and exercise in relation to volume of research attention to exercise effects.[2]

This section, Part VII, designated as the section about avenues to "quality of life," refers to "mental health broadly defined" and "subjective sense of well-being." In the contexts of mental illnesses, diagnoses, or dimensional characteristics for which traditional medical treatments, complementary and alternative medicine (CAM), and "none-of-the-above" have been used, the term "quality of life" has heterogeneous meanings depending on the particular focus of each study ("quality of life" as the sole search term received a total of 181,139 hits, August 28, 2012). Specification in order to frame measurable questions would be required in order to compare strength or weakness of quality of life effects related to a given intervention. That is, to assess how helpful and how much elevation in feelings of well-being appear to have been achieved because of a CAM or a none-of-the-above behavior, measurable indicators would be needed.

One finding consistent across type of anxiety, exercise, and population was that exercise of more than 20 minutes' duration per session is necessary to reduce anxiety levels. Proposed explanations for effects include reducing muscle tension by raising body temperature, a calming effect from release of acetylcholine, and energizing physiologically by increasing adrenaline (epinephrine) levels (Callaghan, 2004).

In a review of research on mental health effects of exercise, Callaghan (2004) noted that exercise reduces anxiety, depression, and negative mood, as well as improves self-esteem and cognitive functioning. However, Callaghan reported that (as of the publication date 2004), exercise was seldom recognized by mainstream mental health services as an effective intervention and was consequently underutilized as such. It would be interesting to learn how much greater the recognition and utilization of exercise with clients has become since that time.

He and colleagues (2012) used stress in rats to induce depression, and found that exercise significantly increased serotonin, dopamine, and norepinephrine in the hippocampus. The findings suggest that exercise reverses and prevents decreases in norepinephrine (noradrenaline)and serotonin as well as restoring dopamine in situations of chronic mild stress (Callaghan, 2004).

Recent studies indicate that men appear to respond particularly well to high-dose exercise as an antidepression strategy, with 85.4% showing improvement in depressive symptoms compared with 39% of women (Trivedi et al., 2011). Comparing 53 individuals suffering from major depressive disorder (MDD) and 53 never-depressed controls, Mata and colleagues (2011) demonstrated gradient effects in that the higher the intensity and the longer the duration of exercise, the greater the benefit among the group of depressed subjects gaining the most benefits.

Blumenthal, Babyak, Doraiswamy, and colleagues (2007) assigned 202 adults (153 women; 49 men) diagnosed with major depression randomly to one of four conditions: supervised exercise in a group setting; home-based exercise; antidepressant medication (sertraline, commercial name Zoloft, 50–200 mg daily); or placebo pill for 16 weeks. After four months of treatment, 41% of the participants achieved remission (no longer met criteria for major depressive disorder). Patients receiving active treatments tended to have higher remission rates than the placebo controls: supervised exercise = 45% remission; home-based exercise = 40%; medication = 47%; placebo = 31% (p = 0.057).

The efficacy of exercise was comparable between patients in the two exercise groups and those receiving antidepressant medication (sertraline). These interventions tended to be better than placebo in patients with MDD. Placebo response rates were high (a not uncommon occurrence with antidepressants), suggesting that nonspecific factors such as patient expectations, ongoing symptom monitoring, and attention determine much of the therapeutic response.

Helmich, Latini, Sigwalt, and colleagues (2011) note that despite growing evidence that exercise can be a preventive and rehabilitative intervention in the treatment of depression, the exact neuronal mechanisms are still unclear. These authors have reviewed physiological relationships between physical activity and depressive disorders to try to identify neurobiological alterations induced by exercise that might lead to relief from depression and other mental challenges.

They searched electronic databases for research on neurobiological as well as clinical effects of exercise on depression for the years 1963 to 2009 (a 45-year span). The data suggested that physical inactivity was associated with higher levels of depressive symptoms, and that exercise training could be as effective as antidepressant medications.

Why "could be"? With respect to identifying neurobiological alterations resulting from exercise, the fairly extensive literature lacked enough sufficiently well designed studies to have confidence in the results. However, Helmich and colleagues state that the *observed* antidepressant actions of exercise are strong enough to use exercise as an alternative to current antidepressant medications in the treatment of depressive disorders, even without a clear map of the neural networks producing the antidepressant effects. Findings that appeared most salient over the 45-year period were summarized as follows (Helmich et al., 2011):

1. Physical activity appears to stimulate neural adaptations of the brain in all age groups; conversely, reducing levels of physical activity leads to higher levels of depressive symptoms; and when physical activity is resumed, depressive symptoms decrease again.
2. Altered blood flow is the main action of exercise on brain function, possibly explaining:
3. Lower risk of cerebrovascular diseases among active people, reduced risk of neurodegenerative and age-related cognitive deficits, and improved learning and memory.
4. Reduced age-related neuronal loss and stimulation of cell proliferation and neurogenesis (growth of new cells).
5. Exercise produces elevations in mood (human), and antidepressant effects in rodents.

Other findings about the effects of exercise reviewed by Helmich and colleagues (2011) include release of proteins and peptides known to improve health and survival of nerve cells. These internal compounds include (but are not limited to) the following: brain-derived neurotrophic factor (BDNF), vascular endothelial growth factor (VEGF), insulin-like growth factor (IGF-1), and the gene nerve growth factor (VGF). These substances are secreted by cells both in and outside the brain to influence specific targets.

Like oxytocin and exercise, BDNF has attracted a large following among health-watchers (see Gabriel, 2010, p. 1, above). BDNF, a protein, binds to receptors in the synapses, increasing electrical activity and signal strength. In cells, it activates genes that produce more BDNF, other needed proteins, and serotonin, the neurotransmitter which in addition to its many other virtues is essential for learning and self-esteem. Low levels of BDNF have been associated with depression and suicide. BDNF improves the function of neurons and helps new neurons grow, while protecting them from stress and cell death. It is strengthened by the physiological processes that take place when we do aerobic exercise (Ratey, 2008).

Both at rest and during exercise, the brain contributes 70–80% of circulating BDNF, suggesting that the brain is a major but not the sole contributor to BDNF levels. Moreover, the importance of the cortex and hippocampus as a source for plasma BDNF becomes even more prominent in response to exercise (Rasmussen, Brassard, Adser et al., 2009).

An additional and potentially very important effect of exercise is to counter the behavioral depressing effects of pro-inflammatory types of cytokines, which are proteins produced by cells. Cytokines interact with cells of the immune system in order to regulate the body's response to disease and infection. They can be either pro-inflammatory or non-inflammatory. There is now considerable evidence that immunoregulatory and proinflammatory cytokines functioning in the immune system (interferon, interleukins, and TNF-alpha) are a significant contributor to depression. Dantzer, Gheusi, Johnson, and colleagues (1999) demonstrated that the insulin-like growth factor IGF-1 can counteract the depression-inducing effects of cytokines. This means that IGF-1 can act as an anti-inflammatory cytokine in the brain. And IGF-1 can also be induced by exercise!

Koob and Le Moal (2008) developed a theory of contravening forces in relation to addiction: an *opponent process* as a motivational theory for the negative reinforcement of drug dependence (continuing to use after the initial pleasure is no longer experienced in order to avoid often highly aversive effects of withdrawal). It is driven not only by decreases in reward neurotransmission by dopamine and opioid peptides in the ventral striatum (location of the nucleus accumbens and ventral pallidum, two pleasure centers), but also by the recruitment of brain stress systems to produce corticotropin-releasing factors (CRFs), noradrenaline, and dynorphin in the extended amygdala.

The usual processes for these structures are hypothesized to be dysregulated in addiction so that they convey the opponent motivational processes that drive dependence. Acute withdrawal from all major drugs of abuse produces increases in reward thresholds (need larger amounts of the drug to feel good), anxiety-like responses, and extracellular levels of corticotropin-releasing factors (CRFs) in the central nucleus of the amygdala. CRF receptor antagonists block excessive drug intake produced by dependence. A brain stress response system is hypothesized to be activated by acute excessive drug intake, to be sensitized during repeated withdrawal, to persist into protracted abstinence and to contribute to stress-induced relapse. The combination of loss of reward function and recruitment of brain stress systems provides a powerful neurochemical basis for the long hypothesized opponent motivational processes responsible for the negative reinforcement driving addiction (Koob and Zorrilla, 2010).

What can we learn from these accounts of the relationship of exercise to mental health and well-being? It's that exercise induces release of *all kinds of good things*—agents related to *neurotrophic factors* (promoting the initial

growth and development of neurons in the central nervous system and peripheral nervous system, and stimulating the repair of damaged neurons in test
tubes); *vascular* substances (pertaining to blood vessels); *insulin-like* compounds (insulin is a hormone that regulates carbohydrate and fat metabolism
in the body); and a *nerve growth factor* (promotes nerve growth). Can exercise
really do all that?

A few researchers on the benefits of exercise are skeptical—maybe exercise
doesn't really counter depression (Mead, Morley et al., 2008), or maybe it's
only a diversion from negative thoughts (LePore, 1997). Mead and colleagues
believe that the design of exercise must be based on research to determine
more specifically what type and conditions of exercise will be beneficial.

So what might happen to us while we wait for this future research, or if
we're just too busy right now to exercise? We don't know, but let's be safer and
find a way to make the time!

Almost all of us want fun, laughter, food, love (with or without sex), or sex
(with or without love), among many pleasurable experiences. These experiences motivate us to stay alive and hold on to hope for the future, despite
struggles and pain.

When we develop tolerance to a particular drug (it no longer gives us pleasure), we often still want it to avoid unpleasant, painful, even excruciating
withdrawal symptoms. Similarly, if people's lives are barren of pleasure, and
these people are our clients, isn't it time to add enhancement of *fun* and
pleasure—even in small amounts—to our intervention goals?

Intake protocols in agencies and hospitals sometimes include inquiries
about a person's sources of fun and enjoyment (the questions being named
"recreation" or "interests" or "leisure time activities"). Do these categories
sound as inviting as "fun" and "pleasure"?

Social workers and therapists from numerous disciplines may use the question "Where are you now, and where would you like to get to?" as an opening
topic of discussion with clients. A companion question later in the introductory interview could be: "While you're on the way to *getting there*, what are
you going to do for fun?" This query is not intended as painful irony, it's a
serious therapeutic issue—enhancing quality of life even in situations of grief
or anger. The concept I'm proposing here is to "prescribe" small behavioral
respites from distress by creatively and collaboratively coming up with a few
rewarding short as well as longer actions the client can engage in, to "grab"
little bits of pleasure along the (hard) way. That is, the next step is to identify
very specific behaviors and contexts that can *help clients get pleasure* as they
work hard to get closer to the "where."

Examples of such pleasure might be to bring a delicious albeit small treat
to have at designated times during the day; *creative pursuits* involving artistic,
musical, theatrical, writing, and many other activities; *exercise* with a *fun* component, such as walking with a friend or friends; or a group sport that perhaps

the individual used to enjoy but hasn't done for years; and *work* that is productive and enjoyable, volunteer or paid (if the latter is available)—but remember, unpleasant or demoralizing work is not likely to help unless it includes moments when pleasure circuits in the brain are activated, and the rewards of this activation are salient enough to balance or outweigh the aversive aspects of the work.

For most of us, the paycheck is the "can't do without it" reinforcer. However, for people experiencing serious unhappiness or pain, work can provide another strong reinforcer, *distraction* from otherwise compelling misery. This kind of reinforcement is called *negative reinforcement* arising from escape from or avoidance of pain arising from injury, illness, grief, ongoing frustration, disappointment, anger—that is, pain from somatic or psychological sources. Although temporary, distractions can provide respite from pain.

None of these ideas are new—the problem is that they do not appear to be a routine part of professional assessment and intervention planning. Thus, it might appear that we as service providers may be missing opportunities to help.

Notes

[1] Although exercise is relatively low in adverse side effects, new exercisers should consult a safe exercise protocol, such as official PAR-Q form, Canadian Society for Exercise Physiology (CSEP), free online, which asks about seven questions to help them determine whether they need a consultation with a physician before starting an exercise program.

[2] We didn't take the time to refine the searches by adding qualifiers and applying MOLES filter terms (see Gibbs, Chapter 9) that would have been required to get an accurate estimate of how many hits would be eliminated because the sets of keywords pulled up topics by chance, not relevant to the topic being searched, that happened to have one of the expressions: *exercise, health,* and *exercise, mental health,* respectively.

49

🏥 Alternatives to Conventional Treatments

DAVID'S MOTHER DRAWS ON NEW KNOWLEDGE
TO FIND BETTER HELP FOR DAVID

Jill V. Haga, Mother and MSW

David was a normally developing child until 15 months. At that time, he began to engage in repetitive behaviors and to withdraw socially. By 18 months, he had lost the ability to communicate and refused to make eye contact with other people. He ignored events happening around him and lived quite happily in his own world. After a series of evaluations, it was determined that he has autism, a disorder characterized by social and communication deficits as well as stereotypical behaviors.

The most recently released data from the Centers for Disease Control and Prevention (CDC) suggest that autism affects 1 in 88 children (CDC, 2012), a higher prevalence than a measure found in some other sources (1 in 150). There are likely multiple contributing factors to autism, and although correlations have been established, straightforward etiologies remain unclear. The website of the Centers for Disease Control and Prevention (2013) is one of several comprehensive resources on autism spectrum conditions that present clear descriptions of, research related to, and explanations of the range of treatments for these disorders. Often, a combination of treatments, not just one type, none of them curative but many helpful, can offer the best chances for optimal functioning for persons with ASD (autism spectrum disorders). There is a nascent body of empirical evidence and a larger body of anecdotal evidence to suggest that there are helpful "alternative" remedies for symptoms of these conditions as well. The first of these treatments used for David was diet therapy. David was placed on a casein- and gluten-free diet that is used to implement an opioid excess theory of autism.).

David had self-limited his diet to only foods containing gluten and casein, and David exhibited the withdrawal reaction to the diet that is similar to withdrawal from other opioids including irritability, sleeplessness, and diarrhea. However, after six weeks these symptoms disappeared, and he began slow but steady improvements. Eventually, it was determined that casein did not have adverse effects on David's behavior, and it was reintroduced into his diet. He remains on the gluten-free diet and shows marked regression when he accidentally ingests gluten.

In a fascinating demonstration of the opioid effect of these foods, when David had a hernia operation, his mother gave him foods containing gluten in lieu of pain medications. David went from barely being able to walk following the surgery to climbing on the furniture following ingestion of the foods with gluten. These foods were discontinued a few days after the surgery.

David was also placed on an anti-yeast regimen involving dietary restrictions, antifungal medications, and the use of probiotic supplements for a short amount of time to eliminate candida yeast from his system. Like many young children, David had chronic ear infections and had been on antibiotics for most of the first 15 months of his life. Introduction of echinacea drops finally eliminated these infections. Again he presented with a regression of symptoms possibly due to release of toxins from a process of die-off of the yeast. Once he finished the treatment, he no longer experienced bursts of hyperactivity that had occurred immediately following meals. David continues to take probiotic supplements to prevent yeast growth as well as a number of vitamin and mineral supplements specifically designed for children with autism.

David's mother used pet therapy to help David develop social skills. His love of cats helped him to develop empathy, and one of his regular household chores involved feeding his own cats. When taking his pets to the veterinarian's office, David routinely offers comfort to his cats and shows empathy by saying, "Ow, ow, ow" when they receive shots. Additionally, David's speech therapist reported bursts of language each time a new pet joined the household.

When David reached puberty, he became more aggressive when frustrated. At 6'1" and 250 lbs., this became a concern among his educators and caregivers. Doctors initially treated him with Inderal and Risperdal. Risperdal was effective but has serious side effects. David eventually began taking Relora, which caused a significant decrease in hand biting, yelling, and hitting.

David continues to receive behavioral therapies through his local school system and attends elementary school alongside his peers with the help of an aide. He is able to communicate his needs and desires verbally and to follow simple instructions. He remains on the gluten-free diet. He shows a remarkable amount of empathy for both animals and humans and engages in imaginative play.

{ REFERENCES }

Addicott MA and Laurienti PJ (2009). A comparison of the effects of caffeine following abstinence and normal caffeine use. *Psychopharmacology (Berl)* 207(3):423–431.

Agdal R, Hjelmborg JV and Johannessen H (2011), Energy healing for cancer: a critical review, *Forschende Komplementarmedizin* 18(3):146–154.

Aguilera G (2011). HPA axis responsiveness to stress: Implications for healthy aging. *Experimental Gerontology* 46(2–3):90–95.

Ainsworth M, Blehar M, Waters E, and Wall S. (1978). *Patterns of Attachment*. Hillsdale, NJ: Erlbaum.

Akirav I (2011). The role of cannabinoids in modulating emotional and non-emotional memory processes in the hippocampus. *Frontiers of Behavioral Neuroscience* 5:34.

Akiskal HS (1996). The prevalent clinical spectrum of bipolar disorders: Beyond DSM-IV. *Journal of Clinical Psychopharmacology* 16(2 Suppl. 1):4S–14S.

Akiskal HS, Judd LL, Gillin JC, and Lemmi H (1997). Subthreshold depressions: Clinical and polysomnographic validation of dysthymic residual and masked forms. *Journal of Affective Disorders* 45(1–2):53–63.

Allen JG (2001). *Traumatic relationships and serious mental disorders*. Chichester: John Wiley and Sons, Ltd.

Alia-Klein N, Parvaz MA, Woicik PA, Konova AB, Maloney T, Shumay E, et al. (2011). Gene × disease interaction on orbitofrontal gray matter in cocaine addiction. *Archives of General Psychiatry* 68(3):283–294.

Alves SE, Akbari HM, Anderson GM, Azmitia EC, McEwen BC, and Strand FL (1997). Neonatal ACTH administration elicits long-term changes in forebrain monoamine innervation. Subsequent disruptions in hypothalamic–pituitary–adrenal and gonadal function. *Annals of the New York Academy of Sciences* 814:226–251.

Amato L, Minozzi S, Pani PP, Solimini R, Vecchi S, Zuccaro P, and Davoli M (2011, December 7). Dopamine agonists for the treatment of cocaine dependence. *Cochrane Database Systematic Reviews* 12:CD003352.

American Psychiatric Association (APA) (1980). *Diagnostic and Statistical Manual of Mental Disorders* (3rd ed.), Washington, DC: Author.

APA (1997). *Diagnostic and Statistical Manual of Mental Disorders* (4th ed. revised). Washington, DC: Author.

APA (2000). *Diagnostic and Statistical Manual of Mental Disorders* (4th ed., text revision). Washington, DC: Author.

APA (2012). DSM-5 (Progress Report) http://www.dsm5.org/Pages/Default.aspx

APA responds to Allen Frances New York Times Op-Ed [Diagnosing the DSM] (2012). http://dxrevisionwatch.wordpress.com/2012/05/31/welcome-to-dsm-5-facts-the-apas-new-pr-site/5/17/2012

APA (May 13th, 2013). *Diagnostic and Statistical Manual of Mental Disorders*, 5th edition (DSM-5).

Anda RF, Felitti VJ, Bremner JD, Walker JD, Whitfield C, Perry BD, Dube SR, et al. (2006). The enduring effects of abuse and related adverse experiences in childhood: a convergence of evidence from neurobiology and epidemiology, *European Archives of Psychiatry and Clinical Neuroscience* 256(3):174–186.

Andari E, Duhamel JR, Zalla T, Herbrecht E, Leboyer M, and Sirigu A (2010). Promoting social behavior with oxytocin in high-functioning autism spectrum disorders. *Proceedings of the National Academy of Sciences USA.*:107(9):4389–4394.

Anderson SC (1994). A critical analysis of the concept of codependency. *Social Work* 39(6):677–685.

Andreasen NC (2001). *Brave New Brain: Conquering Mental Illness in the Era of the Genome.* Oxford: Oxford University Press.

Andrulonis PA, Glueck BC, Stroebel CG, Vogel NG, Shapiro AL, and Aldridge DM (1981). Organic brain dysfunction and the borderline syndrome. *Psychiatric Clinics of North America* 4(1):47–66.

Angier N (1991, January 22). A potent peptide prompts an urge to cuddle. *New York Times*, C1.

Applegate JS and Shapiro JR (2005). *Neurobiology for clinical social work: Theory and practice.* New York, NY: W. W. Norton.

Arlow JA and Brenner C (1964). *Psychoanalytic Concepts and the Structural Theory.* Meriden, Conn, International Universities Press.

Aronson E (2008). *The Social Animal*, 10th ed. New York: Worth.

Atlantic Monthly (editorial) (2013, January). The problem with all of this "overweight people live longer" news. Lindsay Abrams (editor) 1/2/, 2:07 PM ET http://www.theatlantic.com/lindsay-abrams

Bailey CH, Bartsch D, and Kandel ER (1996). Toward a molecular definition of long-term memory storage. *Proceedings of the National Academy of Sciences U S A.* 93(24):13445–13452.

Baldwin AL, Vitale A, Brownell E, Scicinski J, Kearns M and Rand W (2010). The Touchstone Process: an ongoing critical evaluation of Reiki in the scientific literature, *Holistic Nursing Practice*, 24(5):260–276.

Bale TL, Baram TZ, Brown AS, Goldstein JM, Insel TR, McCarthy MM, Nemeroff CB, Reyes TM, Simerly RB, Susser ES, and Nestler EJ (2010). Early life programming and neurodevelopmental disorders. *Biological Psychiatry* 68(4):314–319.

Balleine BW, Delgado MR, and Hikosaka O (2007). The role of the dorsal striatum in reward and decision-making. *Journal of Neuroscience* 27(31):8161–8165.

Barbazanges A, Piazza PV, LeMoal M, and Maccari S (1996). Maternal glucocorticoid secretion mediates long-term effects of prenatal stress. *Journal of Neuroscience* 16(12):3493–3549.

Bardi M, French JA, Ramirez SM, and Brent L (2004). The role of the endocrine system in baboon maternal behavior. *Biological Psychiatry* 55(7):724–732.

Bardi M, Shimizu K, Barrett GM, Huffman MA, Borgognini-Tarli SM, and Bell M (2003). Differences in the endocrine and behavioral profiles during the peripartum period in macaques. *Physiology and Behavior* 80(2–3):185–194.

Barnes PM, Bloom B, and Nahin RL (2008), *National Health Statistics Reports*, #12: Complementary and alternative medicine use among adults and children: United States, 2007, US Department of Health and Human Services, Centers for Disease Control and Prevention.

Bauer PM, Hanson JL, Pierson RK, Davidson RJ, and Pollak SD (2009). Cerebellar volume and cognitive functioning in children who experienced early deprivation, *Biological Psychiatry* 66:1100–1106.

OBatalden PB and Davidoff F (2012). What Is "Quality Improvement" and how can it transform healthcare? http://qualitysafety.bmj.com/

OBateman A and Fonagy P (1999). Effectiveness of partial hospitalization in the treatment of borderline personality disorder: A randomized controlled trial. *American Journal of Psychiatry* 156:1563–1569.

Beless DW (1999b). Foreword, Johnson HC. *Psyche, Synapse and Substance: The Role of Neurobiology in Emotions, Behavior, Cognition, and Addiction for Non-Scientists.* Greenfield, MA: Deerfield Valley Publishing.

Berns GS (2004). Something funny happened to reward. *Trends in Cognitive Science* 8(5):193–194.

Berridge K (2011). "Liking" and "wanting" food rewards: Brain substrates and roles in eating disorders. *Physiology & Behavior* 97:537–550.

Berridge KC (2007). The debate over dopamine's role in reward: the case for incentive salience. *Psychopharmacology (Berl)* 191(3):391–431.

Berridge KC and Robinson TE (2003). Parsing reward. *Trends in Neuroscience* 26(9):507–513.

Berridge KC, Ho CY, Richard, JM, and DiFeliceantonio AG (2010). The tempted brain eats: Pleasure and desire circuits in obesity and eating disorders. *Brain Research* 1350:43–64.

Berridge KC, Robinson TE, and Aldridge JW (2009). Dissecting components of reward: "liking," "wanting," and learning. *Current Opinion in Pharmacology* 9(1):65–73.

Bertalanffy L von (1950), An outline of general system theory, *British Journal for the Philosophy of Science* 1:139–164.

Best PJ and White AM (1999). Placing hippocampal single-unit studies in a historical context. *Hippocampus* 9(4):346–351.

Bettelheim B (1967). *The Empty Fortress: Infantile Autism and the Birth of the Self.* New York: Free Press.

Bhatnagar S and Taneja S (2001). Zinc and cognitive development. *British Journal of Nutrition* 85(Suppl. 2):S139–S145.

Biegel DE, Johnsen JA, and Shafran R (2001). The Cuyahoga County Community Mental Health Research Institute: An academic public mental health research partnership. *Research on Social Work Practice* 11(3):390–403.

Biology Forums (2013). http://biology-forums.com/definitions/index.php?title=Gray_matter

Black JS (1998). How a child builds its brain: Some lessons from animal studies in neural plasticity. *Preventive Medicine* 27:168–171.

Bliss T and Lømo T (1973). Long-lasting potentiation of synaptic transmission in the dentate area of the anaesthetized rabbit following stimulation of the perforant path. *Journal of Physiology* 232(2):331–356.

Blogspot.com (retrieved 2013). http://familiesandaddiction.blogspot.com/2007/10/role-in-families-dealing-with-addiction.html

Blood AJ and Zatorre RJ (2001). Intensely pleasurable responses to music correlate with activity in brain regions implicated in reward and emotion. *Proceedings of the National Academy of Sciences* 98(2):11818–11823.

Blumenthal JA, Babyak MA, Doraiswamy PM, Watkins L. Hoffman BM, Barbour KA, et al. (2007). Exercise and pharmacotherapy in the treatment of Major Depressive Disorder. *Psychosomatic Medicine* 69(7):587–596.

Bolanos CA and Nestler EJ (2004). Neurotrophic mechanisms in drug addiction. *Neuromolecular Medicine* 5(1):69–83.

Bonadonna JR and Ramita (2002). Therapeutic touch. In S. Shannon, ed., *Handbook of Complementary and Alternative Therapies in Mental Health*. San Diego, CA: Academic Press.

Boris NW and Zeanah CH (2005). The work group on quality issues: Practice parameter for the assessment and treatment of children and adolescents with reactive attachment disorder of infancy and early childhood. *Journal of the American Academy of Child and Adolescent Psychiatry* 44(11):1206–1219.

Bos K, Zeanah, CH, Fox NA, Stacy S. Drury SS, McLaughlin KA, and CA (2011). Psychiatric outcomes in young children with a history of institutionalization. *Harvard Review of Psychiatry* 19:15–24.

Bracha HS, Torrey EF, Gottesman II, Bigelow LB, and Cunniff C (1992). Second-trimester markers of fetal size in schizophrenia: a study of monozygotic twins. *American Journal of Psychiatry* 149:1355–1361.

Bradshaw JL (2001). *Developmental Disorders of the Frontostriatal System: Neuropsychological, Neuropsychiatric and Evolutionary Perspectives*. Philadelphia: Taylor and Francis, Inc.

Bradshaw J (2005). *Healing the shame that binds you*. Deerfield Beach, FL: Health Communications. (Original work published 1988).

Brand SR, Brennan PA, Newport DJ, Smith AK, Weiss T, and Stowe ZN (2010). The impact of maternal childhood abuse on maternal and infant HPA axis function in the postpartum period. *Psychoneuroendocrinology* 35:686–693.

Bremner JD (2002). Neuroimaging of childhood trauma. *Seminars in Clinical Neuropsychiatry* 7:104–112.

Bremner JD (2005). *Does Stress Damage the Brain? Understanding Trauma-Related Disorders from a Mind-Body Perspective*. New York: W.W. Norton and Co.

Bremner JD and Vermetten E (2001). Stress and development: Behavioral and biological consequences. *Development and Psychopathology* 13:473–489.

Bremner JD, Staib L, Kaloupek D, Southwick S, Soufer R, and Charney D (1999). Neural correlates of exposure to traumatic pictures and sounds in Vietnam combat veterans with and without posttraumatic stress disorder: A positron emission tomography study. *Biological Psychiatry* 45:806–816.

Breslau N and Anthony JC (2007). Gender differences in the sensitivity to posttraumatic stress disorder: An epidemiological study of urban young adults, *Journal of Abnormal Psychology* 116:607–611.

Breslau N, Chilcoat HD, Kessler RC, Peterson EL, and Lucia VC (1999). Vulnerability to assaultive violence: Further specification of the sex difference in post-traumatic stress disorder. *Psychological Medicine* 29:813–821.

Brewin CR (2001). Invited Essay: A cognitive neuroscience account of posttraumatic stress disorder and its treatment. *Behaviour Research and Therapy* 39:373–393.

Broft AI, Berner LA, Martinez D, and Walsh BT (2012). Bulimia nervosa and evidence for striatal dopamine dysregulation: A conceptual review. *Physiology & Behavior* 104(1):122–127.

Brotman LM, Gouley KK, Huang KY, Kamboukos D, Fratto C, and Pine DS (2007). Effects of a psychosocial family-based preventive intervention on cortisol response to a social challenge in preschoolers at high risk for antisocial behavior. *Archives of General Psychiatry* 64(10):1172–1179.

Brown AS and Susser ES (2008). Prenatal nutritional deficiency and risk of adult schizophrenia. *Schizophrenia Bulletin* 34:1054–1063.

Brown GL, Goodwin FK, Ballenger JC, Goyer PF, and Major LF (1979). Aggression in
human correlates with cerebrospinal fluid amine metabolites. *Psychiatry Research*
1:131–139.

Brubeck M (1999). Social work and the DSM. In FJ Turner, ed, *Adult psychopathology: A
social work perspective* (2nd ed., pp. 121–135). New York, NY: Simon and Schuster.

Buchheim A, Heinrichs M, George C, Pokorny D, Koops E, Henningsen P, O'Connor MF, et al.
(2009). Oxytocin enhances the experience of attachment security. *Psychoneuroendocrinology*
34:1417–1422.

Buie D and Adler G (1982). The definitive treatment of the borderline patient. *International
Journal of Psychoanalysis and Psychotherapy* 9:51–87.

Cacioppo JT (2002), *Foundations in Social Neuroscience.* Cambridge, MA: The MIT Press.

Cadge W (2012), Possibilities and limits of medical science: debates over double-blind clinical trials of intercessory prayer. *Zygon* 47(1):43–64.

Callaghan P (2004). Exercise: a neglected intervention in mental healthcare? *Journal of
Psychiatric Mental Health Nursing* 11(4):476–483.

Caldji C, Diorio J, and Meaney MJ (2000). Variations in maternal care in infancy regulate
the development of stress reactivity. *Biological Psychiatry* 48(12):1164–1174.

Cami J and Farré M (2003). Mechanisms of disease: Drug addiction. *New England Journal
of Medicine* 349(10):975–986.

Cannon CM and Bseikri MR (2004). Is dopamine required for natural reward? *Physiology
and Behavior* 81(5):741–748.

Cantwell D (1972). Psychiatric illness in families of hyperactive children. *Archives of General
Psychiatry* 27:414–417.

Caplan PJ and Hall-McCorquodale I (1985). Mother-blaming in major clinical journals.
American Journal of Orthopsychiatry 55(3):345–353.

Carlson N (2009). *Physiology of Behavior*, 10th ed. Needham Heights, Allyn and Bacon.

Carlson NR (2001). *Physiology of behavior* (7th ed.). Boston, MA: Allyn and Bacon.

Carlson NR (2011). *Foundations of Behavioral Neuroscience*, 8th ed. Boston: Pearson
Education/Allyn and Bacon.

Carpenter LL, Shattuck TT, Tyrka AR, Geracioti TD, Price WH (2011), Effect of childhood
physical abuse on cortisol, *Psychopharmacology* 214:367–375.

Carpenter RW, Tomko RL, Trull TJ, and Boomsa DI (2012). Gene–environment studies and
borderline personality disorder: A review. *Current Psychiatry Reports* 15:336.

Carrera MR, Kaufmann GF, Mee JM, Meijler MM, Koob GF, and Janda KD (2004). From
the cover: Treating cocaine addiction with viruses. *Proceedings of the National Academy
of Sciences USA* 101(28):10416–10421.

Carrión VG, Haas BW, Garrett A, Song S, and Reiss AL (2010). Reduced hippocampal activity in youth with posttraumatic stress symptoms: An fMRI study, *Journal of Pediatric
Psychology* 35(5):559–569.

Carrión VG, Weems CF, Ray RD, and Reiss AL (2002). Toward an empirical definition of
pediatric PTSD: The phenomenology of PTSD symptoms in youth, *Journal of American
Academy of Child and Adolescent Psychiatry* 41:166–173.

Carey B (2004), Can prayers heal? Critics say studies go past science's reach, *New York
Times* 154:1.

Carver CS, Johnson SL, and Joorman J (2008, November). Serotonergic function, two-mode models of self-regulation, and vulnerability to depression: What depression has in common with impulsive aggression. *Psychology Bulletin* 134(6):912–943.

Caspers S, Heim S, Lucas MG, StephanE, Amunts K, andZilles K (2011). Moral set decision strategies to abstract. *Neuropsychology* 48(7):2018–2026.

Cavedini P, Riboldi G, Keller R, D'Annucci A, and Bellodi L (2002). Frontal lobe dysfunction in pathological gambling patients. *Biological Psychiatry* 51(4):334–341.

Chari M, Lam CKL, and Lam TKT (2010). Hypothalamic fatty acid sensing in the normal and disease states. In *Fat Detection: Taste, Texture and Post Ingestive Effects*, Montmayeur JP and le Coutre J (eds). CRC Press, Ch 20.

Charmandari E, Tsigos C, and Chrousos G (2005), Endocrinology of the stress response, *Annual Review of Physiology* 67:259–284.

Charney DS (2004), Psychobiological mechanisms of resilience and vulnerability: Implications for successful adaptation to extreme stress, *American Journal of Psychiatry* 161:195–216.

Chatterjee P, Bailey D, and Aronoff N(2001). Adolescence and old age in twelve communities. *Journal of Sociology and Social Welfare* 28(4):121–159.

Chen FS, Barth ME, Johnson SL, Gotlib IH, and Johnson SC (2011). Oxytocin receptor (OXTR) polymorphisms and attachment in human infants. *Frontiers in Psychology* 2:200.

Chen X, Hastings PD, Rubin KH, Chen H, Cen G, and Stewart SL (1998). Child-rearing attitudes and behavioral inhibition in Chinese and Canadian toddlers: A cross-cultural study. *Developmental Psychology* 34:677–686.

Chersi F (2011), Neural mechanisms and models underlying joint action, *Experimental Brain Research* 211:643–653. http://www.childtrauma.org

Chida Y, Steptoe A, and Powell LH (2009), Religiosity/spirituality and mortality: A systematic quantitative review, *Psychotherapy and Psychosomatics* 78(2):81–90.

Child Welfare League of America (2003). Infomal evaluation of intensive child treatment team program, Tulane–Jefferson Parish Human Services Authority (Louisiana) Infant Team.

Chisholm K (1998). A three year follow-up of attachment and indiscriminate friendliness in children adopted from Romanian orphanages. *Child Development* 69(4):1092–1106.

Chisholm K, Carter MC, Ames EW, and Morrison SJ (1995). Attachment security and indiscriminately friendly behavior in children adopted from Romanion orphanages. *Development and Psychopathology* 7:283–294.

Chugani HT (1997). Neuroimaging of developmental nonlinearity and developmental pathologies. In RW Thatcher, GR Lyon, J Rumsey, and N Krasnegor, eds, Developmental neuroimaging: Mapping the development of brain and behavior (pp. 187–195). San Diego, CA: Academic Press.

Chugani HT, Phelps ME, and Mazziotta JC (1987). Positron emission tomography study of human brain functional development. *Annals of Neurology* 22:487–497.

Cicchetti D (2010), Special article: Resilience under conditions of extreme stress: a multi-level perspective, *World Psychiatry* 9:145–154.

Cicchetti D, Rogosch FA, and Toth SL (2006). Fostering secure attachment in infants in maltreating families through preventive interventions. *Development and Psychopathology* 18(3):623–649.

Cichewicz DL (2004). Synergistic interactions between cannabinoid and opioid analgesics. *Life Sciences* 74(11):1317–1324.

Cintra A, Bhatnagar M, Chadi G, Tinner B, Lindberg J, Gustafsson JA, Agnati LF, et al. (1994). Glial and neuronal glucocorticoid receptor immunoreactive cell populations in developing, adult, and aging brain. *Annals of the New York Academy of Sciences* 746:42–61.

Clark DL and Boutros NN (1999). *The Brain and Behavior: An Introduction to Behavioral Neuroanatomy*. Oxford: Blackwell Science.

Clark L (2010). Decision-making during gambling: an integration of cognitive and psychobiological approaches. *Philosophical Transactions of the Royal Society of London B. Biological Sciences*. 365(1538):319–330.

Clarkin JF, Levy KN, Lenzenweger MF, and Kernberg OF (2007). Evaluating three treatments for borderline personality disorder: A multiwave study. *American Journal of Psychiatry* 164:922–928.

Cochrane Collaboration (2007). *Cochrane Database of Systematic Reviews*, http://www.cochrane.org/cochrane-reviews

Cohen S, Hamrick N, Rodriguez MS, Feldman PJ, Rabin BS, and Manuck SB (2002). Reactivity and vulnerability to stress-associated risk for upper respiratory illness. *Psychosomatic Medicine* 64:302–310.

Collins BG (1993). Reconstructing codependency using self-in-relation theory: A feminist perspective. *Social Work* 38(4):470–476.

Comings DE and Blum K (2000). Reward deficiency syndrome: Genetic aspects of behavioral disorders. *Progress in Brain Research* 126:325–341.

Council on Social Work Education (1995). *Curriculum Policy Statement*. Alexandria, VA: CSWE.

Courchesne E, Chisum H, and Townsend J (1994). Neural activity-dependent brain changes in development: Implications for psychopathology. *Development and Psychopathology* 6(4):697–722.

Cournoyer DE and Johnson HC (1991). Measuring parents' perceptions of mental health professionals. *Research on Social Work Practice* 1(4):399–415.

Cowdry R (1997, January/February). Borderline personality disorder. *NAMI Advocate*, 8–9.

Crick F and Koch C (2003). A framework for consciousness. *Nature Neuroscience* 6(2):119–126.

Crockenberg SC (2003). Rescuing the baby from the bathwater: How gender and temperament (may) influence how child care affects child development. *Child Development* 74(4):1034.

Dackis C and O'Brien C (2003). Glutamatergic agents for cocaine dependence. *Annals of the New York Academy of Sciences* 1003:328–345.

Dahl AA (1994). Heredity in personality disorders—An overview. *Clinical Genetics* 46(1 Spec No):138–143.

Damasio AR, Grabowski TJ, Bechara A, Damasio H, Ponto LL, Parvizi J, and Hichwa RD (2000). Subcortical and cortical brain activity during the feeling of self-generated emotions. *Nature Neuroscencei* 3:1049–1056.

Danese A, Moffitt TE, Pariante CM, Ambler A, Poulton R, and Caspi, A (2008), Elevated inflammation levels in depressed adults with a history of child maltreatment, *Archives of General Psychiatry* 65:409–415.

Dantzer R, Gheusi G, Johnson RW, and Kelley KW (1999). Central administration of insulin-like growth factor-1 inhibits lipopolysaccharide-induced sickness behavior in mice. *Neuroreport* 10(2):289–292.

Dawson KA (2004). Temporal organization of the brain: Neurocognitive mechanisms and clinical implications. *Brain and Cognition* 54:75–94.

De Bellis MD (2001), Developmental traumatology: The psychobiological development of maltreated children and its implications for research, treatment, and policy. *Development and Psychopathology* 13:537–561.

De Bellis MD and Keshavan MS (2003), Developmental trauma Part I. Sex differences in brain maturation in maltreatment-related pediatric posttraumatic stress disorder, *Special Edition of Neurosciences and Biobehavioral Reviews: Brain Development, Sex Differences, and Stress: Implications for Psychopathology* 27:103–117.

De Bellis MD, Baum AS, Birmaher B, Keshavan MS, Eccard CH, Boring AM, Jenkins FJ (1999). Developmental traumatology. Part I: Biological stress systems, *Biological Psychiatry* 45:1259–1270.

De Bellis MD, Hooper SR, Woolley DP, and Shenk CE (2010), Demographic, maltreatment, and neurobiological correlates of PTSD symptoms in children and adolescents, *Journal of Pediatric Psychology* 35:(5):570–577.

De Bellis MD and Keshavan MS (2003). Sex differences in brain maturation in maltreatment-related pediatric posttraumatic stress disorder, Special Edition of *Neurosciences and Biobehavioral Reviews: Brain Development, Sex Differences, and Stress: Implications for Psychopathology* 27:103–117.

De Bellis MD, Keshavan MS, Clark DB, Casey BJ, and Giedd JN, Brain development, *Biological Psychiatry* 45:1271–1284.

De Bellis MD, Keshavan MS, Shifflett H, Iyengar S, Beers SR, Hall J et al. (2002). Brain structures in pediatric maltreatment-related PTSD: A sociodemographically matched study, *Biological Psychiatry* 52:1066–1078.

De Magistris L et al (2010), Alterations of the intestinal barrier in patients with autism spectrum disorders and in their first-degree relatives, *Journal of Pediatric Gastronenterology and Nutrition* 51(4):418–424.

De Sousa A (2010). The pharmacotherapy of alcohol dependence: A state of the art review. *Mens Sana Monographs* 8(1):69–82.

De Vriendt T, Clays E, Moreno LA, Bergman P, Vicente-Rodriguez G, Nagy E, Dietrich S, et al. (2011). Reliability and validity of the Adolescent Stress Questionnaire in a sample of European adolescents - *the HELENA study. BMC Public Health* 11:717.

De Waal F (2013). *The Bonobo and the Atheist: In Search of Humanism among Primates.* New York: WW Norton.

Dear GE (2004). Test-retest reliability of the Holyoke Codependency Index with Australian students. *Psychological Reports* 94(2):482–484.

Diagnostic and Statistical Manual of Mental Disorders: DSM-IV-TR(2000). Arlington, VA: American Psychiatric Association.

Di Dio C and Gallese V (2009). Neuroaesthetics: a review. *Current Opinion in Neurobiology* 19:682–687.

Di Pellegrino G, Fadiga L, Fogassi L, Callese V, and Rizzolatti G (1992), Understanding motor events: a neurophysiological study, *Experimental Brain Research*, 91:176–180.

Diana RA, Yonelinas AP, and Ranganath C. (2007). Imaging the medial temporal lobe: The roles of the hippocampus, parahippocampal cortex, and perirhinal cortex in recollection and familiarity. *Trends in Cognitive Sciences,* 11, 379–386.

Díaz-Marsá M, Carrasco JL, de Anta L, Molina R, Sáiz J, Cesar J, and López-Ibor JJ (2011). Psychobiology of borderline personality traits related to subtypes of eating disorders: A study of platelet MAO activity. *Psychiatry Research 190*(2–3):287–290.

Diego MA, Field T, Hernandez-Reif M, Cullen C, Schanberg S, and Kuhn C (2004). Prepartum, postpartum, and chronic depression effects on new borns. *Psychiatry 67*(1):63–80.

Distel MA, Willemsen G, Ligthart L, Derom CA, Martin NG, Neale MC, Trull TJ, and Boomsma DI (2010). Genetic covariance structure of the four main features of borderline personality disorder. *Journal of Personality Disorders 24*(4):427–444.

Doweiko HE (2012). *Concepts of chemical dependency* (8th ed.). Belmont, CA: Brooks-Cole, Cengage Learning.

Dozier M, Lindhiem O, and Ackerman JP (2005). Attachment and biobehavioral catch up: An intervention targeting empirically identified needs of foster care infants. In LJ Berlin, Y Ziv, L Amaya-Jackson, and MT Greenberg, eds, Enhancing early attachments (pp. 178–194). New York, NY: Guilford.

Dube SR, Anda RF, Felitti VJ, Chapman DP, Williamson DF, and Giles WH (2001). Childhood abuse, household dysfunction, and the risk of attempted suicide throughout the life span: findings from the Adverse Childhood Experiences Study. *Journal of the American Medical Association 286*:3089–3096.

Dubovicky M (2010). *Neurobehavioral manifestations of developmental impairment of the brain.* Bratislava, Slovakia: Institute of Experimental Pharmacology & Toxicology, Slovak Academy of Sciences.

Ducharme S, Fraser R, and Gill K (2012). Update on the clinical use of buprenorphine: In opioid-related disorders. *Canadian Family Physician 58*(1):37–41.

Duman RS, Malberg J, and Nakagawa S (2001). Regulation of adult neurogenesis by psychotropic drugs and stress. *Journal of pharmacology and experimental therapy.* 199:401–407.

Dunbar RIM (1997). *Grooming, gossip, and the evolution of language.* Cambridge, MA: Harvard University Press.

Edelman GM (2004). *Wider than the Sky.* New Haven: Yale University Press.

Edelman GM, Gally JA, and Baars BJ (2011). Biology of consciousness. *Frontiers in Psychology* 2:4. San Diego CA: The Neuroscience Institute.

Eisenberg, D (2012). Integrative medicine in 2021: an imagined retrospective, *EXPLORE: The Journal of Science and Healing 8*(2):81–84.

Emond V, Joyal C, and Poissant H (2009). Structural and functional neuroanatomy of attention-deficit hyperactivity disorder (ADHD) [Article in French]. *Encephale. 35*(2):107–114.

Escorihuela RM, Tobena A, and Fernandez-Teruel A (1994). Environmental enrichment reverses the detrimental action of early inconsistent stimulation and increases the beneficial effects of postnatal handling on shuttlebox learning in adult rats. *Behavioural Brain Research 61*(2):169–173.

Faravelli C, Amedei SG, Rotella F, Faravelli L, Palla A, Consoli G. et al. (2010). Childhood traumata, Dexamethasone Suppression Test and psychiatric symptoms: A trans-diagnostic approach, *Psychological Medicine 40*:2037–2048.

Farlex (2011). Free Online Dictionary, http://www.thefreedictionary.com/).

Farmer RL (2009). *Neuroscience and Social Work Practice: The Missing Link*. Thousand Oaks CA: Sage.

Felitti, VJ (2002). The relationship of adverse childhood experiences to adult health: turning gold into lead. *Zeitschrift und Psychotherapie 48*(4). 359–369.

Field T (1995). Massage therapy for infants and children. *Journal of Developmental and Behavioral Pediatrics 16*(2):105–111.

Fieve RR (1975). New developments in manic-depressive illness. In S Arieti and G Chrzanowski, eds, *New Dimensions in Psychiatry: A World View*. New York: Wiley.

Figueroa EF, Silk KR, Huth A, and Lohr NE (1997). History of childhood sexual abuse and general psychopathology. *Comprehensive Psychiatry 38*(1):23–30.

Fish LS (2000). Hierarchical relationship development: parents and children. *Journal of Marital and Family Therapy 26*(4):501–510.

Fisher PA and Chamberlain P (2000). Multidimensional treatment foster care: A program for intensive parenting, family support, and skillbuilding. *Journal of Emotional and Behavioral Disorders 8*:155–164.

Fisher PA, Ellis BH, and Chamberlain P (1999). Early intervention foster care: A model for preventing risk in young children who have been maltreated. *Children Services: Social Policy, Research, and Practice 2*(3):159–182.

Fisher PA, Gunnar MR, Chamberlain P, and Reid JB (2000). Preventive intervention for maltreated preschool children: Impact on children's behavior, neuroendocrine activity, and foster parent functioning. *Journal of the American Academy of Child and Adolescent Psychiatry 39*:1356–1364.

Flegal KM, Kit BK, Orpana H, and Graubard BI (2013). Association of all-cause mortality with overweight and obesity using standard body mass index categories: a systematic review and meta-analysis. *JAMA 309*(1):71–82.

Fleming SA and Gutknecht (2010), Naturopathy and the primary care practice, *Primary Care 37*(1):119–138.

Frances A (2012, May 11). Diagnosing the DSM [Opinion page]. *New York Times*.

Frankenburg FR and Zanarini MC (2002). Divalproex sodium treatment of women with borderline personality disorder and biopolar II disorder: A double-blind placebo-controlled pilot study. *Journal of Clinical Psychiatry 63*(5):442–446.

Free Dictionary (The) (2012). http://www.thefreedictionary.com/enable, 9/18/2012.

Fu W, Sood S, and Hedges DW (2010). Hippocampal volume deficits associated with exposure to psychological trauma and posttraumatic stress disorder in adults: A meta-analysis. *Progress in Neuro-Psychopharmacology and Biological Psychiatry 34* (7):1181–1188.

Fuller L and Clark LD (1968). Genotype and behavioral vulnerability to isolation in dogs. *Journal of Comparative and Physiological Psychology 66*:151–156.

Fuller RK and Gordis E (2001). Naltrexone treatment for alcohol dependence. *New England Journal of Medicine 345*:1770–1771.

Furlan AD, Yazdi F, Tsertsvadze A, et al (2012). A systematic review and meta-analysis of efficacy, cost-effectiveness, and safety of selected complementary and alternative medicine for neck and low-back pain. *Evidence- Based Complementary and Alternative Medicine*. Article ID 953139, 1–61.2012;2012:953139. Epub 2011 Nov 24. link to abstract: http://www.ncbi.nlm.nih.gov/pubmed/22203884

Fuster JM (2000). Prefrontal neurons in networks of executive memory. *Brain Research Bulletin* 52:331–336.

Fuster JM (2008). *The Prefrontal Cortex*. Amsterdam and Boston: Academic Press/Elsevier.

Fuxe K, Diaz R, Cintra A, Bhatnagar M, Tinner B, Gustafsson JA, Ogren SO, et al. (1996). On the role of glucocorticoid receptors in brain plasticity. *Cellular and Molecular Neurobiology* 16(2):239–250.

Gabriel L (2010). What is BDNF? – Miracle-Gro for the Brain. Thought Medicine http://thoughtmedicine.com/2010/05/bdnf-miracle-gro-for-the-brain/

Gambrill E (2002). *Social Work Practice: A Critical Thinker's Guide*. New York: Oxford University Press.

Gambrill E (2003). Looking back and moving on, and Editor's note. *Journal of Social Work Education* 39(2):164, 169.

Gant L, Been R, Gioia D and Seabury B (2009). Incorporating integrative health services in social work education, *Journal of Social Work Education* 45(3):407–424.

Ganzel BL, Morris PA, and Wethington E (2010). Allostasis and the human brain: Integrating models of stress from the social and life sciences. *Psychology Review* 117(1):134–174.

Garcia FD and Thibaut F (2010). Sexual addictions. *American Journal of Drug and Alcohol Abuse* 36(5):254–260.

Gardner EL (2002). Addictive potential of cannabinoids: The underlying neurobiology. *Chemistry and Physics of Lipids* 121(1–2):267–290.

Gavomali C (2013). Are overweight people likely to live longer? A new study finds that people with higher body mass indexes tend to outlive their more slender peers. *The Week*, January 2:2013. http://theweek.com/editor/articles/chris-gayomali

Geisler S and Wise RA (2008). Functional implications of glutamatergic projections to the ventral tegmental area. *Review of Neuroscience* 19(4–5):227–244.

Genuis SJ and Bouchard TP (2010), Celiac disease presenting as autism, *Journal of Child Neurology* 25(1):114–119.

Georgiadis JR, Kortekaas R, Kuipers R, Nieuwenburg A, Pruim J, Reinders AA, and Holstege G (2006). Regional cerebral blood flow changes associated with clitorally induced orgasm in healthy women. *European Journal of Neuroscience* 24:3305–3316.

Gerdes KE, Segal EA, Jackson KF, and Mullins JL (2011). Teaching empathy: a framework rooted in social cognitive neuroscience and social justice, *Journal of Social Work Education* 47:1:109–131.

Germain CB (1982). Teaching primary prevention in social work: An ecological perspective. *Journal of Education for Social Work* 18(1):20–28.

Germain CB (1987). Human development in contemporary environments. *Social Service-Review* 61(4):565–580.

Gibbs L (2003). *Evidence-based practice for the helping professions: A practical guide with integrated multimedia*. Pacific Grove, CA: Thomson Brooks/Cole.

Giesen-Bloo J, van Dyck R, Spinhoven P, van Tilburg W, Dirksen C, van Asselt T, et al. (2006). Outpatient psychotherapy for borderline personality disorder. *Archives of General Psychiatry* 63:649–658.

Gilbertson MW, Shenton ME, Ciszewski A, Kasai K, Lasko NB, Orr, SP, Pitman RK (2002). Smaller hippocampal volume predicts pathologic vulnerability to psychological trauma. *Nature Neuroscience* 5:1242–1247.

Gillespie CF and Nemeroff CB (2007). Corticotropin-releasing factor and the psychobiological of early-life stress. *Current Directors in Psychological Science* 16:2:85–89.

Gordis EB, Feres N, Olezeski CL, Rabkin AN, and Trickett PK (2010). Skin conductance reactivity and respiratory sinus arrhythmia among maltreated and comparison youth: relations with aggressive behavior. *Journal of Pediatric Psychology* 35:547–558.

Gillman MW, Rifas-Shiman SL, Kleinman K, Oken E, Rich-Edwards JW, and Taverass EM (2008). Developmental origins of childhood overweight: Potential public health impact. *Obesity (Silver Spring)* 16(7):1651–1656.

Ginsberg L, Lackerud L, and Larrison CR (2004). *Human Biology for Social Workers: Development, Ecology, Genetics, and Health.* Boston: Pearson Education.

Giuliano F and Allard J (2001). Dopamine and male sexual function. *European Urology* 40(6):601–608.

Goldman-Rakic P (1995). Structure and functions of the human prefrontal cortex. *Annals of the New York Academy of Sciences* 769:71–84.

Goldstein A (2001). *Addiction from Biology to Policy* (2nd ed.). New York, NY: Oxford University Press.

Goldstein RZ and Volkow ND (2002). Drug addiction and its underlying neurobiological basis: Neuroimaging evidence for the involvement of the frontal cortex. *American Journal of Psychiatry* 159:1642–1652.

Gonzales R, Ang A, Glik DC, Rawson RA, Lee S, Iguchi M, and Methamphetamine Treatment Project Corporate Authors (2011/2012). Quality of life among treatment seeking methamphetamine-dependent individuals. *American Journal on Addictions* 20(4):366–372.

Gottesman II (2001). Psychopathology through a life span-genetic prism. *American Psychologist* 11:867–878.

Gottesman II and Gould TD (2003). The endophenotype concept in psychiatry: Etymology and strategic intentions. *American Journal of Psychiatry* 160:636–645.

Goudriaan AE, Oosterlaan J, de Beurs E, and Van den Brink W (2004). Pathological gambling: A comprehensive review of biobehavioral findings. *Neuroscience Biobehavioral Review* 28(2):123–141.

Gouin JP, Carter CS, Pournajafi-Nazarloo H, Glaser R, Malarkey WB, Loving TJ, Stowell J, et al.(2010). Marital behavior, oxytocin, vasopressin, and wound healing. http://pni.osumc.edu/KG Psychoneuroendocrinology psyneuen.2010.01.009

Gould E (2007). How widespread is adult neurogenesis in mammals? *Nature Reviews Neuroscience* 8:481–488.

Graham KL (2011). Coevolutionary relationship between striatum size and social play in nonhuman primates. *American Journal of Primatology* 73(4):314–322.

Granger DA and Kivlighan KT (2003). Integrating biological, behavioral, and social levels of analysis in early child development: Progress, problems, and prospects. *Child Development* 74(4):1058–1063.

Grant JE, Potenza MN, Weinstein A, and Gorelick DA. (2010). Introduction to behavioral addictions. *American Journal of Drug and Alcohol Abuse* 36(5):233–241.

Griengl H, Sendera A, and Dantendorf K (2001). Naltrexone as a treatment of self-injurious behavior—A case report. *Acta Psychiatrica Scandinavica* 103:234–236.

Grilo CM, Pagano ME, Stout RL, Markowitz, JC, Ansell EB, Pinto A, Zanarini MC, Yen S, and Skodol AE (2012). Stressful life events predict eating disorder relapse following remission: Six-year prospective outcomes. *International Journal of Eating Disorders* 45(2):185–192.

Groza V, Ryan SD, and Cash SJ (2003). Institutionalization, behavior, and international adoption: Predictors of behavior problems. *Journal of Immigration and Health* 5(1):5–17.

Gujar N, Yoo SS, Hu P, and Walker MP (2011).The un-rested resting brain: Sleep deprivation amplifies reactivity of brain reward networks, biasing the appraisal. *Journal of Cognitive Neuroscience* 22(8):1637–1648.

Gunderson JG (1996). The borderline patient's intolerance of aloneness: Insecure attachments and therapist availability. *American Journal of Psychiatry* 153(6):752–758.

Gunderson JG (2009). Borderline personality disorder: Ontogeny of a diagnosis. *American Journal of Psychiatry* 166(5):530–539.

Gunderson JG (2010). Revising the borderline diagnosis for DSM-V: An alternative proposal. *Journal of Personality Disorders* 24(6):694–708.

Gunderson JG and Englund DW (1981). Characterizing the families of borderlines. *Psychiatric Clinics of North America* 4(1):159–168.

Gunderson JG, Berkowitz C, and Ruiz-Sancho A (1997). Families of borderline patients: A psychoeducational approach. *Bulletin of the Menninger Clinic* 61(4):446–457.

Gunderson JG, Stout RL, McGlashan TH, Shea MT, Morey LC, Grilo CM, Zanarini MC, Yen S, Markowitz, JC, Sanislow C, Ansell E, Pinto A, and Skodol AE (2011). Ten-year course of borderline personality disorder: Psychopathology and function from the collaborative longitudinal personality disorders study. *Archives of General Psychiatry* 68(8):827–837.

Gunderson JG, Zanarini MC, Choi-Kain LW, Mitchell KS, Jang KL, and Hudson JI (2011). Family study of borderline personality disorder and its sectors of psychopathology. *Archives of General Psychiatry* 68(7):753–762.

Hajnal A, Smith GP, and Norgren R (2004). Oral sucrose stimulation increases accumbens dopamine in the rat. *American Journal of Physiology—Regulatory Integrative and Comparative Physiology* 286(1):R13, R31–R37.

Haldane E and Ross G, eds (1975). *The philosophical works of Descartes*. Cambridge, UK: Cambridge University Press.

Hameroff S and Penrose R (1996). Conscious events as orchestrated spacetime selections. *Journal of Consciousness Studies* 2:36–53.

Hansen S, Bergvall AH, and Nyiredi S (1993). Interaction with pups enhances dopamine release in the ventral striatum of maternal rats: A microdialysis study. *Pharmacology and Biochemistry of Behavior* 45(3):673–676.

Harmon K (2011). Brain on beauty shows same pattern for art and music. *Scientific American*, July 7th, comments on work of Ishizu and Zeki http://www.scientificameri-can.com/blog/post.cfm? id=brain-on-beauty-shows-same-pattern-2011-07-07).

Harmon-Jones E and Winkielman P (2007). *Social Neuroscience: Integrating Biological and Psychological Explanations of Social Behavior.* New York: The Guilford Press.

Hart H and Rubia K (2012). Neuroimaging of child abuse: A critical review. *Frontiers of Human Neuroscience* 6:52.

Hartman A (1995). Diagrammatic assessment of family relationships. *Families in Society* 76(2).

Hasan H and Hasan TF (2009). Laugh yourself into a healthier person: A cross cultural analysis of the effects of varying levels of laughter on health. *International Journal of Medical Sciences* 6(4):200–210.

Häuser W, Klose P, Langhorst J, Moradi B, Steinbach M, Schiltenwolf M, and Busch A (2010). Efficacy of different types of aerobic exercise in fibromyalgia syndrome: a systematic review and meta-analysis of randomised controlled trials. *Arthritis Research and Therapy* 12(3):R79.

Havermans R (2011). You say it's liking, I say it's wanting. On the difficulty of disentangling food reward in man. *Appetite* 57(1):286–294.

Hayes SC, Luoma JB, Bond FW, and Lillis J (2006). Acceptance and Commitment Therapy: Model, processes and outcomes. *Behaviour Research and Therapy* 44:1–25.

Haynes RB, Sackett DL, Gray JM, Cook DJ, and Guyatt GH (1996). Transferring evidence from research to practice. *ACP Journal Club* 125(3):A14–A16.

Haynes RB, Wilczynski N, McKibbon K, and Sinclair JC (1994). Developing optimal search strategies for detecting clinically sound studies in MEDLINE. *Journal of the American Medical Information Association* 1(6):447–458.

He SB, Tang WG, Kao XL, Zhang CG, and Wong XT (2012). Exercise intervention may prevent depression. *International Journal of Sports Medicine* 33(7):525–530.

Health and Human Services (1999). *Mental Health: A Report of the Surgeon General.* Washington, DC: Department of Public Health, US Department of Health and Human Services.

Heim C and Nemeroff CB (2009). Neurobiology of posttraumatic stress disorder, *CNS spectrums* 14:13–24.

Heim C, Newport DJ, Neit S, Graham YP, Wilcox M, Bonsall R et al. (2000). Pituitary-adrenal and autonomic responses to stress in women after sexual and physical abuse in childhood. *JAMA* 284(5):592–597.

Heishman SJ, Kleykamp BA, and Singleton EG (2010). Meta-analysis of the acute effects of nicotine and smoking on human performance. *Psychopharmacology (Berl)* 210(4):453–469.

Helliwell JF and Putnam RD (2004). The social context of wellbeing. http://faculty.arts.ubc.ca/jhelliwell/papers/Helliwell-Putnam-PTRSL2004.pdf.

Helliwell JF Barrington-Leigh C, Harris A, and Huang H, (2010). International evidence on the social context of wellbeing. http://www.voxeu.org/article/new-evidence-social-context-wellbeing.

Helmich I, Latini A, Sigwalt A, Carta MG, S, Velasques B, Ribeiro P, and Budde H (2010). Neurobiological alterations induced by exercise and their impact on depressive disorders. *Clinical Practice and Epidemiology of Mental Health* 6:115–125.

Henderson L (2000). The knowledge and use of alternative therapeutic techniques by social work practitioners. *Social Work in Health Care* 30(3):55–71.

Henry JP (1997). Cortisol: The right hemisphere and the hypothalamo–pituitary–adrenal axis, an inquiry into problems of human bonding. *Acta Physiologica Scandinavica Suppl.* 640:10–25.

Higashi T, Sone Y, Ogawa K, Kitamura YT, Saiki K, Sagawa S, Yanagida T, et al. (2004). Changes in regional cerebral blood volume in frontal cortex during mental work with and without caffeine intake: Functional monitoring using near-infrared spectroscopy. *Journal of Biomedical Optics* 9(4):788–793.

Hoffman PL and Tabakoff B (1996). Alcohol dependence: A commentary on mechanisms. *Alcohol and Alcoholism* 31(4):333–340.

Hollander E, Allen A, Lopez RP, Bienstock CA, Grossman R, Siever LJ, Merkatz L, and Stein DJ (2001). A preliminary double-blind, placebo-controlled trial of divalproex sodium in borderline personality disorder. *Journal of Clinical Psychiatry* 62(3):199–203.

Hollywell C and Walker J (2009), Private prayer as a suitable intervention for hospitalized patients: a critical review of the literature, *Journal of Clinical Nursing* 18(5):637–651.

Hommer DW, Bjork JM, and Gilman JM (2011). Imaging brain response to reward in addictive disorders. *Annals of the New York Academy of Sciences* 1216:50–61.

Hooper J and Teresi D (1986). *The three-pound universe.* New York, NY: MacMillan.

Hope B, Kosofsky B, Hyman SE, and Nestler EJ (1992). Regulation of immediate early gene expression and AP-1 binding in the rat nucleus accumbens by chronic cocaine. *Proceedings of the National Academy of Sciences U S A* 89(13):5764–5768.

Hughes V (2013). The big fat truth. *Nature News,* http://www.nature.com/news/the-big-fat-truth-1.13039.22.

Hurcom C, Copello A, and Orford J (2000). The family and alcohol: Effects of excessive drinking and conceptualizations of spouses over recent decades. *Substance Use and Misuse* 35(4):473–502.

Hyman SE (2007). Can neuroscience be integrated into the DSM-V? *Nature Reviews Neuroscience* 9:725–732.

Hyman SE (1995, Winter). What is addiction? *Harvard Medical Alumni Review.* Cambridge, MA: Harvard University Alumni Association.

Hyman SE (1997). *Commentary, Science and Treatment* (video). Produced by the National Alliance for the Mentally Ill, Arlington, VA, in conjunction with the National Institute of Mental Health, National Institutes of Health, Rockville, MD.

Hyman SE, Comb M, Lin YS, Pearlberg J, Green MR, and Goodman HM (1988). A common transacting factor is involved in transcriptional regulation of neurotransmitter genes by cyclic AMP. *Molecular Cell Biology* 8(10):4225–4233.

Hyman SE and Malenka RC (2001). Addiction and the brain: The neurobiology of compulsion and its persistence. *Nature Reviews Neuroscience* 2(10):695–703.

Ibanez A, Blanco C, de Castro IP, Fernandez-Piqueras J, and Saiz-Ruiz J. (2003). Genetics of pathological gambling. *Journal of Gambling Studies* 19(1):11–22.

Ichise M, Vines DC, Gura T, Anderson GM, Suomi SJ, Higley JD, and Innis RB (2006). Effects of early life stress on [11C]DASB positron emission tomography imaging of serotonin transporters in adolescent peer- and mother-reared rhesus monkeys. *Journal of Neuroscience* 26(17):4638–4643.

Inclan J and Hernandez M (1992). Cross-cultural perspectives and codependence: The case of poor Hispanics. *American Journal of Orthopsychiatry* 62(2):245–255.

Insel TR (1997). A neurobiological basis of social attachment. *American Journal of Psychiatry* 154:726–735.

Insel TR (2009). Disruptive insights in psychiatry: Transforming a clinical discipline. *Journal of Clinical Investigation* 119(4):700–705.

Insel TR (2010). The challenge of translation in social neuroscience: A review of oxytocin, vasopressin, and affiliative behavior. *Neuron* 65(6):768–779.

Insel TR and Hulihan TJ (1995). A gender specific mechanism for pair bonding: Oxytocin and partner preference formation in monogamous voles. *Behavioral Neuroscience* 109:782–789.

Insel TR and Shapiro LE (1992). Oxytocin receptor distribution reflects social organization in monogamous and polygamous voles. *Proceedings of the National Academy of Sciences USA* 89(13):5981–5985.

Insel TR and Winslow JT (1998). Serotonin and neuropeptides in affiliative behaviors. *Biological Psychiatry* 44(3):207–219.

Integrative Medicine Advisory Council (2012). Recent History of CAM in the United States, 2012. http://www.imacjohnstown.org/cam/recent/recent.htm

Ishijima M and Kurita H (2007). Identical male twins concordant for Asperger's disorder. *Journal of Autism and Developmental Disorder 37* (2):386–389.

Ishizu T and Zeki S (2011). Toward a brain-based theory of beauty. *PLoS ONE 6*(7):e21852. Epub July 6:10.137/journal.pone.0021852.

Jablonka E and Lamm E (2012). Commentary: The epigenotype: a dynamic network view of development. *International Journal of Epidemiology 41*:16–20.

Jackowski AP, de Araujo CM, de Lacerda ALT, de Jesus Mari J, and Kaufman J (2008). Neurostructural imaging findings in children with post-traumatic stress disorder: Brief Review. *Psychiatry and Clinical Neurosciences 63*:1–8.

Jacobs L (2009). Interview with Lawrence Weed, MD—The father of the problem-oriented medical record looks ahead. *Permanente Journal 13*(3):84–89.

Jacobs LF (2003). The evolution of the cognitive map. *Brain, Behavior, and Evolution 62*(2):128–139.

Jacques JP, Zombek S, Guillain Ch, and Duez P (2004). Cannabis: Experts agree more than they admit. *Revue Medicale de Bruxelles 25*(2):87–92.

Jain S and Mills PJ (2010), Biofield therapies: helpful or full of hype? A best evidence synthesis, *International Journal of Behavioral Medicine 17*, 1, 1–16.

James JE and Gregg ME (2004). Effects of dietary caffeine on mood when rested and sleep restricted. *Human Psychopharmacology 19*(5):333–341.

Joels M (2008). Functional actions of corticosteroids in the hippocampus. *European Journal of Pharmacology 583*(2–3):312–321.

Johansen M, Karterud S, Pedersen G, Gude T, and Falkum E (2004). An investigation of the prototype validity of the borderline DSM-IV construct. *Acta Psychiatrica Scandinavica 109*(4):289–298.

Johnson HC (1978). Integrating the problem-oriented record with a systems approach to case assessment. *Journal of Education for Social Work 14*(3):71–77.

Johnson HC (1980). *Human Behavior and the Social Environment: New Perspectives. Vol. I. Behavior, Psychopathology, and the Brain.* New York: Curriculum Concepts.

Johnson HC (1988). Where is the border? Current issues in the diagnosis and treatment of the borderline. *Clinical Social Work Journal 16*(3):243–260.

Johnson HC (1991). Theories of Kernberg and Kohut: Issues of scientific validation. *Social Service Review 65*(3):403–433.

Johnson HC, Cournoyer DE and Fisher GA (1994). Measuring worker cognitions about parents of children with mental and emotional disabilities. *Journal of Emotional and Behavioral Disorders 2*(2):94–108.

Johnson HC (1999a). Borderline personality disorder. In FJ Turner, ed, *Adult psychopathology,* 2nd ed. pp. 430–456). New York, NY: Free Press.

Johnson HC (1999b). *Psyche, Synapse and Substance: The Role of Neurobiology in Emotions, Behavior, Cognition, and Addiction for Non-Scientists.* Greenfield, MA: Deerfield Valley Publishing.

Johnson HC (2004). *Psyche and Synapse: Expanding Worlds,* 2nd ed. Greenfield, MA: Deerfield Valley Publishing.

Johnson HC and Renaud EF (1997). Professional beliefs about parents of children with mental and emotional disabilities: a cross-discipline comparison. *Journal of Emotional and Behavioral Disorders 5*(3):149–161.

Johnson HC, Cournoyer DE, Fisher GA, Flynn M, McQuillan B, Moriarty S, Richert A, et al. (2001). Children's emotional and behavioral disorders: attributions of parental responsibility by professionals. *American Journal of Orthopsychiatry 70*(3):327–339.

Johnson JE, Christie JF, and Yawkey TD (1999). *Play and early childhood development* (2nd ed.). New York, NY: Longman.

Jolly W, Froom J, and Rosen MG (1980). The genogram. *Journal of Family Practice 10:251–255.*

Jones NA, McFall BA, and Diego MA (2004). Patterns of brain electrical activity in infants of depressed mothers who breastfeed and bottle feed: The mediating role of infant temperament. *Biological Psychology 67*(1–2):103–124.

Kaasinen V, Aalto S, Nagren K, and Rinne JO (2004). Expectation of caffeine induces dopaminergic responses in humans. *European Journal of Neuroscience 19*(8):2352–2356.

Kagan J (1994). *The Nature of the Child*, 10th Anniversary Ed. New York: Basic Books.

Kagan J (2003). Biology, context, and developmental inquiry. *Annual Review of Psychology 54:1–23.*

Kagan J and Zentner M (1996). Early childhood predictors of adult psychopathology. *Harvard Review of Psychiatry 3:341–350.*

Kagan J, Snidman N, and Arcus D (1998). Childhood derivatives of high and low reactivity in infancy. *Child Development 69*(6):1483–1493.

Kalivas PW (2004). Glutamate systems in cocaine addiction. *Current Opinions in Pharmacology 4*(1):23–29.

Kamioka H, Tsutani K Mutoh Y, Okuizum H, Ohta M, Handa S, Okada S, et al. (2011). A systematic review of nonrandomized controlled trials on the curative effects of aquatic exercise. *International Journal of General Medicine 4:239–260.*

Kampe KK, Frith CD, Dolan RJ, and Frith U (2001). Reward value of attractiveness and gaze. *Nature 413*(6856):589.

Kamprath K, Romo-Parra H, Häring M, Gaburro S, Doengi M, Lutz B, and Pape HC (2011). Short-term adaptation of conditioned fear responses through endocannabinoid signaling in the central amygdala. *Neuropsychopharmacology 36*(3):652–663.

Kandel E (1998). A new intellectual framework for psychiatry. *American Journal of Psychiatry 155:457–469.*

Kandel E (2011, November 4). Co-host, *Charlie Rose Brain Series 2* Episode 1, PBS.

Kandel ER, Schwartz JH, and Jessell, TM. (2000). *Principles of Neural Science Fourth Edition.* New York N Y: McGraw-Hill. p. 324.

Karls JM and O'Keefe ME (2008). *Person-in-environment system manual* (2nd ed.). Washington, DC: NASW Press.

Karls JM and Wandrei KE (1994). *Person-in-environment system: The PIE classification for social systems.* Washington, DC: NASW Press.

Karr-Morse R and Wiley MS (1997). *Ghosts from the Nursery: Tracing the Toots of Violence.* New York: The Atlantic Monthly Press.

Kazdin A (2001). *Behavior Modification in Applied Settings* (6th ed.). Belmont, CA: Wadsworth Thomson.

Kazdin AE (1981). Drawing valid inferences from case studies. *Journal of Consulting and Clinical Psychology 49*(2):183–192.

Kempe CH, Silverman FN, Steele BF, Droegemueller W, and Silver HK (1962). The battered-child syndrome. *JAMA 181:17–24.*

Kemperman I, Russ MJ, and Shearin E (1997). Self-injurious behavior and mood regulation in borderline patients. *Journal of Personality Disorders 11*(2):146–157.

Kendall KA (1950). Social work education in review. *Social Service Review* 24:296–309.

Kessler RC, Berglung P, Demler O, Jin R, Merkiangas KR, and Walters EE (2005). Lifetime prevalence and age-of-onset distribution of DSM-IV disorders in the National Comorbidity Survey Replication, *Archives of General Psychiatry* 62:593–602.

Kessler RC, Sonnega A, Bromet E, Hughes M, and Nelson CB (1995). Posttraumatic stress disorder in the National Comorbidity Survey. *Archives of General Psychiatry* 52:1048–1060.

Kety S (1979). Disorders of the human brain. *Scientific American* 241:202–214.

King AC, Cao D, Vanier C, and Wilcox T (2009). Naltrexone decreases heavy drinking rates in smoking cessation treatment: An exploratory study. *Alcoholism: Clinical and Experimental Research* 33(6):1044–1050.

Kirk SA and Kutchins H (1992). *The selling of the DSM: The rhetoric of science in psychiatry.* Hawthorne, NY: Aldine de Gruyter.

Knivsberg AM, Reichelt KL, and Nodland M (2001). Reports ondietary intervention in autistic disorders. *Nutrition Neuroscience* 4(1):25–37.

Knoll AT and Carlezon WA Jr (2010). Dynorphin, stress, and depression. *Brain Research* 16(1314):56–73.

Knoll AT, Muschamp JW, Sillivan SE, Ferguson D, Dietz DM, Meloni EG, Carroll FK. et al. (2011). Kappa opioid receptor signaling in the basolateral amygdala regulates conditioned fear and anxiety in rats. *Biological Psychiatry* 70(5):425–433.

Knutson B, Wolkowitz OM, Cole SW, Chan T, Moore EA, Johnson RC, Terpstra J, et al. (1998). Selective alteration of personality and social behavior by serotonergic intervention. *American Journal of Psychiatry* 155:373–379.

Kober H, Barrett LF, Joseph J, Bliss-Moreau E, Lindquist KA, and Wager TD (2008). Functional networks and cortical-subcortical interactions in emotion: A meta-analysis of neuroimaging studies. *Neuroimage* 42, 998–1031.

Kochanska G (1993). Toward a synthesis of parental socialization and child temperament in early development of conscience. *Child Development* 64:325–347.

Kochanska G (2001). Emotional development in children with different attachment histories: The first three years. *Child Development* 72(2):474–490.

Koenen KC and Widom CS (2009). A prospective study of sex differences in the lifetime risk of posttraumatic stress disorder among abused and neglected children grown up. *Journal of Traumatic Stress* 22:6:566–574.

Koepp MJ, Gunn RN, Lawrence AD, Cunningham VJ, Dagher A, Jones T, Brooks DJ (1998). Evidence for striatal dopamine release during a video game. *Nature* 393(6682):266–268.

Koken JA, Bimbi DS, and Parsons JT (2010). Experiences of Familial Acceptance–Rejection Among Transwomen of Color. *Journal of Family Psychology* 23(6):853–860.

Koob GF (2003). Neuroadaptive mechanisms of addiction: Studies on the extended amygdala. *European Neuropsychopharmacology* 13(6):4422–4452.

Koob GF and Zorrilla EP (2010).Neurobiological mechanisms of addiction: focus on corticotropin-releasing factor. *Current Opinion on Investigating Drugs* 1(1):63–71.

Koob GF and Le Moal M (2008). Addiction and the brain antireward system. *Annual Review of Psychology* 59:29–53.

Kranzler HR and Van Kirk J (2001). Efficacy of naltrexone and acamprosate for alcoholism treatment: A meta-analysis. *Alcohol Clinical and Experimental Research* 25(9):1335–1341.

Kranzler HR, Pierucci-Lagha A, Feinn R, and Hernandez-Avila C (2003). Effects of ondansetron in early- versus late-onset alcoholics: A prospective, open-label study. *Alcohol Clinical and Experimental Research* 7:1150–1115.

Kringelbach ML (2005). The human orbitofrontal cortex: linking reward to hedonic experience. *National Review of Neuroscience* 6(9):691–702. Review.

Kringelbach ML and Berridge KC (2010). The functional neuroanatomy of pleasure and happiness. *Discovery Medicine* 9(49):579–587.

Krystal JH, Cramer JA, Krol WF, Kirk GF, and Rosenheck RA (2001). Naltrexone in the treatment of alcohol dependence. *New England Journal of Medicine* 345:1734–1739.

Kumar A (2011). Long-Term Potentiation at CA3–CA1 Hippocampal Synapses with Special Emphasis on Aging, Disease, and Stress. *Frontiers in Aging Neuroscience* 3:7.

Lazar, SW, Kerr, CE, Wasserman, et al (2005), Meditation experience is associated with increased cortical thickness. *Neuroreport* 16:1893–1897.

Leach, MJ and Gillham, D (2011), Are complementary medicine practitioners implementing evidence based practice? *Complementary Therapies in Medicine* 19:128–136.

Lee HJ, Macbeth A H, Pagani J, and Young, 3. (2009). *Oxytocin: the great facilitator of life.* Retrieved from http://www.ncbi.nlm.nih.gov/pmc/articles/PMC2689929 88(2):127–151.

Lenzenweger MF, Lane MC, Loranger AW, and Kessler RC (2007). DSM-IV personality disorders in the National Comorbidity Survey Replication. *Biological Psychiatry* 62(6):553–564.

Lepine JP, Gastpar M, Mendlewicz J, and Tylee A. (1997). Depression in the community: The first pan-European study DEPRES (Depression Research in European Society). *International Clinical Psychopharmacology* 12(1):19–29.

LePore S (1997). Expressive writing moderates the relation between intrusive thoughts and depressivesymptoms. *Journal of Personality Social Psychology* 73(5):1030–103.

Leszcz M, Yalom ID, and Norden M (1986). The value of inpatient group psychotherapy: Patients' perceptions. *International Group Psychotherapy* 85:411–433.

Levine D, Marziali E, and Hood J (1997). Emotion processing in border line personality disorders. *Journal of Nervous and Mental Diseases* 185(4):240–246.

Lewis DO and Balla DA (1976). *Delinquency and Psychopathology.* New York: Grune and Stratton.

Li CY, Zhou WZ, Zhang PW, Johnson C, Wei L, and Uhl G (2011). Meta-analysis and genome-wide interpretation of genetic susceptibility to drug addiction. *BMC Genomics* 12:508.

Lieberman AF and Van Horn P (2009). Giving voice to the unsayable: Repairing the effects of trauma in infancy and early childhood. *Child and Adolescent Clinics of North America* 18:707–720.

Lieberman AF, Compton NC, van Horn P, and Ghosh Ippen C (2003). *Losing a parent to death in the early years.* Washington, DC: Zero To Three.

Lieberman AF, Van Horn P, and Ghosh Ippen C (2005). Toward evidence-based treatment: Child–parent psychotherapy with preschoolers exposed to marital violence. *Journal of the American Academy of Child and Adolescent Psychiatry* 44(12):1241–1248.

Lietman PS (2012), Herbal medicine development: a plea for a rigorous scientific foundation. *American Journal of Therapeutics* 19:351–356.

Lim MM and Young LJ (2006). Neuropeptidergic regulation of affiliative behavior and social bonding in animals. *Hormones* and *Behavior* 50:506–517.

Linden DJ (2011). *The Compass of Pleasure.* New York: Penguin Group, Viking Press.

Linehan MM (1993A). *Skills treatment manual for treating borderline personality disorder.* New York, NY: Guilford.

Linehan MM (1993B). *Cognitive-behavioral treatment of borderline personality disorder.* New York, NY: Guilford.

Linehan MM, Armstrong HE, Suarez A, Allmon D, and Heard H (1991). Cognitive-behavioral treatment of chronically parasuicidal borderline patients. *Archives of General Psychiatry* 48:1060–1064.

Linehan MM, Comtois KA, Brown MZ, Reynolds SK, Welch SS, Sayrs J, and Korslund KE (2002). *DBT vs non-behavioral treatment by experts in the community: Clinical outcomes at one year* (SK Reynolds, Chair, University of Washington treatment study for borderline personality disorder). Symposium conducted at the annual meeting of the Association for Advancement of Behavior Therapy, Reno, NV.

Linehan MM, Comtois KA, Murray AM, Brown MZ, Gallop RJ, Heard HL, Korslund KE, et al.(2006). Two-year randomized controlled trial and follow-up of dialectical behavior therapy vs therapy by experts for suicidal behaviors and borderline personality disorder. *Archives of General Psychiatry* 63:757–766.

Links PS (1993, February). Psychiatric rehabilitation model for borderline personality disorder. *Canadian Journal of Psychiatry* 38(Suppl. 1):S35–S38.

Linnoila M, Virkkunen M, Scheinin M, Nuutila A, Rimon R, and Goodwin FO (1983). Low cerebrospinal fluid 5-hydroxyindoleacetic acid concentration differentiates impulsive from nonimpulsive violent behavior. *Life Sciences* 33:2609–2614.

Littleton J and Zieglgansberger W (2003). Pharmacological mechanisms of naltrexone and acamprosate in the prevention of relapse in alcohol dependence. *American Journal of Addiction* 12(Suppl. 1):S3–S11.

Liu D, Diorio J, Tannenbaum B, Caldji C, Francis D, and Freedman A (1997). Maternal care, hippocampal glucocorticoid receptors, and hypothalamic–pituitary–adrenal responses to stress. *Science* 277(5332):1659–1662.

Livesley WJ, Jang KL, Jackson DN, and Vernon PA (1993). Genetic and environmental contributions to dimensions of personality disorder. *American Journal of Psychiatry* 150(12):1826–1831.

Lorenz K (1952). *King Solomon's Ring: New light on animal ways.* New York, NY: Crowell.

Lucchetti G, Granero-Lucchetti, AL Bassi, and Nobre MRS (2011). Complementary Spiritist therapy: Systematic review of scientific evidence. *Evidence-Based Complementary and Alternative Medicine* 2011; 835945. 1–18.

Lyons-Ruth K and Jacobvitz D (2008). Attachment Disorganization: Genetic Factors, Parenting Contexts, and Developmental Transformation from Infancy to Adulthood,. In J Cassidy and PR Shaver, eds, *Handbook of attachment: Theory, research, and clinical applications* 2nd ed,(pp. 520–554). New York: Guilford.

Macmillan HL, Georgiades K, Duku EK, Shea A, Steiner M, Niec A, et al. (2009). Cortisol response to stress in female youths exposed to childhood maltreatment: Results of the Youth Mood Project. *Biological psychiatry* 66(7):642–648.

Madhavan A, Bonci A, and Whistler JL (2010). Opioid-Induced GABA potentiation after chronic morphine attenuates the rewarding effects of opioids in the ventral tegmental area. *Journal of Neuroscience* 20; 30(42):14029–14035.

Maguire EA, Burgess N, Donnett JG, Frackowiak RSJ, Firth CD, and O'Keefe J (1998). Knowing where and getting there: A human navigation network. *Science* 280 (5365):921–924.

Maguire EA, Gadian DG, Johnsrude IS, Good CD, Ashburner J, Frackowiak RS, and Frith CD (2000). Navigation-related structural change in the hippocampi of taxi drivers. *PNAS* 97(8):4398–4403.

Mannelli P, Peindl KS, and Wu LT (2011). Pharmacological enhancement of naltrexone treatment for opioid dependence: A review. *Substance Abuse and Rehabilitation* 2:113–123.

Manzo M (2013). Personal communication, March 25th, 2013.

Markovitz PJ (2004). Recent trends in the pharmacotherapy of personality disorders. *Journal of Personality Disorders* 18(1):90–101.

Markovitz PJ and Wagner SC (2003). Efficacy of modafinil augmentation in depression with or without personality disorders. *Journal of Clinical Psychopharmacology* 23:207–209.

Marsicano G, Wotjak CT, Azad SC, Bisogno T, Rammes G, Cascio MG, Hermann H, et al. (2002). The endogenous cannabinoid system controls extinction of aversive memories. *Nature* 418(6897):530–534.

Mason BJ (2001). Treatment of alcohol dependent out patients with acamprosate: A clinical review. *Journal of Clinical Psychiatry* 62(Suppl. 20):42–48.

Mason BJ (2005). Rationale for combining acamprosate and naltrexone in the treatment of alcohol dependence. *Journal of Studies on Alcohol* (Suppl.):148–156.

Masten AS, Hubbard JJ, Gest SD, Tellegen A, Garmezy N, and Ramiriez M (1999). Competence in the context of adversity: Pathways to resilience and maladaptation from childhood to late adolescence. *Developmental Psychopathology* 11(1):143–169.

Masters KS and Spielmans GI (2007), Prayer and health: review, meta-analysis, and research agenda, *Journal of Behavioral Medicine* 30:329–338.

Mastripieri D and Zehr JL (1998). Maternal responsiveness increases during pregnancy and after estrogen treatment in macaques. *Hormones and Behavior* 34:223–230.

Matsumoto M, Higuchi K, Togashi H, Koseki H, Yamaguchi T, Kanno M, and Yoshioka M (2005). Early postnatal stress alters the 50-Htergic modulation to emotional stress at postadolescent period of rats. *Hippocampus* 15:775–781.

Mata J, Thompson RJ, Jaeggi SM, Buschkuel M, Jonides J, and Gotlib IH (2011). Walk on the bright side: Physical activity and affect in major depressive disorder. *Journal of Abnormal Psychology* 121(2):297–308.

Mattaini MA (1999). *Clinical Interventions with Families*. Washington, DC: NASW Press.

Mattaini MA (1993). *More Than a Thousand Words: Graphics for Clinical Practice*. Washington, DC: NASW Press.

Matthews, SC, Camacho, A, Lawson, K, and Dimsdale, JE (2003), Use of herbal medications among 200 psychiatric outpatients: prevalence, patterns of use, and potential dangers, *General Hospital Psychiatry* 25(1):24–26.

Matto HC and Strolin-Goltzman JS (2010). Integrating social neuroscience and social work: Innovations for advancing practice-based research. *Social Work* 55:147–156.

Mauri MC, Rudelli R, Somaschini E, Roncoroni L, Papa R, Mantero M, Longhini M, and Penati G (1996). Neurobiological and psychopharmacological basis in the therapy of bulimia and anorexia. *Progress in Neuropsychopharmacology and Biological Psychiatry* 20(2):207–240.

McCrae RR and Costa PT Jr (2003). *Personality in adulthood: A five-factor theory perspective* (2nd ed.). New York, NY: Guilford.

McCrae RR, Costa PT Jr, Martin TA, Oryol VE, Rukavishnikov AA, Senin IG, Hrebickova M (2004). Consensual validation of personality traits across cultures. *Journal of Research in Personality* 38:179–201.

McEwen BS (2007). Physiology and neurobiology of stress and adaptation: Central role of the brain. *Physiological Review* 87:873–904.

McGartland Rubio D, Schoenbaum EE, and Esposito K (2010). Defining translational research: Implications for training. *Academic medicine : Journal of the Association of American Medical Colleges* 86(3):470–475.

McGilloway A, Hall RE, Lee T, and Bhui KS (2010). A systematic review of personality disorder, race and ethnicity: Prevalence, aetiology and treatment. *BMC Psychiatry* 10:33.

McGuire D (2006). *Attitudes and barriers to evidence-based practice in social work.* Unpublished doctoral dissertation, University of Houston, TX.

McKibbon A, EadyA, and Marks S (1999). PDQ *Evidence-Based Principles and Practice.* Hamilton UK: BC Decker.

McLaughlin D, Adams J, Sibbritt D, and Lui C-W (2012), Sex differences in the use of complementary and alternative medicine in older men and women, *Australasian Journal on Ageing* 31(2):78–82.

McManis MH, Kagan J, Snidman NC, and Woodward SA (2002). EEG asymmetry, power, and temperament in children. *Developmental Psychobiology* 41(2):169–177.

Mead GE, Morley W, Campbell P, et al (2008). Exercise for depression. *Cochrane Database Systems Review*(4):CD004366.

Meaney MJ (2001). Maternal care, gene expression, and the transmission of individual differences in stress reactivity across generations. *Annual Review of Neuroscience* 24:1161–1192.

Meaney MJ, Diorio J, Francis D, Widdowson J, LaPlante P, Caldji C, Sharma S, et al.(1996). Early environmental regulation of forebrain glucocorticoid receptor gene expression: Implications for adrenocortical responses to stress. *Developmental Neuroscience* 18(1–2):49–72.

Meaney MJ, Szyf M, and Seckl JR (2007). Epigenetic mechanisms of perinatal programming of hypothalamic-pituitary-adrenal function and health. *Trends in Molecular Medicine* 13:269–277.

MedicineNet.com (2011). Definition of Metabolism. http://www.medterms.com/script/main/art.asp?articlekey=4359

Mehlman PT, Higley JD, Faucher I, Lilly AA, Taub DM, Vickers J, Suomi SJ, et al. (1995). Correlation of CSF 5-HIAA concentration with sociality and the timing of emigration in free ranging primates. *American Journal of Psychiatry* 152:6.

Mercer J (2001). Attachment therapy using deliberate restraint: An object lesson on the identification of unvalidated treatments. *Journal of Child and Adolescent Psychiatric Nursing* 14(3):105–114.

Mercer JA (2013). *Child Development: Myths and Misunderstandings*, 2nd ed., Los Angeles: Sage.

Mereu G, Fa M, Ferraro L, Cagiano R, Antonelli T, Tattoli M, Ghiglieri V, et al. (2003). Prenatal exposure to a cannabinoid agonist produces memory deficits linked to dysfunction in hippocampal long-term potentiation and glutamate release. *Proceedings of the National Academy of Sciences USA* 100(8):4915–4920.

Merriam Webster Online Dictionary (retrieved 2011). http://www.merriamwebster.com/dictionary/hedonism

Merriam Webster Online Dictionary (retrieved 2011). http://www.merriam-webster.com/dictionary/affiliate

Merriam-Webster Online Dictionary (2013). http://www.merriam-webster.com/dictionary/hedonism

Miller BC (1995). Characteristics of effective day treatment programming for persons with borderline personality disorder. *Psychiatric Services* 46(6):605–608.

Miller BL and Cummings JL (2007). *The Human Frontal Lobes*, 2nd ed. New York: Guilford Press.

Miller BL and Cummings JL (2009). *The Human Frontal Lobes, Second Edition: Functions and Disorders (Science and Practice of Neuropsychology)*. New York: Guilford.

Miller, J (2013). Weight and mortality: Harvard researchers challenge results of obesity analysis. Harvard Gazette, February 23rd, http://news.harvard.edu/gazette/story/2013/02/weight-and-mortality/

Miller JG (1978). *Living Systems.* New York: McGraw-Hill.

Miller WR and Rollnick S (2013). *Motivational interviewing: Helping people change* (3rd ed.). New York, NY: Guilford.

Miltenberger R (2012). *Behavior modification: Principles and procedures* (5th ed.). Belmont, CA: Wadsworth/Cengage Learning.

Minzenberg MJ, Fan J, New AS, Tang CY, and Siever LJ (2008). Frontolimbic structural changes in borderline personality disorder. *Journal of Psychiatric Research* 42(9):727–733.

Miresco MJ and Kirmayer LJ (2006). The persistence of mind-brain dualism in psychiatric reasoning about clinical scenarios. *American Journal of Psychiatry* 163:913–918.

Mish FC, ed. (1988).*Webster's Ninth New Collegiate Dictionary.* Springfield, MA: Merriam-Webster, p. 950.

Mitchell PB and Hadzi-Pavlovic, D (2000). Lithium treatment for bipolar disorder. *Bulletin of the World Health Organization* 78 (4):515–7.

Mobbs D, Greicius MD, Abdel-Azim E, Menon V, and Reiss AL (2003). Humor modulates the mesolimbic reward centers. *Neuron* 40(5):1041–1048.

Mobbs D, Hagan CC, Azim E, Menon V, and Reiss AL (2005). Personality predicts activity in reward and emotional regions associated with humor. *Proceedings of the National Academy of Sciences* November 8:2005; 102(45):16502–16506.

Montgomery H (2001). Codependency through a feminist lens. *Praxis* 1:59–65.

Moran J (2004). Wig-Wise. http://www.youtube.com/watch?v=qtl8wRgtCwg.

XMoraska A, Pollini RA, Boulanger K, Brooks MZ and Teitlebaum L (2010), Physiological adjustments to stress measures following massage therapy: a review of the literature. *Evidence-Based Complementary and Alternative Medicine* 7(4) 409–418.

Morris W, ed. (1975). *The American Heritage dictionary of the English language.* Boston, MA: Houghton Mifflin.

Moser, EI; Kropf E, and Moser M-B (2008). Place Cells, Grid Cells, and the Brain's Spatial Representation System. *Annual Review of Neuroscience* 31:69.

Moyer CA, Rounds J, and Hannum JW (2004). A meta-analysis of massage therapy research. *Psychology Bulletin* 130(1):3–18.

Muller RJ (1992). Is there a neural basis for borderline splitting? *Comprehensive Psychiatry* 33(2):92–104.

Murray CJ and Lopez AD (1997). Global mortality, disability, and the contribution of risk factors: Global burden of disease study. *Lancet* 349(9063):1436–1442.

Myers KM and Carlezon WA Jr (2010). Extinction of drug- and withdrawal-paired cues in animal models: Relevance to the treatment of addiction. *Neuroscience & Biobehavioral Reviews* 35(2):285–302.

Nadal M and Pearce MT (2011). The Copenhagen Neuroaesthetics conference: Prospects and pitfalls for an emerging field. *Brain and Cognition* 76:172–183.

National Association of Social Workers Code of Ethics (2008). https://www.socialworkers. org/pubs/code/default.asp.

National Center for Complementary and Alternative Medicine (NCCAM). http://nccam. nih.gov/

National Center for Health Statistics (2007). National health interview survey, Centers for Disease Control and Prevention, Atlanta, GA 30333h.

National Health and Nutrition Examination Survey (NHANES) (2007). See Ogden and Carroll (2007).

National Institute of Child Health and Human Development (2004). Are child developmental outcomes related to before- and after-school care arrangements? Results from the NICHD study of early child care. *Child Development* 75(1):280–295.

National Institute of Mental Health Culture and Diagnosis Group (2013). http://books.google. com/books/about/Culture_and_Psychiatric_Diagnosis.html?id=oTb3SNJGosYC

National Institute of Mental Health (NIMH, 2013). Criteria, borderline personality disorder. http://www.nimh.nih.gov/health/publications/borderline-personality-disorder/ what-is-borderline-personality-disorder.shtml

National Institute of Mental Health (NIMH) Press Office. (2013, February 28). 5 most common mental illnesses share the same genes.

National Institute on Drug Abuse (NIDA) (2004). http://www.nida.nih.gov/

National Institutes of Health (NIH) (2010).Office of Extramural Research, Grans, and Funding RFA-MH-10–02d. The Human Connectome Project (054)

National Scientific Council on the Developing Child (2005). Excessive Stress Disrupts the Architecture of the Developing Brain: Working Paper #3. http://www.developingchild.net.

Nehlig A (2000). Are we dependent upon coffee and caffeine? A review on human and animal data. *Neuroscience and Biobehavioral Review* 23(4):563–576.

Nehlig A and Boyet S (2000). Dose-response study of caffeine effects on cerebral functional activity with a specific focus on dependence. *Brain Research* 858(1):71–77.

Neigh GN, Gillespie CF, and Nemeroff CB (2009). The neurobiological toll of child abuse and neglect. *Trauma, Violence, and Abuse* 10:389–410.

Nelson JD and Panksepp JB (1996). Oxytocin mediates acquisition of maternally associated odor preferences in preweanling rat pups. *Behavioral Neuroscience* 110:583–592.

Nemeroff CB (2004). Neurobiological consequences of childhood trauma. *Journal of Clinical Psychiatry* 65 (supp. 1):18–28.

Nestler EJ (2000). The molecular basis of long-term plasticity underlying addiction. *National Review of Neuroscience* 2:119–128. (Erratum: *National Review of Neuroscience* 2:215).

New AS, Buchsbaum MS, Hazlett EA, Goodman M, Koenigsberg HW, Lo J, Iskander L, et al. (2004). Fluoxetine increases relative metabolic rate in prefrontal cortex in impulsive aggression. *Psychopharmacology (Berl)*. 176(3–4):451–458.

Newcombe NS (2003). Some controls control too much. *Child Development* 74(4):1050–1052.

Nichols DE (2004). Hallucinogens. *Pharmacological Therapy* 101(2):131–181.

Nower L and Blaszczynski A (2004). *Child and Adolescent Social Work Journal* 21(1):25–45.

Nursing Times.net (2013). Overweight people "live longer" study claims. January 7. http:// www.nursingtimes.net/nursing-practice/clinical-zones/public-health/overweight-people-live-longer-study-claims/5053341.article

Nutt DJ, Lingford-Hughes A, and Chick J (2012). Through a glass darkly: Can we improve clarity about mechanism and aims of medications in drug and alcohol treatments? *Journal of Psychopharmacology* 26(2):199–204.

O'Connor TG and Rutter M (2000). Attachment disorder behavior following severe deprivation: Extension and longitudinal follow-up. *Journal of the American Academy of Child and Adolescent Psychiatry* 39:703–712.

O'Connor TG, Bredenkamp D, and Rutter M (1999). Attachment disturbances and disorders in children exposed to early severe deprivation. *Infant Mental Health Journal* 20:10–29.

O'Connor TG, Marvin RS, Rutter M, Olrick JT, and Britner PA (2003). Child–parent attachment following early institutional deprivation. *Developmental Psychopathology* 15:19–38.

O'Doherty J, Winston J, Critchley H, Perrett D, Burt DM, and Dolan RJ (2003). Beauty in a smile: the role of medial orbitofrontal cortexin facial attractiveness. *Neuropsychologia* 41:147–155.

Ocampo B and Kritikos, A (2011). Interpreting actions: the goal behind mirror neuron function. *Brain Research Reviews* 67:260–267.

Ogden, CL and Carroll MD (2007). Prevalence of overweight, obesity, and extreme obesity among adults: United States. National Health and Nutrition Examination Survey (NHANES).

Osaka N and Osaka M (2005). Striatal reward areas activated by implicit laughter induced by mimic words in humans: a functional magnetic resonance imaging study. *Neuroreport* 16(15):1621–1624.

Ozer DJ and Reise SP (1994). Personality assessment. *Annual Review of Psychology* 45:357–388.

Pace, TWW, and Heim, CM (2011). A short review on the psychoneuroimmunology of posttraumatic stress disorder: From risk factors to medical comorbidities. *Brain, Behavior, and Immunity* 25:6–13.

Paladini CA, Mitchell JM, Williams JT, and Mark G (2004). Cocaine self-administration selectively decreases noradrenergic regulation of metabotropic glutamate receptor-mediated inhibition in dopamine neurons. *Journal of Neuroscience* 24(22):5209–5215.

Palmer RL, Birchall H, Damani S, Gatward N, McGrain L, and Parker L (2003). A dialectical behavior therapy program for people with an eating disorder and borderline personality disorder–description and outcome. *International Journal of Eating Disorders* 33(3):281–226.

Palombo J (1983). Borderline conditions: A perspective from self-psychology. *Clinical Social Work Journal* 11(4):323–338.

Paradiso MA, Bear MF, and Connors BW (2007). *Neuroscience: Exploring the Brain.* Hagerstown, MD: Lippincott Williams & Wilkins. p. 718.

Paredes RG and Ågmo A (2004). Has dopamine a physiological role in the control of sexual behavior? A critical review of the evidence. *Progress in Neurobiology* 73(3):179–225.

Paris J (1993). The treatment of borderline personality disorder in light of the research on its long-term outcomes. *Canadian Journal of Psychiatry* 38(Suppl. 1):528–534.

Paris J (1997). Childhood trauma as an etiological factor in the personality disorders. *Journal of Personality Disorders* 11(1):34–49.

Paris J, Zweig-Frank H, Kin NM, Schwartz G, Steiger H, and Nair NP (2004). Neurobiological correlates of diagnosis and underlying traits in patients with borderline personality disorder compared with normal controls. *Psychiatry Research* 121(3):239–252.

Patchev VK, Montkowski A, Rouskova D, Koranyi L, Holsboer F, and Almeida OF (1997). Neonatal treatment of rats with the neuroactive steroid tetrahydrodeoxycorticosterone (THDOC) abolishes the behavioral and neuroendocrine consequences of adverse early life events. *Journal of Clinical Investigation* 99(5):962–966.

Pecina S and Smith KS (2010). Hedonic and motivational roles of opioids in food reward: implications for overeating disorders. *Pharmacology, Biochemistry, Behavior* 97(1):34–46.

Pennington BF (2002). *The development of psychopathology: Nature and nurture.* New York, NY: Guilford.

Pennisi E (2003). Gene counters struggle to get the right answer. *Science* 301(5636):1040–1041.

Perry BD (2002). Childhood experience and the expression of genetic potential: What childhood neglect tells us about nature and nurture. *Brain and Mind* 3:79–100.

Perry BD (2006). Applying principles of neurodevelopment to clinical work with maltreated and traumatized children: the neurosequential model of therapeutics, pp. 27–52 in NB Webb, ed. *Working with traumatized youth in child welfare.* New York: The Guilford Press.

Perry BD and Szalavitz M (2006). *The Boy Who Was Raised as a Dog And Other Stories from a Child Psychiatrist's Notebook: What Traumatized Children Can Teach Us About Loss, Love, and Healing.* New York: Basic Books.

Pertwee RG and Ross RA (2002). Cannabinoid receptors and their ligands (Review). *Prostaglandins Leukot Essential Fatty Acids* 66(2–3):101–121.

Pervanidou P (2008). Biology of post-traumatic stress disorder in childhood and adolescence. *Journal of Neuroendocrinology,* 20:632–638.

Phelps EA and LeDoux JE (2005). Contribution of the amygdala to emotion processing: from animal models to human behaviour. *Neuron* 48:175–187.

Phillips MI and Sierra M (2003). Depersonalization disorder: A functional neuroanatomical perspective. *Stress* 6(3):157–165.

Pidoplichko VI, Noguchi J, Areola OO, Liang Y, Peterson J, Zhang T, and Dani JA (2004). Nicotinic cholinergic synaptic mechanisms in the ventral tegmental area contribute to nicotine addiction. *Learning and Memory* 11(1):60–69.

Pietropaolo S, Branchi I, Cirulli F, Chiarotti F, Aloe L, and Alleva E (2004). Long-term effects of the periadolescent environment on exploratory activity and aggressive behaviour in mice: Social versus physical enrichment. *Physiology and Behavior* 81(3):443–453.

Pimlott-Kubiak, S and Cortina, LM (2003). Gender, victimization, and outcomes: Reconceptualizing risk. *Journal of Consulting and Clinical Psychology,* 71:528–539.

Pinel JPJ (2011). *Biopsychology,* 8th ed. Boston: Pearson Education/Allyn and Bacon.

Poulton R, Milne BJ, Craske MG, and Menzies RG (2001). A longitudinal study of the etiology of separation anxiety. *Behavior Research and Therapy* 39(12):1395–1410.

Proust M (1913). *À la recherche du temps perdu (In Search of Lost Time, also translated as Remembrance of Things Past).* Paris: Bernard Grasset.

PubMed (ongoing updates). National Institutes of Health, http://www.ncbi.nlm.nih.gov/pubmed

Purves D, Augustine GJ, Fitzpatrick D, Hall WC, LaMantia AS, McNamara JO, and White LE (2008). *Neuroscience,* 4th ed. Sunderland, MA: Sinauer Associates.

Purves D, Augustine GJ, Fitzpatrick D, Katz LC, LaMantia AS, McNamara JO, and Williams SM (2001). *Neuroscience* (2nd ed.). Sunderland, MA: Sinauer.

Purves WK, Sadava D, Orians GH, and Heller HC (2001). *Life: The science of biology* (6th ed.). Sunderland, MA: Sinauer.

Raleigh MJ, McGuire MT, Brammer GL, Pollack DB, and Yuwiler A (1991). Serotonergic mechanisms promote dominance acquisition in adult male vervet monkeys. *Brain Research* 559(2):181–190.

Ramsey RF (2011). *Welcome to the PIE website!* http://www.ucalgary.ca/sw/ramsay/#What-is-PIE

Rasmussen P, Brassard P, Adser H, Pedersen ML, Leick L, Hart E, Secher NH, et al. (2009). Evidence for a release of brain-derived neurotrophic factor from the brain during exercise. *Experimental Physiology* 94(10):1062–1069.

Ratey J (2008). *Spark: The Revolutionary New Science of Exercise and the Brain.* New York: Little, Brown, and Co.

Rath LL (2009), Scientific ways to study intercessory prayer as an intervention in clinical research, *Journal of Perinatal and Neonatal Nursing* 23(1):71–77.

Ravven, SE, Zimmerman, MB, Schultz, SK, and Wallace, RB (2011), 12-month herbal medicine use for mental health from the National Comorbidity Survey Replication (NCS-R), *Annals of Clinical Psychiatry* 23 (2):83–94.

Regier DA, Boyd JH, Burke JD Jr, Rae DS, Myers JK, Kramer M, Robins LN, George LK, Karno M, and Locke BC (1988). One-month prevalence of mental disorders in the United States, based on five epidemiologic catchment area sites. *Archives of General Psychiatry* 45(11):977–986.

Regier DA, Kuhl EA, and Kupfer DJ (2013). The DSM-5: Classification and criteria changes. *World Psychiatry* 12(2):92–98.

Reis E (2009). *Bodies in doubt: an American history of intersex*, Baltimore: Johns Hopkins University Press.

Reuter J, Raedler T, Rose M, Hand I, Glascher J, and Buchel C (2005). Pathological gambling is linked to reduced activation of the mesolimbic reward system. *Nature Neuroscience* 8:147–148.

Revenson TA and Seidman E (2002). Looking backward and moving forward: Reflections on a quarter century of community psychology. In TA Revenson, AR D'Augelli, SE French, DL Hughes, and D Livert, eds, *Handbook of community psychology* (pp. 3–31). New York, NY: Kluwer Academic/Plenum.

Richters MM and Volkmar FR (1994). Reactive attachment disorder of infancy or early childhood. *Journal of the American. Academy of Child and Adolescent Psychiatry* 33(3):328–332.

Rinne T, van den Brink W, Wouters L, and van Dyck R. (2002). SSRI treatment of borderline personality disorder: A randomized, placebo-controlled clinical trial for female patients with borderline personality disorder. *American Journal of Psychiatry* 159(12):2048–2054.

Ritvo ER, Freeman BJ, Ornitz EM, and Tanguay PE, eds (1976). *Autism: Diagnosis, Current Research, and Management.* New York: Spectrum.

Rizzolatti, G and Craighero, L (2004). The mirror neuron system. *Annual Review of Neuroscience* 27:169–192.

Robertson J and Robertson J (1989). *Separations and the very young.* London, England: Free Association Books.

Robins CJ and Chapman AL (2004). Dialectical behavior therapy: Current status, recent developments, and future directions. *Journal of Personality Disorders* 18(1):73–89.

Robins CJ and Koons CR (2004). Dialectical behavior therapy for severe personality disorders. In JJ Magnavita, ed, *Treating personality disorders: Theory, practice, and research* (pp. 117–139). New York, NY: Guilford.

Rothbart MK (1989). Temperament and development. In GA Kohnstamm, JE Bates, and MK Rothbart, eds, *Temperament in childhood* (pp. 187–247). Chichester, England: Wiley.

Rothbart MK (2011). *Temperament, personality, and development.* New York, NY: Guilford.

Rothbart MK, Ahadi SA, and Evans DE (2000). Temperament and personality: Origins and outcomes. *Journal of Personality and Social Psychology* 78(1):122–135.

Rothbart MK, Sheese BE, Rosario, Rueda MR, and Posner MI (2011). Developing mechanisms of self-regulation in early life. *Emotion Review* 3(2):207–213.

Rothstein E (2004, March 27). The brain? It's a jungle in there. *New York Times Arts and Ideas*, p. B7.

Rotunda RJ, West L, and O'Farrell TJ (2004). Enabling behavior in a clinical sample of alcohol-dependent clients and their partners. *Substance Abuse Treatment* 26(4):269–276.

Rubak S, Sandbaek A, Lauritzen T, and Christensen B (2005). Motivational interviewing: A systematic review and meta-analysis. *British Journal of General Practice* 55(513):305–312.

Rush CR and Stoops WW (2012). Agonist replacement therapy for cocaine dependence: A translational review. *Future Medicinal Chemistry* 4(2):245–265.

Russ MJ, Campbell SS, Kakuma T, Harrison K, and Zanine E (1999). EEG theta activity and pain insensitivity in self-injurious borderline patients. *Psychiatry Research* 89(3):201–214.

Rutter M, Kreppner J, Croft C, Murin M, Colvert E, Beckett C, Castle J, et al.(2007). Early adolescent outcomes of institutionally deprived and non-deprived adoptees. III. Quasi-autism. *Journal of Child Psychology and Psychiatry* 48(12):1200–1207.

Saal D, Dong Y, Bonci A, and Malenka RC (2003). Drugs of abuse and stress trigger a common synaptic adaptation in dopamine neurons. *Neuron* 37(4):577–582.

Sadock BJ and Sadock VA (2003). *Synopsis of psychiatry* (9th ed.). Philadelphia, PA: Lippincott Williams and Wilkins.

Salamone J, Correa M, Mingote S, and Weber SM (2003). Nucleus accumbens dopamine and the regulation of effort in food-seeking behavior: Implications for studies of natural motivation, psychiatry, and drug abuse. *Journal of Pharmacology and Experimental Therapeutics* 305(1):1–8.

Saleebey D (2001). *The Strengths Perspective in Social Work Practice*, 3rd ed. Boston: Pearson, Allyn, and Bacon.

Salimpoor VN, Benovoy M, Larcher K, Dagher A, and Zatorre RJ (2011) Anatomically distinct dopamine release during anticipation and experience of peak emotion to music. *Nature Neuroscience* 14(2):257–262.

Samuel DB and Widiger TA (2010). Comparing personality disorder models: Cross-method assessment of the FFM and DSM-IV-TR. *Journal of Personality Disorders* 24(6):721–745.

Sanchez NF, Sanchez JP, and Danoff A (2009). Health care utilization, barriers to care, and hormone usage among male-to-female transgender persons in New York City. *American Journal of Public Health* 99(4):713–719.

Sanislow CA, Grilo CM, Morey LC, Bender DS, Skodol AE, Gunderson JG, Shea MT, et al. (2002). Confirmatory factor analysis of DSM-IV criteria for borderline personality disorder: Findings from the Collaborative Longitudinal Personality Disorders Study. *American Journal of Psychiatry* 159:284–290.

Scafidi F and Field T (1996). Massage therapy improves behavior in neonates born to HIV-positive mothers. *Journal of Pediatric Psychology* 21(6):889–897.

Scannapieco, M. and Connell-Carrick, K (2005). *Understanding Child Maltreatment: An Ecological and Developmental Perspective*. Oxford: Oxford University Press.

Schechter DS and Willheim E (2009). Disturbances of attachment and parental psychopathology in early childhood. *Child & Adolescent Psychiatric Clinics of North America* 18(3):665–686.

Schechter DS, Myers MM, Brunelli SA, Coates SW, Zeanah CH, Davies M, Grienenberger JF, et al. (2006). Traumatized mothers can change their minds about their toddlers:

Understanding how a novel use of videofeedback supports positive change of maternal attributions. *Infant Mental Health Journal* 27(5):429–447.

Schechter, DS, Willheim E, Hinojosa C, Scholfield-Kleinman, K, Turner JB, McCaw J, Zeanah CH, and Myers MM (2010). Subjective and objective measures of parent-child relationship dysfunction, child separation distress, and joint attention. *Psychiatry: Interpersonal and Biological Processes* 73(2), 130–144.

Scherag S, Hebebrand J, and Hinney A (2010). Eating disorders: The current status of molecular genetic research. *European Child & Adolescent Psychiatry* 19(3):211–226.

Schloegl H, Percik R, Horstmann A, Villringer A, and Stumvoll M (2011). Peptide hormones regulating appetite—focus on neuroimaging studies in humans. *Diabetes/Metabolism Research and Reviews* 27(2):104–112.

Schlosberg A (1976). Some factors and issues concerning community psychiatry. *International Journal of Social Psychiatry* 22(2):120–129.

Schmahl CG, McGlashan TH, and Bremner JD (2002). Neurobiological correlates of borderline personality disorder. *Psychopharmacology Bulletin* 36(2):69–87.

Schore, AN (2003). *Affect Dysregulation and Disorders of the Self.* New York: W.W. Norton and Company.

Schore AN (1994). *Affect Regulation and the Origin of the Self: The Neurobiology of Emotional Development.* Mahwah, NJ: Erlbaum.

Schore, JR and Schore, AN (2008). Modern attachment theory: The central role of affect regulation in development and treatment. *Clinical Social Work Journal* 36:9–20.

Schriver J (1995). *Human Behavior in the Social Environment*, 2nd ed. Boston: Allyn Bacon.

Schuckit MA (1985). Genetics and the risk for alcoholism. *Journal of the American Medical Association* 254(18):2614–2617.

Schwartz JM, Stoessel PW, Baxter LR Jr, Martin KM, and Phelps ME (1996). Systematic change in cerebral glucose metabolic rate after successful behavior modification treatment of obsessive-compulsive disorder. *Archives of General Psychiatry* 53(2):109–113.

Scientific American. Neurons for good and bad surprises. Podcast. September 20: 2007. http://www.scientificamerican.com/podcast/episode.cfm?id=20BE476F-E7F2-99DF-3A8F766FBB0A19C3

Scott D (2002). Adding meaning to measurement: The value of qualitative methods in practice research. *British Journal of Social Work* 32:923–930.

Searle JR (2000). Consciousness. *Annual Review of Neuroscience* 23:557–578.

Seckl JR (2004). Prenatal glucocorticoids and long-term programming. *European Journal of Endocrinology* 151(suppl. 3):U49–U62.

Segal ZV, Williams JMG, and Teasdale JD (2012). Mindfulness-based Cognitive Therapy for Depression: A New Approach to Preventing Relapse 2nd eds New York: Guilford.

Selye H (1976). *The stress of life.* New York, NY: McGraw-Hill.

Sesack SR and Grace AA (2010). Cortico-basal ganglia reward network: microcircuitry. *Neuropsychopharmacology* 35(1):27–47.

Seung HS (2010). *I am my connectome.* Video TED Talks Sept 28th2010. http://www.ted.com/talks/sebastian_seung.html

Seung HS (2012). *Connectome: How the brain's wiring makes us who we are.* Boston, MA: Houghton Mifflin Harcourt.

Sevilla-Dedieu C, Kovess-Masfety V, Haro JM, Fernandez A, Vilagut G, Alonso, J (2010), Seeking help for mental health problems outside the conventional health care system:

results from the European Study of the Epidemiology of Mental Disorders (ESEMeD), *La Revue canadienne de psychiatrie* 55(9):586–597.

Shalev AY (1996). Stress versus traumatic stress: from acute homeostratic reactions to chronic psychopathology. In van der Kolk BA, McFarlane AC, and Weisaeth L (eds), *Traumatic Stress: The Effects of Overwhelming Experience on Mind, Body, and Society*, pp. yy–101. New York: The Guilford Press.

Shalev AY (2009). Posttraumatic stress disorder (PTSD) and stress related disorders. *Psychiatric Clinics of North America* 32(3):687–704.

Sher L (2003). The placebo effect on mood and behavior: Possible role of opioid and dopamine modulation of the hypothalamic–pituitary–adrenal system. *Forsch Komplementarmed Klass Naturheilkd* 10(2):61–68.

Shippee TP, Schafer MH, and Ferraro KF (2012), Beyond the barriers: racial discrimination and use of complementary and alternative medicine among Black Americans, *Social Science & Medicine*, 74, 1155–1162.

Shizgal P and Arvanitogiannis A (2003). Neuroscience: Gambling on dopamine. *Science* 299(5614):1856–1858.

Sierra A, Encinas JM, and Maletic-Savatic M (2011). Adult human neurogenesis: From microscopy to magnetic resonance imaging. *Frontiers in Neuroscience* 5:47.

Silk KR (2000). Borderline personality disorder: Overview of biological factors. *Psychiatric Clinics of North America* 23:61–75.

Simon NG, Kaplan JR, Hu S, Register TC, and Adams MR (2004). Increased aggressive behavior and decreased affiliative behavior in adult male monkeys after long-term consumption of diets rich in soy protein and isoflavones. *Hormones and Behavior* 45(4):278–284.

Singer F and Zumoff B (1992). Subnormal serum testosterone levels in male internal medicine residents. *Steroids.* 57(2):86–89.

Singh N (2000, April). *Reappraising assessment. Keynote address.* Conference on Family Support and Children's Mental Health, Research and Training Center, Portland State University, Portland, OR.

Slade A, Grienenberger J, Bernbach E, Levy D, and Locker A (2005). Maternal reflective functioning, attachment, and the transmission gap: A preliminary study. *Attachment and Human Development* 7(3):283–298.

Slotkin TA, Barnes GA, McCook EC, and Seidler FJ (1996). Programming of brainstem serotonin transporter development by prenatal glucocorticoids. *Brain Research and Developmental Brain Research* 93(1–2):155–161.

Smail D (1999). Power, the environment and community psychology: The influence of power on psychological functioning: Community psychology perspectives. *Journal of Community and Applied Social Psychology* 9(2):75–78.

Small DM, Jones-Gotman M, and Dagher A (2003). Feeding-induced dopamine release in dorsal striatum correlates with meal pleasantness ratings in healthy human volunteers. *Neuroimage* 4:1709–1715.

Smith College School of Social Work (2008). Relational paradigms and their clinical applications. Celebrating 90 Years of Clinical Social Work Education (special issue). *Smith College Studies in Social Work* 78(2–3).

Smith GT, Fischer S, Cyders MA, Annus AM, Spillane NS, and McCarthy DM (2007). On the validity and utility of discriminating among impulsivity-like traits. *Assessment* 14:155–170.

Smyke AT, Dumitrescu A, and Zeanah CH (2002). Disturbances of attachment in young children: I. The continuum of caretaking casualty. *Journal of the American Academy of Child and Adolescent Psychiatry* 41(8):972–982.

Soloff P, Nutche J, Goradia D, and Diwadka Vr (2008). Structural brain abnormalities in borderline personality disorder: A voxel-based morphometry study. *Psychiatry Research* 164(3):223–236.

Solstad T, Boccara CN, Kropff E, Moser MB, and Moser EI (2008). Representation of geometric borders in the entorhinal cortex. *Science* 322(5909):1865–1868.

Soyka M and Chick J (2003). Use of acamprosate and opioid antagonists in the treatment of alcohol dependence: A European perspective. *American Journal of Addiction* 12(Suppl. 1):S69–S80.

Springer T and Silk KR (1996). A review of inpatient group therapy for borderline personality disorder. *Harvard Review of Psychiatry* 3(5):268–278.

Squire, LR (1992). Memory and the hippocampus: a synthesis from findings with rats, monkeys, and humans. *Psychological Review* 99(2):195–231.

Stalenheim EC, von Knorring L, and Oreland L (1997). Platelet monoamine oxidase activity as a biological marker in a Swedish forensic psychiatric population. *Psychiatry Research* 69(2–3):79–87.

Stanley B, Molcho A, Stanley M, Winchel R, Gameroff MJ, Parsons B, and Mann JJ (2000). Association of aggressive behavior with altered serotonergic function in patients who are not suicidal. *American Journal of Psychiatry* 157:609–614.

Steegers-Theunissen RP, Obermann-Borst SA, Kremer D, Lindemans J, Siebel C, Steegers EA, Slagboom PE, and Heijmans BT (2009). Periconceptional maternal folic acid use of 400 microg per day is related to increased methylation of the IGF2 gene in the very young child. *PLoS One* 4:e7845.

Steeves TDL, Miyasaki J, Zurowski M, Lang AE, Pellecchia G, Van Eimeren T, Rusjan P et al. (2009). Increased striatal dopamine release in Parkinsonian patients with pathological gambling: a [^{11}C] raclopride PET study. *Brain* 132(Pt 5):1376–1385.

Stein A. (2007). *Prologue to Violence: Child Abuse, Dissociation, and Crime.* Mahway: The Analytic Press.

Stein DJ, Hollander E, Cohen L, Frenkel M, Saoud JB, DeCaria C, Aronowitz B, Levin A, Liebowitz MR, and Cohen L (1993). Neuropsychiatric impairment in impulsive personality disorders. *Psychiatry Research* 48(3):257–266.

Stien PT and Kendall JC (2004). *Psychological Trauma and the Developing Brain: Neurologically Based Interventions for Troubled Children.* New York: The Haworth Press, Inc.

Steinberg BJ, Trestman R, Mitropoulou V, Serby M, Silverman J, Coccaro E, Weston S, de Vegvar M, and Siever LJ (1997). Depressive response to physostigmine challenge in borderline personality disorder patients. *Neuropsychopharmacology* 17(4):264–273.

Stellar JR, Kelley AE, and Corbett D (1983). Effects of peripheral and central blockade on lateral hypothalamus self-stimulation: Evidence for both reward and motor deficits. *Pharmacology, Biochemistry, and Behavior* 433–442.

Stice E, Spoor S, Bohon C, and Small DM (2008). Relation between obesity and striatal response to food is moderated by TAQI A1 allele. *Science* 322:449–452.

Stice E, Yokum S, Burger KS, Epstein LH, and Small DM (2011a). Youth at risk for obesity show greater activation of striatal and somatosensory regions to food. *Journal of Neuroscience* 31(12):4360–4366.

382 References

Stice E, Yokum S, Zald D, and Dagher A (2011b). Dopamine-based reward circuitry responsivity, genetics, and overeating. *Current Topics in Behavioral Neuroscience* 6:81–93.

Stien PT and Kendall JC (2004). *Psychological Trauma and the Developing Brain: Neurologically Based Interventions for Troubled Children*. New York: The Haworth Press, Inc.

Stone MH (1987). Psychotherapy of borderline patients in light of long-term follow-up. *Bulletin of the Menninger Clinic* 51(3):231–247.

Stone MH (1994). Characterologic subtypes of the borderline personality disorder. With a note on prognostic factors. *Psychiatric Clinics of North America* 17(4):773–784.

Stone MH (2006). Management of borderline personality disorder: A review of psychotherapeutic approaches. *World Psychiatry* 5(1):15–20.

Stovall KC and Dozier M (2000). The development of attachment in new relationships: Single subject analyses for ten foster infants. *Development and Psychopathology* 12:133–156.

Strohman RC (2003). Genetic determinism as a failing paradigm in biology and medicine: Implications for health and wellness. *Journal of Social Work Education* 39(2):169–191.

Suomi SJ and Harlow HF (1971) Monkeys without play. in Bruner JS, Jolly A and Sylva K, eds. (1976). *Play: Its Role in Development and Evolution*. New York, Basic Books.

Sussman S and Sussman AN (2011). Considering the definition of addiction. *International Journal of Environmental Research and Public Health* 8(10):4025–4038.

Sutoo D and Akiyama K (2004). Music improves dopaminergic neurotransmission: Demonstration based on the effect of music on blood pressure regulation. *Brain Research* 1016(2):255–262.

Szabo B, Siemes S, and Wallmichrath I (2002). Inhibition of GABAergic neurotransmission in the ventral tegmental area by cannabinoids. *European Journal of Neuroscience* 15(12):2057–2061.

Takayanagi Y, Yoshida M, Bielsky IF, Ross HE, Kawamata M, Onaka T, Yanagisawa T, et al. (2005). Pervasive social deficits, but normal parturition, in oxytocin receptor-deficient mice. *Proceedings of the National Academy of Sciences USA* 102:16096–16101.

Talbot M (1998, May 24). Attachment theory: The ultimate experiment. *New York Times Magazine*, pp. 24–54.

Tashiro T and Mortensen L (2006). Translational research: How social psychology can improve psychotherapy. *American Psychologist* 61: 959–966.

Tashiro T and Mortensen L (2008). Translational research: how social psychology can improve psychotherapy. *American Psychologist* 61(9):959–966.

Taylor E (2003). Practice methods for working with children who have biologically based mental disorders: A bioecological model. *Families in Society* 84(1):39–50.

Taylor EH (1989). Schizophrenia: Fire in the brain. *Social Work* 34:258–261.

Taylor EH (2006). The weaknesses of the Strengths Perspective: Mental health as a case in point. *Best Practices in Mental Health* 2(11):1–29.

Taylor SE and Gonzaga GC (2007). Affiliative response to stress: a social neuroscience model. In Harmon-Jones E and Winkielman P, *Social Neuroscience: Integrating Biological and Psychological Explanations of Social Behavior*, pp. 454–473. New York: The Guilford Press.

Teicher MH, Ito Y, Glod CA, Andersen SL, Dumont N, and Ackerman E (1997). Preliminary evidence for abnormal cortical development in physically and sexually abused children using EEG coherence and MRI. *Annals of the New York Academy of Sciences* 821:160–175.

Teicher MH, Andersen SL, Polcari A, Anderson CM, and Navalta CP (2002). Developmental neurobiology of childhood stress and trauma. *Psychiatric Clinics of North America* 25:397–426.

Teicher MH, Dumont NL, Ito Y, Vaituzis C, Giedd JN, and Andersen SL (2004). Childhood neglect is associated with reduced corpus callosum area. *Biological Psychiatry* 56:80–85.

Tekur P, Nagarathna R, Chametcha S, Hankey A, and Nagendra HR (2012). A comprehensive yoga programs improves pain, anxiety and depression in chronic low back pain patients more than exercise: an RCT. *Complementary Therapeutic Medicine* 20(3):107–118.

Terkelsen K (1983). Schizophrenia and the Family II. Adverse effects of family therapy. *Family Process* 22;191–200.

Terr L (1990). *Too scared to cry.* New York: Basic Books.

Thomas A and Chess S (1977). *Temperament and development.* New York, NY: Brunner/Mazel.

Thomas P, Jones J, Evans, JM, and Leslie SJ (2012), Factors influencing the use of complementary and alternative medicine and whether patients inform their primary care physician, *Complementary Therapies in Medicine* 20:45–53.

Thompson AM, Swant J, Gosnell BA, and Wagner JJ (2004). Modulation of long-term potentiation in the rat hippocampus following cocaine self-administration. *Neuroscience* 127(1):177–185.

Thompson PM, Hayashi KM, Simon SL, Geaga JA, Hong MS, Sui Y, Lee JY, et al. (2004). Structural abnormalities in the brains of human subjects who use methamphetamine. *Journal of Neuroscience* 24(26):6028–6036.

Tizard B and Rees J (1974). A comparison of the effects of adoption, restoration to the natural mother, and continued institutionalization on the cognitive development of four-year-old children. *Child Development* 45(1):92–99.

Torgersen S, Lygren S, Oien PA, Skre I, Onstad S, Edvardsen J, Tambs K, and Kringlen E (2000). A twin study of personality disorders. *Comprehensive Psychiatry* 41(6):416–425.

Torrey EF (1992). *Freudian Fraud: The Malignant Effect of Freud's Theory on American Thought and Culture.* New York: HarperCollins.

Tottenham N and Sheridan MA (2010). A review of adversity, the amygdala and the hippocampus: a consideration of developmental timing. *Frontiers in human neuroscience* 3:68:1–18.

Trickett PK, Noll JG, Susman EJ, and Shenk CE, and Putnam FW (2010). Attenuation of cortisol across development for victims of sexual abuse. *Development and psychopathology* 22:165–175.

Trivedi MH, Greer TL, Church TS, Carmody TJ, Grannemann BD, Galper DI, Dunn AL, et al. (2011). Exercise as an augmentation treatment of nonremitted major depressive disorder: a randomized, parallel dose comparison. *Journal of Clinical Psychiatry* 72(5):677–684.

Tse WS and Bond AJ (2002). Serotonergic intervention affects both social dominance and affiliative behaviour. *Psychopharmacology (Berl)* 161(3):324–330.

Twardosz S and Lutzker JR (2010). Child maltreatment and the developing brain: A review of neuroscience perspectives. *Aggression and Violent Behavior* 15:59–68.

Tzschentke TM and Schmidt WJ (2003). Glutamatergic mechanisms in addiction. *Molecular Psychiatry* 8(4):373–382.

United States Centers for Disease Control and Prevention (CDC) (2012). Autism prevalence data.

University of Washington Digital Anatomist Program, Seattle (2011). Website. www9.biostr. washington.edu/da.html

U.S. Department of Health and Human Services (2009). Child Maltreatment, 2007. Washington, DC: Government Printing Office. Retrieved August 2011 from http://www. acf.hhs.gov/programs/cb/pubs/cm07/cm07.pdf

U.S. Department of Health and Human Services (2010). *How tobacco smoke causes disease: The biology and behavioral basis for smoking-attributable disease: A report of the Surgeon General.* Atlanta, GA: U.S. Department of Health and Human Services, Centers for Disease Control and Prevention, National Center for Chronic Disease Prevention and Health Promotion, Office on Smoking and Health.

U.S. Department of Health and Human Services (1999). *Mental health: A Report of the Surgeon General.* Washington, DC: Department of Public Health, Department of Health and Human Services.

Uzuner O, Mailoa J, Russell Ryan R, and Sibanda T (2010). Semantic relations for problem-oriented medical records. *Artificial Intelligence in Medicine 50*(2):63–73.

Vadakkan KI (2011). A possible mechanism of transfer of memories from the hippocampus to the cortex. *Med Hypotheses 77*(2):234–243.

Valjent E, Pages C, Herve D, Girault JA, and Caboche J (2004). Addictive and non-addictive drugs induce distinct and specific patterns of ERK activation in mouse brain. *European Journal of Neuroscience 19*(7):1826–1836.

Van den Boom DC (1994). The influence of temperament and mothering on attachment and exploration: An experimental manipulation of sensitive responsiveness among lower-class mothers with irritable infants. *Child Development 65*:1457–1477.

van der Kolk BA (1996). The body keeps the score: approaches to the psychobiology of posttraumatic stress disorder. In van der Kolk, BA, McFarlane, AC, and Weisaeth, L, eds, *Traumatic Stress: The Effects of Overwhelming Experience on Mind, Body, and Society* (pp. 214–241). New York: The Guilford Press.

van der Kolk BA (2003). Posttraumatic stress disorder and the nature of trauma. In M Solomon and D Siegel (eds.), *Healing Trauma* (pp. 168–195). New York: W.W. Norton.

van der Kolk BA (2009). Developmental trauma disorder: towards a rational diagnosis for chronically traumatized children. *Praxis der Kinderpsychologie und Kinderpsychiatrie 58*(8):572–586.

van der Kolk, BA (2006), Clinical implications of neuroscience research in PTSD, *Annals New York Academy of Sciences 1071*:277–293.

van der Kolk BA (2009). Developmental trauma disorder: towards a rational diagnosis for chronically traumatized children. *Praxis der Kinderpsychologie und Kinderpsychiatrie 58*(8):572–586.

van der Vaart, HB, Gijsen, VMGJ, de Wildt, SN and Koren, Gideon (2009), A systematic review of the therapeutic effects of Reiki, *The Journal of Alternative and Complementary Medicine 15*(11):1157–1169.

van Eimeren T, Ballanger B, Pellecchia G, Miyasaki JM, Lang AE, and Strafella AP (2009). Dopamine agonists diminish value sensitivity of the orbitofrontal cortex: A trigger for pathological gambling in Parkinson's disease? *Neuropsychopharmacology 34*(13):2758–2766.

Vandenschuren LJ, Niesink RJ, Van J, and Ree M (1997). The neurobiology of social play behavior in rats. *Neuroscience and Biobehavioral Review 21*(3):309–326.

Van Elzakker, MB; Fevurly RD, Breindel T, and Spencer RL (2008). Environmental novelty is associated with a selective increase in Fos expression in the output elements of the hippocampal formation and the perirhinal cortex. *Learning & Memory* 15(12):899–908.

Van Voorhees E and Scarpa A (2004). The effects of child maltreatment on the hypothalamic-pituitary-adrenal axis. *Trauma, Violence, and Abuse* 5(4):333–352.

Vasterling JJ and Brewin CR, eds (2005). *Neuropsychology of PTSD: Biological, Cognitive, and Clinical Perspectives.* New York: The Guilford Press.

Vazquez-Borsetti P, Celada P, Cortes R, and Artigas F (2011). Simultaneous projections from prefrontal cortex to dopaminergic and serotonergic nuclei. *International Journal of Neuropsychopharmacology* 14(3):289–302.

Ventura R, Alcaro A, Mandolesi L, and Puglisi-Allegra S (2004). In vivo evidence that genetic background controls impulse-dependent dopamine release induced by amphetamine in the nucleus accumbens. *Journal of Neurochemistry* 89(2):494–502.

Verkes RJ, Fekkes D, Zwinderman AH, Hengeveld MW, Van der Mast RC, Tuyl JP, Kerkhof AJ, et al.(1997). Platelet serotonin and [3H]paroxetine binding correlate with recurrence of suicidal behavior. *Psychopharmacology (Berl)* 132(1):89–94.

Verkes RJ, Pijl H, Meinders AE, and Van Kempen GM (1996). Borderline personality, impulsiveness, and platelet monoamine measures in bulimia nervosa and recurrent suicidal behavior. *Biological Psychiatry* 40(3):173–180.

Vermetten E and Bremner, JD (2002). Circuits and systems in stress: preclinical studies. *Depression and Anxiety* 15:126–147.

Volkmar FR and Greenough WT (1972). Rearing complexity affects branching of dendrites in the visual cortex of the rat. *Science* 176(42):1145–1147.

Volkow ND, Fowler JS, and Wang GJ (2002). The addicted human brain: insights from imaging studies. *Journal of Clinical Investigation* 111(10):1444–1451.

Volkow ND, Fowler JS, and Wang GJ (2003). The addicted human brain: insights from imaging studies. *Journal of Clinical Investigation* 111(10):1444–1451.

Volkow ND, Wang GJ, and Baler RD (2011). Reward, dopamine and the control of food intake: Implications for obesity. *Trends in Cognitive Sciences* 15(1):37–46.

Volkow ND, Wang GJ, Fowler JS, and Telang F (2012). Overlapping neuronal circuits in addiction and obesity: Evidence of systems pathology. *Philosophical Transactions of the Royal Society of London. Series B, Biological Sciences* 363(1507):3191–3200.

Volkow ND Wang GJ, Fowler JS, Tomasi D, and Baler RD (2012). Reward, dopamine and the control of food intake: Implications for obesity. *Trends in Cognitive Sciences* 15(1):37–46.

Volkow ND, Wang GJ, Fowler JS, Logan, J, Jayne, M, Franceschi D, Wong (2002). "Nonhedonic" food motivation in humans involves dopamine in the dorsal striatum and methylphenidate amplifies this effect. *Synapse* 44:175–180.

Volkow ND, Wang GJ, Fowler JS, Tomasi D, Telang F, and Baler R (2010). Addiction: Decreased reward sensitivity and increased expectation sensitivity conspire to overwhelm the brain's control circuit. *Bioessays* 32(9):748–755.

Volkow ND, Wang GJ, Tomasi D, and Baler RD (2012). Obesity and addiction: Neurobiological overlaps. *Obesity Reviews*:14(1):2–18.

Von Bertalanffy L (1950). See Bertalanffy L von.

Von Bertalanffy L (1951). *General system theory—A new approach to unity of science Symposium* 23:303–361.

Wakefield JC (1992). Disorder as harmful dysfunction: A conceptual critique of DSM-III-R's definition of mental disorder. *Psychological Review* 99(2):234–247.

Waldinger R (1987). Intensive psychodynamic therapy with borderline clients: An overview. *American Journal of Psychiatry* 144(3):267–274.

Walters D, Connors JP, Feeney GJ, and Young RM (2009). The cost effectiveness of naltrexone added to cognitive behavioral therapy in the treatment of alcohol dependence. *Journal of Addictive Diseases* 28(2):137–144.

Wang GJ, Geliebter A, Volkow ND, Telang FW, Logan J, Millard LJ, Jayne MC, et al. (2011). Enhanced striatal dopamine release during food stimulation in binge eating disorder. *Obesity* 19(8):1601–1608.

Wang GJ, Volkow ND, Thanos PK, and Fowler JS (2009). Imaging of brain dopamine pathways: Implications for understanding obesity. *Journal of Addiction Medicine* 3(1):8–18.

Wang HR, Gao XR, Zhang KG, and Han JS (2003). Current status in drug addiction and addiction memory (abstract). *Sheng Li Ke Xue Jin Zhan* 34(3):202–206 (article in Chinese).

Warren K, Franklin C, and Streeter CL (1998). New directions in systems theory: chaos and complexity. *Social Work* 43(4):357–372.

Watamura SE, Donzella B, Alwin J, and Gunnar MR (2003). Morning-to-afternoon increases in cortisol concentrations for infants and toddlers at child care: age differences and behavioral correlates. *Child Development* 74(4):1006–1020.

Waters E, Merrick S, Treboux D, Crowell J, and Albersheim L (1997). Attachment security in infancy and early adulthood: A twenty-year longitudinal study. *Child Development* 71(3):684–689.

Watts-English T, Fortson BV, Gibler N, Hooper SR, and DeBellis MD (2006). The psychobiology of maltreatment in childhood. *Journal of Social Issues* 62:4:717–736.

Webb. NB (2006). The impact of trauma on youth and families in the child welfare system. In Webb NB (ed.), *Working with traumatized youth in child welfare*, pp. 13–26. New York: The Guilford Press.

Wechsler RT, Morss, AM, Wustoff, CJ, and Caughey, AB (2004). *Blueprints: Notes & Cases: Neuroscience.* Oxford: Blackwell Publishing. p. 37.

Weinberger DH (2011). Genes and Mental Illness, Brain/Behavior Workshop, Brain Disorders Intramural Research Program, NIMH, May 23. Educational presentation.

Weiss SJ (2007). Neurobiological alterations associated with traumatic stress. *Perspectives in Psychiatric Care* 43:3:114–122 http://www.childtrauma.org

Wender PH (1971). *Minimal Brain Dysfunction.* New York: Wiley-Interscience.

Werner EE (1989). Children of the Garden Island. *Scientific American* 260(4):106–111.

Westfall JM, Mold J, and Fagnan L (2007). Practice-based research—"blue highways" on the NIH roadmap. *JAMA* 297(4):403–406.

Weze C, Leathard HL, Grange JM, Tiplady P, and Stevens G (2004). Evaluation of healing by gentle touch in thirty-five clients with cancer. *European Journal of Oncology Nursing* 8(3,4):September/December.

Whitfield CL (1987). *Healing the child within: Discovery and recovery for adult children of dysfunctional families.* Deerfield Beach, FL: Health Communications. (Reprinted 2006)

Whitfield CL (1991). Co-dependence: Healing the human condition. Deerfield Beach, FL: Health Communications.

WHO Report on the Global Tobacco Epidemic (2008). The MPOWER package. Geneva, Switzerland: World Health Organization. http://www.who.int/tobacco/mpower/en/

Widiger TA (2006). Psychometric properties of an abbreviated measure of the five-factor model. *Assessment* 13:119–137.

Widiger TA and Mullins-Sweatt SN (2009). Five-factor model of personality disorder: A proposal for DSM-V. *Annual Review of Clinical Psychology* 5:197–220.

Wiesemann C, Ude-Koeller S, Gernot H. Sinnecker G, and Thyen U (2010) Ethical principles and recommendations for the medical management of differences of sex development (DSD)/intersex in children and adolescents. *European Journal of Pediatrics* 169(6):671–679.

Wilson BDM, Hayes E, Greene GJ, Kelly JG, and Iscoe I (2003). Community psychology. In DK Freedheim, ed, *Handbook of psychology: History of psychology* (Vol. 1, pp. 431–449). New York, NY: John Wiley.

Winslow JT and Insel TR (2002). The social deficits of the oxytocin knockout mouse. *Neuropeptides* 36:221–229.

Winslow JT, Noble PL, Lyons CK, Sterk SM, and Insel TR (2003). Rearing effects on cerebrospinal fluid oxytocin concentration and social buffering in rhesus monkeys. *Neuropsychopharmacology* 28(5):910–918.

Winters BD, Gurses AP, Lehmann H, Sexton JB Carlyle J Rampersad CJ, and Pronovost PJ (2009) Clinical review: Checklists—translating evidence into practice. *Critical Care* 2009, 13:210.

Wismer Fries AB, Zigler TE, Kurian JR, Jacoris S, and Pollak SD (2005). Early experience in humans is associated with changes in neuropeptides critical for regulating social behaviour. *Proceedings of the National Academy of Sciences USA* 102:17237–17240.

Wolfe SH (2013). *Public citizen, health research group* (Newsletter Worst Pills, Best Pills). Washington, DC.

Woolf SH (2008). The meaning of translational research and why it matters. *Journal of the American Medical Association* 299(2):211–213.

Woods WJ (1975). Community psychiatry. *Australian Nurses Journal* 4(10):28–31.

Wootton JC and Sparber A (2003), Surveys of complementary and alternative medicine usage: a review of general population trends and specific patient populations, *Seminars in Integrative Medicine* 1(1):10–24.

World Health Organization (1992a). *Basic Epidemiology*. Geneva, Switzerland: Author.

World Health Organization (1992b). *The ICD-10 classification of mental and behavioral disorders: Clinical descriptions and diagnostic guidelines*. Geneva, Switzerland: Author.

World Health Organization (2002). The World Health Report 2002—Reducing risks, promoting healthy life. Geneva, Switzerland: Author. http://www.who.int/whr/2002/en/

World Health Organization (2004). *Report of global burden of disease update*. Geneva, Switzerland: Author.

World Health Organization (2011). World No Tobacco Day celebrates WHO framework convention on tobacco control: WHO Report on the Global Tobacco Epidemic.

World Lung Foundation and American Cancer Society (2010). *The tobacco atlas* (3rd ed.).

Xiao L, Cousins G, Courtney B, Hederman L, Fahey T, and Dimitrov BD (2011). Developing an electronic health record (EHR) for methadone treatment recording and decision support. *BMC Medical Informatics and Decision Making* 11:5.

Xu MQ, Sun WS, Liu BX, Feng GY, Yu L, Yang L, He G, Sham P, Susser E, St Clair D, and He L. (2009). Prenatal malnutrition and adult schizophrenia: Further evidence from the 1959–1961 Chinese famine. *Schizophrenia Bulletin* 35:568–576.

Yang PC, Wu MT, Hsu CC and Ker JH (2004). Evidence of early neurobiological alternations in adolescents with posttraumatic stress disorder: a functional MRI study *Neuroscience Letters* 370(1):13–18.

Yang Y, Zheng X, Wang Y, Cao J, Dong Z, Cai J, Sui N, et al. (2004). Stress enables synaptic depression in CA1 synapses by acute and chronic morphine: Possible mechanisms for corticosterone on opiate addiction. *Journal of Neuroscience* 24(10):2412–2420.

Yapko M (1994). *Suggestions of abuse: True and false memories of childhood sexual trauma.* New York, NY: Simon and Schuster.

Yehuda R (2009). Status of glucocorticoid alterations in post-traumatic stress disorder, *Annals of the New York Academy of Sciences* 1179:56–69.

Yehuda R, Engel SM, Brand SR, Seckl J, Marcu, SM and Berkowitz GS (2005). Transgenerational effects of posttraumatic stress disorder in babies of mothers exposed to the World Trade Center attacks during pregnancy. *JCEM* 90:4115–4118.

Yehuda R, Halligan SL, and Bierer LM (2002). Cortisol levels in adult offspring of Holocaust survivors: relation to PTSD symptom severity in the parent and child. *Psychoneuroendocrinology* 27:171–180.

Young LJ, Lim MM, Gingrich B, and Insel TR (2001). Cellular mechanisms of social attachment. *Hormonal Behavior* 40(2):133–138. Review.

Young LJ, Murphy AZ, Young KA, and Hammock EA (2005). Anatomy and neurochemistry of the pair bond. *Journal of Comparative Neurology* 493(1):51–57.

Zametkin AJ, Nordahl TE, Gross M, King AC, Semple WE, Rumsey J, Hamburger S, and Cohen RM (1990). Cerebral glucose metabolism in adults with hyperactivity of childhood onset. *New England Journal of Medicine* 323(20):1361–1366.

Zanarini MC (2004). Update on pharmacotherapy of borderline personality disorder. *Current Psychiatry Reports* 6(1):66–70.

Zanarini MC (2008). Reasons for change in borderline personality disorder (and other axis II disorders). *Psychiatric Clinics of North America* 31(3):505–515, viii.

Zanarini MC and Frankenburg FR (2003). Omega-3 fatty acid treatment of women with borderline personality disorder: A double-blind placebo-controlled pilot study. *American Journal of Psychiatry* 160:167–169.

Zanarini MC, Frankenburg FR, DrLuca CJ, Hennen J, Khera GS, and Gunderson JC (1998). The pain of being borderline: Dysphoric states specific to being borderline. *Harvard Review of Psychiatry* 6:201–207.

Zanarini MC, Frankenburg FR, Reich DB, and Fitzmaurice G (2010). The 10-year course of psychosocial functioning among patients with borderline personality disorder and axis II comparison subjects. *Acta Psychiatrica Scandinavica* 122(2):103–109.

Zanarini MC, Reichman CA, Frankenburg FR, Reich DB, and Fitzmaurice G (2010). The course of eating disorders in patients with borderline personality disorder: A 10-year follow-up study. *International Journal of Eating Disorders* 43(3):226–232.

Zanarini MC, Ruser T, Frankenburg FR, and Hennen J (2000). The dissociative experiences of borderline patients. *Comprehensive Psychiatry* 41(3):223–223.

Zeanah CH and Fox NA (2004). See also Bos, Zeanah et al (2012).

Zeanah CH, Boris NW, Bakshi S, and Lieberman AF (2000). Attachment disorders in infancy. In JD Osofsky and HE Fitzgerald, eds, WAIMH handbook of infant mental health, Volume Four: Infant mental health in groups at high risk (pp. 93–122). New York, NY: Wiley.

Zeanah CH, Larrieu JA, Heller SS, Valliere J, Hinshaw-Fuselier S, Aoki Y, and Drilling M (2001). Evaluation of a preventive intervention for maltreated infants and toddlers in foster care. *Journal of the American Academy of Child and Adolescent Psychiatry* 40(2):214–221.

Zeanah CH, Scheeringa MS, Boris NW, Heller SS, Smyke AT, and Trapani J (2004). Reactive attachment disorder in maltreated toddlers. *Child Abuse & Neglect* 28:877–888.

Zeanah CH, Smyke AT, and Dumitrescu A. (2002). Attachment disturbances in young children: II. Indiscriminate behavior and institutional care. *Journal of the American Academy of Child and Adolescent Psychiatry* 41(8):983–989.

Zeanah CH, Smyke AT, Koga SF, and Carlson E (2005). The BEIP Core Group. Attachment in institutionalized and community children in Romania. *Child Development* 76(5): 1015–1028.

Zeisel SH (2008). Genetic polymorphisms in methyl-group metabolism and epigenetics: Lessons from humans and mouse models. *Brain Research* 1237:5–11.

Zhang Y, von Deneen KM, Tian J, Gold MS, and Liu Y (2011). Food addiction and neuroimaging. *Current Pharmaceutical Design* 17(12):1149–1157.

Ziauddeen H and Fletcher PC (2013). Is food addiction a valid and useful concept? *Obesity Reviews* 14(1):19–28.

Zimbardo P and Formica R (1963). Emotional comparison and self-esteem as determinants of affiliation. *Journal of Personality* 31(2):142–162.

Zimmerman M, Chelminski I, and Young D (2008). The frequency of personality disorders in psychiatric patients. *Psychiatric Clinics of North America* 31(3):405–420, vi.

{ INDEX }

Pagani, J., 223
Pagano, M. E., 294
PAI-BOR, 294
pair-bonding, 94, 211, 213, 227
Palombo, J., 290, 310
parallel systems, 36, 77
parental PTSD, as risk factor, 159
parents: "Bad Parenting" (BP), 28; perception of
    by professional helps, 28; toxic parenting,
    46, 207, 275, 315. *See also* family/families;
    mothers
Paris, J., 289, 290
Parkinson's disease, 130, 196
paroxetine (Paxil), 93, 226
pars reticulata (PR) neurons, 192
partial hospitalization, for BPD, 314
Pat (case study), food struggles and mental
    challenges, 200–206, 295, 296–303, 319–325
Pavlov, Ivan, 208
PDD (pervasive developmental disorder), 41, 231
Peindl, K. S., 190
Pennisi, E., 48
peptides, 78, 94, 105, 152, 179, 191, 211, 344, 345
Percik, R., 141
Perry, B. D., 145, 146, 147
personality disorders, 27, 280, 281, 288, 289,
    290, 291
personality factors, 331
personal responsibility, as component of
    successful treatment, 197
person-in-environment (PIE), 15, 16, 69, 278
pervasive developmental disorder (PDD), 41, 231
PET (positron emission tomography), 29
pharmacology, as diagnosis-driven, 33
phenotypes, 46
PHS (US Public Health Service), 280
physical addiction, distinguished from
    psychological addiction, 176
physical versus psychological, as false
    dichotomy, 42
Pijl, H., 296
Pilates, 332, 338
pituitary gland, 74, 77–79, 94, 150, 155
plasticity, of the brain, 251
platelet monoamine oxidase activity, 296, 307
Pleasure, as example of natural neural network, 117
pleasure pathway, 136, 172, 178
pleasure(s): also called reward, 122; as a result of
    brain ingenuity, 123–132
policy-making, brain system's, 121–122
polygenetic effects, 48
polygenetic pathway, 46
polymorphisms, 212
polypeptides, 94
polypharmacy, 304

pons, 74, 83, 93, 133
PORs (problem-oriented client records), 54
positive reinforcement, 132, 191, 228, 242,
    243, 340
positron emission tomography (PET), 29
posterior, 76
postsynaptic membrane, 86, 95, 97
posttraumatic stress disorder (PTSD), 4, 41, 79,
    144, 145, 146, 148, 150, 153, 154, 157, 158, 159,
    176, 195, 229, 233, 236, 281, 302, 308, 336
posttraumatic stress symptoms (PTSS), 159
Poulton, R., 251
Powell, L. H., 339
prayer, 332, 339
precursor substances/precursors, 88, 99, 100
pre-Freudian beliefs, 27
prefrontal cortex (neocortex), 9, 73, 75, 76, 91, 132,
    136, 141, 150, 151, 152, 154, 158, 172, 173, 179,
    188, 195, 270, 283, 300, 306
presynaptic membrane, 86, 97, 101, 186
prevention, importance of regarding trauma, 158
primary motor cortex, 75, 76
primary sensory cortex, 155
"primitive" brain, 79
privileged memories, 173, 176
problem-oriented client records (PORs), 54
protective factors: in biological
    environments, 40; defined, 18, 52, 171;
    interaction of with risk factors, 18;
    Midsummer Night, 20; sources of, 19
Proust, Marcel, 137
Prozac (fluoxetine), 93, 306
psychiatric rehabilitation, for BPD, 314
psychic dysregulation, 286
psychic phenomena, 23
psychoanalytic thought, 208
psychodynamic therapy, 311
psychoeducation, 26, 185, 310, 311, 315, 316
psychological addiction, distinguished from
    physical addiction, 176
psychological problems, 27, 29
psychosocial environment, 14
psychosocial treatments/interventions, 197, 198
psychotherapy, 28, 111, 232, 233, 234, 290,
    310, 311
psychotropic medications, 304, 305, 307
PTSD (posttraumatic stress disorder). *See*
    posttraumatic stress disorder (PTSD)
PTSS (posttraumatic stress symptoms), 159
PubMed (database), 23, 30, 46, 59, 60, 133, 179,
    302, 305, 313, 317
Purves, D., 71 (footnote)
putamen, 74, 82, 83, 91, 129, 130, 131, 133, 137, 140,
    173, 195, 298
Putnam, R. D., 331